# Essays on
# Ayn Rand's *Anthem*

# Essays on
# Ayn Rand's *Anthem*

Edited by
Robert Mayhew

LEXINGTON BOOKS
*Lanham • Boulder • New York • Toronto • Oxford*

LEXINGTON BOOKS

Published in the United States of America
by Lexington Books
An imprint of The Rowman & Littlefield Publishing Group, Inc.
4501 Forbes Boulevard, Suite 200, Lanham, Maryland 20706
www.lexingtonbooks.com

P.O. Box 317, Oxford OX2 9RU, United Kingdom

British Library Cataloguing in Publication Information Available

**Library of Congress Cataloging-in-Publication Data**

Essays on Ayn Rand's Anthem / edited by Robert Mayhew.
    p. cm.
    Includes bibliographical references and index.
    ISBN 0-7391-1030-6 (cloth : alk. paper) — ISBN 0-7391-1031-4 (pbk. : alk. paper)
    1. Rand, Ayn. Anthem. I. Mayhew, Robert.
PS3535.A547A734 2005
813'.52—dc22

                                                                    2005002801

Printed in the United States of America

⊗™ The paper used in this publication meets the minimum requirements of
American National Standard for Information Sciences—Permanence of Paper
for Printed Library Materials, ANSI/NISO Z39.48-1992.

# Contents

# Preface

During the first half of the twentieth century, owing largely to the existence of totalitarianism in Soviet Russia and later in Nazi Germany, there appeared a number of 'anti-Utopia' works of fiction, among the most well-known being Yevgeny Zamyatin's *We* (1921), Aldous Huxley's *Brave New World* (1932) and George Orwell's *1984* (1949). Ayn Rand's novella *Anthem* (1938) is a similar work (though unique in many crucial respects); but whereas *We*, *Brave New World*, and especially *1984* have received substantial scholarly attention, *Anthem* has not. A book-length study of *Anthem* is long overdue; the present collection fills this need.

*Anthem* was written in the summer of 1937, during a break Ayn Rand took from writing her novel *The Fountainhead*. *Anthem* was first published in England in 1938, and a revised edition appeared in the United States in 1946. Part I of this volume is devoted to the history of *Anthem*. The opening chapter is Shoshana Milgram's "*Anthem* in Manuscript: Finding the Words," which examines the outline and draft of the novella. The second chapter is Richard Ralston's "Publishing *Anthem*," which describes Ayn Rand's struggles (especially in the United States, during America's "Red Decade") to find a publisher. A revised edition of *Anthem* was published in 1946; Ayn Rand made hundreds of revisions in preparing it. My chapter, "*Anthem*: '38 & '46," examines the changes she made and offers a detailed discussion of those revisions that might appear to reveal a change in philosophical outlook. In the fourth chapter, "Reviews of *Anthem*," Michael S. Berliner surveys dozens of the reviews *Anthem* received, covering those that first appeared in England in 1938 and up to a recent 2002 review of an audio-book version of *Anthem*. Although there has been a great deal of interest in adapting *Anthem* over the years—primarily into film—there has unfortunately been only one adaptation. Jeff Britting's "Adapting *Anthem*: Projects That Were and Might Have Been" surveys the one realized adaptation and the many others that were discussed but never actualized. Part I of this collection ends with Jeff Britting's "*Anthem* and 'The Individualist Manifesto'," which compares *Anthem* to its "nonfiction twin brother" (in Britting's words): Ayn Rand's first extended nonfiction essay in English, "The Individualist Manifesto" (written in 1941, but never published).

Part II examines *Anthem* as a work of literature and as philosophy. The first chapter of this part is Tore Boeckmann's "*Anthem* as a Psychological Fantasy," which provides a detailed literary analysis of *Anthem* and the integration of its story and theme; explains why Ayn Rand considered *Anthem* a psychological fantasy and a poem; and compares *Anthem* to another work in the genre of psychological fantasy, namely Ibsen's *Peer Gynt*. Most comparisons of *Anthem* with other literary works focus on anti-utopia fiction. This is the subject of the next chapter, Shoshana Milgram's "*Anthem* in the Context of Related Literary Works: 'We are not like our brothers'," which contrasts *Anthem* with a wide range of works: not only *We*, *Brave New World*, and *1984*, but also H. G. Wells's *The Time Machine*, Stephen Vincent Benét's "The Place of the Gods," and several others.

John Lewis's "'Sacrilege toward the Individual': The Anti-Pride of Thomas More's *Utopia* and *Anthem*'s Radical Alternative" compares *Anthem* and *Utopia* from both the point of view of literature and especially their different moral philosophies. It thus provides a transition from the literary comparisons contained in the previous two chapters to the five chapters on philosophical themes that follow. Darryl Wright's "Needs of the *Psyche* in Ayn Rand's Early Ethical Thought" places *Anthem* in the context of the first stages in the development of her moral philosophy, from her arrival in the United States in 1926 through the publication of the first edition of *Anthem* in 1938. The next two chapters chart the progress of the hero of *Anthem*, though from different angles. Onkar Ghate, in "Breaking the Metaphysical Chains of Dictatorship: Free Will and Determinism in *Anthem*," reveals the relationship between determinism and dictatorship, and free will and political freedom, as found in *Anthem*. Gregory Salmieri's "Prometheus' Discovery: Individualism and the Meaning of the Concept 'I' in *Anthem*" provides a detailed description of the steps required, epistemologically and morally, for the hero of *Anthem* to discover the concept "I" and the moral philosophy associated with that concept. The last two chapters in Part II focus on political philosophy. Amy Peikoff's "Freedom of Disassociation in *Anthem*" discusses the nature, purpose and consequences of the rejection, by the society in *Anthem*, of the freedom to be alone. Andrew Bernstein's "*Anthem* and Collectivist Regression into Primitivism" describes the connection in *Anthem* between the society's totalitarianism and its lack of advanced technology.

This collection contains two other essays: an epilogue by Harry Binswanger, "*Anthem*: An Appreciation," which is based on a talk the author gave in New York City in 1998 as part of a celebration of the 60th anniversary of the publication of *Anthem*; and an appendix by Lindsay Joseph, "Teaching *Anthem*: A Guide for High School and University Teachers," which should be useful not only to the growing number of teachers who assign *Anthem* in their classes but to anyone interested in Ayn Rand's novella.

At the time of this volume's publication—in the centenary year of Ayn Rand's birth—annual sales of *Anthem* have passed the 100,000 mark, and total sales have reached 3,500,000 copies. *Anthem* is and deserves to be a book for all times—a permanent fixture in the Western canon. And as we are living in an age when that canon and the civilization it embodies are under attack, from within and from without, there is no better time to study *Anthem*, which portrays so simply and eloquently the foundation that Western civilization requires, and what will result if that foundation is destroyed.

Robert Mayhew
Seton Hall University
February 2005

# Acknowledgments

I wish to thank Leonard Peikoff (Executor of the Estate of Ayn Rand) for permission to use previously unpublished material of Ayn Rand, and Jeff Britting (Archivist of the Ayn Rand Archives) for his assistance in accessing this material. Thanks also to the staff at Lexington Books for their work on this volume, and to Neil Erian for preparing the index. I am grateful to both the Ayn Rand Institute and the Anthem Foundation for Objectivist Scholarship for grants that supported this project. Finally, special thanks are due the Ayn Rand Institute for sponsoring a very productive colloquium at which four authors discussed their contributions to this collection.

# Bibliographical Note

Unless otherwise indicated, quotes from Ayn Rand's *Anthem* will be followed by page number(s) in parentheses in the text and not by an endnote. Pagination refers to the fiftieth anniversary paperback edition (New York: Signet, 1995).

In some chapters, the author quotes from, and refers to information contained in, a series of biographical interviews that Ayn Rand gave in 1960–1961, the tapes and transcripts of which are in the Ayn Rand Archives. References will appear in the endnotes as: Biographical interviews (Ayn Rand Archives).

# I

## THE HISTORY OF *ANTHEM*

# 1

## *Anthem* in Manuscript: Finding the Words

*Shoshana Milgram*

There is some error, one frightful error, in the thinking of men. What is that error? We do not know, but the knowledge struggles within us, struggles to be born.

Today, the Golden One stopped suddenly and said:

"We love you."

But then they frowned and shook their head and looked at us helplessly.

"No," they whispered, "that is not what we wished to say."

They were silent, then they spoke slowly, and their words were halting, like the words of a child learning to speak for the first time:

"We are one . . . alone . . . and only . . . and we love you who are one . . . alone . . . and only."

We looked into each other's eyes and we knew that the breath of a miracle had touched us, and fled, and left us groping vainly.

And we felt torn, torn for some word we could not find. (86–87)

Two young lovers walk through the Uncharted Forest, knowing intensely the horror they have escaped but not yet conceptually aware of its cause or its cure. The Golden One tries to express her love for the man she has named "The Unconquered," but discovers that she cannot do so adequately without the singular pronouns designed to name unique individuals. As Howard Roark tells Dominique Francon in *The Fountainhead*, "To say 'I love you' one must know first how to say the 'I'."[1] Lacking the prerequisite, the Golden One cannot say "I love you." And being able to say "I love you" is indeed important. For complete understanding, one needs "that full, luminous finality which is a thought named in words."[2]

Long before composing the book, Ayn Rand had grasped the main concept of *Anthem*—the role of individualism in human life. During the weeks of composition she was not groping vainly for the substance behind the

3

breath of that miracle. She wrote this work quickly, from a one-page outline, with the aim of immediate magazine publication. There are fewer large differences (in total, and even in proportion) between the manuscript and the published version than was the case for any of the full-length novels.[3] Whereas, for example, the manuscript of *We the Living* has traces of an affair between Victor Dunaev and Rita Eksler, and the manuscript of *The Fountainhead* includes a long, philosophical conversation between Ellsworth Toohey and Roark, the manuscript of *Anthem* contains no episodes that were not ultimately included in the text (with the minor and partial exception of the hero's memories of events from the time before the opening of the narrative proper).

The manuscript, however, shows numerous smaller-scale changes (and Ayn Rand was to make additional small-scale changes in revising the 1938 text for the second edition in 1946). The differences include revisions that are apparent directly on the page (cross-outs and additions) as well as those that can be inferred from a comparison of the manuscript with the published text. In writing *Anthem*, Ayn Rand made continual revisions in vocabulary, syntax, and details.

Why did she make so many small-scale changes, by contrast with the paucity of large-scale changes? She did not need to make large-scale changes because she knew her theme well, and because she had had in mind, for more than a decade, the basic idea: a future world that has lost the use of the singular pronouns. But she found herself needing to make numerous small-scale changes partly because, as she said, "the attempt to have that semi-archaic style was very difficult," and she did not always know how to achieve her desired effect.[4] Not yet fully confident in her command of English, she was endeavoring to write in two additional foreign languages: not only English, but also the language of the collectivist society of *Anthem*, and, later, the language of the hero after he has discovered the word and concept he had been missing.

Not only that, but she was attempting to present the first-person perspective (in her only first-person fictional work of any length) of a noble soul whose conscious convictions are false and at war with the principles by which he lives. What he *says* is not always what *is*—and even he knows it. In the passage above, he is "torn for some word we could not find" (and it is not even clear if the "we" refers to one person or two). It is not surprising that his author, writing about him in multiple foreign languages, also looks for words she does not immediately find, and that the manuscript shows that search.

Why did Ayn Rand initially include numerous narrative and descriptive details that she eventually omitted? Perhaps she intended from the beginning to write more than she needed. The draft, in fact, is approximately twice as long as the length she stated in her outline. In the case of *The Fountainhead,* she said that she intentionally wrote more than she expected to retain, and she made the decisions about what was to be cut only after its completion.[5] With that novel, her cuts led to omissions of entire episodes and even characters. With *Anthem*, by contrast, her cuts do not affect the story line. The omitted passages are, for the most part, appropriate for *Anthem*, and appear to be omitted in the spirit of "less is more." In a few cases, though, the omissions or modifications of details show her eliminating a possibly confusing implication or guiding the reader firmly to a powerful realization.

By examining the manuscript, we observe the alternatives she considered, the difficulties she encountered, and the decisions she made.

She began with a one-page, hand-written outline:

<u>Plan</u>

    I. We are sinners. We should not write, but we cannot help it. It is a crime to write. [*crossed-out*: Only writers and secretaries can do it.] Where we are. What he is doing and why. How he gets there. His day. How he missed his career. [*crossed-out*: his sins and his plan of redemption. It is bad to feel so always]

    II. Liberty 5–3000. Who she is, where he saw her. First incident of her interest in him. His guilt. About the mating. About his friend smiling.

    III. The general vague fear in the House and his joy in the tunnel. He was reprimanded for singing. His sin of joy. The Saint of the [*crossed out*: Unspeakable] Unmentionable Word.

    IV. Incident with [crossed out: Liberty] the Golden One. (the names)

    V. The Light. Pride of self. His [matchless?] value. Plans about the Council.

    VI. He is caught. The torture. His waiting for the Council.

    VII. In the forest. Account of Council meeting.

    VIII. His days in the forest. Hunger. Hunting. The brook and the wreath.

    IX. The Golden One joins him. Love scene. His doubt about the truth of others. [Pride]

    X. They find the abandoned mansion. He will read the books.

    XI. His new philosophy. [*crossed-out*: Their new worries.]

    XII. Gives new names. Laws for the future. Their child. The crowd will gather. What they will fight for. History. We shall all die, but we shall be glad to die. The word that will never die.

[*crossed-out*: 5 typewritten pages per entry. (about 7 written) About 50 pages (12,500 words).]

She followed the essence of this outline: the journal written in the tunnel, the two values (love and the light), the threat to the light, the escape, the union with the beloved, the discovery of the house and the word, the dedication to fight for the future of Man. The only substantial change in order is that in the outline, a second encounter with Liberty followed the memory of the Saint, whereas in the text, the memory of the Saint is followed by the account of the discovery of the light.

She modified subtly the atmosphere of the conclusion. She intended to write about the couple's "new worries," but removed that concern from her plan. Perhaps in a similar spirit, she intended to have her hero expect to die (as did Kira Argounova in *We the Living*) physically defeated but spiritually triumphant; later, she removed that expectation as well. In the text, Prometheus is confident of ultimate victory.

She did not follow her projected restrictions on length: in the novel itself, the chapters were not equal in length, and the total length exceeded her estimate. Nor does the actual content of each chapter correspond to the content indicated in the outline: for example, the hero was originally supposed to remember the death of the Saint in the third chapter—rather than in the second.

The hand-written manuscript itself is in two parts, chapters 1–5 and chapters 6–12. Part 1 concludes with page 72, and the pagination starts again with part 2, which concludes with page 66. (For clarity, I identify pages in the first part with the page number plus A, and pages in the second part with page number plus B.) There are no gaps in the text, but there is evidence of missing pages. For example, there was once another page between 14A and the following page (on which the number has been changed from 16 to 15). Judging from the crossed-out lines on the top of page 15, the missing material had to do with Council elections. The manuscript is longer than the version published in 1938 (which itself is longer than the edition published in 1946), and it includes passages that are crossed out on the page and others that were omitted before publication. In editing, Ayn Rand did much more cutting than expanding. (The only substantial addition to the manuscript—a passage that appears in the 1938 edition and has no equivalent in the manuscript—is the description of the alleged achievements of the Council. This passage, which appears on pages 14–15 of the 1938 edition, was not included in the 1946 text.)

The handwriting is often very hard to read, especially when the words have been crossed out. Looking at the changes, though, is worth the effort. What Leonard Peikoff wrote about the changes from one edition to the next applies as well to the changes in the manuscript: "If (ignoring the concrete issue of biblical style) you study the changes, asking 'Why?' as you proceed, there is virtually no limit to what you can learn about writing—Ayn Rand's or your own."[6]

One can begin with the editing for vocabulary and syntax, where the meaning appears substantially the same. A purposeful change in wording is the substitution of "toil" for "work" in the phrase "to lighten the burden of their toil, to do their toil for them" (A68). The word "work" emphasizes the goal, the purpose, the productiveness; the word "toil" emphasizes the strain, the effort, the pain (and, accordingly, "toil" is the word used repeatedly in the text). The expression "to do their work" is the ordinary mode of expression; to write instead "to do their toil" is to call attention to the oddness of the language and the corresponding oddness of the world. The entire sentence, originally included in what is now the central paragraph on p. 75 of the 1938 edition, was ultimately dropped, but the book retains the emphasis on the drudgery of "toil."

A more significant purposeful change pertains to the sacred word "I." Originally, the crime of the Saint of the pyre was that he knew and invoked the "Unmentionable Word" (A53), a locution analogous to the term "Unmentionable Times" (which denotes the unchronicled and dimly remembered time period before the world's decline). But using the same adjective for both the word and the times did not allow Ayn Rand to highlight the significance of the word "Ego" itself, which denotes the concept of the self. The erasure of historical facts is bad, but the loss of a concept (especially that particular concept) is much worse, and much more important. For "Unmentionable Word" (which she crossed out) she substituted "Unspeakable Word," which she had at first written in the outline, and which not only makes a distinction between the word and the times but coheres with the religious network of images. The "unspeakable word" in some religious traditions (e.g., the Tetragrammaton in Judaism) is the name of God, and so it is here. When the hero finally learns and speaks the unspeakable word, he identifies it, clearly and repeatedly, as a god:

> And now I see the face of god, and I raise this god over the earth, this god whom men have sought since men came into being, this god who will grant them joy and peace and pride.
> This god, this one word:
> "I." (97)

A change from active to passive voice increases the emphasis on the passivity of the denizens of the degraded world. The adult men and women were originally said to "go to the City Palaces of Mating"; this phrase was crossed out. Instead, they "are sent there" (A41). The change in voice enhances the meaning.

But the manuscript shows, in addition to this sort of editorial improvement (i.e., making the writing clearer and stronger), evidence of a struggle with language that is more severe than anything in the existing drafts of the other novels. For example, Ayn Rand wrote a line between "we" and "against" (B8) and later filled in the word "lunged." She wrote extremely awkward sentences, which she eventually omitted, e.g., "We have done these things, and they give us no shudder" (A32) and "We were not a thing which lived, but only a thing which ran" (B18). She chose, then rejected, awkward words. In the manuscript, a Council member calls the hero "You scum and filth of the swines" (B14), which in the published 1938 text became "You scum of the swines" (p. 92) and which was omitted entirely from the 1946 text.

The manuscript also shows her deliberations about adopting the style of the King James Bible. On the one hand, she frequently uses archaic syntax, and she makes changes on the page to increase this use: for example, "we do not think" becomes "we think not," and "do not frighten us" becomes "frighten us not" (both on A40). Several archaisms, as Robert Mayhew observes, were dropped for the 1946 text.[7] But the manuscript also shows that she wrote, and then omitted, some phrases that referenced not only the style of the Bible, but actual Biblical phrases. For example, she initially wrote (as the creed of the collectivist world): "Ours is the power and the glory and the truth forever" (A3), which was replaced by "one, indivisible and forever." The reference is to Matthew 6:13. (John Galt refers to the same Biblical verse in his speech: "They had known that theirs was the power. I taught them that theirs was the glory."[8]) She wrote, and removed, the statement (as part of the society's beliefs) that "there is no will on earth save good will to all men" (A46), which refers to Luke 2:14. She occasionally used a Biblical phrase such as "pass understanding" (Philippians 4:7), which appears in the description of the Saint: "there was a pride in them and a calm which pass understanding" (p. 58 in the 1938 edition). In the 1946 edition, though, she removed this phrase, and she generally avoided the specific quotation of a recognizable Biblical formulation.

The manuscript shows, finally, that she had to correct herself to avoid inadvertent singulars. She wrote "body" instead of "bodies" (A12), "The will of my [instead of "our"] brothers be done" (A17), "There is [instead of "are"] Fraternity 2–5503" (A49), and (in an error re-introduced into the fiftieth anniversary edition, 50), "they led him [instead of "them"] to the Pyre" (A53). Much as, in her outline, she wrote "he" rather than "they" or "we" for her hero, she wrote in the manuscript, at several points, the correct singular word rather than the plural mandated by the language of the Damned.

There is some evidence that she deliberated about the setting or action appropriate to the characters. On the very first page, for example, there was "wind in the tunnel, coming from we know not where. Perhaps it is [rushing?] to some city lost under the earth," and, because of the wind, "The candle trembles in the wind" (A1). But she crossed out the passage about the wind, along with the hint of the lost city. She wrote instead, on the same page: "It is dark here. The flame of the candle stands still in the air. Nothing moves here. We are alone under the earth." This version emphasizes the speaker's aloneness. In a silent world, only he speaks. In a static world, only he moves.

Another example is the response of the Golden One when the hero calls her "our dearest one." Ayn Rand initially wrote: "Then the Golden One laughed suddenly, and shook [*crossed-out*: her] their head, and looked away from us, as if to hide some fear of their own, and their laughter was troubled. And they spoke fast, as if they wished words to conceal things rather than reveal them" (A63). This version shows that she is nervous, knowing that there is no place in their world for the emotion they experience. This, of course, is nothing new, and her nervous behavior makes the reader a bit uncomfortable. In the revised version, she replies with an implicit expression of love. Silent, with her palms open in submission, she looks at the hero, and then brings him water.

Numerous other changes, on the level of sentences and paragraphs, involved the selection or modification of narrative or descriptive details. Many of the revisions concern passages that are appropriate, but were ultimately deemed superfluous. For example, the hero, in the manuscript, describes as follows the House of the Infants:

> [*crossed-out*: It was the tallest building of the City, for it had six floors. Each year was different to us, for each year we were moved to live one storey higher, while new babies came to the first floor the fall of each year.] The sleeping halls there were white and clean and bare of all things save one hundred beds. [*crossed-out*: As we moved higher, the beds grew larger and we could see more roofs from our windows. In all else there was no change.] (A6)

Of this description, only the sentence about the sleeping halls was retained; the rest was cut.

Similarly omitted were the circumstances under which he fought with the other children: "We kicked them when they came to be in our way, standing in line for the swimming pools and when they [pushed ahead?] of us in the line for supper" (A6). This information does not add to the basic fact (that he fought with the others, and was the only one to commit such a "transgression"). Although his fighting appears to be motivated by a desire to protect his rights and his privacy, to ward off interference, the incidents, as described, might even weaken the characterization by implying that he was impulsive or impatient.

In the manuscript, he recalls that he yawned when hearing the history of the Councils, and would have been lashed if a "kindly spirit" had not kept him from being seen (A13). In the published text, he says only that he did not listen well to that history. Although mentioning the yawning adds some sensory detail to the passage, sensory detail is in fact not a prominent factor in the first part of *Anthem* (with the major exceptions of the descriptions of the Golden One, the light, and the torture). In the second part, after his escape from the City of the Damned, the world is more worth seeing, and he describes it in more detail. It is possible, too, that Ayn Rand wanted to omit his mystical belief in a "kindly spirit" (a mysticism that on p. 17 of the 1938 edition is suggested by the reference to "demons," which was dropped for the 1946 edition).

The manuscript contained additional information about the reports of the Councils of Trades. Crossed out, for example, was the following passage:

> Then the Councils of the houses of the other Trades mount the pulpit to tell us about their Trades, for all the workers must know about all the work of the world. So they tell us about the work of the Plumbers, and how they do it, or the work of the Tailors, or the work of the Musicians. And two of our Council of Street Cleaners are away, telling at the Houses of those other Trades about Street Cleaning. (A21–22)

Originally the program of Social Recreation, which in the published text consisted of plays, included songs and stories as well:

> [*crossed-out*: The chorus from the House of the Musicians sings the hymns for us on the stage. Then the Readers come onto the stage and read to us, together in one voice, a chapter from the latest story written by the House of the Authors. The stories are about the different trades and the good work they do.]

There follows a brief description of the plays, as in the published versions. Later, Ayn Rand decided that the plays were enough to describe the program of Social Recreation, and she cut from the description of the plays the following sentences:

> Sometimes evil men are shown in the plays. The evil are always alone and they wear black tunics with scarlet horns on their head. They have committed the crimes of laziness or preference, in that they [illegible] to like one brother more than the others. For that they are always punished and the two great choruses turn their backs upon them in scorn. The plays are good and teach us to know what we must not do. (A22)

She originally had her hero recall the time limit of his "education."

> [*crossed-out*: We had not learned all that is prescribed for us to learn when we came to the age of fifteen. This was because there were too many children in our class who could not learn very fast. This is the law: if a class is not fast, it cannot stay in the House of the Students longer than [illegibly crossed out]. Ten years is the time allowed for learning, not one day more and not one day less. If a class is not fast, we all leave the House of the Students with our program unfinished. They cannot remain there longer, for they must make room for the new students who come each spring, and they must go to work when their work is needed. Otherwise, it would impede the plans of the Central Council of World Planning and the world would come to an end.] (A11)

This passage makes the specific point that the good students are held back by the slow learners, and that the schedule of completion is considered more important than the acquisition of knowledge. But, given the nature of what the hero learns, it is possible that Ayn Rand omitted the description not only because we already know that collectivism is bad for learning, but because the passage might remind readers of the old joke: "The food in this restaurant is simply awful. Not only that, but the portions are too small."

In editing the manuscript, Ayn Rand also removed a passage emphasizing the prohibition against preference in studies, and the statement that toil for the State is the universal goal:

> Each morning, as we came into the classroom, the Teachers said to us: "Now begin the day, our children, and give equal care to each art and science you learn. For all the arts and sciences were prescribed for you by the Council of Education, and are of equal importance, so that should you show a preference for one over another, you would be rebelling against the wisdom of the Council of Education." Furthermore, it is evil to show preference for any one man, beast or thing on earth, for all things are equal." That did the Teachers tell us, and also this: "You are not learning here because it pleases you. You are learning so that you may become useful toilers of your State." (A12)

Both of these points (the sin of preference and the ideal of service) are made elsewhere, in numbing repetition, and hence could be omitted here without loss.

Ayn Rand initally included (but crossed out on the page) information about vigorous physical activity, e.g., "Then we run around a track, and we jump over wooden barriers, and we throw a big ball to one another" (A21); the 1938 text (pp. 22–23) includes only the more moderate exercise of standing in rows and stretching (and even this exercise was removed for the 1946 edition). Why these cuts? Possibly because running and jumping are signs of health, and health— even if it is said to be for the purpose of working for the collective—is a value incompatible with the diseased metaphysics of the world of the Damned.

In recounting his memories, Equality 7-2521 reported, in the original text, on two particularly horrifying aspects of his society, both of which are no more than hints in the published version. The first has to do with the List of the Damned:

> It was when we had come to our twelfth year that we, Equality 7-2521, began to fear the List of the Damned. When a class ends its learning, at the age of fifteen, the Council of the Teachers meets and composes the List of the Damned. No men know who the Damned are or why. Only the Teachers know. It is said that the Damned are those who are not like their brothers and who will never be like their brothers. So that they have to be destroyed. There is a great iron cellar under the Temple of the World Council and in the spring of each year all the men and all the children of the City gather in the great square of the Temple of the World Council. Then the Damned are led down to the cellar and the iron door is closed. There is a great fire in the cellar and two small barred windows. We all of the City stand and watch the smoke rising from the windows. It is a blue smoke

The text cuts off here, on A9, and A10 is missing. The next page, A11, continues: "Solidarity 2-3650 was not dismissed from their post and we were not put down on the List of the Damned" on the missing page. Apparently, Equality recounts an incident in which he came close to being placed on the List.

If Ayn Rand had removed the burning of the Damned in between the first and second editions, one might assume that she was trying to avoid the implication of a specific reference to the Nazi concentration camps. But she removed this passage in 1937, while writing (and left only the reference, earlier in the text, to being locked in a Dark Place, A7). Maybe the reason is that physical force is not the primary agent of control. Perhaps, too, this episode was removed in order to reserve the term "the Damned" for those who are truly damned.

It is possible, too, that the idea of the List of the Damned was introduced in order to set up an episode with Solidarity 2-3650 (an episode described on a page that has not been preserved), and that, when Ayn Rand decided to cut the episode, she omitted the List as well. One might imagine, finally, that if there were a list of those who are different from their brothers, Equality's name would certainly be on it, and that would be the end of the story. There would be no plausible explanation of how he managed to avoid being burned in the cellar; he cannot blend, no matter how he tries.

Another painful passage, written in the manuscript but crossed out, concerns the Madness:

> And as we all undress at night, in the dim glow of the candles, our brothers do not look into one another's eyes, for they all fear the Madness. It is whispered that the Madness is a new disease, for it came into being since the Great Rebirth. It strikes as lightning, without warning. And they whom it has stricken, scream of a sudden, and gnash their teeth, and froth runs from their mouth, and their face is no human face, but only a mangled, howling face of raw hatred, and it is hatred with their brothers. They leap upon the men around them and they kill as many as they can reach. Then they must be seized and put to death, for nothing can (cuts off here, on A49).

This is followed by what appears to be an alternative version, also crossed out:

> We have seen the Madness once in our sleeping hall. It struck Solidarity 3–2294, who were the gentlest lad in the House, shy and devoid of all harm. We have heard the scream, and we wish to forget it. We have seen their face, and it was no human face, but only a mangled, shapeless thing of raw hatred. And it was hatred for all their brother men. We saw them choke three men in the hall, with their bare hands upon their throats, they, Solidarity 3–2294, who had been feeble and fragile. And we saw them, as the guards carried them away, bite the hands of the guards and howl like a beast. (the text cuts off here, on A50.)

The description of the Madness—the transformation of even the meek into savage beasts who attack their "brothers"—is, in the text, reduced to the statement that people scream in the night. Possibly the scream is enough to convey the psychological trauma of life under collectivism. Possibly, too, Ayn Rand reconsidered the implications of having people become stronger through illness and hatred.

The hero's observations in the tunnel were originally conveyed with more detail—probably cut for space. For example: "[*crossed-out*: And there were braided cords running along the walls, but they were not cords, for they felt soft and gummy under our fingers and like no substance we had ever touched]" (A28). Later:

> [*crossed-out*: Then we looked about us, at the tunnel, and at the walls of the tunnel, and suddenly we understood. Those glass bulbs on the wall. . . . The men who had built the tunnel must have had light under the ground, yet we found no candles and no torches and no places to hold torches, but those glass bulbs were spaced in such manner that they would have lit the tunnel, had they given light. And now we knew. They had given light. And the light had been carried to them by the copper wires. And it had been the light of the power of the sky, the same light which glowed before us.
>
> We know not how this was done, nor whence their power came. But what matters it! We know that it was done. We can do it again.] (A67)

This passage may have been cut for space, or for the statement that not knowing how the bulbs worked does not matter, or for the implied over-confidence in his belief that he can make light bulbs even though he does not know how. The following, too, may have been cut for over-confidence.

> [*crossed-out*: We shall wait for the World Council of Scholars. The Scholars will understand.] Just one last month. Then our road will be open to us. Our road without end. Our road to be traveled with the power of the sky lighting the way. Nothing can stop us now. Nothing is impossible to us. (A71)

The manuscript has a paragraph, crossed out, about the hero's reception on his return to his House:

> The Council of the House were waiting for us in the entrance hall. There was no light in the windows. The House slept, and all those in the House, but not the Council. We stood before them, and they had been looking at the door when we entered, and so their eyes did not move, nor their faces. And then the oldest of the Council asked us, without moving:
>
> "Where have you been?" (B1-2)

This passage may have been edited out for space, or for the implication that the House Council members are good at their job, i.e., are purposefully watchful.

In the following sequence, in which the hero, despite being tortured, refuses to say where he has been, the manuscript included gruesome sensory metaphors of torture. Ayn Rand commented that she had some "concern with torture," and she speculated that it may have begun when she read in Maurice Champagne's *The Mysterious Valley* (1914) about Cyrus's defiance in the face of the threat of torture.[9] The climax of *Atlas Shrugged* was her final fictional torture scene; this scene in *Anthem* is the first. Among the phrases written, and crossed out, are: "And we felt we were being ground through a red grill" (B4) and "And two thin needles whirred in our ears, whirling and grinding and burrowing deeper into our brain, and we wondered when they would meet" (B5). The command that Equality shall be lashed "till the pulp of their body is fit to feed to the hogs" is crossed out and replaced by "until there is nothing left under the lashes" (B14). In revising the torture sequence for the 1946 edition, Ayn Rand removed still more of the gory details.

Also crossed out is a passage in which a judge expresses amazement at the hero's tenacity in maintaining his silence:

> The three greatest judges of the City came and stood looking upon us as if they could not believe the sight of their eyes.
> "Wretch," the oldest said to us, "had we not been Judges and known that as such we cannot be stricken with madness, we would think now that our senses have gone from us. For no creature such as you has ever been beheld by men, nor is possible. To defy the will of the Councils and to refuse them is not a thing to be uttered in words, yet you have done this thing. What will can be holding your tongue, wretch, when there is no will on earth save the will of our brothers?"
> "We know not," we answered, "but we cannot speak." (B7)

This scene, while not necessary for the story, is emotionally powerful. Perhaps it was cut because the judge is admitting puzzlement. To do so is implicitly to acknowledge the value of understanding, i.e., of the mind. But the leaders of the world of the Damned depend on denying the mind its role in existence. The speech of the oldest judge, moreover, contains an explicit singular, i.e., "no creature such as you has." The hero's defiance comes close to triggering the return of the language (and the concept) of the singular person.

The sequences following his escape contain several passages that were cut for the first published version, and some of these were shortened still further for the second edition. In the manuscript, for example, the hero describes as follows the first time he saw his own image:

> We sat still and we held our breath not to frighten the picture away. [*crossed-out*: Then we moved our hand, and the hand in the water moved also, and we knew that it was our face and our body before us.] [The rest of the paragraph continues as on p. 104 of the 1938 text. Following this paragraph:]

[*crossed-out*: We forgot to drink for a long time. Then we drank, and sat still again, waiting for our picture to return. And we looked and looked upon it, and our thirst for it was greater than for water. We knew how evil it is for men to have concern for their own bodies, and we said so to ourselves. But the lips on the face in the stream were smiling.] (B24–25)

The material crossed out in the manuscript has no equivalent in the text; possibly the passage crossed the line from pride to self-absorption. In the manuscript and in the 1938 version, there follows a paragraph, dropped for the 1946 edition, in which the hero adorns himself with a wreath.

Here is another post-escape passage that appears only in the manuscript—with some sentences crossed out on the page, and others excluded later. The hero celebrates the experience of freedom.

[*crossed-out*: We walked till we were tired, and we rested when we wished, and we walked again. We gathered wild berries on our way, ripe and bursting with juice. We ate when we were hungry. We drank when we were thirsty. We stopped to look upon each other, when our happiness seemed too great to bear and made us doubt the truth of what had befallen us; then we stopped to be certain, to let our eyes tell us that we were still together.] And as we walked, our heart would not believe that we were now free to look upon the Golden One whenever we wished, to speak to them aloud and not whisper, to touch their body and have no fear. [*crossed-out*: and no one to stop us. We know we had no right to this. But our heart laughed at all rights.] (B31)

The entire paragraph is cut (probably for space) in the published text, which proceeds directly—and with good reason—to the couple's first night together.

Here are two more omitted passages, similarly positive in spirit:

[*crossed-out*: For this life and the joy of this life pass all understanding, and the mind which was our mind in the City would not have believed nor conceived of it. We have always thought without questions that to live was to feel pain, and to be weary, and to hate, and to obey. But we have found that this is not true. We have found that joy is not a word that means only less pain, but that it is a thing real and true and possible.] (B33)

[*crossed-out*: We have found that the earth is beautiful, and the air of the earth is sweet. We awaken in the morning and we wish that our day would not end. We fall asleep at night, and we wish for the morning to come. We have learned to be strong, to be proud, to be free. We are free. Now we have written it. It is a strange word which keeps coming to us, again and again, as a call, as a portent. There is some secret in this word, which we can not fathom.] (B34)

In editing, Ayn Rand also omitted description of the closets and rugs in the house from the Unmentionable Times. Closets, as a luxury feature, are unknown to the hero, who has lived only in a time when there was no need for a place to store an individual's clothes. "We opened doors which opened upon holes cut in the wall" (B40). Similarly unfamiliar are the rugs:

> And there were great pieces of velvet upon the floors, soft and sinking under our feet, and we both laughed at this, for it seemed that they had been put there for no reason save to make men's steps a pleasure, which could not be, for men do not do things for a reason such as this. (B39)

To indicate how unfamiliar the hero is with rugs, Ayn Rand has him use one of them as a blanket or bedspread. After the Golden One falls asleep and he carries her to bed:

> [*crossed out*: We put the strange light covers of the bed over their body, but we wished them to be warm, so we took the velvet piece from the floor and added it to the covers.] (B43)

This incident also shows his tenderness toward the woman he loves. Nonetheless, the prospect of placing a rug (even a velvet rug) over the body of the beloved is a bit incongruous, and cutting it avoids unintentional humor.

The description of the details of the house, to be sure, is significant. This passage about beauty is itself beautiful, and coheres well with the theme of *Anthem*. The hero identifies pleasure as the purpose of these strange objects, and the contrast between his pleasureless world (because, after all, pleasure is an individual experience, and his world does not recognize the individual) and the world of the past is an important one. In a passage crossed out in the manuscript, he infers that the house itself is evidence of the will that formed it.

> [*crossed-out*: But the great wonder is that this house had been made beautiful. It did not happen to be so, it had been made so. It was not accident, it was a will which had made these rooms, for the joy of the eyes of men, and for the comfort of their bodies. Never had we known that a house could be beautiful or comforting to men.] (B40)

His explicit statement is not only an acknowledgment of beauty and comfort as implicit in the old world and as absent in his, but a non-mystical version of the Argument from Design, which states that the existence of a divine creator can be inferred from the order of the universe. Here, the hero infers from the nature of the house the existence—and the values—of the man or men who built it.

There are two small changes in detail after the hero discovers the concept "I." The first is that in the manuscript, he originally communicated his discovery immediately to his beloved; one can see on the page, though, that Ayn Rand added in the sentence: "Then I read many books for many days" (B56). The phrase "many days" may be a dramatic exaggeration. (What was the Golden One doing, during those days? If she didn't see him, wouldn't she have wondered where he was? And if they did see each other, how could he have held his tongue?) Nonetheless, the point is that his thirst for knowledge and understanding—especially at the time of the great discovery—exceeds even his love for the Golden One, and that this was an important point to make. In a similar spirit, Roark tells Gail Wynand that what he feels when he walks through a building is much greater than being in love.[10]

The second small change is the way the hero thinks of his fight against the world of the Damned. In the manuscript and in the published text, he speaks of returning to the City for the friends he left behind, and of building a protective barrier of wires: he intends, in other words, to give sanctuary to those who share his values, and to prevent intrusion by those who do not. In the manuscript, though, he also speaks of new weapons: "And strange weapons shall I build for myself, and strange new engines of power" (B59). It is, of course, true that he would be capable of constructing weapons far more effective than any the Council of Scholars is likely to devise, but mentioning military ammunition is anticlimactic in the context of the greater issues and the fiercest battle ahead.

In addition to the passages analyzed so far, all of which reveal Ayn Rand's purpose and purposefulness, there are some passages of particular philosophical interest, in that the changes show her avoiding philosophically confusing implications. Most of these occur in the final chapters, after the discovery of "ego," but one earlier passage, from the description of education, is as follows:

> And we learned about the bones of men, and the fur of beasts and the wings of the birds. And we learned not to believe the Old Ones in the House of the Useless, when they whisper that in the Unmentionable Times before the Great Rebirth men could fly like the birds. We know that this cannot be. (A14)

The hero acquires knowledge of objective reality—the physical make-up and capacity of the human body—that contradicts the true but vague statements of the Old Ones. But there are, in reality, no contradictions. The truth is that—as he eventually learns—men could fly, but not by their unaided bodies, only in the machines they built. But this passage, by itself, might suggest that knowledge is a negative, and is thus misleading.

Another possibly misleading passage occurs when he speaks, in the first part, of his "curse," including his "cursed" preference of a particular woman:

> [*crossed-out*: It is the curse in us which whispers in our heart and teaches us to say 'Yes' and 'No' to all things. But men may say nothing save 'Yes,' for all must agree with all.] (A39–40)

This passage is, I believe, related to a later passage in *Anthem*: "All things come to my judgment, and I weigh all things, and I seal upon them my 'Yes' or my 'No'" (p. 128 in the 1938 edition; as Robert Mayhew points out, this passage is reminiscent of Nietzsche's style and was excluded from the 1946 edition[11]). The passage is crossed out in the manuscript, perhaps, because it does not make literal sense. People in the City of the Damned obviously do say "No." The point was that people were forbidden to have individual preferences and judgments, but the point is made elsewhere more clearly.

The most extensive philosophically significant changes and cuts in the manuscript occur, as one would expect, in the final two chapters. In the first of these chapters, the hero speaks of his discovery of the concept "I" and, in general terms, of its meaning to him and to his life. In the second, he addresses his plans for the future struggle, i.e., the specific existential consequences of his discovery.

Among the passages omitted from Chapter XI is the following:

> [*crossed-out*: It is shameful for man to have a master. But the shame is multiplied ten thousand fold if he has ten thousand masters. It is agony for man to have his desires commanded unto him by another man. But the agony is multiplied ten thousand fold if his desires are at the mercy of ten thousand other men. It is a disgrace to man if his thoughts are received by him second-hand from the mind of another man. But the disgrace is multiplied ten thousand fold if his thoughts are received by him ten-thousand-hand from ten thousand other minds.] (B52–53)

This passage may have been cut because it is an exaggeration and because it appears to emphasize numbers as such. Its implications are not clear. Granted, collectivism is monstrous—but second-handedness itself is evil in principle regardless of the numbers involved.

Another omitted passage, also confusing in its implications, appears to undercut objective truth:

> [*crossed-out*: There is no Truth for all, and no eyes to see nor a voice to speak the Truth for all. There is only the Truth of the one and his Truth for each one. I am the guardian of my truth.] (B47)

In a later passage (also eventually omitted), the hero states that truth is individual in the way that joy, values, and choice are individual.

> I am. I think. I will. I am, for I know joy in living. But there is no joy for all, and no [way?] to know joy for all. There is only the joy of the one, and his joy for each one. But if the joy of the one is forbidden, then all joy is forbidden on earth.
>
>     I think, for I judge and I choose my truth. But there is no Truth for all, [*crossed out*: and no eyes to see for all,] nor a mind to judge for all. There is only the

Truth of the one, and his Truth for each one [*crossed out*: if he is such as can fathom this word of Truth]. But if the thought of the one is forbidden, then all thought is forbidden on earth.

[*crossed-out*: I live, for I think. But there is no brain which thinks for all.]

I will, for I know my desires, and I am free in that which I desire. But there is no will for all, and no heart to desire for all, and no hand to [reach?] the desired. There is only the will of the one, and his will for each one. But if the will of the one is forbidden, then all will is forbidden on earth. (B53–54)

In the 1938 text, some of these implications survive in the hero's statement that he is the beginning and end of all Truth (128); the 1946 edition removes the confusing implication that one can choose one's own truth.

Another philosophically significant revision concerns the statement, crossed out and omitted from the same chapter, that he came to understand "why my body knew the truth which my mind had been taught not to grasp" (B56). There follows a statement retained in the 1938 text: "For there is truth in my body, and no centuries of chains and lashes can kill this truth in the body of man" (136–37). (The 1946 edition eliminated the reference to the body.) The hero appears to be saying that there is a clash between the mind and the body. What Ayn Rand meant to imply, I believe, is that there was a conflict between his healthy, rational sense-of-life (or preconceptual grasp) and the mistaken conscious convictions he had adopted as a result of his education. Describing the subconscious/conscious conflict as a mind/body split is a stylistic device that may reflect Nietzsche's style, as Robert Mayhew points out;[12] it is clearly problematic, though, in view of Ayn Rand's eventual formulation of mind/body integration (which, as I will shortly point out, she was already approaching in this text).

A related passage is found in the first part of *The Fountainhead*:

> He felt at times as if the beams and girders were shaping themselves not into a house, but into a barricade to stop him; and the few steps on the sidewalk that separated him from the wooden fence enclosing the construction were the steps he would never be able to take. It was pain, but it was a blunted, unpenetrating pain. It's true, he would tell himself; it's not, his body would answer, the strange, untouchable healthiness of his body.[13]

Even if the mind/body split is a misleading way to describe the situation, the situation can exist: sometimes the subconscious is right and the conscious mind wrong. But the misleading implication does not mean that Prometheus or Ayn Rand failed to recognize the crucial value of reason. The hero understands that the mind is his means of survival, and the cause of the victory he anticipates over the world of the Damned. The manuscript in fact shows the explicit identification. Initially, his discovery is "I am. I live. I will." But, right on the page, the discovery becomes: "I am. I think. I will" (B46).

My final topic, in examining the manuscript in the light of the outline, is the matter of the hero's willingness to suffer and die, and his expectation that he will do so. The outline stated: "We shall all die, but we shall be glad to die." But this is not the last word on the subject.

Along the way, the author progressively removes the emphasis on possible martyrdom. Consider, for example, a passage cut from the first part:

[*crossed-out*: We have lost all fear of the laws. The Council may take our body, and they may have it broken and they may have it torn apart till our blood runs onto the earth. But something will be left to us, unbroken and untouched. That thing is our curse, our evil curse which we are blessing.] (A41–42)

He sounds like Rostand's Cyrano de Bergerac, proud to cherish and brandish his *panache* even as he loses all else, including life. He sounds like Kira in *We the Living*, holding on to her vision of life as her life's blood drains from her body. But the hero of *Anthem* is not Cyrano or Kira.

In the manuscript, he initially makes a distinction between his body and his discovery of the light, as if the body is nothing and the light is everything. He states: "We care not about our body, but our Light is above all things to us" (A71) and "[*crossed-out*: We cared not about our body and the punishment which awaited our body, but we could not betray the tunnel]" (B1). In the published text, there is a crucial change:

We care not about our body, but our Light is . . .
Yes, we do care. For the first time do we care about our body. For this wire is as a part of our body, as a vein torn from us, glowing with our blood. Are we proud of this thread of metal, or of our hands which made it, or is there a line to divide these two? (p. 77 of the 1938 edition)

The mind and the body are a unit; his work is an expression of his self. The work should live, and so should the man who did it.

The 1938 version, to be sure, includes some statements (omitted for the 1946 version) that indicate a willingness to die if necessary. He believes that he "may not be here to see" the final victory (146), and he says that he and his chosen friends "may fail" and "may perish" (147), as the first have perished in the past. But, even in the manuscript, he emphasizes the glory and nobility of the very moment he has reached, along with the glorious future he expects.

[*crossed-out*: I have read many books, and I have learned much, and I know that I shall learn much more as I read and work. The earth and the story of the earth are re-born in me. It is a great story, though it had its dark places, its sins and its sorrows. But it is the story of man's spirit and of the great struggle of man's spirit. Then a black abyss opened before man and swallowed the story. I stand on the other shore and I am ready to carry it on. These books are the bridge over the abyss of the dark ages behind me.] (B57–58)

Then here, upon this mountain top, with the world below me and nothing above me save the sun, I shall live my own truth. As a challenge to the lies of my brothers will it be, this life of mine—and as a reproach. [*crossed-out*: My home will be the haven of all those who are strong, who are proud, who are free among men. My home will be the beginning of the world's re-birth and the coming of a new race of men.] (B59–60)

[*crossed-out*: And the years which unrolled slowly behind men taught them but one lesson: that all their good, and all their wisdom had come drop by drop from the spirit of one, from some man, some one man who appeared here and there through the ages; that all their evil and all their folly had come as floods from the many, the many men who knew no thought and no power save in their numbers. For all truth comes from one. And all evil comes from the many. And those who stood alone brought their light to the world, but the many fought against all light, be it the light of an artist or the light of the scholar. And those who stood alone suffered and perished at the hands of the many. But their light and their truth did not perish, for even in their defeat and in the death of their bodies they were the winners and the conquerors. And with each victory they won, mankind took a step forward in spite of itself. This is what the old books call civilization. It was the work of the few. The many contributed nothing to it, save the impediments. But the few moved forward, and the human race moved with them. [Then come the sentences, included in the 1938 text on p. 141, explaining what freedom is.] And dimly men saw that their goal and the road to their happiness was in setting man free, each man free of all chains, that the best of them may fulfill their destiny, and the others may gain by the gifts of their betters in spirit. And so man fought the battle of freedom through the ages.] (B61–62)

The paragraphs above were cut from the manuscript, possibly for space, possibly because the explicit discussion of the issues was more appropriate for the scale of Roark's speech (which is anticipated here). But the ideas in these paragraphs are the ideas that inspire the hero, who faces his battle in the spirit conveyed by the statement: "anyone who fights for the future, lives in it today."[14]

Ayn Rand decided to conclude *Anthem* in a spirit not of martyrdom and anxiety, but with the hero's solemn, self-dedicated nobility, suspended between the heroism of Kira's death in action and the heroism of Roark's and Galt's triumphs. Prometheus would have been willing to die, but he expects to live, as a man. And the manuscript ends, as does the published work, with the sacred word "Ego." Like Roark and Galt, he stands, after much struggle, with the woman he loves, and at a height.

In examining the manuscript of *Anthem*, we observe fewer philosophically significant changes than is the case for the full-length novels. Not surprisingly, the author's philosophical grasp of the issues did not change in the time between writing the first page of the manuscript in the late summer of 1937 and publishing the first edition in 1938. She did, however, wrestle with matters of language, and we see on the pages the marks of that struggle. Her hero struggled, too—and not only because he lacked the word and the concept of the ego, but because he had been taught that it "is a sin to write this," i.e., that it was wrong to write for himself alone, and that it was wrong to live for his own sake. She also carefully pared down the narrative and descriptive details; it was, as she told Rose Wilder Lane, a poem.[15] Poems are characterized by concise, distilled, emotional intensity.

Small in length, *Anthem* is not small in subject. Even in a work designed for magazine publication, Ayn Rand was not capable of writing anything trivial, or of giving her ideas less than her best and fiercest efforts. This book presented distinct challenges that she labored to meet. It had, as she wrote to Paul Winans, "the same theme and spirit [as *The Fountainhead*], though in an entirely different form. In relation to THE FOUNTAINHEAD, ANTHEM is like one of those preliminary sketches that artists draw for their future large canvases."[16]

Why did Ayn Rand decide, during the writing, to emphasize her hero's confidence in his eventual triumph rather than his willingness to die in battle? She did not say, and I do not know. She was, in her larger project, trying to solve her plot problem with *The Fountainhead* in order to be able to conclude the novel with Roark's complete and ultimate triumph rather than with Toohey's temporary victory, i.e., the Stoddard Temple, the destruction of which Roark accepts (much as Prometheus would have accepted a valiant death). She was several months away from devising the episode of the Cortlandt explosion, which allowed her to show Roark winning over everyone and everything—but, even without the specific means of showing his victory, she knew that victory was the only possible outcome for *The Fountainhead*. And if that is true for a novel set in a real time and place, how much more so for a story set in a universe invented by her. Prometheus could and should win, and he could and should know it. It was surely no sin to write that.

And, having written *Anthem*, Ayn Rand went on to plan and compose *The Fountainhead*. Not far from the end of that novel, she wrote, for Wynand, a paragraph that speaks for the hero of *Anthem* and for its author as well:

He thought—while his hand moved rapidly—what a power there was in words; later, for those who heard them, but first for the one who found them: a healing power, a solution, like the breaking of a barrier. He thought, perhaps the basic secret the scientists have never discovered, the first fount of life, is that which happens when a thought takes shape in words.[17]

## NOTES

1. Ayn Rand, *The Fountainhead* (New York: Bobbs-Merrill, 1943; Signet fiftieth anniversary paperback edition, 1993), 376.

2. Ayn Rand, *Atlas Shrugged* (New York: Random House, 1957; Signet thirty-fifth anniversary paperback edition, 1992), 347.

3. The manuscript and outline of *Anthem* are found in the Ayn Rand Papers at the Library of Congress. I have made use of the bound volume of the photocopies of the papers, at the Ayn Rand Archives. For pages A52–55 and A61–65, the copies of which were entirely dark, Fred Bauman of the Library of Congress made copies for me of the originals.

4. Leonard Peikoff, introduction to the fiftieth anniversary American edition of *Anthem*, by Ayn Rand (New York: Signet, 1995), xi.

5. Biographical interviews (Ayn Rand Archives), and Ayn Rand, *The Art of Nonfiction: A Guide for Writers and Readers*, ed. Robert Mayhew (New York: Plume, 2001), 162–63.

6. Peikoff, introduction, xi.

7. Robert Mayhew, "*Anthem*: '38 & '46," in the present volume, p. 33–37.

8. Rand, *Atlas Shrugged*, 967.

9. Biographical interviews (Ayn Rand Archives).

10. Rand, *Fountainhead*, 550–51.

11. Mayhew, "*Anthem*: '38 & '46," p. 39.

12. Mayhew, "*Anthem*: '38 & '46," p. 39.

13. Rand, *Fountainhead*, 175–76 .

14. Ayn Rand, "Introduction," *The Romantic Manifesto: A Philosophy of Literature*, revised edition (New York: Signet, 1975), viii.

15. Michael S. Berliner, *Letters of Ayn Rand* (New York: Dutton, 1995), 293.

16. Ayn Rand Papers (unpublished), September 9, 1946, Ayn Rand Archives.

17. Rand, *Fountainhead*, 642.

# 2

## Publishing *Anthem*

*Richard E. Ralston*

Ayn Rand intended *Anthem* as a story or serial in a magazine. But Ann Watkins, her literary agent, pitched it to publishers as a book in 1937. She was not successful. As with *We the Living*, a book critical of collectivism was unlikely to be well received by many New York publishers in the 1930s. This is confirmed by correspondence Ayn Rand had in 1947 with Archibald Ogden (at Bobbs-Merrill) regarding *Anthem*. When he told her he doubted *Anthem* was rejected for political reasons in 1937, she replied:

> Ann Watkins submitted it to three publishers. I do not know (but suspect) the reasons why two of them rejected it; but I know the reason given by Macmillan who were my publishers then [of *We the Living*]. They said that *I did not understand socialism*. I think you are probably in a position to see right now how well I understood it.[1]

Unsuccessful in the United States, Watkins sent the manuscript to Cassell, the British publisher of *We the Living*, who had actively been soliciting additional titles from Ayn Rand. They published *Anthem* in 1938 and kept it in print for many years. Originally, Newman Flower at Cassell proposed an illustrated edition. Ayn Rand responded in a January 2, 1938 letter:

> in the case of illustrations I should like to offer my suggestions to the artist in order to keep the spirit of the book intact, in text and appearance. I would not ask for this if this story were not more precious to me than anything I have ever considered writing.
>
> It is so very personally mine, it is in a way, my manifesto, my profession of faith. The essence of my entire philosophy.[2]

You may quote my saying this in the advance publicity for the book if you find it advisable.[3]

In his reply (of January 12, 1938), Flower indicated that there would be no illustrations, as they would hold up publication, and added:

> I was intensely stirred by this piece of work. I thought the writing marvelous. I am not going to say we shall sell a lot of the book. One can never tell, of course—books being the biggest gamble in the world—but it is a book I should certainly not have liked to have passed. I regard it as an ornament to our list.[4]

It is unclear how long Watkins tried to secure an American publisher for *Anthem*, though it is likely that finding a publisher for *The Fountainhead* soon replaced any attempts to publish *Anthem*. In any case, after the publication of *The Fountainhead* in 1943, Ayn Rand no longer wanted to publish *Anthem* as a book in the United States. She wrote to the Ann Watkins agency on February 1, 1944:

> In reply to your inquiry about *Anthem*, I must say that I have not done anything with it, so far—because I think it would be wrong to publish it at this time. It is too short a book, on the same theme, to come out right after *The Fountainhead*. It might spoil the market which *The Fountainhead* has created for me. I have not shown it to Bobbs-Merrill at all and do not think it would be advisable right now.
>
> If you feel that you can arrange for a magazine publication of *Anthem* and you want to handle it let me know.[5]

In fact, the first publication in the United States was in pamphlet form, published by Pamphleteers, Inc., an organization whose purpose was stated in the foreword of the pamphlet: "to further the cause of freedom and individualism." Leonard Read, in this publisher's foreword (later reprinted in the Caxton edition), described a meeting in Ayn Rand's home in Chatsworth, California, during which he and William Mullendore, an executive at Southern California Edison, learned of *Anthem*, its theme, and its British publishing history. That meeting led to their decision to publish the novel in the Pamphleteers series of pamphlets, which previously included only nonfiction essays in politics or economics.

This occasioned the many revisions to the British edition discussed in chapter 3 of this volume, which are reflected in all later editions. As usual, Ayn Rand paid close attention to the design and promotion of the pamphlet. In a letter to Pamphleteers on June 24, 1946, for example, she suggested many minor changes to the advertisement copy, much of which she liked: "At the top of page 2, the line, 'Too daring for 1937,' is very good, and intriguing, but the line following it, 'too incredible,' weakens the effect by qualifying it. I suggest you eliminate this last."[6] Rand edited and approved advertising, including a poster and counter display card, and in at least one instance she personally reimbursed Pamphleteers for the cost of a poster. A first printing of 5,000 copies was soon followed in February of 1947 with a reprinting of 1,500 copies. In November of 1946 she received a detailed list of 175 bookstores that ordered the pamphlet.[7]

The original intention to publish *Anthem* in a magazine was eventually realized when it was published in the June 1953 issue of *Famous Fantastic Mysteries*. (The magazine had requested publication rights much earlier. On November 30, 1945, Rand had written to Alan Collins at her new agent, Curtis Brown Ltd., asking, "Could you let me know whether this is a legitimate, respected magazine?"[8]) This attractively illustrated version likely reached a new and larger audience for the book. It was almost immediately followed by the first American publication in book form.

The hardcover edition by the Caxton Printers was published in 1953, reproducing the edits and foreword of the Pamphleteers edition. (This edition is still in print, and has sold more than 100,000 copies.)

Once again, Ayn Rand took a "hands-on" approach to promotion of the book. For example, in a December 23, 1952, letter to J. H. Gipson, the president of Caxton, she wrote:

> Thank you for the advertising material on *Anthem*, which you sent me. I am enclosing copies of it, which I have revised and retyped, and am also returning your original copies, so that you may see what particular changes I have made.
>
> I have attempted to follow the form of the original material, but to stress the positive theme of Individualism, rather than the negative aspect of an expose of the Collectivist State. This last might give readers the impression that *Anthem* is merely another sordid story on the order of Orwell's *1984* (which, incidentally, was written many years after *Anthem* had been published in England).
>
> I have rewritten the copy about the story because I felt that it was both too detailed and too confused, and that it suggested the tone of a non-fiction political treatise. I can't say that I blame the young man who wrote it, however—it was a terribly difficult job to do, even for me.
>
> You will note that I have included in this copy a brief mention of the publishing history of *Anthem*. I consider it most essential that we do not mislead the public and do not give the impression that *Anthem* is a *new* novel by me, written later than *The Fountainhead*. It is essential that all our publicity mention the fact that this is a new edition, not a new work.
>
> As a small publicity suggestion, I would not feature the description "tender and terrific" out of the context of Ruth Alexander's review. It is good and impressive in the review, but not right when given without quotes (*Anthem* is anything but tender).
>
> Under separate cover, I am returning the sketch of the jacket design. It is excellent and I like it very much for its dignified simplicity. The only suggestion I would make here is that the color yellow tends to give the lettering a faded, "yel-

lowed" look. A pale green or blue-green would be infinitely better. Yellow and black is a bad combination, it suggests lifelessness.[9]

It was no longer a challenge to find a publisher for any novel by Ayn Rand after the success of *The Fountainhead* and *Atlas Shrugged*. Caxton licensed New American Library to publish a paperback edition of *Anthem* in 1961, and this quickly achieved far greater sales than all previous editions combined.

Since *Anthem*'s initial publication in the 1930s, many translations have appeared, in languages including Hebrew, Romanian, Finnish, Dutch, Swedish, Norwegian, Turkish, German, Italian, Spanish, Danish, and Chinese. In 1947, Ayn Rand received a sales report from the Spanish publisher indicating 6,339 copies had been sold—about the same as U.S. sales by that time.[10] However, as with most of Ayn Rand's books, foreign sales have never been a significant fraction of sales in the United States, and translations seldom remained in print for many years. Translations of *Anthem* in print at this writing include German and Italian.

The publication history of the English language editions of *Anthem* merged when in 1995 New American Library published a Fiftieth Anniversary Edition (celebrating the first American edition of 1946). This special edition includes an introduction by Leonard Peikoff, and an appendix consisting of a complete facsimile reproduction of Ayn Rand's 1946 edits to her copy of the original 1938 British edition.

Total sales to date of New American Library and other Penguin editions of *Anthem* have reached more than 3,500,000 copies, and more than 100,000 copies are currently sold each year. This is a remarkable record for a book that Ayn Rand completed during the summer of 1937 as "a kind of rest" from working out plot problems in *The Fountainhead*.[11]

## NOTES

1. Michael S. Berliner, ed., *Letters of Ayn Rand* (New York: Dutton, 1995), 473.

2. Note that these observations were made years in advance of the publication of *The Fountainhead* and *Atlas Shrugged*.

3. Unpublished material (Ayn Rand Archives).

4. Unpublished material (Ayn Rand Archives).

5. Unpublished material (Ayn Rand Archives).

6. Berliner, *Letters*, 285.

7. Unpublished material (Ayn Rand Archives).

8. Unpublished material (Ayn Rand Archives).

9. Berliner, *Letters*, 494–95. The color was changed to blue-green.

10. Unpublished material (Ayn Rand Archives).

11. Biographical interviews (Ayn Rand Archives).

# 3

## *Anthem*: '38 & '46

*Robert Mayhew*

Ayn Rand wrote *Anthem* during the summer of 1937. It was first published in England in 1938, by Cassell and Company (who had published the British edition of *We the Living* a year earlier). *Anthem* would not have an American publisher until 1946, after the publication of *The Fountainhead*. The American version was a significantly revised edition. To give one indication of the difference between the two, the word-count of the 1946 edition is 19,190—approximately 18 percent fewer words than in the 1938 edition (23,484).[1]

Ayn Rand made her changes by hand to a copy of the 1938 edition, which she then sent to her publisher. (A facsimile of this hand-corrected copy has been reprinted as an appendix to the fiftieth anniversary edition of *Anthem*.[2])

On at least three occasions she described the kinds of revisions she needed to make in preparing the American edition. In a February 28, 1946, letter to Leonard Read, she wrote that before it could be re-issued, "I'd want to edit the story a little first; it's old and there are some passages which I think are bad writing and which I'd like to straighten out."[3] She provided more details elsewhere about what she thought was wrong. In her April 1946 foreword to the American edition, she wrote:

> I have edited it for this publication, but have confined the editing to its style; I have reworded some passages and cut out some excessive language. No idea or incident was added or omitted; the theme, content and structure are untouched. The story remains as it was. (xiv)

Finally, in an interview in the early sixties, she explained her main concerns:

> Precision, clarity, brevity, and eliminating any editorial or slightly purple adjectives. You see, the attempt to have that semi-archaic style was very difficult. Some of the passages were exaggerated. In effect, I was sacrificing content for style— in some places, simply because I didn't know how to say it. By the time I wrote *The Fountainhead*, I was in full control of my style and I knew how to achieve the same effect, but by simple and direct means, without getting too biblical.[4]

This essay is a survey of the revisions Ayn Rand made in bringing *Anthem* to its final form—revisions which range from minor changes in punctuation to significant changes made to avoid unintended philosophical implications. As we shall see, although she did on the whole limit her changes to style, and "no idea or incident was added or omitted," some ideas and incidents were revised and some *descriptions* were added and others omitted.

In his introduction to the fiftieth anniversary American edition of *Anthem*, Leonard Peikoff writes: "If (ignoring the concrete issue of biblical style) you study her changes and ask 'Why?' as you proceed, there is virtually no limit to what you can learn about writing—Ayn Rand's or your own" (xi). This essay should prove useful in such a study.

(It is worth mentioning at the outset that in what follows, I often speculate about why Ayn Rand cut a particular passage without replacing it with anything else. In such cases, one obvious reason for the cut—which may be the only reason—is that the passage was simply unnecessary, i.e., it was redundant or otherwise did not contribute to the story and its theme. Keep this possibility in mind whenever omitted material is discussed.)

## MINOR REVISIONS

As far as I can tell, none of the changes Ayn Rand made was the correction of a typographical error.[5]

Twenty-four changes were made in order to transform the British English of the 1938 edition into American English. Nine of these are changes in spelling from "ou" to "o", e.g., hono[u]r (19/25), odo[u]r (53/46), labo[u]r (59/50), smo[u]lder (112/84). Fourteen are changes from the hyphenated (British) to the un-hyphenated (American) spelling of "today," "tomorrow," and "tonight" (see, e.g., 46/42, 86/67, 73/59).[6]

Ayn Rand inserted paragraphing twenty-two times.

I recorded six changes in punctuation. In three cases, she inserted a comma (35/35, 46/42, 51–52/45–46), and in a single case, she eliminated a comma (140/100). Slightly more interesting—as it reflects her overall attitude toward revising *Anthem*—is the fact that she twice replaced an exclamation point with a period (56/49, 91/70).

Few revisions were made to correct grammatical errors; but in four cases, she originally used "as" where "like" would be better (89/69, 112/84–85, 113/85 [twice]). Here are two examples:

> For you do not look [as] <like> a Scholar. (89/69)
> The days before us are without end, [as] <like> the forest. (113/85)[7]

## REVISED DETAILS

In at least three cases, details were changed (as opposed to omitted). I refer here to minor changes in content, not in style. First, Equality 7-2521's[8] height is changed from six feet one inch to six feet (7/18). Ayn Rand may have concluded that six feet one inch was too precise a measurement for such a primitive culture, and changed it on those grounds.

Second, Rand changed the number of tables, cups, and plates in the dining hall of the street sweepers.

> The shadow on the sundial marks off a half-hour while we dress and eat our breakfast in the dining hall, [which has three] <where there are five> long tables with [one hundred] <twenty> clay plates and [one hundred] <twenty> clay cups on each table. (22/27)

So the three hundred street sweepers of the original edition were reduced to one hundred. Perhaps she concluded that three hundred were too many for the size of the city she envisioned (and the size of the dining hall where they all ate their meals), and one hundred were too many for one table.

Third, the name of someone called "Equality 4-6998" was changed to "Democracy 4-6998" (93/72). I assume she originally thought that giving this character the same "first" name as the hero, with only the numbers differing, would underscore the anonymity and lack of individuality of the institution of state-given names in *Anthem*. But she decided to make the change, no doubt to avoid confusion.

In five cases, Ayn Rand *omitted* details:

> (1) *Cut*: we stand in rows, and stretch our arms and bend our bodies while the Council beats a drum. This we do in order that our bodies may be healthy and fit and good for work. (22–23/27)

I am not sure why she made this change. It's possible she did not want to convey the idea that the state actually did something to promote the health of these people (as opposed to their bare subsistence), though the notion that the people were made "fit and good for work" would not seem to raise any problems.

> (2) And we take no heed of the law which says that men [are to receive one hundred lashes, if they are found to be taking notice of any among women, and if they survive the lashes, they are sent for ten years to the Palace of Detention. [Man] may not think of women, save at the Time of Mating. (45/41)

The important point is that men by law are not allowed to think of women, unless permitted to do so, and that Equality ignores this law. The rest distracts from this point, and is unnecessary.

The remaining three examples—all cut from the original—involve clothing and other adornments worn by the hero and/or heroine.

> (3) Never have men worn adornments of any kind, for it is evil to adorn one among the others. But we gathered leaves and twigs, there, by the stream, and we wove a wreath of them. We know not how such a thought came to us. But we put the wreath upon our head and we looked into the water. And we thought that it was beautiful. Then we said to ourselves that we were vain and foolish, so we threw the wreath away, and we left the stream, and walked on. (104/80)

Ayn Rand mentions a wreath scene in her original plan for *Anthem*,[9] and I imagine she thought it was important in that it shows Equality doing something creative and against the spirit of the society he recently escaped. But it also portrays him as ignorant of what motivates him, and feeling guilty about such things. Further, I do not think this gesture quite fits the masculinity of a typical Ayn Rand hero.[10]

> (4) Our tunics and sandals had long since fallen to shreds. We both wore the skins of the beasts we had killed, we carried our bow and arrows over one shoulder, and the glass box with the power of the sky in our arms. (117/88)

My guess is that however admirable it is for Equality and Liberty 5-3000[11] to make their own clothing, there is something esthetically objectionable about the move from white tunics to the garb of cavemen.

I think that by cutting the bulk of the next passage, greater emphasis is placed on Liberty looking at herself in the mirror, which is no doubt where Ayn Rand wanted it; further, this is what we would expect Equality to stress in his diary.

> (5) We did this work alone, for no words of ours could take the Golden One away from the big glass which is not glass. They stood before it and they looked and looked upon their own body. [They had found a small casket in the sleeping room, and it was full of jewels, such as no men had ever touched, save upon the great mosaics of the Palace of the World Council. The Golden One put long

strings of rubies on their shoulders, and circles of gold upon their arms, and clusters of diamonds on their ears. These things must have been made for such use, only we could not have guessed it, but the Golden One guessed. And they stood before the magic glass, and they looked, and the sun sent fires to dance upon the jewels, and sparks of all colours glittered in the fur which wrapped the body of the Golden One.] (123–24/92)

Another objection to this passage—which I discuss later—is its reference to the great mosaics of the Palace of the World Council.


## BREVITY

Ayn Rand made dozens of revisions aimed at brevity—i.e., conveying the same meaning with fewer words and without redundancy. (These are cases of her removing excessive language, though not exaggerated Biblical language, which I cover later). Here are eight examples, which speak for themselves:

(1) We walked [down the aisle towards] <to> the dais (20/25).
(2) We came together to the great ravine [which is] behind the Theatre. It is empty [of all things] save <for> trees and weeds. (28/30).
(3) We [fell on our knees] <knelt> (30/32).
(4) keep [your mouth closed forever about this] <silent> (33/34).
(5) The eyes of our brothers are [not clear, but veiled and lustreless] <dull> (52/46).
(6) the wire glowed! It came to life, it turned [to a faint shadow of red, and the shadow grew, and it became] red [red as molten metal] (74/59).
(7) We picked a stone and we sent it as an arrow at [the body of] a bird. (103/79).
(8) raze [to the ground] the cities of the enslaved (146/104).[12]


## PRECISION, CLARITY, ACCURACY

There were around one hundred instances of word replacement. Some words were replaced to remove unwanted philosophical connotations (more on those later); others were replaced for accuracy—here are three examples:

(1) There is green [moss] <mould> in the grooves of the letters and yellow streaks [up]on the marble. (8/19)

This is simply an issue of accuracy: one more likely finds mould (note the spelling, not "mold," which is currently the standard American usage) than moss in the grooves of letters carved in marble.

(2) We felt the [tendons] <cords> of our neck. (20/26)

"Tendons" is in fact more precise than "cords," but it suggests a level of knowledge that neither Equality nor anyone else in that culture possesses, and thus was less accurate in this context.

(3) We burn the [sticks] <wood> we find in the ravine. (36/35–36)

The original is unnecessarily narrow. In building a fire, Equality would not have limited himself to sticks. Further, in writing about it in his diary, it sounds primitive or childish for him to describe the wood he gathers as "sticks."

In roughly two dozen cases, a word was replaced to achieve greater grammatical correctness and/or precision. Here are a couple of examples:

We exist through, by and for our brothers [which] <who> are the State. (12/21)
then we knew that we were looking [upon] <at> the squares of the iron grill in the door. (82/65)

Similarly, a couple of verb-changes were made for greater accuracy. For example:

We knew suddenly that this place [had been] <was> left from the Unmentionable Times. (31/32)

Whereas "had been" puts the focus on someone having done something, "was" makes the line more a description of a fact.

Finally, here are some assorted examples of revisions that fall under this heading:

And then we saw iron rings as steps leading <down a shaft> into [the heart of the earth] <a darkness without bottom>. (29/31)
We have stolen candles from the [larder of the] Home <of the Street Sweepers>. (35/35)
Our body was not like the bodies of our brothers, for our limbs were straight <and thin> and hard and strong. (104/80)
we saw great peaks before us <in the west>. (116/88)


## ELIMINATION OF EXCESSIVE AND BIBLICAL LANGUAGE

The style of *Anthem* is unique among Ayn Rand's novels. *Anthem* is written in the form of a diary, and describes an individual's discovery of the concept "I" and his emergence out of a primitive collectivist culture. Rand attempted, she tells us, to give it a "semi-archaic style." Yet when she came to revise *Anthem*, she decided she needed to remove the "slightly purple adjectives" and passages that were "exaggerated" and "too biblical."[13]

I begin with some formulas that Ayn Rand decided should not be employed. The first type is certainly Biblical (that is to say, in the style of the King James Version of the Bible). In at least seven cases, she had used a "holy of holies" formula for emphasis.

> But it is [the] <a> sin [of sins] to give men names which distinguish them from other men. (45/41)
> the fire [of fires,] which is called the Dawn of the Great Rebirth (56/48)
> *Cut*: Great Mercy of all human mercies (56/49)
> And that night we knew that to hold the body of women in our arms is neither ugly nor shameful, but the <one> ecstasy [of ecstasies] granted to the [human] race of men. (111/84)
> *Cut*: This is the sacrament and the holy of holies. (127/94)
> *Cut* (where "it" refers to the hero's happiness): It is the reason of reasons. (130/95)
> For in [his heart of hearts and in] the [sanctuary] <temple> of his spirit, each man is alone. (132/96)

Note, however, that she did not object to every use of this formula. In the opening chapter, Equality's reference to "our crime of crimes" is retained (10/20).[14]

In at least a dozen cases, Ayn Rand eliminated a slightly Biblical formula involving a verb plus the word "not." Here are two examples:

> We <do not> think [not] of them as Liberty 5–3000 any longer. (45/41)
> We <do not> care [not]. (93/72)

In over a dozen cases, she replaced "upon"—which has a more archaic feel—with "on." For example: "Nothing moves in this tunnel save our hand [upon] <on> the paper" (6/17). Similarly, in the following passages, the word "forth" has a Biblical tone that is unnecessary, and could simply be removed: "the Students so assigned go [forth] to work" and "those Students go [forth] into the Home of the Leaders" (19/25).

Toward the beginning of the final chapter, when the hero is talking to Liberty—and only in this chapter and in this context—Ayn Rand originally used some typically Biblical pronouns:

> I love [thee] <you>. (137/98)
> It shall be [thy] <your> name. (137/99)
> Let this be [thy] <your> name, my Golden One, for [we have a new world to build and thou art] <you are> to be the mother of a new [race] <kind> of gods. (138/99)

Ayn Rand likely used these second person singular pronouns because they were archaic and *singular*. The revisions, however, make the style of these lines more consistent with the rest of *Anthem* (in its revised form), without sacrificing the romance, grandeur, and poetry of the scene.

The following six passages were all eliminated and not replaced with anything else. I believe they are all examples of Ayn Rand in the original "sacrificing content for style."

> (1) Thus did Liberty 5–3000 walk toward us in the field that day, as a thin flame in the wind, as a swaying white mist, as a scourge, as a miracle. (41/39)

Rand had already described Liberty walking toward Equality; adding that she did so "as a thin flame," etc., adds nothing.

> (2) And the curse in us cries in a voice of thunder that we would rather see all our brothers, yes, all the thousands and thousands of them, die in agonies unspeakable, than see one golden hair hurt on the head of Liberty 5–3000. And these words, which should burn the paper we write them on, by the fire of their evil, these words frighten us not. (44–45/41)

This passage occurs in Chapter 2, when Equality first encounters Liberty and recognizes that his thoughts about her represent his "second Transgression of Preference" (41). But the language and the thought about seeing thousands of men dying "in agonies unspeakable" is exaggerated and distracts from the emphasis on what he feels for Liberty. It may also have been too early in the novella for Equality to choose a great value over all of his brothers (which he won't do in the revised version until Chapter 7, when he chooses his invention over society).

> (3) The Light! . . .
>     Here, under our hands, at our bidding, the light of the sky, the light to set the earth aglow, the Light smokeless and flameless and unquenchable! . . . (73/59, ellipses in the original)

This was originally the opening of Chapter 3, which gives an account of the hero's rediscovery of electricity and re-invention of the electric light. But Ayn Rand chose to cut it and instead to begin with what follows this passage. The result is a simpler, more straightforward, more effective—though still slightly archaic—opening: "We made it. We created it. We brought it forth from the night of the ages." (59). Moreover, with this opening, the emphasis is placed on the hero and the fact that *he* is the source of the achievement.

(4) It glowed! It glowed like a star fallen from heaven upon the Council table. (90/70)

This passage was preceded by the line "Then the wire glowed," which was enough.

(5) *Collective 0–0009 to Equality*: You scum of the swines! (92/71)

The combination of scum and swine sounds strange in English, and in fact makes no sense if taken literally.

(6) It was as if dawn had come to the night of my soul, and the sun had risen. And every thing became clear to me. (136/98)

Originally, these were the first two lines of the second paragraph of Chapter 12, in which Equality announces his discovery of the word "I." It is followed by: "I understood the blessed thing which I had called my curse." This understanding is what Rand wants to convey—and she decided it was best to do this simply, without the metaphor of dawn coming to the night of his soul.

In a number of cases, Rand *revised* her formulation to achieve a more direct, less exaggerated, style. Here are three such revisions, all involving positive emotions:

We [rejoice in writing] <wish to write> this name. (39/38)
we . . . [rejoice] <are glad> to be living. (53/47)
But the only [two] things which [set our soul on fire was] <taught us joy were> the power we created in our [glass box] <wires>, and the Golden One. (114/86)

In the first two cases, she may have come to regard "rejoice" as too biblical. Further, in the first case, the change to "wish" improves the line by putting the focus on Equality's will. In the third, not only does the revision simplify the line, it also better connects Equality's feelings to the previous line, which discusses joy explicitly: "There is no joy for men, save the joy shared with all their brothers" (114/86).

Chapter 6 describes Equality's time in the Palace of Corrective Detention, where he is whipped for refusing to tell the Council where he had been, after he was discovered arriving home late. The whipping scene was revised. Although this scene is not exaggerated in the original (in that it conveys what happened to Equality as accurately as the revised scene), it is "too much" in another sense (more on this shortly), and thus I think it appropriate to discuss it here. There were four significant revisions to the whipping scene:

The first blow of the lash felt as <if> [a thin iron collar which cut into our flesh, and the folds of pain unrolled from it as a mantle, over our body, to the tips of

our toes, and we thought] our spine had been cut in two. The second blow [tore the mantle off] <stopped the first>, and for a [blinding] second we [could feel] <felt> nothing, [and] then the pain struck us in our throat and fire ran in our lungs without air. (81/64)
*Cut*: We felt once as if iron teeth had ripped our thigh open, and then our chest. (81–82/64)
*Cut*: And then we felt a thin trickle, heavy and warm, from our waist, running down our legs. But we did not cry out. (82/65)
[Then t]<T>he lash whistled again[, and we thought we were floating, floating away, and that soft thing writhing upon the stones concerned us not any longer]. We wondered who was sprinkling burning coal dust upon the floor, for we saw [little red beads lighting and lying and] <drops of red> twinkling on the stones around us. [We wondered whence that strange sound was coming, the dull sound of a stick beating upon soft, wet mud.] (83/65)

I assume Ayn Rand revised this scene extensively because it was too gory, and thus distracting. Further, she may have concluded that the revisions make the passage more consistent with what Equality would have written about this ordeal in his diary.[15]


## NIETZSCHEAN CONNECTIONS

As a transition between revisions of exaggerated language and revisions of philosophically unclear or dubious lines, I turn to those passages in *Anthem* that may reflect the influence—stylistically if not philosophically—of Friedrich Nietzsche.

Ayn Rand read all of the major works of Nietzsche, in Russian translation, before she left for the United States, and she had a positive reaction to certain aspects of his philosophy. In 1926, in America, she purchased an English translation of *Thus Spake Zarathustra*, and in the 1930s continued to have a favorable view of some aspects of it.[16]

Usually the Nietzschean influence evident in *Anthem* is purely stylistic, and the changes she made of this sort fall under the heading of revisions to exaggerated or Biblical passages. (Note that in the early sixties, she said that "*Zarathustra* is very much like the Bible; it's written poetically."[17]) With a couple of exceptions, the relevant passages all come around or after Equality's discovery of the concept "I," which should not come as a surprise, as this is when he is most triumphant and explicitly or outspokenly heroic—triumphant heroism being very much a part of the spirit of *Thus Spake Zarathustra*.

One section of *Thus Spake Zarathustra* is entitled "Old and New Tables" (with "tables" or "tablets" used in the sense of a moral code—an obvious

example being the Ten Commandments). Here are some passages from
*Zarathustra*, in the English translation Ayn Rand owned and read:[18]

> Here do I sit and wait, old broken tables around me and also new half-writ-
> ten tables.
> Behold, here is a new table; but where are my brethren who will carry it with
> me to the valley and into the hearts of flesh?
> O my brethren, break up, break up for me the old tables!
> O my brethren, a *new nobility* is needed, which shall be the adversary of all
> populace and potentate rule, and shall inscribe anew the word "noble" on new
> tables.[19]

Compare these passages to two that Rand cut from *Anthem*:

> This moment is a warning and an omen. This moment is a sacrament which calls
> us and dedicates our body to the service of some unknown duty we shall know.
> Old laws are dead. Old tables have been broken. A clean, unwritten slate is now
> lying before our hands. Our fingers are to write. (125–26/93)
> I leave broken the tables of my brothers, and my own tables do I now write for
> my own spirit. (134/97)

These two passages are similar in style and in content to the ones from
*Zarathustra* quoted above—especially in the idea of breaking the old tables
(i.e., the old moral code) and replacing them with new ones. Why did Ayn
Rand cut these passages?

I think there are two major reasons: (1) She did not replace these passages with anything else, which means they were cut for the same reason
other exaggerated or Biblical passages were. (2) Although the major problem is stylistic, there were also philosophical reasons for cutting them.
First, "a sacrament which calls us and dedicates our body to the service of
some unknown duty" implies that duty and service are (at least in some
cases) good. As the theme of *Anthem* makes clear, duty—an unchosen
moral obligation—and service are not part of Rand's moral code.[20] She
probably had in mind Equality's intransigent devotion to his task: to reach
the concept he is on the verge of discovering (I, ego) and to define the
moral code—and to work toward the building of a new kind of society
and culture—based on this concept. But she came to recognize the erroneous implications of this line.

Second, the idea of writing a new moral code, as stated, is philosophically
dubious. In Nietzsche's case, as far as I understand him, human beings with
great souls should write a new, noble moral code upon new tables. Such
men are beyond good and evil and will create (not discover, because there
is no objective moral truth) a new code of what constitutes the good (and impose it on others by force).[21] There is no evidence that Ayn Rand embraced

this view of morality, even in the mid-1930s. But what Equality is here talking about is discovering—or to use the language of Hugh Akston in *Atlas Shrugged, defining*—a new code of morality, one that recognizes the nature of man.[22] But one could read these passages (as originally written) as advocating a Nietzschean relativism, and so they were cut.

Similar concerns apply to the following passage on the creation or discovery of truth:

> It is my eyes which see, and the sight of my eyes grants beauty to the earth. It is my ears which hear, and the hearing of my ears gives its song to the world. [All things come to my judgment, and I weigh all things, and I seal upon them my "Yes" or my "No." Thus is Truth born. Such is the root of all Truth and the leaf, such is the fount of all Truth and the ocean, such is the base of all Truth and the summit. I am the beginning of all Truth. I am its end.] <It is my mind which thinks, and the judgment of my mind is the only searchlight that can find the truth. It is my will which chooses, and the choice of my will is the only edict I must respect.> (128/94)[23]

I think she revised this passage primarily to remove the philosophically problematic lines "Thus is Truth born. . . . I am the beginning of all Truth," which might suggest that the source of truth is not objective reality (grasped by a mind), but the human being alone, who creates truth. It is most likely that her precise meaning was distorted by the exaggerated style, and that what she in fact meant was that truth had to be discovered by men like Equality (as he had re-discovered the truth about electricity and the electric light). Perhaps at this point in her philosophical development she did not see clearly how to express the difference between a human mind *creating* truth and *discovering* it—at least not in a way that avoided misleading subjectivist implications. Further, I think the revision improves the metaphor ("the judgment of my mind is the only searchlight that can find the truth" as opposed to "I weigh all things, and I seal upon them my 'Yes' or my 'No'"). A searchlight better fits the particular kind of search for truth that Equality is engaged in (in secret, in a tunnel at night, experimenting with electricity).

Ayn Rand revised the following passage for similar reasons.

> [For there is truth in my body, and no] <I understood that> centuries of chains and lashes [can kill this truth in the body of man] <will not kill the spirit of man nor the sense of truth within him>. (136–37/98)[24]

The important change Rand makes is from "body" (and "body of man")—which is not where truth resides—to "man" which is where it does reside (at least in a metaphorical sense).[25]

The emphasis on will is strong in Nietzsche—and will in the sense of a powerful faculty that acts independently within a person (and even outside any particular person and within a culture). For example:

> so willeth it my creating Will;
> Willing emancipateth;
> But to man doth it ever impel me anew, my fervent creative will;
> Yea, something invulnerable, unburiable is with me, something that would rend rocks asunder: it is called *my Will*.[26]

There is a strong emphasis on will in *Anthem*, no doubt because there is so much emphasis on the will of all men, the will of our brothers, the will of the Councils,[27] which conflict with the will of the hero, Equality. Ayn Rand's revisions do not lessen this emphasis. But she did revise some of the passages in which Equality's will is described. As long as he is asserting his will, there is no problem (as we shall see: e.g., "I will it"). But she cut those passages in which the will might seem to be a separate driving force within a person. Here are two passages:

> [Where I go, there does my will go before me. My will, which chooses, and orders, and creates. My will, the master which knows no masters. My will, the liberator and the conqueror. My will, which is the thin flame, still and holy, in the shrine of my body, my body which is but the shrine of my will.] Many words have been granted me, and some are wise, and some are false, but only three are holy: "I will it!" (129/94–95)
> *Cut*: And so I hail my will! And so I guard my will before I guard my life. Let no man covet my will and the freedom of my will. Woe to them who have tried. (131/95)

Again, it is not clear to me what caused her to write these lines in the original. Two possibilities come to mind: (1) this is simply a case of style distorting content, so that when she wrote this, she was not able to express clearly the difference between her conception of man (and his will) and the Nietzschean conception; or (2) when she wrote this, she had (at least temporarily and/or partially) a more Nietzschean conception of the will—clearly not in the sense of a will *opposed* to reason and of a separate Will to Power that moves not only human beings but entire groups and cultures, but in the limited sense of a separate will within an individual. I think that (2) is unlikely, however, or else we would have seen more signs of it in her earlier writings (and especially in the 1936 edition of *We the Living*).

According to Ayn Rand's philosophy, independence is *not* non-conformity. A rational person does not act in order to be like others; neither does he act to be unlike others.[28] In Nietzsche, however, striking out on one's own and creating one's own set of values—different from that of others—and acting accordingly is stressed and considered good. (See for example *Beyond Good and Evil*, section 212.) One line from the original edition of *Anthem* which was subsequently cut reveals a possible Nietzschean influence along these lines: "I wish no man to be like me, nor do I wish to be like any man" (131/96). She may have only wanted to convey that, unlike the dictates of the society that worshiped We, Equality possessed independence and wished not to have to be like others. But as written, the original blurs the distinction between genuine individualism and pseudo-individualism.

In at least three cases, Ayn Rand cut or revised a passage that could be taken to imply an erroneous Nietzschean conception of rule[29] that was completely inconsistent with her political philosophy:

> *Cut*: The earth seems waiting, waiting for some order which is to come from us. This world is new, this world is ours to rule. (125/97)
> *Cut*: My will, which chooses, and orders, and creates. My will, the master which knows no masters. My will, the liberator and the conqueror. (129/94)
> And the day will come[, though I may not be here to see it, when my race will conquer] <when I shall break all the chains of> the earth. (146/104)

Throughout *Anthem*, Equality's ambition is to be free—free to discover scientific truths about the world, to love and be with the one woman he loves, free to reside with her in a home of their own where they can raise a family of their own, free to live. His ambition is clearly not to rule, i.e., to have political power over others. Even the desire to be the leader of a society with a proper political system is not his ambition. As he says in Chapter 1: "But we wished not to be a Leader, even though it is a great honor. We wished to be a Scholar" (19/25). Elsewhere in *Anthem*, Rand makes clear her anti-Nietzscheanism on this point (in both versions): "I shall choose [companions from] <friends> among [my brothers] <men>, but neither slaves nor masters" (132/96). Thus the passages referring to rule—which may have been the result of a Nietzschean influence, and which may simply have been meant to convey that Equality would win out in the end and be in charge of his life with no masters over him—had to be changed.

Nietzsche is saddled (often unfairly) with the racist doctrines later adopted by the Nazis.[30] He did, however, often speak in terms of the different races of men and their different cultural characteristics, and it is not always clear whether he is referring to conditions of their birth and blood or chosen elements within a culture. In any case, Ayn Rand revised three passages in the last chapter of *Anthem* to remove the reference to race. (Note that she clearly never uses "race" in *Anthem* in any ethnic sense of the term.) The first refers to Liberty as follows: "the mother of a new [race] <kind> of gods" (138/99). A few pages later, Rand changed "race of men" to "men" (144/103), and in a passage quoted earlier, she replaces "my race will conquer the earth" with "I shall break all the chains of the earth" (146/104). There is no reason to think that a Nietzschean influence led her to use "race" in the original versions of these passages. But whatever her reasons for using this term, by 1946 she recognized that "race" was too collectivist in connotation.

As a last thought on Nietzsche and *Anthem*, let me offer as a possibility a more positive influence—one that was not later revised or removed. I have in mind a possible influence on the idea for the novel itself—which was first conceived while she was still in Russia. In *Thus Spake Zarathustra*, in the section entitled "Neighbor-Love," Nietzsche writes:

> Ye flee unto your neighbor from yourselves, and would fain make a virtue thereof: but I fathom your "unselfishness."
>
> The *Thou* is older than the *I*; the *Thou* hath been consecrated, but not yet the *I*; so man presseth nigh unto his neighbor.[31]

Perhaps Ayn Rand's reflections on this passage—on a culture in which Thou (i.e., other people) has been consecrated, but not I—and on how a person might emerge from a Thou culture and discover the I—in part led her to write or shaped how she wrote *Anthem*. But this is pure speculation. In any case, note that the end of *Anthem* is a consecration of I: "over the portals" of his fort, Equality tells us, he will "cut into stone . . . The sacred word: EGO" (147/105).

## EQUALITY 7-2521'S DEVELOPMENT

In the original, Equality is sometimes presented too negatively, either in general—given his moral character and psychology—or in relation to how far along we are in the story. This was revised accordingly. I present the relevant passages in the order in which they appear.

(1) [We are ashamed of] <But we cannot change> our bones <nor> [and of the things inside] our body[, but we cannot change them]. (7–8/18)

This revision removes any reference to, and thus emphasis on, shame.

(2) *Cut*: It is said that before the Great Re-birth men were blind and ignorant as beasts, for they had to seek the truth. This is strange and fearful to us, for our age has found it. (9/19)

To have Equality claim that his age has found the truth contradicts his own ongoing search for it. At this point in the story he has not re-discovered truths about electricity or the electric light or man's ego; yet he has discovered the tunnel and he has the sense that there is much to learn about the world that cannot be learned in his society. But I think the main reason the passage was cut is because seeking after truth is clearly *not* strange and fearful to him.

(3) We know not [what demons sit inside our skull and] <why our curse> make<s> us seek we know not what, ever and ever. But we cannot resist [them] <it>. [They] <It> whisper<s> to us that there are <great> things [undreamed] on this earth of ours, and that we can know them if we [but] try, and that we must know them. We ask<,> [the demons] why must we know, but [they have] <it has> no answer to give <us>. We must know that we may know. [We cannot understand this evil wish of ours, but neither can we conquer it.] (17–18/24)

The suggestion—even if it is Equality's own, in his diary—that he is in some sense possessed by demons is disturbing and clashes too much with Rand's view of volition. Further, the whole idea of being possessed by demons would be more likely to arise in someone living in a religious society, not in the collectivist society of *Anthem*. Finally, cutting the reference to demons and employing instead the idea of a curse makes this passage a better fit with the rest of Chapter 1, in which Equality regularly refers to his curse.[32]

(4) *Cut*: To-night, we shall write it down upon this paper, and face it and acknowledge it, even though we are afraid. We shall write down the thought which has tortured us for two years. It has been coming to us, even though we tried not to know it and not to listen. And while we said to ourselves that we held no such thought, it formed itself into words, and the words rang in our ears as a bell of alarm within our mind. (61/52)

This passage was the original opening of Chapter 3, wherein Equality describes his re-discovery of electricity. With the removal of the passage, the chapter opens not with a description of the tortured existence of the past couple of years, but with a statement of pride (while recognizing that others regard him as wrong):

We, Equality 7-2521, have discovered a new power of nature. And we have discovered it alone, and we are alone to know it.
It is said. Now let us be lashed for it, if we must. (61/52)

(5) *Cut*: Now we look upon these words and we cannot believe that our hand has written them. It cannot be, we cannot be as evil as this. But we are. If only, we pray, if only we could suffer as we say this. Could we but suffer remorse, we would know that there is a spark of good left in us. But we suffer not. Our hand is light. Our hand and the thought which drives our hand to write, laugh at us and know no shame. (66/54)

Again, this passage (with which Chapter 3 originally ended) is too negative. Equality at this point in the story is not completely certain of the correctness of what he is doing; he is torn. But here he sounds as if he doubts whether "there is a spark of good" within him.

> (6) *Cut*: This is vain and base, for we are nothing. But are we? Are we? What is this new pride which rises as a fog to strangle the breath in our throat, and as a song to ring in our ears? What has befallen us? But what matters it? This Light is above all things. And the being in whom it is born . . . Oh, what matters it? We raise our arms over the flaming wire, we throw our head back, and our spirit is as a hymn within us. We hold the Light, we, Equality 7-2521.
> 　　Whatever we are, we hold the Light! (78/62)

This passage was originally the ending of Chapter 5. Equality has just stated, in strong terms, his pride in his new invention (the electric light). Ayn Rand apparently concluded that that statement of pride should not be undercut— and certainly not by the claim that Equality is nothing.

> (7) *Cut*: And as we lay alone through hours without end, we thought that our brothers had done right. We know no anger against our brothers, and no hatred. We knew we had deserved the lash and the cell and the agony of our body. Yet our curse and the Light born of our curse kept our lips sealed. (84–85/66)

This passage described Equality's thoughts, while in the Palace of Corrective Detention, following his whipping and shortly before his escape. Again, it is too negative: it does not quite fit his development to say, at this point in the story, that he knows he deserved to be whipped and imprisoned, and that he feels no anger at his brothers.

> (8) And we [know the evil of it. We] have heard of the [abysmal] corruption to be found in solitude. (98/76)

The change here is significant: the original says he knows that the solitude he prizes is evil, and he has heard that it is an abysmal corruption. According to the revised version, he has merely heard of its corruption (which leaves his evaluation of it open—which, at this point, it probably was).

　　The next three passages—which convey a lack of understanding or reason on Equality's part—were cut:

> (9) Strange are the ways of life. We understand them not, nor the meaning hidden behind them. (100/78)

> (10) We sat up, and we brushed the leaves off our face, and we said to ourselves that we know not our body any longer, nor could we understand it. (102/79)

> (11) And we threw our head back in a pride senseless and unreasoning. (104/80)

　　In at least one case, Ayn Rand *added* a line to clarify the state of Equality's self-evaluation. This is from when he is alone in the forest:

(12) And suddenly, for the first time this day, we remembered that we are the Damned. We remembered it, and we laughed. (105/80)

Chapter 8 ends as follows:

(13) We are writing this [up]on the [last of the] paper we had hidden in our tunic together with the written pages we had brought for the World Council of Scholars, but never given to them. [In the days to come, we shall gather the long, white strips of tree bark which we have seen, and we shall write upon them with charred sticks.] We have much to speak of to ourselves, and we hope we shall find the words for it in the days to come. Now, we cannot speak, for we cannot understand.

[We cannot understand our heart, nor this day which has passed. We know that we should feel sin, and guilt, and shame. But we feel it not. For never—if there be one who can understand this, may they give us the answer!—never have we felt more true, more proud, more clean.] (105/80)

I think the second paragraph was cut not because it conveys ignorance on Equality's part—the preceding does that as well—but because it is not only repetitious but overemphasizes or exaggerates the degree of the ignorance or just what he does not understand.

This final passage, from near the very end of *Anthem*, also conveys too much ignorance—but in this case, ignorance about the state of the world. Ayn Rand radically revised it to make Equality know exactly what error made possible the society he had recently escaped.

(14) What brought it to pass? What disaster [struck the earth and] took their reason away from men? What whip lashed them to their knees in shame and submission? [I know not. The books do not speak of it. The books are very old. When the twilight came, men wrote no longer, neither did they read. So the story of man's fall is dark for ever, dark as the hearts of those who brought it about.] <The worship of the word "We."> (142–43/102)

In the revised edition, Equality sees that the evil and destruction of the worship of We is a corollary of the good and creativity connected to the discovery of the concept I.

## OTHER PHILOSOPHICALLY INTERESTING CHANGES

*Anthem* is set against a background of a completely collectivist society which has sunk to a primitive state because of its lack of the concept I. In five passages in the original, certain aspects of the society are presented too positively, and they were revised accordingly.

(1) *Cut*: The world of men is but kindness and love. (13/22)

No, it isn't. Moreover, Equality at some level must have known that it isn't. He could at this point in the story accept, abstractly, that the Councils are just (see the following item). But he dealt every day with his fellow men, and he could not—especially in his diary—characterize them as kind and loving. (This is not to say that they are unkind and feel hate. On the contrary, most of his brothers don't feel much of anything.)

> (2) *Cut*: This is just,[33] for the Councils have a great duty to carry, and they who have the duty must also have the power. It is the Councils who hold the reins of the world, who feed us all and clothe us and shelter us in our sleep. None among men go hungry, nor do they tremble, homeless, in the autumn rains— upon this wonderful earth of ours. Down the roads of the world heavy carts stream day and night, carrying men's sustenance to men; fields of wheat ripen in the sun; wheels turn, and axes bite into forests, and pits split the granite of the earth—and each blow, each tensed muscle, each trembling green blade of wheat is under the great wisdom of our fathers' hand, our fathers who are the Councils; these Councils who bend their sage, tireless heads in the candle light over miles and mountains of maps, that each morsel of food may find its way on time to the humblest stomach. But to do this, our Councils hold the power to command their life work unto each among men. Else what order would there be upon earth? (14–15/22)

It is possible that in his youth, on some level, Equality believed this propaganda, which he must have heard endlessly while growing up. But it is unlikely that he would have believed it at this point in his life to such an extent as to record it in his diary in this admiring way. Moreover, he cannot have seen that "Down the roads of the world heavy carts stream day and night," because this didn't happen. Later in Chapter 1, we read: "It is dark in the streets and no men are about" (34–35/35).

> (3) And there they [learn many things] <study> for many years. (19/25)

One can study the Bible or Koran for many years, and still learn nothing. That is the nature of "study" in the society of *Anthem*.

> (4) We stopped when we felt hunger. [We watched this with curiosity. We had never known hunger save as a word.] (102/79)

Whatever propaganda he has heard about material abundance—see (2) above—it is inconceivable that in such a primitive society Equality would never have known hunger. The people in this society lived in a primitive fashion, not much above a hand-to-mouth existence. One bad harvest and everyone would have felt hunger.

(5) *Cut*: They had found a small casket in the sleeping room, and it was full of jewels, such as no men had ever touched, save upon the great mosaics of the Palace of the World Council. (123/92)

It is possible that a primitive, stagnant society could have buildings and people bedecked with jewels (e.g., as in ancient Egypt and India). But Ayn Rand is presenting a society which has rejected or lost virtually every remnant of past glory and achievement, and which would not have its citizens take the trouble to create jewelry. Further, purely esthetically, such jewels clash with the simple, Spartan existence of the society in *Anthem*.

I turn now to some interesting changes involving masculinity and femininity.

In 1969, more than thirty years after the publication of the first edition of *Anthem*, Ayn Rand wrote the following about the nature of femininity:

For a woman *qua* woman, the essence of femininity is hero worship—the desire to look up to man. "To look up" does not mean dependence, obedience, or anything implying inferiority. It means an intense kind of admiration; and admiration is an emotion that can be experienced only by a person of strong character and independent value judgments. A "clinging vine" type of woman is not an admirer, but an exploiter of men. Hero worship is a demanding virtue: a woman has to be worthy of it and of the hero she worships. Intellectually and morally, i.e., as a human being, she has to be his equal; then the object of her worship is specifically his *masculinity*, not any human virtue she might lack.[34]

In *Anthem*, in the relationship between Liberty and Equality—and especially after she joins him in the forest—how Rand presents what Liberty feels for him comes close to this statement about femininity. But in a number of passages in the original, she went too far in her presentation of hero-worship, making it at least sound like dependence and obedience. Thus, she later revised them. (In the first three passages, "they" refers to Liberty.)

*Cut*: And they spoke on, and their head was bowed.
"We have come to you," they said, "for we have no will but your will, and no thought but your thought, and no breath save the breath you give us. We have come, for you are our master, and we cannot leave you." (108–109/82)
Then they knelt, and <bowed> their golden head [was bowed] before us[, and their hands lay at our feet, palms up, limp and pleading]. (110/83)
They approach us, and they stop, [and their eyes worship us in silence,] <laughing, knowing what we think,> and they wait obediently, without questions, till it pleases us to turn and go on. (113/85)

In three passages in which Liberty originally refers to Equality as master, the "master" was cut:

> Do as you please with us, [our master,] but do not send us away from you. (110/83)
> Your will be done, [our master] (123/92)
> It shall be [thy] <your> name, [my master] (137/99)

I imagine the major reason for these revisions was to make the presentation of the masculinity and femininity of the hero and heroine more consistent with the novella's thematic emphasis on individualism. Recall that Equality earlier said (in the 1938 edition): "I shall choose companions from among my brothers, but neither slaves nor masters" (132). Revising these passages makes it clearer that this also refers to Liberty, whose individualistic spirit is what first attracted Equality.

In her discussion of connotation in *The Art of Nonfiction*, Ayn Rand states: "Watch out for philosophical implications, too. For example, if someone writes, 'He had an instinct for courage,' he may only want to convey, 'He is brave.' But the actual, and improper, implication is that courage is an instinct."[35] Ayn Rand replaced some words and revised some passages in *Anthem* to avoid improper philosophical implications.

As far as I can tell, she replaced over a dozen words to avoid such implications. Here are four examples.

> (1) Their eyes were dark and hard and glowing, with no fear in them<,> [and] no kindness and no [shame] <guilt>. (40/39)

This passage describes Equality's first encounter with Liberty. "Guilt" refers to the fact of having done something wrong; "shame" refers to the awareness of wrongdoing (either self-awareness and/or awareness of what others might think). "Guilt" is the better term here because a person can feel no shame, but still be guilty as hell (and that is clearly not what Rand has in mind).

> (2) I need no [reason] <warrant> for being, and no word of sanction upon my being. I am the [reason] <warrant> and the sanction. (128/94)[36]

What Ayn Rand wants to convey here is the idea that a man is an end in himself (and in that sense, she does believe that one needs no reason to exist). But to say that one needs no reason for being might also suggest that one may exist without any purpose, which is of course a view she rejects.

> (3) in the [sanctuary] <temple> of his spirit, each man is alone. (132/96)

Though both "sanctuary" and "temple" suggest religious reverence and respect, the former suggests a place one withdraws into with an expectation of help. The latter avoids this unwanted implication, and connotes simply a place of worship or the location of what one worships.

> (4) I shall rebuild the [wonders] <achievements> of the past. (139/99)

The difference here is subtle but important, for "wonders" gives the slight suggestion that the achievements of the past are beyond understanding or comprehension, and of course does not underscore the fact that they are *achievements*. Further, "wonders" stresses the subjective reaction (of being amazed), "achievement" the objective fact (i.e., what was accomplished).

Those were some examples of word-replacement; I conclude with three passages which were revised owing to unintended philosophical implications.

> (1) *Cut*: For great are the evils of this earth, but none so great as the evils which come from men. (132/96)

This line implies that some evils are not man-made, which further implies a malevolent view of the universe—all of which Ayn Rand rejects (as does Equality).

> (2) But I am done with this [reign of folly, for my eyes are opened] <creed of corruption>. (134/97)

This line comes at the end of the penultimate chapter. Equality here explicitly rejects the moral code of the society he has left. But to call this code a "reign of folly" suggests that it was the result of stupidity rather than evil; and the reference to Equality's eyes being closed implies that he was blind not to recognize this folly. Cutting "for my eyes are opened" removes any suggestion that his lack of the concept of self was the result of blindness or in any way his fault; on the contrary, the discovery of ego was a spectacular achievement—the philosophical and psychological equivalent of rediscovering electricity. And replacing "reign of folly" with "creed of corruption" makes clear that the source of this moral code is not stupidity or ignorance, but evil.

> (3) *Cut*: We shall know no fear and no doubt. Ours will be a holy war, the holy, the blessed and the last. We may perish, but our truth will go on. We may fall, but our torch is too bright ever to die again. What if we perish? The first have always perished.[37] But I think not of danger. I look ahead through the years to the sun of my victory. I laugh. I sing to my victory. (147/104)

This was the last paragraph cut in Ayn Rand's revision of *Anthem*. I assume it was cut not only because it was unnecessary (it was not replaced with anything else), but because it is both too negative and too positive: too negative because defeating a stagnant, corrupt collectivist society should not require a great war—such is the impotence of evil; and too positive because defeating this collectivist society will not ensure victory forever—the price of liberty is eternal vigilance, and the constant and active defense of egoism and a philosophy of reason.

As with the other philosophically interesting revisions discussed in this essay, these last three passages in the original were the result of (1) putting style over content or (2) the fact that Ayn Rand had not (in the 1930s) formulated precisely in every case some philosophical idea that she was developing. But less than ten years later, she knew even more about both philosophy and writing, and so was able to improve *Anthem*, though without having to change its essence. Or as she put it: "The story remains as it was. I have lifted its face, but not its spine or spirit; these did not need lifting" (xiv).[38]

## NOTES

1. A word on the notation employed in this essay: Whenever two numbers are given (e.g., 46/42), the first refers to the page number(s) in the 1938 edition, the second to the page number(s) in the 1996 paperback edition. With rare (and obvious) exceptions, square brackets [ ] indicate a deletion, pointed brackets < > an addition.

2. The changes in the hand-corrected copy do not match the revised edition exactly. I counted twenty-seven differences between what Ayn Rand indicated in handwritten corrections, and what appeared in the published revised edition. Twenty-two are cases in which she did not indicate changes from British to American spelling, though she did sometimes indicate such changes (more on British-American differences under Minor Revisions). In three cases, she did not indicate—or changed her mind about—the insertion of a comma (35/35, 46/42, 115/86–87). In one case, a change from "may" to "might" is not indicated (68/55); in another, she writes "want" in her handwritten changes, but "wish" appears in the published revised edition (37/36).

Here are some other differences (presenting what is in the original edition, the hand-corrected copy, and the revised edition—in that order):

(1) they drew pictures upon the walls and upon the floors (27)
they drew pictures upon the walls and the floors (hand-corrected copy)
they drew pictures upon the walls (29)

(2) Then we were up on our feet once more, and we ran. We ran. (96)
Then we were up on our feet once more, and we ran." (hand-corrected copy)
Then we ran. (75)

(3) The bird fell before us, and quivered, and lay still. (103)
The bird fell before us. (hand-corrected copy)
It fell before us. (79)

(4) And then we found a room with walls made of shelves, and upon them stood rows and rows of manuscripts. (121)
We found a room with walls made of shelves, which held rows and rows of manuscripts. (hand-corrected copy)
We found a room with walls made of shelves, which held rows of manuscripts. (91)

The above leads us to the unsurprising conclusion that the hand-corrected copy corresponded to the manuscript an author normally turns in to the publisher, and that Rand had other opportunities to make changes.

3. Michael S. Berliner, ed., *Letters of Ayn Rand* (New York: Dutton, 1995), 262.

4. Biographical interviews (Ayn Rand Archives). Quoted in Leonard Peikoff, introduction to fiftieth anniversary American edition to *Anthem*, by Ayn Rand (New York: Signet, 1995), x.

5. I initially thought that there were three possible typographical errors corrected for the 1946 edition. In two cases, "no thing" was changed to "nothing" (18/24, 98/76)—for example: "For men may wish no[ ]thing" (18/24). In the third case, at the end of *Anthem*, Equality 7-2521 says that he will fight for man's freedom and honor, and "For his right<s>" (146/104). But Shoshana Milgram informed me that the drafts make clear that "right" and (in both cases) "no thing" were all intended by the author and only later changed. (Thus, I assume "no thing" in the original was an attempt at archaic style.)

There seems to have been a typographical error introduced between the hand-corrected copy and the published revised edition (note the difference between "force" and "forces"):

For they have nothing to fight me with, save the brute force of their numbers. (hand-corrected copy; see the appendix to the 1996 edition, p. 140)
For they have nothing to fight me with, save the brute forces of their numbers. (100)

At least two typographical errors were introduced by the publisher into the fiftieth anniversary edition: (1) "They brought the Transgressor out into the square and they led him to the pyre" (50)—where "him" should be "them." (2) In the following paragraph, "likeliness" is a mistake; it should be "likeness" (50). (See pp. 58 and 59 of the 1938 edition, and all versions of the revised edition prior to the fiftieth anniversary edition.)

6. I originally thought the following word replacement fell under the category of British to American changes: "There are Fraternity 2-5503, a quiet [lad] <boy> with wise, kind eyes" (53/47). But Ayn Rand wrote "lad" in her original draft, so that cannot be the reason for the revision (unless she *later* concluded that "lad" was too British).

7. This sort of change was prevalent in her revisions to the 1936 edition of *We the Living*. See Robert Mayhew, "We the Living: '36 & '59," in *Essays on Ayn Rand's We the Living*, ed. Robert Mayhew (Lanham, MD: Lexington Books, 2004), 189. As I there note, the Russian word for both "as" and "like" is the same: *kak*.

8. From this point on, I refer to the hero of *Anthem* as Equality.

9. See Shoshana Milgram, "*Anthem* in Manuscript: Finding the Words," in this volume, p. 5.

10. I make the same point about a detail cut from a scene in *We the Living*. See Robert Mayhew, "*We the Living*: '36 & '59," ed. Mayhew, 200.

11. From this point on, I refer to the heroine of *Anthem* as Liberty.

12. In addition, over twenty times Ayn Rand cut the initial "And" of a sentence—for example, from this line: "And in five hours time, when the sun is high, we return to the Home. . ." (22/27).

13. Biographical interviews (Ayn Rand Archives). Peikoff, "Introduction," x.

14. Writing the first version of *Anthem* was not the only occasion in which Ayn Rand employed this formula. In the first notes she wrote in preparation for *The Fountainhead*—dated December 4, 1935, a year and a half before writing *Anthem*—we find the following: "sum of sums" and "the holiest of holies and the reason of reasons." In the December 26, 1935, entry, she refers to Howard Roark as "the end of ends." See David Harriman, ed., *Journals of Ayn Rand* (New York: Dutton, 1997), 78, 80–81, 88.

15. In *We the Living*, she made similar changes to Stepan Timoshenko's description of what a revolution requires. See Mayhew, "*We the Living*: '36 & '59," 199–200.

16. Biographical interviews (Ayn Rand Archives). She also had an immediate negative reaction to his *Birth of Tragedy*, with its opposition of reason and emotion.

17. Biographical interviews (Ayn Rand Archives).

18. Friedrich Nietzsche, *Thus Spake Zarathustra* (New York: Dover, 1999). This is a reprint edition of the Thomas Common translation, first published in 1911 by Macmillan and in 1917 as a Modern Library edition (the edition Rand owned). Nietzsche's *Also sprach Zarathustra* was originally published in four parts between 1883 and 1885. A Russian translation was published in St. Petersburg in 1898. See Richard D. Davies, "Nietzsche in Russia 1892–1919: A Chronological Checklist," in *Nietzsche in Russia*, ed. Bernice Glatzer Rosenthal (Princeton: Princeton University Press, 1986), 359.

19. Nietzsche, *Zarathustra*, 136, 138, 141.

20. For her mature statement on this issue, see Ayn Rand, "Causality versus Duty," in her *Philosophy: Who Needs It* (New York: Bobbs-Merrill, 1982; Signet paperback edition, 1984).

21. Nietzsche, *Zarathustra*, 11: "Whom do they hate most? Him who breaketh up their table of values, the breaker, the law-breaker:—he, however, is the creator." See also Friedrich Nietzsche, *Beyond Good and Evil*, sec. 211.

22. Ayn Rand, *Atlas Shrugged* (New York: Random House, 1957; Signet thirty-fifth anniversary paperback edition, 1992), 677. The important point—in contrast to Nietzsche—is that the good "must be discovered, not invented, by man" (Ayn Rand, *Capitalism: The Unknown Ideal* [New York: New American Library, 1966; expanded paperback edition, Signet, 1967], 22).

23. Note that in her collection *For the New Intellectual*, which consisted of a long essay and selections from her fiction, Ayn Rand included most of Chapter 11 of *Anthem* (revised version, of course); but this entire passage was omitted. I don't know whether this omission was the result of further doubts about the passage. See Ayn Rand, *For the New Intellectual* (New York: Random House, 1961; Signet paperback edition, 1961), 64–65.

The original passage bears a resemblance to the language of some passages from Nietzsche. For example:

from thee they want a Yea or Nay (*Zarathustra*, 32);
alas for every living thing that would live without dispute about weight and scales and weigher! (*Zarathustra*, 79);
I honour [those who] have learned to say "I" and "Yea" and "Nay" (*Zarathustra*, 135);
quietly and quickly will I put the "truth" upside down (*Zarathustra*, 217);
Formula for my happiness: a yes, a no, a straight line, a *goal*. . . . (*Twilight of the Idols*, "Maxims and Barbs" # 44, translated by Duncan Large [Oxford: Oxford University Press, 1998], 10.)

24. Compare this to the following passage from *Thus Spake Zarathustra*:

The body is a big sagacity, a plurality with one sense. . . . An instrument of thy body is also thy little sagacity, my brother, which thou callest "spirit"—a little instrument and plaything of thy big sagacity. . . . Behind thy thoughts and feelings, my brother, there is a mighty lord, an unknown sage—it is called Self; it dwelleth in thy body, it is thy body. (19)

25. See Milgram, "*Anthem* in Manuscript," in this volume, p. 18.

26. Nietzsche, *Zarathustra*, 56–57, 75. See also *Beyond Good and Evil*, section 19.

27. See *Anthem*, 20, 25, 26, 34, 36, 44, 46, 47, 72.

28. See Ayn Rand, "Selfishness without a Self," in her *Philosophy: Who Needs It*, and Nathaniel Branden, "Counterfeit Individualism," in Rand, *The Virtue of Selfishness: A New Concept of Egoism* (New York: New American Library, 1964).

29. See Nietzsche, *Zarathustra*, 76–77, 147; *Beyond Good and Evil*, sections 22, 61, 199, 230, 260.

30. See, for example, Nietzsche, *Beyond Good and Evil*, sections 28 and 48, and also Robert C. Solomon and Kathleen M. Higgins, *What Nietzsche Really Said* (New York: Schocken Books, 2000), 8–13.

31. Nietzsche, *Zarathustra*, 38. I should mention, however, that Ayn Rand did not underline this passage in her own copy of *Zarathustra*.

32. Note that in the manuscripts, Ayn Rand referred to a "kindly spirit" that prevented Equality from being caught yawning during a history lesson. See Milgram, "*Anthem* in Manuscript," in this volume, p. 9.

33. "This is just" refers to the preceding passage, which the Teachers had spoken to them all:

Dare not choose in your minds the work you would like to do when you leave the Home of the Students. You shall do that which the Council of Vocations shall prescribe for you. For the Council of Vocations knows in its great wisdom where you are needed by your brother men, better than you can know it in your unworthy little minds. And if you are not needed by your brother men, there is no reason for you to burden the earth with your bodies (13–14/22).

34. "About a Woman President" (1969), in Ayn Rand, *The Voice of Reason: Essays in Objectivist Thought*, ed. Leonard Peikoff (New York: New American Library, 1988), 268.

35. Ayn Rand, *The Art of Nonfiction: A Guide for Writers and Readers*, ed. Robert Mayhew (New York: Plume, 2001), 119.

36. Cf. Nietzsche, *Gay Science*, edited by Bernard Williams, translated by Josefine Nauckhoff (Cambridge: Cambridge University Press), section 276: "what thought shall be the reason, warrant, and sweetness of the rest of my life!" (157).

37. On the idea that "the first have always perished," see Nietzsche, *Zarathustra*: "O my brethren, he who is a firstling is ever sacrificed. Now, however, are we sacrificed" (139). (This was marked off by Ayn Rand in her copy.) Cf. Ayn Rand, *The Fountainhead* (New York: Bobbs-Merrill, 1943; Signet fiftieth anniversary paperback ed., 1993), 679.

38. I should like to thank Allan Gotthelf who, in the mid-1980s, first brought to my attention the question of a possible Nietzschean influence on the 1938 edition of *Anthem*. I wish also to thank Tore Boeckmann, Onkar Ghate, Shoshana Milgram and Greg Salmieri for their extensive comments on earlier versions of this draft.

# 4

# Reviews of *Anthem*

*Michael S. Berliner*

The unusual publishing history of *Anthem* resulted in an unusual history of reviews, covering more than sixty years.[1] The first edition was published in England by Cassell and Co. in 1938 and was widely reviewed in the United Kingdom. Not until 1946 was the novella published in the United States, a substantially revised softcover edition brought out by a small pro-freedom group calling themselves the Pamphleteers. Seven years later, Caxton, a small Idaho publisher, released a hardcover edition. The first edition by a major U.S. publisher came in 1961, with a mass-market paperback by New American Library, whose (later) parent company, Penguin, issued, in 1995, both hardcover and paperback editions that included a facsimile of the 1938 edition with the handwritten changes Ayn Rand made in preparation for the 1946 version.

The 1938 British edition was the only edition of *Anthem* to attract significant attention from reviewers. The print run of the first U.S. edition was small and the publisher minor, and because the first major release of *Anthem* came fifteen years after its initial publication (or twenty-three years if one counts the British edition), it was no longer a publishing "event."

## 1938 BRITISH EDITION: CASSELL AND CO.

With the peril of National Socialism looming in Europe, Ayn Rand's novella warning against collectivism was reviewed in major publications throughout the United Kingdom. Surprisingly, almost all of the reviews were highly positive. The *Sunday Times* (May 8, 1938; reprinted in the *Montrose Review*, May 27) assigned the book to noted film critic and classicist Dilys Powell, who, calling it "a curious little novel," accurately recounted the story and ended her review: "This parable against the submergence of the individual in the State has the merits of simplicity and sincerity."[2] The *Times Literary Supplement* went further, their unnamed reviewer terming *Anthem* a "fantasia" with the moral that "the collectivist tyranny threatening us, whether labeled Communism or Fascism, will kill not only freedom but it will kill most of man's power to guide nature." In the context of both criticism and the history of ideas, this is a most unusual identification, for it recognizes what most intellectuals still deny: that philosophically, Communism and Fascism are essentially the same and that technology (i.e., the application of reason to nature) depends upon freedom. The *Birmingham Post* (May 3) reviewer described the story as a "short, imaginative fantasy" and "the author's profession of faith in the individual and a striking counter to the modern ideas of race." (One can only speculate that by "modern" the reviewer was sarcastically referring to the racial views of Nazism.)

In the *Daily Telegraph* (May 10), *Anthem* was reviewed by Malcolm Muggeridge, the renowned cynic who became editor of *Punch*. Muggeridge called the book a "grisly forecast of the future," where collectivization and mechanism are carried to their limits. It is, wrote Muggeridge, "a cri du Coeur after a surfeit of doctrinaire intolerance." *Anthem*, he acknowledged, "has its charm; but the weakness of all these nightmare Utopias reversed, as of beautific Utopias, is that they are inconceivable, since experience shows that no tendency ever is carried to its limit, that man remains man in spite of everything." Muggeridge's cynicism and implicit anti-intellectualism are apparent: since ideas are basically irrelevant, it is of no value to identify essentials and what they would mean if acted on consistently. But another reviewer, with the pen name Fidus Achates, writing in the Church of England newspaper (May 13), understood what Muggeridge didn't:

> Ayn Rand, who gave us *We the Living*, has written . . . a tribute to the meaning and value of finite individuality and the vindication of the unique status of man. . . . [C]ertain tendencies and forces now at work amongst us and certain ideologies have been allowed to work themselves out to their logical conclusion in the complete elimination from the earth of the rights and liberties of the individual.

A short review in the *East Anglian Daily Times* (May 16) notes merely that the book "contains much food for thought. It is original and powerful, and the author has made good use of the theme." However, the reviewer fails to mention what that theme is. The *Edinburgh Citizen* (June 10) considered the story "a fine piece of imaginative work." Its neighbor, the *Edinburgh Evening News* (May 16) was more philosophical, describing the world of *Anthem* as a place "where the right of the individual is non-existent." The hero's determination, continued the reviewer in a passage highlighted by Ayn

Rand's underlining, "overcame all obstacles and he finally discovers the full glory of individuality—the word Ego and its meaning—and the beauty of true love. The writer explains that the book is his (sic) own profession of faith which accounts for the sincerity of its telling." The *Eastern Daily Press* in Norwich (June 15) found *Anthem* to be "very ingenious" and—unaware of Ayn Rand's life under the Soviets—thought it to be merely "anti-Fascist" but "less knowledgeable" and "more emotional" than Aldous Huxley's *Brave New World.*

Young Marlow (likely a pseudonym derived from a character in Oliver Goldsmith's *She Stoops to Conquer*), writing in the *Reynolds News* of London (May 22), correctly identified the theme: "if the totalitarian State developed without check, a time might come when individuality would be altogether crushed, no thought permitted which is not the thought of all." "The intention," he wrote, "is to declare that individuality is the only thing that makes life worth living. Ayn Rand makes this declaration in an impressive way. The [hero's] fight against conditions of mass slavery is vividly pictured." In *The Weekly Review* (formerly *GK's Weekly*, the "GK" referring to G. K. Chesterton), Michael Burt wrote that at its beginning, *Anthem* reads like a satire— "but a satire with no laughter in it." Rather, it is a "strikingly conceived dream of the world in the very distant future," when man "has thrown away his most precious attribute—his individuality." "This is," wrote Burt,

a strange little book, and manifestly the product of an unusual mind. It is written with vigour and sincerity, and it may be regarded as a timely warning to a generation that seems intent on doing its best either to procure or to ignore the extinction of individual liberty. All such considerations apart, however, "Anthem" is to be commended as an outstandingly beautiful piece of pure literature.

## 1946 AMERICAN EDITION: THE PAMPHLETEERS

It wasn't until eight years later that *Anthem* was published in America, by the Pamphleteers. This is the standard, authorized edition. There were few reviews. In fact, *Anthem* did not even come to the attention of *Book Review Digest*, which excerpts major reviews every year. The only major and lengthy review appeared in the *Columbia Missourian* (February 14, 1947), whose reviewer, "A. F.," summarized both the story and the new preface, and concluded:

Miss Rand's forceful dramatization of the principles of collectivism and the ultimate consequences to which they lead, is challenging. She has no patience with people who seek to excuse their acceptance of what is actually serfdom by hiding behind the mask of ignorance. A ruder awakening is her medicine for them, and in 'Anthem' she pours it on bitterly.

A brief review in the *Los Angeles Herald Examiner* (September 22, 1946) advised the reader that "What might happen in a world in which collectivism has reached its ultimate is dramatically told by Ayn Rand, Los Angeles author, in 'Anthem.'" A Bombay newspaper, *India International,* highly praised the book, urging that it be read by "the wisest and most humanized" people, the "humblest and meekest" and even the "most wicked and the most crooked," who should "be able to understand the utter insignificance of their own miserable lives."

Most of the reviews of *Anthem* among Ayn Rand's papers were from small, conservative publications. In the June 1946 issue of the "Economic Council Review of Books," Rose Wilder Lane wrote:

> it is unlike anything ever written before. It is a projection, nominally into the future but actually out of space and time, of the basic principle of collectivism. I can't call it a work of imagination; it is pure abstract thought, an idea presented in terms of action, imaginatively. I can't say it's fiction, though ostensibly a masculine atom of a collective tells his life experience, which includes meeting a feminine atom, and their escape from the social whole to a discovery of human personality. I give up; read it yourself. It is unique; it is remarkable. And if you think of books in this way, someday this first edition will be a collector's item; Ayn Rand is a phenomenon in literature.[3]

In his September 1946 issue of "Analysis," a four-page broadsheet later merged into *Human Events,* conservative Frank Chodorov understood Ayn Rand's moral message, writing:

> It takes a strong imagination, and a considerable amount of instransigence, to conjure up a society in which men are without sense of individual dignity. Ayn Rand has both, plus a vigorous style, and in her story, *Anthem,* she shows what happens to the human being who is coerced, under pain of extinction, into becoming a social means rather than an end in himself. Pride, hope and even the striving for better things is crushed. The first person singular ceases to have meaning; all life is described in terms of "we." The collectivity wipes out the person; the two cannot live together.

## 1953 AMERICAN EDITION: CAXTON

Seven years later, in 1953, the first hardcover edition was published by Caxton, a small right-wing publishing house. Apparently, the only full-scale newspaper review was in the *Buffalo Evening News* (July 25, 1953) by G.G., who had the insight to realize that "Ayn Rand saw in 1937 that Nazism, Fascism and Communism are all manifestations of totalitarianism and the subjugation of the individual." *Anthem* was also publicized by Dr. Ruth Alexander (a long-time supporter of Ayn Rand) as part of a story about the publisher in her syndicated column (New York *Sunday Mirror*, December 9, 1951).[4] Wrote Alexander:

> Among our great Libertarians is the Russian-born Ayn Rand, who knows about communism first hand and whose earlier novel, "The Fountainhead," was a brilliant dramatization of individualism. [Jim] Gipson has just brought out a tender and terrific short novel by Miss Rand, entitled "Anthem." It crystallizes the belief of all true Americans—"Depend upon it, the lovers of freedom will be free."[5]

A lengthy review of Caxton's 1953 reissue appeared in "Facts Forum News" (August, 1955), a conservative newsletter. Reviewer Joan DeArmond compared *Anthem* to other dystopias, opining that

> Anthem is different—inspiringly different. Most satires [on the evils of mass conformity] have presented the collectivized society in terms of its physically brutal aspects. These writers have done little more than parody twentieth century tyrannies. Ayn Rand portrays the mental state that lies beyond the tyranny, beyond slavery. Gone is the physical brutality, the purges, and the tortures—yet the Collective of Anthem is intellectually more repellent, even, than the cruelty and inhumanity that must have gone before. The stagnation has become voluntary, the transition to the peaceful Collective apparently complete. Lost is all sense of individual worth and identity. . . . As all individual thought and action are forbidden, the fruits of individual inspiration are unknown. . . . This is the most beautiful, the most inspiring novel this reviewer has ever read. It is an ethical and philosophical rather than a religious dedication to freedom and the individual.

In "All-American Books" ("A Quarterly Review of Books Every American Should Read"), the unnamed reviewer contrasts *Anthem* favorably with George Orwell's *1984* (published in 1948): *Anthem*, wrote the reviewer, goes "a good deal beyond" Orwell's book and, unlike *1984, Anthem* is "a hopeful story," in which the hero's "rebellion brought hope for the redemption of the human race from the slough of despondence into which it had fallen."

Finally, there was a positive 250-word review by Rand's associate, Nathaniel Branden, in *The Freeman* (September 21, 1953). Branden identified the nature of the on-going conflict between individualism and collectivism as "the struggle between those who assert that man's duty is to exist for others and those who uphold his right to exist for his own happiness."

## THE FIFTIETH ANNIVERSARY AND BEYOND

After 1953, the number of reviews of subsequent versions continued to dwindle. I could find no reviews of the first major publication in the U.S., a 1961 paperback by New American Library. The fiftieth anniversary edition (in 1996) merited a brief mention in *Library Journal* (August 1995), where Michael Rogers referred to it as a "dark portrait of the future."

Upon the release of the unabridged audio book in 2002, *AudioFile*'s D. B. opined that "its allegory is crudely transparent, and the ideas have lost their political urgency." Apparently he believes that political philosophy is of no relevance now that the Soviet Union had collapsed. The audio book also received a negative review from *Library Journal* (November 2002), whose Mark Pumphrey—reflecting the relativist's fear of absolutes—criticized the "extremist tone" compared to other dystopias and branded *Anthem* a "long-forgotten exercise in paranoia." Pumphrey is wrong on at least two counts: Given the millions of people slaughtered by the Nazis and Communists (and now by their Muslim descendants), a warning about the evils of collectivism is far from paranoid. Second, nearly seventy years after it was written, this "long-forgotten" book sells more than 100,000 copies per year and is the subject of more than 8,000 entries submitted annually in a high-school essay contest sponsored by the Ayn Rand Institute.

*Anthem*, like its hero, prevails despite the opposition.

## NOTES

1. For more on Ayn Rand's attitude toward reviews generally, see Michael S. Berliner, "Reviews of *We the Living*," in *Essays on Ayn Rand's* We the Living, ed. Robert Mayhew (Lanham, MD: Lexington Books, 2004), 145–46.

2. Most of the reviews cited reside in the Ayn Rand Archives. Some reviews she had clipped herself, while others, e.g., those of the British edition, were sent to her by a clippings service.

3. As of the completion of this essay, this edition of *Anthem*—originally $1.00— ranges in price from $85 to $1250 at used and rare book stores.

4. The 1951 date for this column is indeed correct, although the Caxton edition carries a 1953 copyright. Alexander was likely given an advanced copy of the book, and perhaps publication was delayed.

5. At this time, "libertarian" was honorific and referred to supporters of individual rights; the term was later taken over by anarchists and others whom Ayn Rand characterized as "hippies of the right." See Ayn Rand, *Philosophy: Who Needs It* (New York: Bobbs-Merrill, 1982; Signet paperback edition, 1984), 13 and 202.

# 5

## Adapting *Anthem*: Projects That Were and Might Have Been

*Jeff Britting*

*Anthem* has a long history as the inspiration for derivative works. From the 1940s to the mid-1960s, twenty adaptations were proposed, including several live action and animated films, ballets, and an opera. Only one project, a 1950 radio drama, was realized. While the evidence of these actual and possible uses is fragmentary, the proposals demonstrate *Anthem*'s impact on a small group of artist-readers. And the first of these artists may have been Ayn Rand herself.[1]

*Anthem* was first envisioned as a stage play in Soviet Russia during the 1920s. The story remained an unrealized idea until it was written as a novella in America in 1937. Little is known about the early theatre origin of *Anthem*. It was conceived as a four-act play, probably during Ayn Rand's college years at the University of Leningrad. The story was to have taken place entirely within a city of the future. The hero would lead a revolt against a society that had lost all memory of the word "I." There was no Uncharted Forest. One item remaining from this early version is a reference to a citizen who breaks down and cries out in the night. The original Russian title is not known. However, as indicated on the earliest existing draft, the first English title was "Ego." The work was eventually published in Great Britain as *Anthem*. The genesis of the novella is, perhaps, the first example of its "adaptation."[2]

### *ANTHEM* AS FILM

By the mid-1940s, Ayn Rand was the successful author of *The Fountainhead* and working in the second phase of her Hollywood screenwriting career. One goal was to promote awareness of *Anthem* in Hollywood as material for film adaptation. A total of ten parties considered *Anthem* as a film project. None of these projects was made and the reasons are not currently known.

Interest surfaced shortly after the novella's 1946 American publication. Two companies that discovered the work through the Pamphleteer edition were Vanguard Films (David O. Selznick's production company) and Columbia Pictures. At times, Rand's own appeals to various Hollywood film producers displayed her concern with the *visual means* of translating *Anthem* onto the screen.[3]

In a letter to Walt Disney, she writes that *Anthem*

> would be a complete departure from the conventional Hollywood film, and that is why I thought it worthwhile to call it to your personal attention. You might see it as I do, because you have never been afraid to venture into new fields and to do the different and the unusual. . . . If this story can be translated to the screen, I would like to see it done in *stylized drawings*, rather than with living actors.[4]

*Anthem*'s potential as an animated film was also suggested in a brief proposal received some fourteen years later from Charles Dee Emmert, a "Motion Picture Consultant" and producer who had amassed a collection of two thousand artworks. The assembly of these works into either a one-hour or a ninety-minute television presentation of *Anthem* would be accompanied by the music of composer Leon Kirschner.

Warner Bros. considered *Anthem* as a short film. Ayn Rand's attorney Bert Allenberg related that Jack Warner had sent the novella to the Warner Bros. short-subject producer Gordon Hollingshead. Hollingshead's report was negative. *Anthem* would be too expensive to make. Its revenue, he claimed, would not justify the investment.[5]

Ayn Rand communicated personally with Henry Blanke, another Warner Bros. filmmaker and the producer of the forthcoming film adaptation of *The Fountainhead*:

> The enclosed is a personal present to you, rather than a submission of a story for pictures, but you might be one of the few who would like it as a picture possibility.
>
> It is, in a way, an ancestor of THE FOUNTAINHEAD. I wrote it in 1937, when I was working on THE FOUNTAINHEAD, and it has the same theme, though in an entirely different form and on a much smaller scale. This is its first publication in America.
>
> So I thought you might be interested in it, and I wanted you to have it, to put on your bookshelf next to its child.[6]

Ayn Rand also wrote to Hal Wallis, a former Warner Bros. producer and her employer at Paramount Pictures: "I don't suppose you will be interested in this for pictures, but I want you to see it, so that you won't accuse me of disloyalty if someone else decides to buy it."[7] One other "solicitation" included Richard Mealand, a one-time story editor for Paramount Pictures and former supervisor during Rand's employment as a professional film reader. She writes: "I don't want to rush you about reading *Anthem*—I know that reading is the hardest of all jobs for a writer, I hardly have time to read anything myself."[8]

Perhaps the most intriguing inquiry came from outside of Hollywood entirely. As relayed to Ayn Rand by a Hollywood friend, screenwriter Albert Mannheimer, the U.S. State Department appeared interested in filming *Anthem* for use as "pro-capitalist propaganda."[9]

As a rule, these inquiries and responses are brief and cryptic. Rand left no notes or journal entries expanding upon these discussions. One remaining letter, however, does provide additional insight into the nature of the visual stylization Rand sought.

In 1946 Rand wrote to director Cecil B. DeMille, her first American employer, about a possible joint venture. Her reasons were political and esthetic.

Both DeMille and Rand were prominent voices in Hollywood anti-communist circles. Rand saw *Anthem* as a possible "contribution to the cause of freedom." In a previous conversation, DeMille had asked her how America might be saved from collectivism. She replied (in her letter) that filming *Anthem* was the answer:

> we have a tremendous medium such as the screen at our command—we should use it, if we want to serve our cause and our country. We should use it openly, dramatically, full blast. Organizations, speeches or editorials are almost futile, when compared to the power of the screen in presenting ideas and reaching the conscience of people.

Rand's letter reveals significant clues as to her vision:

> I see it as a picture on the grand scale, as a dramatic fantasy, on the order of the magnificent spectacles which you made in the silent days. It would be completely different from any picture made now. . . . I would have to expand the story into greater detail, and give it a more complex plot; perhaps, add a modern story to it, running parallel, showing our present day trends and their ultimate counterparts in the story of the future—using the method you used in *The Ten Commandments*.[10]

The first part of *The Ten Commandments* (1923) was filmed in an early version of Technicolor. The story adapts the biblical story of Moses, who leads the Israelites from slavery in Egypt to freedom in the Promised Land. After Moses climbs Mt. Sinai to receive the Ten Commandments from God, he returns and finds that the Israelites, having forsaken the true God, are now worshipping a Golden Calf. The second part of the motion picture, shot in black and white, is a contemporary treatment of the same issue: the initial rejection yet ultimate triumph (and therefore relevance) of the Ten Commandments to modern life.[11] DeMille's film exhibited "[t]heatricality . . . on the grandest scale, with masterly lighting and art direction sustaining large gestures."[12]

Despite Ayn Rand's obvious enthusiasm, her personal papers contain no conclusive evidence of DeMille's reaction to her film proposal, other than the fact that DeMille had enjoyed the work as literature. As with the previous film proposals, a film project did not materialize. Ultimately, Hollywood did not provide the opportunity for her ideas that the medium promised.[13]

## *ANTHEM* AS RADIO DRAMA

Despite the failure of Hollywood to adapt *Anthem*, an adaptation did occur as a result of her time in Hollywood. In 1950 *Anthem* was presented as a radio drama, and she was pleased with the production.

In August 1950 she received a letter from Howard M. Conner, Director of Radio for Spiritual Mobilization, a conservative pro-American educational organization funded by the First Congregational Church of Los Angeles.[14] Conner was writer and producer of Spiritual Mobilization's weekly radio program called *The Freedom Story*. Fascinated by *Anthem*, he discovered the novella on the library shelf of Herb Cornuelle, a mutual friend of Conner and Rand. Conner contacted Rand to suggest a radio adaptation of *Anthem*.[15]

By August 21 an agreement had been drawn up and the conditions were favorable to the author. Ayn Rand would have approval over the script, the words of all the actors, the announcer, including those of Dr. James W. Fifield. During production on the program, she would have final authority to approve the casting, direction, and the master copy of the program.[16]

The broadcast opened with Dr. Fifield's introductory comments, and featured an announcer as well as actors portraying "Equality," "Teacher," and "Collective." The production included a musical accompaniment. The script was eight double-spaced pages in length. Approximately six of those pages comprised the drama while two pages were devoted to opening and closing remarks. The story dramatizes Equality's "great crime" of working alone, his rediscovery of electric light and his subsequent rejection by the Collective. The script ends with a highly condensed version of the last two chapters of the novella, where Equality rediscovers the word "I" and celebrates the "sacred" word "ego." Interestingly, the closing remarks delivered by Fifield bear a strong resemblance to "The Individualist Manifesto": "All wonders of our modern age, all the material benefits which you now enjoy, have come from one source—from the work of a free human mind. The mind does not and cannot work under compulsion. If you destroy the freedom of the mind, all its achievements will vanish too, and mankind will fall back into primitive savagery."[17]

Ayn Rand expressed her personal evaluation of the final result in a letter to actor Tony Barrett concerning his portrayal of Equality:

> Thank you for your wonderful performance in *Anthem*. I feel that I want you to know that this was the first time I have ever heard my own words read by an actor in a manner which made me proud to hear them. . . . If you remember, I said to you that you would have to supply the emotional element which the script could not provide in view of its brevity. I did not expect to hear it provided as perfectly as you have done—and for this I am very grateful.[18]

As to the program's impact, a September 1950 letter to Rand from Conner mentions a favorable reaction throughout the country. The broadcast was provoking much discussion. This venture would be her first and only public involvement with American religious conservatives. It would also be the only *authorized* adaptation of *Anthem* during her lifetime.

## THE MUSICAL *ANTHEM*: OPERA AND BALLET

The most fragmentary evidence concerns *Anthem* as the basis for derivative musical works. Interest began shortly after the 1946 publication of the American edition of the book and continued well into the 1960s.

At some point during 1946–1947, Rand exchanged letters with Franklin Brewer, a librettist described as a "long-time friend." Brewer was interested in writing an opera libretto for *Anthem*. Apparently this proposed project had been preceded by the idea of *Anthem* as subject matter for a ballet. An undated letter from Brewer mentions Rand's view that expressing the idea of *Anthem* in ballet form would be impossible. However, he does express his own opinion that *Anthem* would make a "magnificent" opera. On librettos in general, Rand would later write: "In operas and operettas, the esthetic base is music, with the libretto serving only to provide an appropriate emotional context or opportunity for the musical score, and an integrating line for the total performance. (In this respect, there are very few good librettos.)" Once again, the proposed opera failed to move ahead.[19]

The idea of *Anthem* as the basis of an original ballet was revisited briefly four more times.

In 1947 Donald Hayne, executive assistant to Cecil B. DeMille, wrote to Rand, acknowledging the receipt of her novel. Hayne also relayed the reaction of DeMille's daughter, who suggested that *Anthem* would make a "wonderful" ballet and she recommended that Rand discuss the idea with her cousin, choreographer Agnes DeMille. No record of such a discussion exists.[20]

In 1964, after a period of fifteen years, two admirers of *Anthem*, Sharon Kopsky and Yvonne Hudlow, submitted separate requests for permission to adapt the work into a ballet. Both requests were declined. A letter to Hudlow from Rand's secretary at the time gives a brief, somewhat vague explanation as to the reason why:

> In reply to your letter of November 24, 1964, Miss Rand has asked me to inform you that she does not give you permission to write a ballet on a theme from *Anthem*. She does not consider such a request appropriate to the nature of her story.[21]

Rand's answer is unusual in view of a completely separate request received—and actually entertained—during the same period. Writing in his "Introduction" to the fiftieth anniversary edition of *Anthem*, Dr. Leonard Peikoff, Rand's literary executor, writes:

> in the mid-1960s, as I recall—she received a request from Rudolf Nureyev, who wanted to create a ballet based on *Anthem*. Ordinarily, Miss Rand turned down requests of this kind. But because of the special nature of *Anthem* (and because of her admiration for Nureyev's dancing), she was enthusiastically in favor of his idea. (Unfortunately . . . a ballet [never] materialized.) (viii)

The details of this request are unknown. However, because of Rand's respect for Nureyev, she was apparently willing to make an exception. In an unpublished 1965 letter to the *New York Times*, she defended Nureyev against criticisms expressed by Allen Hughes in an article entitled "Shadow and Substance." Hughes compared Nureyev's esthetic choices unfavorably with those of dancer-choreographer Martha Graham, criticizing the Russian dancer's outmoded nineteenth century–esthetic ideals and lack of contemporary relevancy. Protesting Hughes's "gratuitous abuse on a superlative artist," Rand describes her personal view of the performance in question as an "incomparable aesthetic experience," which provoked an "authentic, spontaneous and exultant" ovation from the audience.[22]

## UNAUTHORIZED ADAPTATION

The final entry in this survey of adaptations of *Anthem* is also the first evidence of *unauthorized* use. Material from *Anthem* appeared in a concert phonograph album entitled *Stuarti Arrives at Carnegie Hall*, and featured in a song called "Prelude."

A memo to Ayn Rand dated May 4, 1964, relates that *Exodus,* a film dealing with the effort to establish a Jewish homeland in Israel, had recently appeared in theatres with a musical score by composer Ernest Gold. Shortly thereafter, the film's popular theme music was set to lyrics and performed by singer Pat Boone (in a song called "This Land Is Mine"). In a spoken introduction, Enzo Stuarti implies that Boone was also the composer of the music for "Prelude," set to lyrics "inspired" by Stuarti's friend, Frank Lovejoy.

The lyrics of "Prelude" begin: "I know not if this earth on which I stand is the core of the universe or if it is but a speck of dust lost in eternity." This is identical to a line in *Anthem* (95). After approximately 150 words the lyrics conclude: "And my treasures, I guard my treasures: my thought, my will, my land, and my freedom. And the greatest of these is freedom." In *Anthem* the line reads: "I do not surrender my treasures, nor do I share them. The fortune of my spirit is not to be blown into coins of brass and flung to the winds as alms for the poor of the spirit. I guard my treasures: my thought, my will, my freedom. And the greatest of these is freedom."[23] Among Rand's remaining papers there is no record of any attempt to contact the principals involved.

## CONCLUSION

The twenty proposed adaptations of *Anthem* reveal the novella's attention-grabbing impact on a tiny fraction of the 2.5 million readers to date. Those who proposed these adaptations were concerned with translating the literary work into media as varied as dance, music and film. Among all of Ayn Rand's works, *Anthem*'s appeal to potential adapters is unusual. Perhaps this appeal is explained by *Anthem*'s condensed form, or its poetic style. Or maybe it is the dramatic tension produced in the reader by the ubiquitous "We" and its subsequent release in the affirmation of "I"—or all the above.

To underscore, one last time, *Anthem's* susceptibility to adaptation: late in life Ayn Rand herself borrowed from another medium to explain her work. In 1979 when asked by a high school class why she chose *Anthem* as a title, she answered with a *musical* metaphor:

"Because this story is my *hymn* to man's ego."[24]

## NOTES

1. This paper describes proposed adaptations, summarizing such esthetic intentions as are known. It is limited to the evidence contained in the Ayn Rand Papers (ARP) at the Ayn Rand Archives, a special collection of the Ayn Rand Institute. Also cited are reproductions of original manuscripts of Ayn Rand's novels located at the Manuscript Division, Library of Congress (available at the Special Collections [SC], Ayn Rand Archives). Whenever possible, the earliest dated literary typescripts or earliest handwritten versions will be cited.

I would like to thank Robert Mayhew for his editorial suggestions as well as Michael S. Berliner, Shoshana Milgram, Marc Baer, and Donna Montrezza for their helpful comments.

2. Biographical interviews (Ayn Rand Archives).

3. Ayn Rand to Bert Allenberg, November, 15 1946, and October 23, 1946, ARP 122-26-11-A, Ayn Rand Archives.

4. Ayn Rand to Walt Disney, September 5, 1946 (emphasis added). Michael S. Berliner, ed., *Letters of Ayn Rand* (New York: Dutton, 1995), 317. Rand observed the integrity of the film medium by adjusting the form through which her vision would be realized.

5. Ayn Rand to Bert Allenberg, October 23, 1946, Ayn Rand Archives.

6. Ayn Rand to Henry Blanke, September 5, 1946. Berliner, *Letters*, 315.

7. Ayn Rand to Hal Wallis, September 5, 1946. Berliner, *Letters*, 316.

8. Ayn Rand to Richard Mealand, January 20, 1947. Berliner, *Letters*, 358. Mealand replied that he liked *Anthem* for its "explosive parable" and disliked it for "its too extreme simplicity. . . . I think it should not have been a story but a poem." (Richard Mealand to Ayn Rand, Feb. 11 [1947?], ARP 149-33-M-D) Rand responded: "In your comment on *Anthem* you said it should have been a poem. Well, that is exactly what it is." Ayn Rand to Richard Mealand, July 31, 1947. Berliner, *Letters*, 371–72.

9. Albert Mannheimer to Ayn Rand, October 20, 1951, ARP 149-33-M-B, Ayn Rand Archives.

10. Ayn Rand to Cecil B. DeMille, September 5, 1946. Berliner, *Letters*, 316–17.

11. The device of mixing historical periods continued to hold Rand's fascination. After the publication of *Atlas Shrugged*, she lost interest in contemporary story settings due to the increasing irrationality of twentieth century culture. Towards the end of her life, she had considered a story on the theme of self-sacrifice, set in the Middle Ages. The final chapter of the story would jump centuries ahead to the present—its characters' modern dress thinly disguising their persisting philosophical errors. (Leonard Peikoff, interview by Richard Ralston, tape recording, Special Collections, Ayn Rand Archives.)

12. As quoted in John Wakeman, ed., *World Film Directors*, vol. 1, 1890–1945 (New York: The H. W. Wilson Company, 1987), 215. Paul Iribe, DeMille's chief art director on the film (throughout the 1920s as well) was a French born painter, stage designer and illustrator. A member of the French *avant-garde* associated with Jean Cocteau, Iribe is described as the chief architect of the "continental" visual style associated with Paramount Pictures for the next two decades. Iribe combined biblical and modern elements in his production design. His own pictorial style was akin to Art Nouveau. The combination of modern and oriental influences is also a feature of the fashion illustration of Rand's younger sister Eleanora Rosenbaum, an aspiring artist, set designer, and later exhibit designer. Known as "Nora," she and Rand shared an early interest in the "glamorous" silent films of DeMille. For samples of her work, see Jeff Britting, *Ayn Rand* (New York: The Overlook Press, 2005), 32.

13. In "Art and Cognition," Rand writes: "Potentially, motion pictures are a great art, but that potential has not as yet been actualized, except in single instances and random moments. An art that requires the synchronization of so many esthetic elements and so many different talents cannot develop in a period of philosophical-cultural disintegration such as the present. Its development requires the creative co-

operation of men who are united, not necessarily by their formal philosophical convictions, but by their fundamental view of man, i.e., by their sense of life." In Ayn Rand, *The Romantic Manifesto: A Philosophy of Literature*, revised edition (New York: Signet, 1975), 72.

14. Howard Conner to Ayn Rand, August 3, 1950, ARP 143-33-C-5, Ayn Rand Archives.

15. Rand also had an association with Spiritual Mobilization's Vice President, James C. Ingebretsen, an early admirer of *The Fountainhead*. They first met in 1943 at a dinner in Los Angeles hosted by future publisher of *The Freeman,* Leonard Read. Read's best friend was Ingebretsen, who at the time was General Council of the United States Chamber of Commerce. Ingebretsen was also an associate of Pamphleteers, the American publisher of *Anthem*. (Leonard Read to Ayn Rand, December 17, 1943, ARP 144-33-F-1, Ayn Rand Archives.)

16. Howard Conner to Ayn Rand, August 21, 1950, ARP 53-10-07, Ayn Rand Archives.

17. "The Freedom Story," Script #46-B "Anthem" (*The Ayn Rand Papers*), ARP 54-10-09, Ayn Rand Archives. See also: Jeff Britting, "*Anthem* and 'The Individualist Manifesto,'" in the present volume, p. 70.

18. Ayn Rand to Tony Barrett, August 25, 1950. Berliner, *Letters*, 475–76.

19. Rand, *Romantic Manifesto*, 71. Also during this period, a letter from Rand to Brewer reveals another potential venture involving Edmond Rostand's play *Chantecler* (1910). Rand thought the fable would make a good libretto and considered writing one. Unfortunately, an opera based on this material had already been composed and produced. Rand writes: ". . . this shows, at least, that I had a good idea."

20. Donald Hayne to Ayn Rand, March 10, 1947, ARP 109-24-12-C, Ayn Rand Archives.

21. Daryn Kent to Sharon Kopsky, September 3, 1964, ARP 42-07-06-D, Ayn Rand Archives. Daryn Kent to Yvonne Hudlow, September 3, 1964, ARP 42-07-07-H, Ayn Rand Archives.

22. Rand to editor, Sunday Theatre Section, *New York Times*, May 20, 1965, ARP 107-24-05, Ayn Rand Archives. Hugh's article contrasts Martha Graham's visionary voice of "our time" with Nureyev's desire to "resign from the twentieth century." In reply, Rand writes: "Here, it must be stated that Martha Graham represents a static, tired, semi-private cult of anti-Romanticism—a fad of no greater significance than 'modernistic' furniture or theosophy. Her followers are entitled to their 'fun' and deserve it—but to elevate *that* into the voice of the century is worse than absurd."

23. Pat Boone's "Prelude" performed by Enzo Stuarti from *Stuarti Arrives at Carnegie Hall,* Jubilee JGM-2-5055 (1964), two record set. (Memo to Ayn Rand [author unknown], May 4, 1964, ARP 54-10-21, Ayn Rand Archives.)

24. Ayn Rand, "Questions and Answers on Anthem," in *The Ayn Rand Column*, ed. Peter Schwartz (New Milford, CT.: Second Renaissance Books, 199), 123 (emphasis added).

# 6

## *Anthem* and 'The Individualist Manifesto'

*Jeff Britting*

Speaking through the voice of Prometheus in the final chapter of *Anthem*, Ayn Rand writes:

> When I shall have read all the books and learned my new way, when my home will be ready and my earth tilled, I shall steal one day, for the last time, into the cursed City of my birth. . . . I shall call to me all the men and the women whose spirit has not been killed within them and who suffer under the yoke of their brothers. . . . And here, in this uncharted wilderness, I and they, my chosen friends, my fellow-builders, shall write the first chapter in the new history of man. (100–101)

Had Prometheus returned to the "cursed City" of his birth, in what form would his "new way" have been presented to those still living there? *Anthem* does not say. However, Ayn Rand's personal papers allow us to speculate. An obscure 1941 essay called "The Individualist Manifesto" suggests a possible form. With certain adjustments, one can imagine Prometheus slipping into the City and distributing this essay among his "fellow-builders." Apparently, Ayn Rand conceived the manifesto with a similar end in mind; only her audience lay in twentieth century America.

"The Individualist Manifesto" was Ayn Rand's first extended nonfiction essay in English. Its theme is the political philosophy presented in *Anthem*. Interestingly, there are traces of the manifesto and thus of *Anthem* in *The Fountainhead*. Ayn Rand nowhere states that these three works are linked as a group. Yet, evidence encompassing the years 1937 through 1946 in her personal papers suggests that these works *are* linked and that *Anthem* is their intellectual source. Ayn Rand once referred to *The Fountainhead* as the child of *Anthem*. If so, the manifesto might be best described as *Anthem's* nonfiction twin brother.[1]

70

"The Individualist Manifesto" was written in 1941, approximately two and one-half years after the publication of *Anthem* and two years before the publication of *The Fountainhead*. The essay was intended as the mission statement for a conservative intellectual union proposed by Ayn Rand and Channing Pollock, a playwright and conservative activist.[2] Rand wrote the manifesto in order to rouse the post–Wendell Willkie, anti–New Deal conservatives of the time with a *moral* defense of capitalism. The document, she writes, would "present the whole groundwork of our 'Party Line' and be a basic document, such as the *Communist Manifesto* was on the other side." In a letter to Pollock, she writes: "Evasion and compromise have killed all pro-capitalist movements so far. I think the tragedy of Capitalism from the beginning has been the lack of a consistent ideology of its own." Referring to the pre-existing "hodgepodge" of "Collectivist-Christian-Equalitarian-Humanitarian concepts," she asked: "Are we to be the ones who will clear it up?"[3]

By 1943 *The Fountainhead* was the most complete statement in print of Rand's moral philosophy and its detailed application to human life. However, it was not the first statement of her moral philosophy. In 1938, five years before the publication of *The Fountainhead*, she writes in a letter that *Anthem* is "in a way, my manifesto, my profession of faith, the essence of my entire philosophy."[4] She expresses this view again eight years later in a 1946 letter to Leonard Read, publisher of the American edition of *Anthem*: "my whole theory of ethics is contained in *Anthem*. That was my first statement of it on paper. Everything I said in *The Fountainhead* is in *Anthem*, though a briefer, less detailed form, but there explicitly, for all to see who are interested in ideas."[5]

Inserting a "whole theory of ethics" in a literary work is a new development for Rand. *Anthem* is her first attempt to do so. And as we shall see, "The Individualist Manifesto" expands upon the political implications of her ethics.

*Anthem* is a major intellectual turning point. It presents a "whole theory." By contrast, the philosophical content of pre-*Anthem* fiction is indirect and unsystematic. *We the Living, Ideal,* the screenplays, scenarios, and short stories *apply* individualism, a morality *assumed* to be true. The stories dramatize how individualism is enacted and expressed—or show what happens to people and to their societies in its absence. But they do not define a moral code. They are not concerned with good and evil *per se*.[6] By contrast, *Anthem* makes the *re-defining* of good and evil an integral part of the story's structure.

*Anthem* is a chronicle of good and evil. The story is told, initially, in the first person plural and is set in a world that has lost its memory of the concept "I." An aspiring young scientist, assigned by the state to become a street sweeper, recounts in his journal his discovery of the electric light. According to the world's moral code—one that holds the collective as the standard of the good—both his diary and his discovery are sins. By thinking independently and by affirming personal preference, he has defied the ethics of collectivism. Conscientiously, he admits his "sin." However, he is unable to deny his love and pursuit of knowledge. Thus, he is unable to reconcile his pursuit with a moral code that regards it as evil. The hero faces a dilemma. He aspires to act morally. (He is not amoral.) Yet, his effort to act morally only further unravels his connection to the world and its collectivist code. The final break occurs when, as an act of absolution, he brings his invention to the attention of the governing "World Council." In doing so, he believes he acts to benefit the collective. However, the Council recoils and seeks to destroy him. He escapes with his life—a value his existing moral concepts do not recognize and, therefore, cannot defend or uphold. Later, in the relative solitude of the final two chapters, the hero rediscovers the missing component of a proper morality: the *concept* of the thinking, willing "ego" or "I." In doing so, he answers the world of collectivism and discovers the philosophical foundation of *political individualism*.

In a letter to Lorine Pruette, Ayn Rand writes that "[t]he last two chapters are the actual anthem."[7] In these final chapters, she presents her "whole theory of ethics" and its political consequences. The presentation involves two steps:

First, in the penultimate chapter, Rand presents the philosophic foundation of her ethics (94–97). Here the hero discovers three crucial facts: the "primacy" of his existence, the fact that he thinks, and that he is capable of personal preference and judgment. ("I am. I think. I will.") Thereafter, he describes man's approach to truth and happiness. "Truth" is not an impersonal, detached realm; nor is "happiness" subjective and cut off from truth. As the kind of being that he is—the existing, thinking and judging being that he knows himself to be—he *must* seek truth, if he is to live. And he is able to pursue happiness, which motivates his continued living.

Second, in the final chapter, Rand presents the social consequences of her ethics (98–105). Here the hero explains that a proper society requires the concept of inalienable, individual *rights*. As the events in *Anthem* demonstrate, the concept of "rights" enables man to preserve his life in a social setting. *His* thought, *his* judgment, *his* independence—and their enactment in a productive life—has only one social requirement: that his rights remain inviolable. If these rights are spelled out and their protection delegated to the state, man's freedom to act is protected from the threat of force. He can pursue his own life without the fear that force initiated by others will imperil him without recourse.

Ayn Rand elaborates the political implications of *Anthem* at length in "The Individualist Manifesto." The manifesto advocates the primacy of the individual over the collective. And it defends capitalism as a moral ideal.[8]

The manifesto opens with a one page platform of principles followed by a thirty-two page analysis of the "the basic issue of the world today." "In the name of Man's dignity, Man's honor and the integrity of Man's spirit," the manifesto affirms the principle of "inalienable individual rights" and its various forms: "the right of life," "the right of liberty," "the right to the pursuit of happiness." The "unconditional" possession of these rights by the individual "precede and limit" any claims by any "collective" of men: "these rights are granted to Man not by the Collective nor *for* the Collective, but *against* the Collective; that these rights are Man's protection against all other men." "That the State exists for Man and not Man for the State."

Following this credo is an analysis of totalitarianism ("the greatest threat to mankind and civilization") and how not to fight this trend ("Once men have accepted the enemy's faith—it is bankrupt"). The essay identifies the proper weapon ("a positive credo") embodied by "individualism." After several pages on the fallacy of "the common good" ("a holy absolute without limitations that made all tyrants possible"), the manifesto proposes a two-part division of proper human activity. There is "the Creative" sphere which embraces every productive activity, including the creation of culture. There is "the Political" sphere which concerns men and their relations with other men. Properly defined, these two spheres are complementary. The Individual, as the source of wealth and production is the active force which the political sphere encourages by allowing the individual to function. Government is a limited instrument designed to protect individual rights: "States and Governments have never contributed anything to civilization—except in a negative manner, in allowing the Individual to function." And the source of the great productive burst in the West during the past 150 years, the development of "Capitalism," confirms that the source of man's well-being is civilization: "every page of history screams to us that there is and ever has been but one source of civilization: *Individual Man in Individual Freedom.*"

The middle section of the manifesto identifies two *conflicting* principles from history. They are the "Active Man" versus the "Passive Man": The "Active Man" principle "is the desire for independence, for responsibility, for personal achievement, and a hatred of all compulsion. The second ["Passive Man" principle] is the desire to rest, to be safe, to be told by a kind father and to submit. The degree to which we follow the first and submerge the second is the degree of our worth as human beings." A society geared to the requirements of the Passive Man destroys not only the Active Man, but Passive Man as well. However, a society geared towards the Active Man raises everyone, including the Passive Man. "The basic requirement of the Active Man is freedom." After a look at the societies that result from each principle, the manifesto asks: "What, then, is the best and highest system of society? Let us have the courage to say it: THE HIGHEST SYSTEM OF SOCIETY IS THE CAPITALIST SYSYEM."

What follows is a moral analysis of the elements of capitalism. Interestingly, it shows that profit, personal choice, prices and wages, wealth and its creation, physical and mental labor, capital, production, private property are not merely economic considerations. They are tied to the requirements of human life:

> And one of the greatest achievements of the Capitalist system is the manner in which a man's natural, healthy egoism is made to profit both him and society. Capitalism does not demand a preposterous reversal of all human instincts, which is not possible and would not be desirable if it were possible. It does not require a miracle to be performed upon human nature. It takes this nature as it is and offers it a fair, sane, decent way of functioning. It does not attempt to emasculate the human spirit. Selfishness is a magnificent force. A system which makes use of it, which allows us to exercise it without injury to our brothers is a noble system.

The next section discusses the alleged improvements proposed by collectivist planning and the actual impact of such planning on civil rights, security, and the management of industry—as well as their ultimate impact upon human beings.[9] The section concludes with a refutation of the collectivist charge of capitalism's alleged abuses: poverty, waste and duplication, unemployment.

The final section of the manifesto analyzes the reasons why capitalism has been eroded and why its defenders are in a state of self-doubt, despite capitalism's unmatched record of producing material abundance. The manifesto argues that capitalism's alleged abuses are flaws made possible by an encroaching collectivism. Even a false ideal such as "the common good" shows the power of morality, which is why a moral defense of a truth like capitalism is necessary: "Collectivism is not new. It is the principle of the Dark Ages and of primitive barbarism. Capitalism is new and very young. . . . The Collectivist developments within the Capitalist System were not an inherent necessity of the system. They were merely the backward pull, the resistance of the old, the reversal to the easier, habitual methods of the Passive type of humanity." "Capitalism has never found its 'ideology.' It has been rushing along, too busy to think. But the time has come for it to speak, to formulate its own faith and its own ideal." The manifesto's final pages return to the basic choice: individualism *versus* collectivism, which includes the invitation: "Individualists of the World, Unite!"

The similarities between *Anthem* and the manifesto are numerous. Both works view man as a solitary, thinking individual. Both state that proper social relations require respect for rights. Neither of the works objects to human society as long as it is a proper one. The hero in *Anthem* affirms the benefits of living among other individuals. He even speaks of returning to the world he has fled in order to save his friends, that they might join him in creating a society that respects individual rights. Likewise, the manifesto affirms, in the name of man's "spirit" or ego, the same "inalienable, individual rights" referred to in *Anthem*, rights which are the moral basis of a proper defense of capitalism.

But the similarities do not end here. They extend to *The Fountainhead* as well.

In a letter to Samuel B. Pettengill, former congressman and the head of the Transportation Association of America, Ayn Rand writes:

> I shall be eager to hear your opinion of *The Fountainhead*. It is actually an illustrated message, in fiction form, of my "Individualist Manifesto." I have taken the basic principles of the "Manifesto" and shown them in concrete action and in human terms, how they work, what they do to people, what are their psychological roots and their practical consequences.[10]

*Anthem*, "The Individualist Manifesto" and *The Fountainhead*, while stand-alone works, do share proximity of creation. The planning of one (or more) work precedes or follows the completion of another.[11] Therefore, one can read in two different directions: either from *Anthem* to the manifesto (and *The Fountainhead*) or from *The Fountainhead* back to the manifesto (and *Anthem*). These connections reveal Rand's intellectual focus on egoism and its political implications. Even so, their order of publication affirms more than a coincidental relationship. It suggests an order of development. Ideas originated in *Anthem* are developed further by its twin brother, the manifesto. Then they reach their culmination in *Anthem's* son, *The Fountainhead*.[12]

The literary and philosophic similarities among these three works are striking. There are reoccurring concepts such as the "dark ages," "light," "truth," "legends," the "individual," "spirit," "happiness," "the Collective." There is also similarity of style. Within sections of each work, the writing is in the form of an appeal—as a credo, a manifesto, a defense. Certain situations are expressed and re-expressed from work to work: there is the lone inventor in *Anthem*; the "Creative Man" of the manifesto; Howard Roark, the first-hander of *The Fountainhead*. In opposition are philosophical antagonists, respectively: "The Collective" in *Anthem*; the "Passive Man" in the manifesto; Ellsworth Toohey, the "second hander" of *The Fountainhead*.

Numerous passages appear to flow uninterrupted from one work to the other.

In *Anthem,* the hero reinvents the electric light and brings it before the elected World Council. The manifesto refers to a "Final Planning Board, the Economic ruler of the World," which

> is elected by a free and general vote of all men and that it is composed of the greatest specialists and the best minds of mankind. Let us suppose that a new invention is offered to this Board. It is startling and revolutionary, as all great

innovations have always been. The Board has to decide by collective judgment—by a majority vote.[13]

In *Anthem* the World Council rejects the light as evil and the hero escapes with his life. The manifesto ponders a similar situation:

> But what happens if the Planning Board of a Collectivist society rejects an invention? That is the end. The inventor has no place to go, no action to take, no help to find. He is alone—and utterly helpless—against the will of the majority.

The manifesto draws the point to its ultimate consequences:

> What if such a Board had rejected just one innovator—Pasteur? Ask the millions who would have died by now but for his discoveries.[14]

On the issue of happiness, *Anthem* states:

> My joy is not the means to any end. It is the end. It is the reason of reasons. This earth is mine. This earth exists but as a field for my desires and for the choice of my will. I am upon this earth but for the joy I wrest from it. What blind vanity, what folly can command me to live for pain? But there is no joy unless it be my joy. (236)

Similarly, in the manifesto, Rand writes about happiness:

> A man's happiness is not anti-social, but un-social; it is a private domain which society has no right to touch. A general happiness cannot be created out of general suffering and self-sacrifice. The only happy society is a society of happy Individuals.[15]

Regarding the mythic figure of Prometheus in *Anthem*, Rand writes:

> I have read of a man who lived many thousands of years ago, and of all the names in these books, his is the one I wish to bear. He took the light of the gods and he brought it to men. . . . And he suffered for his deed as all bearers of light must suffer. His name was Prometheus. (243)

In *The Fountainhead,* Prometheus reappears:

> That man, the unsubmissive and first, stands in the opening chapter of every legend mankind has told about its beginning. Prometheus was chained to a rock and torn by vultures each day—because he had stolen the light of the gods.[16]

Passages concerning martyrs and truth also link *Anthem*, the manifesto, and *The Fountainhead*.

On martyrs, *Anthem* states:

Now I look ahead. My future is clear before me. The Saint of the pyre had seen the future when he choose me as his heir, as the heir of all the saints and all the martyrs who came before him and who died for the same cause, for the same word, no matter what name they gave to their cause and their truth. (244)

Likewise the manifesto states:

The Collective has contributed nothing to Man's progress—save the impediments. The history of mankind's benefactors is the history of martyrs. Most of them were fought, opposed and ridiculed for years before they won their battle.[17]

This theme appears in *The Fountainhead* as follows:

It is an algebraic formula. History will give you the specific figures to insert. The history of mankinds [sic] benefactors is the history of martyrs. In all the centuries that followed there were men who took first steps down new roads armed with nothing but their own vision. Their goals and their truths were different, but they all had this in common: that the step was first, the road new, the vision un-borrowed and the response they received—hatred.[18]

On "truth," several statements link all three works. From *Anthem*:

It is my eyes which see, and the sight of my eyes grants beauty to the earth. It is my ears which hear, and the hearing of my ears gives its song to the world. All things come to my judgment, and I weigh all things, and I seal upon them my "Yes" or my "No." Thus is Truth born. (234)

From the manifesto:

Not a single great genius has ever been actuated by the motive of "service." Not one of them was moved by a selfless devotion to his fellow-men. Every genius is motivated by a profoundly *selfish* devotion to his own convictions, to the integrity of his own thought, to his own truth.[19]

And, finally, from *The Fountainhead*:

This truth was his only concern and his only motive. His own truth as he saw it, and his own work to achieve it his own way. A symphony, a book, an engine, a philosophy, an airplane or a building—that was his goal and his life.[20]

If *Anthem* defined a "whole new theory of ethics," then in "The Individualist Manifesto," Ayn Rand elaborated a view of politics on the basis of which she could defend capitalism as a moral ideal. Although her manifesto did not rally conservatives as she had hoped, this nonfiction twin brother of *Anthem* was not completely unrealized. In a highly condensed form, the manifesto was eventually published for a mass audience.[21] In 1945, Burt

MacBride, senior editor of *Reader's Digest*, wrote to Ayn Rand, soliciting from her a short essay for the magazine's column, "Drama in Everyday Life."[22] After sending her several samples to provide the "dope" on the column, Rand responded in March of 1946, apologizing for the delay and expressing her interest in doing articles for the magazine: "I have several ideas in mind which, I think, would interest you. . . ." She asked to leave the matter open due to a pressing work schedule.[23]

In July 1946 she wrote to MacBride suggesting *Anthem* in lieu of a new article. MacBride's response was mixed: he praised *Anthem* but indicated that something more factual in the way of a critique of communism was needed. Rand's response, interestingly, recapitulates issues raised in "The Individualist Manifesto." She writes:

> Thank you for your very interesting letter. One paragraph in it startled me as an instance that belongs in the "thought transference" or "funny coincidence" department. In case you have not kept a copy of your letter. I quote:
> 'What is needed is an abecedarian, primer-like question-and-answer pamphlet that is absolutely clear, straight to the point, and hard-hitting because it presents facts. Who is there who will write that sort of eye-opener for Joe Zilch and his wife?'
> Well, you will find the answer enclosed [referring to the content of her letter].

Ayn Rand continues her letter, pointing out the need for new *ideas*:

> That is why true and factual books about the horrors of Soviet Russia are and will continue to be ineffectual. That is why they will not cure Americans of sympathy for the Kremlin, nor check the trend toward collectivism in America. *Facts alone won't do it. Only the proper philosophy derived from the facts,* will."[24]

Although MacBride did not accept Rand's offer of *Anthem,* he did, at an earlier point, accept a revision of "The Individualist Manifesto." After Rand submitted a shortened draft renamed "The Individualist Credo," the essay was ultimately published by the *Reader's Digest* in 1944 as "The Only Path to Tomorrow."

In *Anthem*, Ayn Rand asks how "men who knew the word 'I,' could give it up and not know what they lost." Perhaps, she writes, men of "clear sight and clean soul" had "cried out in protest and in warning. But men paid no heed to their warning" (103). Perhaps. Or maybe these protestors knew the facts "I" and "ego" but not the "proper philosophy derived from the facts." By contrast, Ayn Rand published *Anthem* and "The Individualist Manifesto" in her own "cursed City" of twentieth century politics. She offered "fellow-builders" (those whose spirits have "not been killed") a "proper philosophy" based on man's ego and, therefore, the promise of human life.[25]

## NOTES

1. Ayn Rand, "The Individualist Manifesto," c. 1941: 23, version ARP 32-06-90-A, Ayn Rand Archives. This essay was privately circulated in 1941 and has not been republished. For *The Fountainhead* as the "child" of *Anthem*, see Ayn Rand to Henry Blanke, September 5, 1946. Michael S. Berliner, ed., *Letters of Ayn Rand* (New York: Dutton, 1995), 315.

I would like to thank Robert Mayhew for his valuable editorial suggestions, Shoshana Milgram for her historic insight, as well as Michael S. Berliner, Marc Baer, and Donna Montrezza for their helpful comments.

2. Ayn Rand wrote "The Individualist Manifesto" in April 1941, thirteen months after the last dated entry in the first draft of *The Fountainhead* (May 11, 1940, *The Fountainhead*, first draft, *Ayn Rand Papers at the Library of Congress*, Reel 12, Part A (223), *Special Collections*, Ayn Rand Archives). Work on *The Fountainhead* would not resume until December 11, 1941, a work stoppage of almost 19 months. After resuming the novel, the first draft of Roark's speech is dated November 14, 1942, a scant two months before her contracted delivery date of the entire manuscript—over one and one-half years *after* completing "The Individualist Manifesto." The manifesto was composed when *The Fountainhead* lay unfinished. The philosophy in *The Fountainhead* had yet to be stated explicitly, while the philosophy in *Anthem* had been stated.

3. Ayn Rand to Channing Pollock, May 1, 1941. Berliner, *Letters*, 46.

4. Ayn Rand to Newman Flower, January 2, 1938, ARP 86-18-15, Ayn Rand Archives.

5. Ayn Rand to Leonard Read, May 18, 1946. Berliner, *Letters*, 275.

6. I am indebted to Shoshana Milgram for this observation.

7. Ayn Rand to Lorine Pruette, October 28, 1946. Berliner, *Letters*, 336.

8. Rand, "Manifesto," 1–33. This endnote encompasses the six paragraph summary that follows.

9. In a cogent example, she writes: "Three million peasants died of starvation in the great Soviet famine. We know that the famine was deliberately planned. But the Communists claim that it was due merely to a mistake of the government. Let us accept their explanation. It is more horrible. A ruling authority whose single mistake can take three million lives is a monster unequaled in history." Rand, "Manifesto," 26.

10. Ayn Rand to Samuel B. Pettengill, June 13, 1943. Berliner, *Letters*, 76.

11. This overlap is true of a considerable portion of Ayn Rand's work preceding *Atlas Shrugged*.

12. A word about a separate unfinished work: "The Moral Basis of Individualism." (See David Harriman, ed., *Journals of Ayn Rand* [New York: Dutton, 1997], 244–310.) "The Moral Basis" concerns ethical egoism and *its* foundations.

*The Fountainhead*'s publisher, Bobbs-Merrill, suggested a companion book which would present the novel's moral and political ideas in non-fiction form. Ayn Rand's working title was "The Moral Basis of Individualism." Work on the book began in 1943 and continued, alongside other projects, until 1946. It was never finished. As recounted by David Harriman:

> There seem to be two reasons why she lost interest in writing [*The Moral Basis of Individualism*]. Years later, she recalled that in the early stages of planning she had concluded

that "it was useless to present a morality without a metaphysics and epistemology." Second, her primary interest was fiction writing.

She explained that,

> The idea of writing a philosophical nonfiction book bored me; in such a book, the purpose would actually be to teach others, to present my ideas to *them*. In a book of fiction the purpose is to create, for myself, the kind of world I want and to live in it while I am creating it; then, as a secondary consequence, to let others enjoy this world, if, and to the extent that, they can. (Harriman, *Journals*, 243)

The unfinished "Moral Basis" is a transitional work and it likely clarified the need to address metaphysics and epistemology, subjects later taken up by "Galt's speech" in *Atlas Shrugged*. Her final novel, *Atlas Shrugged*, can be viewed as the systematic fulfillment of the (moral) philosophy first presented in *Anthem*. Only now, by introducing metaphysics and epistemology, the literary and artistic scope of her novel increased accordingly *and necessarily*.

13. Rand, "Manifesto," 22.

14. Rand, "Manifesto," 23.

15. Rand, "Manifesto," 21.

16. The excerpts cited here and in notes 18 and 20 are from the earliest draft of Roark's speech because they are the closest to "The Individualist Manifesto" in the order of creation. (See note 2.) Rand, *The Fountainhead, Library of Congress,* Reel 14, Part A (569). Cf. Ayn Rand, *The Fountainhead* (New York: Bobbs-Merrill, 1943; Signet fiftieth anniversary paperback edition, 1993), 679.

17. Rand, "Manifesto," 7.

18. Rand, *The Fountainhead, Library of Congress,* Reel 14, Part A (569). Cf. Rand, *Fountainhead*, 679.

19. Rand, "Manifesto," 7 (emphasis added).

20. Rand, *The Fountainhead, Library of Congress,* Reel 14, Part A (571). Cf. Rand, *Fountainhead*, 680.

21. The failure of the "The Individualist Manifesto" to rally conservatives is best explained by the incoherence of the conservatives' philosophical views. Capitalism requires a philosophical base of reason and ethical egoism, not religious faith and altruism. For Rand's view of the conservative movement, see "Conservatism: An Obituary," in *Capitalism: The Unknown Ideal* (New York: New American Library, 1966; Signet expanded paperback edition, 1967).

22. Burt MacBride to Ayn Rand, December 20, 1945, ARP 149-33-M-A, Ayn Rand Archives.

23. Ayn Rand to Burt MacBride, March 23, 1946, ARP 149-33-M-A, Ayn Rand Archives.

24. Ayn Rand to Burt MacBride, July 30, 1946, ARP 149-33-M-A, Ayn Rand Archives (emphasis added).

25. Ayn Rand, "The Only Path to Tomorrow," in *The Ayn Rand Column,* ed. Peter Schwartz (New Milford, CT: Second Renaissance Books, 1991), 114. I would like to thank Shoshana Milgram for her suggestion to situate "The Individualist Manifesto" into the narrative of *Anthem,* which I have done in the opening and closing paragraphs of this essay.

# II

## *ANTHEM* AS LITERATURE AND AS PHILOSOPHY

# 7

## *Anthem* as a Psychological Fantasy

*Tore Boeckmann*

The opening of *Anthem* takes the reader into strange territory.

"It is a sin to write this," writes the narrator. "It is as if we were speaking alone to no ears but our own. And we know well that there is no transgression blacker than to do or think alone" (17). This is an arresting formulation of a peculiar sentiment; but the real shock comes with the revelation of who is referred to by the plural pronoun. "We are alone here under the earth," the narrator says—"there is nothing here save our one body, and it is strange to see only two legs stretched on the ground, and on the wall before us the shadow of our one head" (17).

The reader has been introduced to a mind unlike any to be encountered in normal experience—the mind of a man who, lacking the concept "ego," or "I," refers to himself as "we."[1] *Anthem* is the story of how this man discovers his ego.

In addition to its lack of realism, this central story premise has one striking characteristic: its purely mental orientation. The hero of *Anthem* goes from ignorance to knowledge of a fact about his own consciousness.

*Anthem*, in Ayn Rand's own words, is a *psychological fantasy.*[2]

The genre of *Anthem* follows from its central premise, and these in turn determine all of the novel's other distinctive features. Take, for instance, the *setting*. To explain the hero's predicament, Ayn Rand places him in a future collectivist "utopia" where the word "I" has been eradicated and everyone refers to himself as "we" and to another individual as "they."[3] The utopia's

83

philosophy is expressed in the words cut in marble over the portals of the Palace of the World Council:

*We are one in all and all in one.*
*There are no men but only the great WE,*
*One, indivisible and forever.* (19)

The hero has been taught this philosophy since childhood. His acceptance of it is the bar to his forming a concept of the ego.

The term "ego," in Leonard Peikoff's formulation, "designates the mind (and its attributes) considered as an individual possession."[4] In this regard, observe that the word "I" can be used as a noun; one may speak of "the I," meaning the mind or self of an individual, whereas "we" is merely a pronoun. But for the collectivist utopia in *Anthem*, the human mind is, fundamentally, a collective possession. Thus it is "we" that gets to be a noun—"the great WE"—and "I" is not even a pronoun.

If the collective mind has metaphysical primacy, then it is logically the arbiter of truth and goodness. Thus the hero of *Anthem* writes that "the World Council is the body of all truth" (19), and "the Councils are the voice of all justice, for they are the voice of all men" (22). Further, as the body of truth and the voice of justice, the collective mind is entitled to *reverence*. In nightly Social Meetings, the inhabitants of the collectivist utopia sing the Hymn of the Collective Spirit (27–28).

This context explains not only why the hero of *Anthem* lacks the concept "ego," but also why his discovering that concept will be a prodigiously difficult task.

Note that he does have some awareness of himself as an individual. He can directly perceive his own body: "two legs stretched on the ground." He has been given the name Equality 7-2521, and although this combination of a collectivist slogan and a number is meant to eradicate his individuality, it still distinguishes him from, say, Equality 7-2522. More significantly, when he says that "there is no transgression blacker than to do or think alone," he knows that such is exactly what he is doing. "It is a sin to think words no others think and to put them down upon a paper no others are to see" (17). But this is the very sin he is committing. It is precisely for the individual exercise of the human mind that Equality condemns himself in the novel's opening.

However, he *does* condemn himself—and there lies his problem.

Whereas the collective mind is (supposedly) metaphysically normal, epistemologically potent, morally good, and worthy of reverence, Equality has been taught that any individual exercise of the mind is just the opposite: a transgression and a sin. Add to this the fact that a man experiences his mind, not as a perceptible object, but as a continuous stream of perceptions, thoughts, feelings, memories, etc. To grasp these as constituting an *ego* is difficult enough in the ordinary case.[5] But so long as Equality regards his own mental actions as aberrant, impotent, evil, and loathsome, his isolation and integration of them into the concept of an enduring, autonomous *self* is impossible to him.

To form such a concept, Equality must first learn the true nature and significance of his mind.

He must live through the story of *Anthem*—the events of which correspond to the novel's theme: "the meaning of man's ego."[6]

## THE INTEGRATION OF STORY AND THEME IN *ANTHEM*

### The Tunnel

The first chapter of *Anthem* is the story of a crime.

"We were born with a curse," Equality writes in his diary. "It has always driven us to thoughts which are forbidden. It has always given us wishes which men may not wish" (18). And it has "brought us step by step to our last, supreme transgression, our crime of crimes hidden here under the ground" (20). That crime is Equality's clandestine research in the old subway tunnel.

Written as Equality's own retrospective on the steps which brought him to his crime, the first chapter poses two major puzzles, to Equality himself no less than to the reader. The first concerns Equality's motive: why does he do that which he thinks is wrong? "We know that we are evil," he says, "but there is no will in us and no power to resist [our curse]. This is our wonder and our secret fear, that we know and do not resist" (18). Compare Equality to Andrei in *We the Living*, who says: "If it's right and you don't want to do it—you don't know what right is and you're not a man."[7] This is how one expects an Ayn Rand hero to talk. By contrast, Equality is a mystery to himself, like the tormented St. Paul, who said: "For the good that I would I do not: but the evil which I would not, that I do" (Romans 7:19).

The second puzzle of the first chapter concerns the emotional effect of Equality's crime: unlike Paul, Equality is *not* tormented. The retrospective that begins with his consciousness of sin ends with his consciousness of a profound lack of guilt. "The evil of our crime is not for the human mind to probe," writes Equality.

> And yet there is no shame in us and no regret. We say to ourselves that we are a wretch and a traitor. But we feel no burden upon our spirit and no fear in our heart. And it seems to us that our spirit is clear as a lake troubled by no eyes save those of the sun. And in our heart—strange are the ways of evil!—in our heart there is the first peace we have known in twenty years. (36–37) [Equality is twenty-one.]

But the ways of "evil" are not as strange as Equality thinks. For what is his curse? It is "our cursed wish to know" (29). And what is the essence of Equality's crimes and transgressions? The exercise of his individual mind in struggling to understand the world.

In the Home of the Infants, he writes, "we fought with our brothers" (20). One can infer that this was the only way an independent but (at that age) intellectually helpless mind could resist the conformist pressure of the pack. In the Home of the Students (after the age of five), the nature of Equality's transgression changes: he is too bright. It "is a great sin, to be born with a head which is too quick" (21). Equality tries to be like Union 5-3992, "a pale boy with only half a brain" (21), but the teachers see through him and he is lashed. "We wished to know," Equality relates. "We wished to know about all the things which make the earth around us. We asked so many questions that the Teachers forbade it" (23).

It is his desire to know that leads Equality to the grave Transgression of Preference: he wishes to be sent to the Home of the Scholars. But the Council of Vocations, no doubt informed about his active mind, makes him a street sweeper instead. He resolves to accept the decision: "we would work for our brothers, gladly and willingly, and we would erase our sin against them, which they did not know, but we knew" (26). This is his "victory over ourselves" (26)—his attempt, in Paul's terms, to do "the good that I would" rather than "the evil which I would not."

Equality sustains his resolve for four years. His life in those years is described in *Anthem*'s longest paragraph, a monotonous catalog of bleak regimentation, stuporous routine, exhausting toil, and mindless propaganda—all of which leaves not a moment's room for thought.[8] "Such would have been our life," says Equality, "had we not committed our crime which changed all things for us" (29).

Triggered by his accidental discovery of the old tunnel from the Unmentionable Times, Equality's crime consists of his claiming the tunnel for himself, as his clandestine base for scientific research. For two years, he sits in his tunnel each night, melting strange metals and mixing acids; and in those years "we have learned more than we had learned in the ten years of the Home of the Students" (36). Although he judges his action as a sin, he is at peace with himself. "We wish nothing, save to be alone and to learn, and to feel as if with each day our sight were growing sharper than the hawk's and clearer than rock crystal" (36). Still, as we have seen, he cannot explain his deeper motive. "We ask, why must we know [the things on this earth], but [our curse] has no answer to give us. We must know that we may know" (24).

The actual answer, which Equality will eventually discover, is that he *has* a mind and that its nature is to perceive reality and guide his actions. To exercise his mind or not is his deepest choice—and *not* to exercise it is to blank himself out of existence. He is implicitly aware of this, since for four years his mind *did* lie dormant—as idle and irrelevant as the mind of Union 5-3992 (who had become his fellow street sweeper). And what he experienced in those years was not existence as a human being. This implicit knowledge is what makes him grab without a second thought at the fortuitous chance to conduct his research. Although he believes his desire and action to be evil, to act as he does is ultimately *not* a breach of integrity, since without his crime, there literally is no *him* whose convictions he could betray.

It is for the same reason that his "evil" brings him not a psychological punishment, but a psychological reward. He *has* an individual mind, and its function is to perceive, explore, and come to know reality. Each day in which his sight grows "sharper than the hawk's" is a day when his mind, and thus his *self*, is brought into its proper relationship to existence, and brought to life—which is the ultimate source of serenity and happiness. Equality is a long way from grasping all of this—because his *real* curse is not the wish to know, but his lack of a concept of the ego. However, the two puzzles he confronts in this chapter are themselves the first pieces of evidence in the chain that will eventually lead him to form such a concept, and thus to answer the puzzles.

It is clear how the events of the first chapter relate to *Anthem*'s theme—"the meaning of man's ego"—and to the core premise of showing a man who lacks, and then discovers, the word "I." A subtler issue is how the same events fit the novel's *genre*.

Observe first that Equality's adversary, the collective, is a faceless mass who hardly notices his existence. The obstacle posed by the councils to Equality is structural rather than dynamic: they *would* stop him if they knew what he was doing, so he is forced to act in secret. But they take no active measures against him, and he has little practical trouble in eluding their grasp. "It is easy to leave the Theatre" at night and to run through the darkness to his tunnel, and later "it is easy" to fall back in line as the column of street sweepers leaves the Theatre (35). Aspiring writers of suspense thrillers have nothing to learn from Ayn Rand's literary technique here.

Next observe that the big turning point in Equality's life is triggered by an accident. Once he finds the tunnel, he uses it purposefully to conduct his research. But he does not actively seek such a hiding place; he stumbles upon it. In this, Equality is unlike the typical Ayn Rand hero, who never lets his life course be determined by happenstance.

However, suppose Equality had not chanced upon the tunnel but, say, had dug a secret hole for his research, like the escape tunnel dug by the Allied prisoners of war in *The Great Escape*. Equality would then have been responding to a central conflict—the collective versus himself—with an assertive plan of action designed to overcome practical obstacles. The result would have been logical plot connections, melodramatic suspense, a stronger existential *story*—and a fatal displacement of focus away from Equality's *mind*.

In a plot story, like Ayn Rand's other novels, the link between the theme and the events is the element which Ayn Rand called the plot-theme. She described this as "the central conflict or 'situation' of a story—a conflict in terms of action, corresponding to the theme and complex enough to create a purposeful progression of events [i.e., a plot]."[9] By contrast, *Anthem*'s equivalent of a plot-theme is not an action conflict, but the premise of a man who lacks, and then discovers, the concept "ego." What facilitates the novel's integration of story and theme is a psychological gimmick. This precludes the introduction of a central action conflict and a plot.[10] *Two* integrating premises is a contradiction—it is *dis*integration.

Ayn Rand has to maintain a careful balance in *Anthem*. She needs a coherent story, but she cannot let the elements of existential storytelling start to cohere on their own terms. In literature, physical action exerts a stronger claim on the reader's attention than introspective revelation, and any emergent *existential* basis of integration will wipe out a mental one. Therefore, to keep the focus on Equality's mental progression—to keep the "we" in his mind, and the eventual "I," from becoming mere stylistic garnish to an action drama—Ayn Rand downplays the existential conflict and makes a key turning point accidental.

Her stylistic treatment of the events serves the same purpose. It is Equality's *accidental* discovery of the tunnel that is dramatized across several pages, while his purposeful utilization of the tunnel to circumvent the collective—an action that follows logically from the preceding events—is merely synopsized in a few paragraphs.

Here, too, Ayn Rand demonstrates her grasp of what she is writing: a psychological fantasy.


## Liberty 5-3000

"We do not know why we think of them," writes Equality of Liberty 5-3000. "We do not know why, when we think of them, we feel of a sudden that the earth is good and that it is not a burden to live" (41).

Equality's love for Liberty 5-3000 confronts him with new puzzles. For one thing, he has been taught that "all men must be alike" (19), but Liberty, and her response to him, prove that they are not. She tells him:

> "You are not one of our brothers, Equality 7-2521, for we do not wish you to be."
> We cannot say what they meant, for there are no words for their meaning, but we know it without words and we knew it then.
> "No," we answered, "nor are you one of our sisters." (43)

What makes Liberty differ from her sisters? "Their eyes were dark and hard and glowing, with no fear in them, no kindness and no guilt," Equality writes of his first sight of her. "They threw seeds from their hand as if they deigned to fling a scornful gift, and the earth was as a beggar under their feet" (39).

And what makes Equality differ from his brothers? "Your eyes are not like the eyes of any among men" (44), Liberty tells him in their first conversation. Later in the novel, she specifies:

> Your eyes are as a flame, but our brothers have neither hope nor fire. Your mouth is cut of granite, but our brothers are soft and humble. Your head is high, but our brothers cringe. You walk, but our brothers crawl. (82–83)

Equality and Liberty see in each other the exact same characteristic: an indomitable *pride.* It is a trait Equality has not yet consciously identified in himself. Yet his response to seeing such pride in Liberty is instantaneous: love at first sight. "And we stood still that we might not spill this pain more precious than pleasure" (39).

As Aristotle put it, in a passage that could have been written specifically about Equality,

> it is both a most difficult thing, as some of the sages have said, to attain a knowledge of oneself, and also a most pleasant thing. . . . And so, as when we wish to see our own face, we do so by looking into the mirror, in the same way when we wish to know ourselves we can obtain that knowledge by looking at the one we love. For the one we love is, as we say, another self. If, then, it is pleasant to contemplate oneself, and it is not possible to do this without having someone else whom one loves, the self-sufficient man *will* need someone to love.[11]

Equality is introspectively groping to conceptualize his self, but he is merely at the beginning of a long and torturous process. However, in Liberty he can perceive his self simply, directly, without groping, in an object of the external world.

His emotional response to this perception is no less intense for being, to him, mysterious. On the day when he first speaks to Liberty, he starts to sing without reason. "We are singing because we are happy," he tells the member of the Home Council who reprimands him. He is answered: "How else can men be when they live for their brothers?" (45).

Yet Equality can see that his brothers are not happy. "The heads of our brothers are bowed," he writes that night in his tunnel.

> The eyes of our brothers are dull, and never do they look one another in the eyes. The shoulders of our brothers are hunched, and their muscles are drawn, as if their bodies were shrinking and wished to shrink out of sight. And a word steals into our mind, as we look upon our brothers, and that word is fear. (46)

Clearly, his brothers are neither happy nor proud.

It is no literary coincidence that Equality meets Liberty after he has spent two years conducting research in his tunnel, i.e., after he has objectively earned the pride that is the bond between them. And it is probably no coincidence that his reflection on the state of his brothers occurs on the night after he has first spoken to Liberty. Through his relationship to her, he has gained a clearer sense of what he is, which has drawn his attention to the fact that "our brothers are not like us" (47).

For Equality, the evidence is accumulating. And it is precisely *as* evidence of Equality's ego that his and Liberty's love relate to the totality of the story. Observe that Ayn Rand abstains from turning the forbidden love into a melodramatic aspect of the conflict between Equality and the collective. To avoid detection, he and Liberty are forced to communicate partly by glances and gestures—but the subterfuge is elementary. By contrast, if Equality had stolen away in disguise at night for secret assignations with Liberty, the focus would have been displaced from his mental progression to the existential story. So Ayn Rand instead has him simply waiting for a fortuitous opportunity to speak to Liberty again.

When that opportunity comes, he gains another clue.

Equality and Liberty's love constitutes a celebration of their egos. This they do not explicitly understand, but at least Equality can name the emotional quality of what he experiences: it is a "pain more precious than pleasure" when he first sees Liberty, and "happiness" when he has first spoken with her. But in their next encounter, they both experience something he is unable to express directly in words.

The encounter takes place after Equality has discovered electricity, and thus has gained an even greater appreciation of his mental efficacy. He and Liberty exchange the names they have given each other in their thoughts: the Golden One and the Unconquered. At the end of their encounter, the Golden One stands before Equality "as if their body were delivered in submission to our eyes" (56–57).

> Then they knelt by the moat, they gathered water in their two hands, they rose and they held the water out to our lips.
> We do not know if we drank that water. We only knew suddenly that their hands were empty, but we were still holding our lips to their hands, and that they knew it, but did not move.
> We raised our head and stepped back. For we did not understand what had made us do this, and we were afraid to understand it.
> And the Golden One stepped back, and stood looking upon their hands in wonder. Then the Golden One moved away, even though no others were coming, and they moved stepping back, as if they could not turn from us, their arms bent before them, as if they could not lower their hands. (57–58)

With its motif of submissive offering and exalted acceptance, this physical seal on Equality and the Golden One's love has the form of a religious rite, performed in reverence for the highest and most uplifted—but by worshipers who act like sleepwalkers, evoking the drugged trance of an Oriental ceremony. The scene is written as if Equality and the Golden One are the sacred vessels of something far beyond their conscious understanding.

And at this point, that is what they are.

## The Power and the Light

"We, Equality 7-2521, have discovered a new power of nature. And we have discovered it alone, and we are alone to know it" (52).

Equality has rediscovered electricity—and it was not a lucky chance. Unknown to himself, he has duplicated the experiments of Galvani, Volta and Franklin. The nature of this research is related in a highly essentialized way, which keeps the focus on the meaning of his discovery for Equality's mental progression.

Equality is now able to draw two conscious conclusions. The first is that "the Council of Scholars is blind" and that the "secrets of this earth are not for all men to see, but only for those who will seek them" (52). The second conclusion is an even more profound overturn of everything Equality has been taught. "No single one can possess greater wisdom than the many Scholars who are elected by all men for their wisdom. Yet we can. We do" (54).

If this constitutes a puzzle for Equality, he does not dwell on it. Although "it frightens us that we are alone in our knowledge" (54), his main emotional reaction is one of assured confidence in his individual mental powers and of dismissive contempt for the Scholars. "So much is still to be learned! So long a road lies before us, and what care we if we must travel it alone!" (54).

When Equality reinvents the electric light, his attitude changes.

For one thing, he reacts to his own invention with a delirious excitement not in evidence when he discovered electricity. "We made it. We created it. We brought it forth from the night of the ages. We alone. Our hands. Our mind. Ours alone and only" (59). This change of tone reflects the difference between a scientific and a technological achievement. The discovery of electricity is a simple recognition of reality, and a testament to the *cognitive* efficacy of Equality's mind; the invention of the electric light is an extension of himself into physical reality and a testament to his *creative* efficacy.

> We stretched our hands to the wire, and we saw our fingers in the red glow. We could not see our body nor feel it, and in that moment nothing existed save our two hands over a wire glowing in a black abyss. (60)

In the darkness of the tunnel, it is his own ego that Equality sees glowing.

The implications of his invention are immediately clear to Equality. The new power "can be made to do men's bidding" (60), he writes. "We can light our tunnel, and the City, and all the Cities of the world with nothing save metal and wires" (60). He realizes that his discoveries cannot be extended or applied on the scale they deserve—in a secret hole in the ground. While earlier he was content to travel the road of learning alone, he now decides to bring his secret "into the sight of men" (60). He will resolve the main conflict of the novel,[12] the conflict that has forced him into the role of an outcast. He will present his light to the World Council of Scholars. "They will see, understand and forgive," he thinks. "For our gift is greater than our transgression" (61).

Equality's decision to abandon the secrecy follows from his revolutionary *technological* invention. But since Ayn Rand is writing a psychological fantasy, not a plot story, Equality's diary entry on his invention does not end with a plan of action logically connected to the preceding events. Instead, the focus is brought back to Equality's mind.

> Men never see their own faces and never ask their brothers about it, for it is evil to have concern for their own faces or bodies. But tonight, for a reason we cannot fathom, we wish it were possible to us to know the likeness of our own person. (61–62)

After reinventing the electric light, and deciding to resolve the conflict that has shaped his entire life, Equality's concluding thought for the night is—the wish for a mirror. That this does not come across as vain or ludicrous, but as appropriate, inevitable, and moving, is a tribute to Ayn Rand's sustained focus on her novel's primary concern: Equality's mental struggle to grasp his ego.

## The Whipping

"The first blow of the lash felt as if our spine had been cut in two," Equality remembers. "The second blow stopped the first, and for a second we felt nothing, then the pain struck us in our throat and fire ran in our lungs without air. But we did not cry out" (64).

Equality finds himself in the torture room of the Palace of Corrective Detention partly by accident. On the night when he invents the electric light, he forgets to watch the time and returns to the City Theatre too late to join the departing street sweepers. The World Council of Scholars will not meet for another month. If Equality hides in his tunnel, he and his light will be discovered by lesser representatives of the collective. So to protect his light from destruction, he turns himself in. He is lashed until he blacks out, but refuses to reveal where he has been. Then, on the night before the Council meets, he escapes from the Palace, runs back to his tunnel, and awaits the morning.

This whole sequence plays no role in the progression of the existential story of *Anthem*. At the end of chapter six (his diary entry on his torture),

Equality is precisely where he was at the end of chapter five: sitting in his tunnel with the resolution to show the scholars his light. In terms of his existential position, the only thing that has changed is the passage of time. Moreover, as noted, the whipping episode is set off from the rest of the story by arising from an accident. While it is logical that Equality would turn himself in *given* that he has forgotten the time, the forgetfulness itself is not determined by the previous events (although it is plausibly explained by Equality's emotional state at the time).

Also, while Equality's *escape* from the Palace does follow logically from his previous resolution to go to the scholars, the escape involves no melodrama. Just as it has been "easy to leave the Theatre" and run to the tunnel, so it is now

> easy to escape from the Palace of Corrective Detention. The locks are old on the doors and there are no guards about. There is no reason to have guards, for men have never defied the Councils so far as to escape from whatever place they were ordered to be. (66–67)

Equality's obstacle is not the collectivist state as such, but his lack of a concept of the ego. And the self-contained nature of the whipping episode stresses its real purpose: not to form a link in a melodramatic chain of events, but to demonstrate something about Equality's *mind.* That he gives himself up, presumably knowing that he may be lashed, and then resists the torture, proves to himself and to the reader the *intensity* with which Equality values his invention of electric light—the foremost product of his ego.

Ayn Rand once stated that her literary "concern with torture" came from the adventure story *The Mysterious Valley,* which profoundly influenced her as a child.[13] The hero of that novel, Cyrus Paltons, remains defiant when threatened with a whipping by an evil Hindu. Ayn Rand would include a torture scene not only in *Anthem,* but also in her greatest novel, *Atlas Shrugged.* And both of these scenes add an element of characterization that only the depiction of physical torture can accomplish.

As an aspect of consciousness, intensity of valuing cannot be measured by a general standard like inches or pounds. A story may show a character giving up one value for another and thus indicate their relative importance *to him,* as when Howard Roark in *The Fountainhead* turns down the Manhattan Bank Company commission to preserve his artistic integrity. He values his integrity more than the commission. But the intensity with which Roark values the commission is something the reader can estimate only approximately from the general context of the story.

Pain provides a more direct standard. As a *sensation,* it has the same quality and meaning for all men: it is self-evidently bad, and it can itself be measured in terms of intensity and duration. The reader can empathize directly with each racking blow that lands on Equality's back. Even if the reader himself has never been lashed, he can know by projection from his own experience of pain the strength of resolve that makes Equality refuse to speak. And he can know exactly what Equality feels when he regains consciousness in his cell, and smiles—"for we thought of the light and that we had not betrayed it" (66).

The literary use of torture to measure intensity of valuing can be appropriate in any kind of story, but it is particularly suited to a psychological fantasy like *Anthem*. Had Ayn Rand instead confronted Equality with a dramatic choice between two *existential* values—say, his light and the life of the Golden One—this would have displaced the story's focus from Equality's mind. In *Anthem*, the hero's commitment to his highest value is best measured against another phenomenon of his *consciousness*—the pain Equality triumphs over in the torture scene.

This does not mean that Equality's whipping is irrelevant to his later actions. On the contrary, after resisting physical torture, Equality will not abandon his light because of a prison door with an old lock, or any equivalent.

And he will soon have another opportunity to prove it.

### The Scholars

"We saw a great painting on the wall over their heads, of the twenty illustrious men who had invented the candle" (68).

As Equality walks into the meeting of the World Council of Scholars, this painting symbolizes to him the reason why he is there. Earlier, he has condemned the scholars as "blind" and has concluded that he himself has "greater wisdom" than they do. But he still retains some respect for their powers of thought. After all, "the great modern inventions come from the Home of the Scholars, such as the newest one, which we found only a hundred years ago, of how to make candles from wax and string" (23–24). This is the technological precursor of Equality's own electric light, which may be why he thinks of "our brother Scholars" and wants "their wisdom joined to ours" (60). But when he demonstrates his new invention to them—when he closes the circuit and the wire glows—terror strikes the scholars. "They leapt to their feet, they ran from the table, and they stood pressed against the wall, huddled together, seeking the warmth of one another's bodies to give them courage" (70).[14]

Of the scholars, the first to move forward from the wall is Collective 0-0009. He asks Equality, "How dared you think that your mind held greater wisdom than the minds of your brothers?" (71). The "oldest and wisest of the Council" (69), and the closest Equality ever has to a personal antagonist, Collective is a complete cipher. His name may be Ayn Rand's private joke. In *We the Living*, the heroine responds to the idea that society is a "stupendous whole" by saying, "If you write a whole line of zeroes, it's still—nothing."[15]

Ayn Rand could well have had this remark in mind when, in writing *Anthem*, she combined "Collective" with a string of zeroes (concluded by a "9," a digit visually close to a zero).

The other scholars follow Collective in moving from the wall—and in condemning Equality. He shall be burned at the stake, they say, or lashed. But Collective, appropriately, has the best grasp of proper collective decision making. "No such crime has ever been committed," he says, "and it is not for us to judge" (72). He passes the buck to a higher council.

Equality asks what will happen to his light.

("What is not thought by all men cannot be true" (73), says Collective—after he has *seen* the wire glow.) "What is not done collectively cannot be good" (73), says another scholar. Many scholars "have had strange new ideas in the past," says yet another, "but when the majority of their brother Scholars voted against them, they abandoned their ideas, as all men must" (73).

In this scene, Equality can see first-hand the nature of the collective mind at its highest development. He can see what is *really* symbolized by the painting of the twenty men who invented the candle. And, probably, he can see the motive that makes Collective point to the box containing his invention and say, "This thing must be destroyed" (74).

But Equality does not yet have all the evidence required to understand fully what he has seen, nor the time to think about it. In this respect, compare him to John Galt in *Atlas Shrugged*, who is present at the *formation* of a collectivist society which claims him—and, by implication, his revolutionary new invention—as its property. When Galt stands up and says, "I will put an end to this, once and for all," his voice is "clear and without any feeling."[16] Galt knows exactly what is wrong with collectivism; he has the intellectual basis for calm determination. Equality does not. He has only his rage. When the other scholars follow Collective's lead and cry, "It must be destroyed!" Equality, rage choking his voice, cries, "You fools! You fools! You thrice-damned fools!" (75). Then he swings his fist through the windowpane and escapes with his invention.

He runs to the Unchartered Forest, which "men never enter" (48). In doing so, Equality resolves the main conflict of the novel, although not in the way he had expected. He breaks unequivocally with the collective.

This is not a conscious decision, which would presuppose conclusions Equality has not yet drawn (and would make his escape too much of a plot event). Rather, Equality's escape is a *subconsciously* driven action. "We had not thought of coming here, but our legs had carried our wisdom, and our legs had brought us to the Unchartered Forest against our will" (75). However, after the fact Equality's action does give him conscious knowledge of something he had not been clear about previously. "We have not built [our] box for the good of our brothers. We built it for its own sake. It is above all our brothers to us, and its truth above their truth" (76).

Equality's confrontation with the scholars has not merely shown him the nature of the collective mind, but also taught him something crucial about his own.

## The Forest

"The moss is soft and warm," writes Equality. "We shall sleep on this moss for many nights, till the beasts of the forest come to tear our body. We have no bed now, save the moss, and no future, save the beasts" (68).

Equality's first night in the forest is marked by tired resignation. Although glad to be away from his fellow men, he thinks he is doomed. And the reason for his resignation is not a fear of wild beasts.

At this point, Equality knows that he can *think* alone. He knows that he can *create* alone. What he does not yet know is that he can *be*, alone. He has learned the efficacy of his individual mental actions, but not the fact that he, as an individual, has metaphysical primacy over the collective. Consequently, Equality expects "the corruption to be found in solitude. We have torn ourselves from the truth which is our brother men, and there is no road back for us, and no redemption" (76).

Equality's sense of doom vanishes in the morning.

His first impulse on waking is "to leap to our feet, as we have had to leap every morning of our life" (78). But then he remembers that he is now free from the collective's regimentation. "We thought suddenly that we could lie thus as long as we wished, and we laughed aloud at the thought" (78). Then he leaps up and throws himself into an ecstatic frenzy of joyous motion— and "we heard suddenly that we were laughing, laughing aloud, laughing as if there were no power left in us save laughter" (79).

Humor, in Ayn Rand's words, "is the denial of metaphysical importance to that which you laugh at."[17] But Equality's laughter in this scene, while metaphysical, is not humor. It is what Robert Mayhew has called "a special kind of laughter which transcends humor: laughter in response to a benevolent universe."[18] Such laughter may imply a relief that one does not have to take the negative seriously—but the laugher's focus of attention is the positive.

Equality's sense of a benevolent universe—one auspicious to a being of his nature—is confirmed as he walks further into the forest that he had so recently thought menacing. "The trees parted before us, calling us forward. The forest seemed to welcome us" (79). When Equality feels hungry, he proves his efficacy by killing and cooking a bird. He feels a "strange new pride in eating" (79). And later, it is precisely an impression of practical efficacy that strikes him when, on the surface of a stream, he sees his own likeness for the first time. His limbs are "straight and thin and hard and strong. And we thought that we could trust this being who looked upon us from the stream, and that we had nothing to fear with this being" (80).

Equality now has the evidence to conclude that he can survive on his own in the forest, and wider, that he is the kind of *being* that is fit for existence. He has the evidence—but not the concept that would facilitate the full, conscious conclusion. So he says that he cannot yet speak, "for we cannot understand" (80). But in his joyous laughter, his emotions speak for his implicit knowledge. And they speak as well when, at nightfall, "we remembered that we are the Damned. We remembered it, and we laughed" (80).

This time Equality's laughter *is* humorous. He is denying the metaphysical importance of an erroneous metaphysical viewpoint: that the individual cannot exist apart from the collective.

## The Golden One

"We stood together for a long time. And we were frightened that we had lived for twenty-one years and had never known what joy is possible to men" (83).

Equality already knows that he can *survive* apart from the collective. When the Golden One joins him in the forest, he learns that he can be *happy* apart from it.

Early in *Anthem*, at the end of his first conversation with her, Equality had decided that he would never let the Golden One be sent to the Palace of Mating, the collective's breeding institution. But on the night of his escape from the city, he had put any thought of her aside, believing he was "one of the Damned" (77). So when the Golden One joins him, having heard of his escape, it is on her own initiative.

This is important for reasons of both genre and theme. First, for Equality to steal back into the city to "rescue" the Golden One would, qua melodrama, derail the psychological fantasy. Second, if the Golden One's escape is to be thematically congruent, she must make as independent a break with the collective as Equality has done. After all, what keeps her in the city is not guards or barbed wire, which Equality could help her defeat. The collective's hold on her is *mental*. To break it, she must assert her own ego by means of loyalty in action to a strong personal value. And she does. Just as Equality has his light, the Golden One has Equality. He escapes to protect his light, she to join the man she loves.

The Golden One's acting from love does not make her a dependent character. Like Equality, she lacks a concept of the ego. Given what she has (and has not) been taught, for her to break with the collective in the name of a personal value like love requires heroic independence. And in one sense, the Golden One's break is even more heroic than Equality's: it is a fully conscious action. Equality's legs "brought us to the Unchartered Forest against our will." The Golden One knows where she is going.

If Equality keeps his resolution to save the Golden One from the Palace of Mating, it is by the example he sets in escaping from the city. But she follows that example only because she is worthy of him.

It is no coincidence that Equality is reunited with the Golden One on his *second* day in the forest, not the first. Sex, in Ayn Rand's words, is "a celebration of [one]self and of existence."[19] In order to celebrate his self's efficacy in the universe, Equality must first possess ample evidence of it, as he does after a day alone in the forest. "There is no danger in solitude," he tells the Golden One. "It is our own world, Golden One, a strange, unknown world, but our own" (83–84).

On the basis of this knowledge does Equality go on to learn that "to hold the body of women in our arms is neither ugly nor shameful"—as it was in the collective's breeding rooms—"but the one ecstasy granted to the race of men" (84).

In the following days, Equality thinks about the evidence he has gathered.

> There is no joy for men, save the joy shared with all their brothers. But the only things which taught us joy were the power we created in our wires, and the Golden One. And both these joys belong to us alone, they come from us alone, they bear no relation to our brothers, and they do not concern our brothers in any way. (86)

He concludes that there is some "frightful error in the thinking of men" (86). He gets his next clue from the Golden One, who is struggling with the same issues from her own distinct perspective.

> Today, the Golden One stopped suddenly and said:
> "We love you."
> But then they frowned and shook their head and looked at us helplessly.
> "No," they whispered, "that is not what we wished to say."
> They were silent, then they spoke slowly, and their words were halting, like the words of a child learning to speak for the first time:
> "We are one . . . alone . . . and only . . . and we love you who are one . . . alone . . . and only."
> We looked into each other's eyes and we knew that the breath of a miracle had touched us, and fled, and left us groping vainly.
> And we felt torn, torn for some word we could not find. (86–87)

In *The Fountainhead*, Howard Roark says, "To say 'I love you' one must know first how to say the 'I.'"[20] The Golden One could not come closer without having the word.

In fact, she and Equality *do* here grasp everything essential to the concept "ego"—ephemerally. All they lack for a full conscious grasp is the material sound of a word to anchor this mental content and make it a constant in their minds.

Equality is clearly on the verge of forming the concept "ego." He has the evidence he needs.

Yet there is one more event to come before he does form the concept—an event which provides evidence not primarily of the ego's existence, but of its full meaning.

## The House

"Never had we seen rooms so full of light," writes Equality of the house he has found. "The sunrays danced upon colors, colors, more colors than we thought possible, we who had seen no houses save the white ones, the brown ones and the grey" (90).

Why does Equality find the old house from the Unmentionable Times? Earlier, he had planned to some day "stop and build a house, when we shall have gone far enough" (84–85). But this proves unnecessary when he finds one ready-made. And as with the tunnel, he finds the house by accident. Would it not be a more individualistic action if he built a house himself?

There are several reasons, relating to style, theme, and genre, why Equality finds a house rather than builds one. The reason of style is the simplest: the books in the library of the old house will enable Equality to learn the word "I" in the language in which *Anthem* is written—as opposed to his coining a new word of his own, which would be stylistically awkward. The books also give Equality knowledge of history and mythology, which he refers to in the last chapter. But these matters could have been handled differently.

The thematic reason is a more profound one. A house that Equality built for himself could be only a frontiersman's cabin, which would not provide a good contrast to the primitive life in the collectivist city. Such a contrast has been hinted at in the old legend of "the towers which rose to the sky in those Unmentionable Times" (19), as against "the Home of the Leaders, which is the greatest house in the City, for it has three stories" (25). But to grasp the full meaning of man's ego, Equality must experience first-hand the difference between an individualist and a collectivist way of life.

Ayn Rand held that she could not have identified reason as man's means of survival without the evidence of the Industrial Revolution. Similarly, Equality has not yet had full proof that his box with glowing wires is more than just an interesting gadget, like the toy steam engines of Ancient Rome. The house from the Unmentionable Times gives him the proof. It is a concrete structure with Frank Lloyd Wright—like windows that continue straight around the corners, and with mirrors, printed books, crystal bottles, silk flowers, colors—and electric lighting. Such a house, Equality learns from the sleeping arrangements, was built for only two people.

Nothing could better concretize for him the scope of achievement and luxury made possible by man's ego.

At the age of twenty-one, Equality has rediscovered electricity and reinvented the electric light. He need not prove his self-reliance by building a log cabin. What he does need is what the house gives him: evidence that man's ego is not only his means of thought, creation, survival, and happiness—it is a cause of *splendor.*

The third reason why Equality finds a house, rather than builds one, follows from *Anthem*'s nature as a psychological fantasy. As we have seen, the core premise of *Anthem* is the device of showing a man who lacks the concept "ego"—and his mental journey toward its discovery. Throughout, Ayn Rand takes great care not to let the existential events dominate over Equality's mental progress as the locus of primary interest. Thus, in the novel's first two-thirds, she never lets the conflict between Equality and the collective develop into a plot structure of logically connected events.

After the resolution of this conflict and his escape from the city, Equality faces no existential obstacles whatever. There is no "rise to the climax" in *Anthem*, in the sense of a progressive intensification of existential conflict leading to a climactic resolution. Instead there is a complete cessation of conflict long before the novel's end. (One could say that Equality's traveling is motivated by the desire to avoid pursuit. But his primary motive is probably psychological rather than practical: "each day added to the chain of days between us and the City is like an added blessing" [84]. And even considered as a faint aftereffect of the main conflict, Equality's traveling has achieved its purpose by the time he discovers the house: "we knew that no men would ever follow our track nor reach us here" [88].)

Not only does Equality face no conflict after his escape from the city, his escape is followed by the systematic removal of any urgent existential need on his part. He easily learns how to survive on his own in the forest. He is reunited with his beloved. And he finds a large, well-equipped house, providing him with material comfort and relieving him from any immediate practical effort.

For Equality to stop and *build* a house would be a fatal break with this pattern. Unlike the merely transitional act of traveling, building a house would constitute the existential inauguration of Equality's new life as an individualist. And by the nature of *Anthem*, Equality's new life—with all its attendant struggles and efforts—cannot start before its full *intellectual* inauguration: his discovery of the concept "ego."

That discovery is the essence of *Anthem*'s climax—of the final resolution of the hero's struggles.

Throughout the novel, Equality has been struggling to understand—to understand why he pursues a course he thinks is evil, why he feels no guilt, why he is successful and happy while his brothers are not. Implicitly, he has been struggling to know the existence and meaning of the ego. But so long as this mental struggle occurred in the context of conflict and existential effort, its resolution would have been diluted and anticlimactic. As a *mental* breakthrough, the climax of *Anthem* must be prepared for by the removal of all practical concerns and a concomitant intensification of focus on the hero's psychological need. Only then will the climax have its maximum effect.

As we get our last view of him before the climax, Equality—in an existential context of harmony, rest, and fulfillment—exclaims in his diary: "May knowledge come to us! What is the secret our heart has understood and yet will not reveal to us, although it seems to beat as if it were endeavoring to tell it?" (93).

His only longing now is mental.

## ANTHEM AND PEER GYNT

The closest literary counterpart to *Anthem* is *Peer Gynt*.[21] Yet the mental road traveled by the protagonist of Ibsen's play leads in the opposite direction of Equality's: Peer Gynt starts by professing pride in his ego, but in the end discovers that an ego is precisely what he lacks.

Set in early nineteenth-century Norway, the play's first half presents Peer as a penniless country boy—with enormous aspirations. He has what people colloquially describe as "a big ego."

> Just you wait, I'll take in hand
> Something—something really grand! . . .
> I'll become a king, an emperor.[22]

Yet Peer pursues no goals beyond dreaming elaborate daydreams and spinning fantastic tales about invented exploits. He is a complete whim-worshiper. At a wedding party, he falls in love with Solveig, an innocent young girl; but moments later, on a whim, he runs off to the mountains with the bride—whom he discards the next morning, remembering Solveig. He is declared an outlaw, and Solveig, breaking with her Pietist family, joins him at his cabin in the woods (much as the Golden One joins Equality). But Peer tells Solveig he is going out on an errand—and instead of coming back, he leaves the country.

This is the realistic business of the first three acts—but the telling is far from realistic. Not only do Peer's reveries and tall tales have scant basis in fact; the dramatic action itself consists partly of fantastic scenes of introspective symbolism, conveyed by figures of Norwegian folklore. One such scene—a feverish dream of Peer's—takes place in the hall of the Mountain King. Peer is bargaining about terms for marrying the troll king's daughter, who has aroused his lust. He agrees to everything, including the demand that he let himself be turned into a troll—but he balks when told that he can never go back to being human. He says to the Mountain King:

> To be like a mountain troll all of one's days,
> Forever cut off from retreat to old ways—
> *This* is a point which is close to your heart,
> Whereas for me it's the cue to depart.

By contrast, when Solveig joins Peer in the woods, she tells him, "That road I have stepped on never turns back."

Solveig's line is realistic (though metaphorical); Peer's encounter with the Mountain King is decidedly not. This indicates the pattern of the first half of *Peer Gynt*: a fairly coherent, realistic progression of events—broken up by fantasy sequences exploring Peer's psychology. Why does Ibsen shatter the realism? Because he is writing a psychological fantasy.

This becomes fully apparent in act four, where any semblance of logical story progression is abandoned. Peer is now introduced as a middle-aged bon vivant and former slave trader—on his way to assist, for profit, the Turks in their war against Greek independence. His goal, he tells some acquaintances on the coast of Morocco, is to become emperor of the world by means of his riches. In pursuing his old ambition, he is, as he sees it, being true to himself. And when asked, What *is* the Gyntian self? he answers:

> The Gyntian *self*, it's that entire
> Array of whims and feelings of desire—
> The Gyntian self, it is that land
> Of impulse, appetite, demand—
> To cut it short, it's all the things which give
> *My* lungs their breath, so I, qua me, can live.

The Turkish affair falls apart. For a while, Peer dreams of founding a colony in Morocco—"Gyntiana," with the capital "Peeropolis." He forgets about this when he is embraced as a prophet by a tribe of Arabs. The role of prophet soon bores him, and, attracted to a Bedouin chief's daughter, he fancies himself a great lover. But when the girl flees with all of his valuables, he decides to become a great historian. At the end of the fourth act, Peer is crowned "emperor of the self" in a madhouse in Cairo.

In act five, he returns to Norway an old man. Looking back on his life, he starts peeling a wild onion, each layer representing one of his "selfs": historian, prophet, bon vivant, slave-trader, etc.

> What a lot of layers!
> Won't the core soon come to light?
> No, damn, all the way it's
> Only layers, growing slight.

With the remark "Nature is witty!" Peer throws away the onion. But soon he is staggering through the wilderness, confronting his lack of a firm self through symbolic conversations with an array of fantasy figures from national and religious folklore, or purely of Ibsen's making. Foremost among these is the Button-Molder, who has come from "the Master" to collect Peer's crippled soul for the "metal value." Peer's spirit is to be melted into the mass from which new souls are molded like buttons. He reacts with horror.

> This molding transaction, this Gyntish cessation,
> Fills my innermost soul with acute perturbation.

Peer does not want to give up his self. The Button-Molder answers that Peer has never had one. He has a spirit; but by never remaining loyal to any personal value, he has failed to give his spirit a definite, lasting *identity*.

The basic *message* of *Peer Gynt*—that loyalty to external values is the key to personal identity—is obviously consonant with *Anthem*'s. In *Anthem*, Equality's journey toward a concept of the ego depends on an intransigent loyalty to his values (his research and his light). Equality's constancy is what gives his ego the firm identity which in turn allows him to grasp that ego conceptually— and such constancy is precisely what Peer defaults on, leaving him with no sense of a distinct self.

When Peer visits the madhouse in Cairo, he states that he is "myself in everything," whereas, he presumes, the inmates have lost their selves. The madhouse director replies that Peer is wrong; in the madhouse, everyone is "himself and nothing else."

> All lock themselves up in the casks of self
> And stop the bungholes with the bungs of self;
> They swell the wooden lining of the wells
> Of self, then climb down all the rungs of self.

The inmates live completely within their own minds; their thoughts, desires, and actions have no basis in the external world. This is what makes them insane. And it is what makes them similar to Peer, whose tall tales and daydreams have no foundation in reality, whose extravagant ambitions are not pursued in reality, and who acts on the random whims of his consciousness. Peer is not mad; but he is, like madmen, an implicit exponent of what Ayn Rand called the "primacy of consciousness"—the idea that consciousness has metaphysical primacy over existence and that existence is a derivative phenomenon.[23] To Peer, if he *thinks* he will do great things, then he will; he need not actually *do* anything. If he *thinks* he is a prophet, a lover, a historian, then he is; he need not pursue these vocations in action across time. If he *thinks* he has an ego, then he does.

But in fact he doesn't, as Ibsen shows.

Leaving Ibsen's own view aside for a moment, what Peer's fate demonstrates is the mistakenness of the primacy of consciousness. The true principle is the "primacy of existence": existence exists, and consciousness is simply the faculty of perceiving it. Apart from its awareness of reality, consciousness is nothing—and thus it is no wonder that a mind like Peer's, which divorces itself from reality, fails to develop a distinct ego.

Nor is it any wonder that, in *Anthem*, Equality *does* develop an ego—by consistently perceiving reality, forming reality-based values, and pursuing these *in* reality. Ironically, Equality gains his firm sense of self from his implicit refusal ever to regard his own mind—or any mind—as the metaphysical primary.[24] Observe that the councils in *Anthem* uphold the primacy of consciousness—"What is not thought by all men cannot be true"—but they think that the *collective* mind has primacy over both reality and the individual mind. Unable even to conceive of the primacy of existence, the councils in effect regard Equality as a kind of Peer Gynt. But in fact Equality's opposition to the collective is never a subjective rebellion; he is always guided by reality. And his vocation—science—is especially suited to demonstrating his reality-orientation. (The point would have required more elaboration if Equality had been, say, an artist like Howard Roark in *The Fountainhead*.)

While *Peer Gynt* demonstrates the corruption of upholding one's own mind's metaphysical primacy, Ibsen does not ultimately share Ayn Rand's primacy-of-existence premise. The scenes with the Button-Molder imply that Peer's ultimate default is a failure to have intuited, and then acted on, the purpose that "the Master" had in mind for him. In other words (and whether the Master represents God or Hegel's *Geist*), Peer's real treason is not to existence, but to the one supreme consciousness that *really* has primacy. However, this philosophical difference with *Anthem* is not stressed in *Peer Gynt* to the point of negating the overall thematic consonance of the two works.

In terms of *genre*, *Peer Gynt* and *Anthem* are not merely consonant, but identical. The link between the theme and the events of *Peer Gynt* is a mental premise: a man who believes he has an ego discovers that he does not. As in *Anthem*, this kind of central premise leads to a psychological fantasy, in which the focus is kept on the mental progression through the lack of a strongly coherent existential story—and, in *Peer Gynt*, through introspective fantasy segments. Moreover, the elements of conventional story progression in *Peer Gynt* diminish in the build-up to the climax—or, rather, they vanish abruptly, the last two acts being entirely episodic and/or fantastic. As in *Anthem*, there is a "rise of the mental" as the exclusive focus of interest—in preparation for a special kind of climax.

The crux of that climax is simple: although Peer has no distinct ego, Solveig does. Having remained flawlessly loyal in her love, she is still waiting for Peer at the cabin. When Peer discovers this, he concludes, "*Here* was my empire!"—an empire he went his whole life without gaining. But to Peer's desperate, tormented question, Solveig has an answer:

PEER GYNT
Where was I, as myself, as the whole and the true?
Where was I, with God's stamp on my forehead?
SOLVEIG
Why, you
Were in my faith, in my hope and in my love.

Solveig's constancy—combined with Peer's final acknowledgment of his own default—opens the way for Peer's potential redemption. Peer is saved from the Button-Molder, who warns that he will be back at "the final cross-roads"—"and *then* we shall see."

As a psychological fantasy—the story of a mental progression—*Peer Gynt* needs a mental resolution, and has one. Peer's ultimate fate will be up to himself (and will depend on his mode of existential action). However, in the context of the story, his predicament has been resolved—primarily by an act not of his own mind, but of Solveig's.

## THE CLIMAX OF *ANTHEM*

The theme of an Ayn Rand novel is never left opaque, a mystery for literary scholars to divine. Typically, the abstract meaning of the events is expounded in a speech near the novel's end. A good example is *The Fountainhead* and Howard Roark's courtroom speech. The theme of *The Fountainhead* is "individualism versus collectivism, not in politics, but in man's soul"[25]—and Roark goes straight to the essence when he says: "the mind is an attribute of the individual. There is no such thing as a collective brain. There is no such thing as a collective thought."[26]

Ayn Rand wrote *Anthem* in the summer of 1937, as a break from her work on *The Fountainhead*. But *Anthem*, while admittedly much shorter than *The Fountainhead*, has the same theme. Why, then, write it at all?

The key to the answer lies in the concluding abstract expositions of the two novels.

Consider these two quotes from Roark's courtroom speech:

The first right on earth is the right of the ego. Man's first duty is to himself. His moral law is never to place his prime goal within the persons of others. His moral obligation is to do what he wishes, provided his wish does not depend *primarily* upon other men. This includes the whole sphere of his creative faculty, his thinking, his work. But it does not include the sphere of the gangster, the altruist and the dictator.[27]

Men have been taught that their first concern is to relieve the suffering of others. But suffering is a disease. Should one come upon it, one tries to give relief and assistance. To make that the highest test of virtue is to make suffering the most important part of life. Then man must wish to see others suffer—in order that he may be virtuous. Such is the nature of altruism.[28]

Observe that Roark is impersonal, arguing his case in general terms (in fact, he never uses the pronoun "I" until the last section of his speech, which deals with the specific charges against him). His wording is abstract ("right," "duty," "moral law," "obligation"), and he is methodical in relating his abstractions to one another in a structured argument. He is didactic: he argues his case in strictly literal language without metaphors; and in the first quote, he carefully delineates the scope of his main generalization. He is polemical: in the second quote, he points out a logical absurdity in the contrary position.

Compare Roark's style with the following two passages from Equality's statement in chapter eleven of *Anthem*.

I stand here on the summit of the mountain. I lift my head and I spread my arms. This, my body and spirit, this is the end of the quest. I wished to know the meaning of things. I am the meaning. I wished to find a warrant for being. I need no warrant for being, and no word of sanction upon my being. I am the warrant and the sanction. (94)

Neither am I the means to any end others may wish to accomplish. I am not a tool for their use. I am not a servant of their needs. I am not a bandage for their wounds. I am not a sacrifice on their altars. (95)

Equality is saying the same things that Roark says. But whereas Roark is impersonal, Equality refers to himself in every sentence. His wording is concrete where Roark's is abstract; he is metaphorical where Roark is literal. His structure is broadly thematic where Roark's is intellectually involved. He is unconcerned with polemics. He asserts where Roark argues. Whereas Roark is rhetorical, Equality is *poetic*.

Now consider the opening of Roark's speech:

Thousands of years ago, the first man discovered how to make fire. He was probably burned at the stake he had taught his brothers to light. He was considered an evildoer who had dealt with a demon mankind dreaded. But thereafter men had fire to keep them warm, to cook their food, to light their caves. He had left them a gift they had not conceived and he had lifted darkness off the earth.[29]

Roark shows a strong consciousness of struggle, suffering, and injustice. He begins by discussing a martyr to the cause of the ego, as quoted above, then follows this example with three others: the inventor of the wheel,

Prometheus and Adam. (This use of examples from history and legend is another indication of his didactic approach.)

Compare Roark's opening with Equality's:

> I am. I think. I will.
> My hands . . . My spirit . . . My sky . . . My forest . . . This earth of mine. . . . (94)

There is no consciousness here of struggle or suffering. Instead, Equality's words represent pure exaltation. They are the opening words of a hymn—of an *anthem.*

A hymn is a song of praise, glorification, and worship of the highest value to which a man dedicates himself. Traditionally, that value is God or one's country. But Equality's hymn is unique: its object is the ego.

The Hymn of the Collective Spirit, which Equality had been forced to sing for most of his life, was a travesty. What deserves a hymn, he has learned, is not a nonexistent collective spirit, but the only spirit there is and thus the true source of everything exalted: man's individual mind.

Those thoughts, desires, and actions which Equality had thought were evil because they came from "one" and not from "the many"—those were good, he now understands, because they came from *the one* and not from *many*. Being metaphysically an attribute of the individual, man's mind performs its proper function only when it is exercised independently. Then and only then can man achieve truth, goodness, success, happiness, and splendor.

What is actually aberrant, impotent, evil, and loathsome is not the individual mind, but the idea of collective thought, and what follows from such an idea. The word "we," Equality now knows, "must never be placed first within man's soul, else it becomes a monster, the root of all the evils on earth, the root of man's torture by men, and of an unspeakable lie" (96–97).

He knows this, but he does not say it at the beginning of his statement. A hymn evokes the emotion of contemplating the most sacred and perfect, and cannot focus on the negative. Equality's statement therefore opens with and maintains an ecstatic focus on his own exalted ego. Only toward the end does he deal with "the monster of 'We'" (97), dismissing it with the words "But I am done with this creed of corruption" (97).

An opening like Roark's, which dwelt on struggle and suffering, would be totally wrong for a hymn. Conversely, an opening like Equality's would be inappropriate for Roark's speech. Even if Roark *could* experience a state of rapture in the courtroom, it would be a presumption for him to display that emotion to the jury. Roark's speech is by its nature a forensic exercise: he is aiming to convince an audience. Therefore, his style is rhetorical as opposed to poetic. Befitting a hymn, Equality's style is just the opposite. A hymn cannot argue, only affirm.

The nature of Roark's and Equality's concluding statements is determined by the contexts. In *The Fountainhead*, Roark is on trial. The jury's verdict will resolve, one way or the other, the conflict between him and society, and his speech is his attempt to influence this outcome. In other words, Roark's speech, qua physical action, forms an integral part of the novel's climax.

This is no coincidence. A speech given *before* the climax could not expound on the abstract meaning of the novel as a whole, but only on some delimited part or aspect (as does Francisco d'Anconia's "money speech" in *Atlas Shrugged*). More importantly, a speech given *after* the climax would not be an event of the story. Suppose Roark refused to testify at his trial, were acquitted on a technicality, and *then* gave his speech, say, to a convention of architects. The speech would be mere philosophical commentary on the novel's events, read for its abstract content alone. Roark would have turned literary scholar. To be more than just commentary—to serve a function in the resolution of the novel's conflicts, and thus in the plot—Roark's speech must be delivered before those conflicts are fully resolved.

The fact that Roark gives his speech in the context of conflict is what makes him stress the aspect of struggle and injustice, as illustrated by the martyrdom of Prometheus, Adam, and mankind's great inventors. The fate of these figures is a live issue for Roark, and their suffering an appropriate topic for his opening remarks—since he *himself* is still struggling and still a victim of the injustice inflicted on all men of independent mind. (He is on trial for an act of integrity and independence.)

Roark could not at this point deliver a hymn like Equality's: one does not experience an unmixed exaltation in the midst of a conflict situation.[30] Observe that Ayn Rand usually evokes such exaltation only in brief vignettes *after* the climax:[31] in *The Fountainhead*, when Dominique rises to Roark at the top of the Wynand Building; in *Atlas Shrugged*, when Galt stands with Dagny "on the highest accessible ledge of a mountain,"[32] declaring their return to the world. Similarly, when Equality formulates an exalted hymn, it is after—long after—all conflict has ceased. His hymn is the emotional summing up of a firmly established record of success, happiness, and splendor, and thus presupposes the post-conflict chapters dealing with his efficacy in the forest, his reunion with the Golden One, and his discovery of the house. Equality's hymn does constitute the resolution of a struggle—but that struggle is precisely his quest to understand the *cause* of his success and happiness.

Equality's hymn is a peculiar literary phenomenon. As exaltation, it follows, as it must, the end of conflict; as expository statement, it does not follow the climax, as it cannot (or it would be a mere appendage to the story). Rather, Equality's hymn *is* the climax.

What kind of climax can *follow*, rather than constitute, the end of existential conflict? A *mental* one. Equality's discovery of the concept "ego," and the hymn that is his statement about his discovery, are the mental resolution of his mental struggle.

Equality's hymn is not a diary entry; his words are words in his mind—they are *thoughts*. Observe that no immediate physical context is provided for the statement, beyond the words "I stand here on the summit of the mountain. I lift my head and I spread my arms" (94). This minimal "stage direction" has the same ascent motif as the concluding vignettes of Ayn Rand's two major novels, a motif congruent with the projection of exaltation. But the main function of the stage direction is to mark a break with the diary form of the novel, i.e., to remove any implication that Equality's words are now physically written down. If he spreads his arms, he is not writing.

The most striking feature of Equality's hymn is of course the word "I." What was startling at the novel's beginning—Equality's use of the "singular 'we'"—has long since become familiar to the reader, just as a king's use of the royal "we" would become familiar. Now it is Equality's use of "I" that is startling.

But it is the hymn that is presented directly to the reader, not Equality's initial grasp of the word "I." This has taken place some time earlier. (At the beginning of chapter twelve, Equality relates that he saw the word in a book, and "when I understood this word, the book fell from my hands, and I wept" [98]—i.e., he did not immediately formulate an exalted hymn.)

Merely to show Equality grasping the word "I" would have been an inadequate resolution to his mental struggle. A Tarzan-like "Me Equality, you Golden One" would not have gone far enough beyond the Golden One's earlier statement that "We are one . . . alone . . . and only . . . and we love you who are one . . . alone . . . and only." And the climax has to involve much more than this. *Anthem* is not the story of a man who corrects a pronominal deficiency; it is the story of a man who discovers the true meaning of man's ego.

Observe that when Equality first uses the word "I," he does so to make a statement: "I am. I think. I will." This is just another way of saying, "It is *I* who am. It is *I* who think. It is *I* who will." The mind is an individual possession, and—as Equality goes on to identify—the glories of the human spirit flow from this ego, which is entitled to reverence.

By the nature of Equality's struggle, he must come to do exactly what he does: formulate a hymn to the ego. And by the nature of *Anthem* as a psychological fantasy, that hymn must be a mental event: *the ego identifying itself and its own glory.*

*Anthem* does not end purely in Equality's mind; the twelfth and last chapter reintroduces the existential context.

Equality first narrates how he discovered the word "I." He then explains this word to the Golden One, and she is finally able to tell him, "I love you." This resolves the last piece of unfinished business from the previous story.

Equality and the Golden One choose new names: Prometheus and Gaea—
an act which serves as their official baptism as explicit individualists. (Their
action has only this symbolic function in the novel, since nothing more is
done with their new names, except that Equality (or Prometheus) uses "Gaea"
in his one further reference to the Golden One. One might ask why they need
the new names, since they have already given each other personal names—
the Unconquered and the Golden One—to replace the collectivist tags they
were known by in the city. But these latter are nicknames too personal to
share with the world; they pertain only to the intimate context of mutual love.
Having discovered the concept and meaning of "ego," Equality is ready to de-
marcate the spheres of public and private.)

Equality then turns to his future plans—he will "rebuild the achievements
of the past and open the way to carry them further" (99)—and his tone now
regains much of the hymnal quality of the penultimate chapter. Although his
content is somewhat less spiritual and abstract, he is continuing his hymn to
the ego. (Ayn Rand once said about *Anthem* that "The last two chapters are
the actual anthem."[33])

When Equality reflects on human history and on how men came to lose
the word "I" (he has learned about the past from the books in his library), his
tone has at times a touch of bitterness, in keeping with the facts. But in the
spirit of an anthem, his fundamental tone is triumphant and exalted—and
when future conflict is projected, it is with assurance of victory: "And the day
will come when I shall break all the chains of the earth, and raze the cities of
the enslaved, and my home will become the capital of a world where each
man will be free to exist for his own sake" (104).

Appropriately for a psychological fantasy written on the primacy-of-
existence premise, *Anthem* ends with physical action—projected by the
hero's mind. Having discovered the concept and meaning of man's ego,
Equality plans to translate his new worship of "I" into material existence,
practically and symbolically.

He will establish a new world based on individualism. And just as the
creed of collectivism was cut in marble over the portals of the Palace of the
World Council, so Equality will cut in stone over the portals of his home
"the word which is to be my beacon and my banner" (104): EGO.


## *ANTHEM* AS A POEM

*Anthem*, Ayn Rand once wrote in a letter, "has the same relation to *The
Fountainhead* as the preliminary sketches which artists draw for their future
big canvases. I wrote it while working on *The Fountainhead*—it has the
same theme, spirit and intention, although in quite a different form."[34]

The essential difference between a sketch and a "big canvas" is the former's freedom from a concern with *detail*.[35] In this regard, consider Ayn Rand's definition of art as "a selective re-creation of reality according to an artist's metaphysical value-judgments."[36] For instance, every aspect of a painting, from choice of theme and subject to the last strand of every brushstroke, is selected by the artist to express his view of man's relation to the universe. (Even when the artist does *not* fully control his brushstrokes, as with Rembrandt or Van Gogh, *that* is a means of expressing his view.) But there are certain forms of art which are anomalous: they present not a full, but only a partial, re-creation of reality. A sketch is one example—it has no brushstrokes.

Neither does *Anthem*. As Leonard Peikoff puts it, the novel shows "relatively little attempt to re-create perceptual, conversational, or psychological detail."[37]

Compare the scene where Equality confronts the scholars with the scene in the first chapter of *The Fountainhead* where Roark meets with the Dean. First the openings of the two scenes, starting with *Anthem*:

> We saw nothing as we entered, save the sky in the great windows, blue and glowing. Then we saw the Scholars who sat around a long table; they were as shapeless clouds huddled at the rise of the great sky. There were men whose famous names we knew, and others from distant lands whose names we had not heard. We saw a great painting on the wall over their heads, of the twenty illustrious men who had invented the candle.
>
> All the heads of the Council turned to us as we entered. These great and wise of the earth did not know what to think of us, and they looked upon us with wonder and curiosity, as if we were a miracle. (68–69)

> The Dean's office looked like a chapel, a pool of dreamy twilight fed by one tall window of stained glass. The twilight flowed in through the garments of stiff saints, their arms contorted at the elbows. A red spot of light and a purple one rested respectively upon two genuine gargoyles squatting at the corners of a fireplace that had never been used. A green spot stood in the center of a picture of the Parthenon, suspended over the fireplace.
>
> When Roark entered the office, the outlines of the Dean's figure swam dimly behind his desk, which was carved like a confessional. He was a short, plumpish gentleman whose spreading flesh was held in check by an indomitable dignity.
>
> "Ah, yes, Roark," he smiled. "Do sit down, please."
>
> Roark sat down. The Dean entwined his fingers on his stomach and waited for the plea he expected. No plea came. The Dean cleared his throat.[38]

In one passage, a room has "great windows," a "long table," and a painting on a wall. In the other, a room has "a tall window of stained glass," with curtains representing the garments of stiff, decorative saints, which have "arms contorted at the elbows;" there is a desk "carved like a confessional," and, beneath a picture, an unused fireplace flanked by squatting gargoyles. The first room is lighted by the blue and glowing sky in the windows. In the second room, twilight flows in through the stained glass and the saints' garments—and in addition there is a "red spot of light and a purple one" resting on the gargoyles, and a green spot on the picture.

In other words, the Roark passage, while only slightly longer than the Equality one, provides much more detail.

Equality's scholars are described only metaphorically—"they were as shapeless clouds huddled at the rise of the great sky"—and their elevated status is merely asserted: "men whose famous names we knew." By contrast, Roark's Dean is short and plumpish, his figure appears to swim dimly in the twilight, his spreading flesh is "held in check by an indomitable dignity." The last touch also indicates (and undercuts) his elevated status, as does his pompous greeting—"Ah, yes, Roark"—and the action of his hands: "The Dean entwined his fingers on his stomach and waited for the plea he expected."

As a function of the greater amount of detail, the sentences in the Roark passage are more closely integrated in terms of their material content than the sentences in the Equality passage. For instance, when the Dean's figure "swam dimly," this builds on the "pool of dreamy twilight" entering the room through the stained glass. Similarly, when the scholars "were as shapeless clouds huddled at the rise of the great sky," this builds on "the sky in the great windows, blue and glowing." But in the first case, the connection is concrete; in the second, metaphorical and abstract.

The Dean and the scholars are equally baffled by the hero. But the Dean's bafflement is conveyed by a physical detail: he "cleared his throat." The implication of this—that Roark acts unlike what the Dean expects and thus brings him out of balance—depends on previous detail: "The Dean entwined his fingers on his stomach and waited for the plea he expected. No plea came." And here again, the implication of a self-satisfied mediocrity who would enjoy the supplications of an ostensible inferior depends on the previous detail about "a short, plumpish gentleman whose spreading flesh was held in check by an indomitable dignity," and on the pompous "Ah, yes, Roark." In other words, as an indication of his bafflement, the Dean's throat-clearing is woven into a rich tapestry of concrete, material detail.

By contrast, the scholars' bafflement is first simply asserted—"These great and wise of the earth did not know what to think of us"—then described in general terms—"and they looked upon us with wonder and curiosity"—followed by a metaphor unconnected to the material description—"as if we were a miracle."

Now compare the following passages from later in the same two scenes, first from *The Fountainhead*, then from *Anthem*.

[The Dean speaking:] "There is a treasure mine in every style of the past. We can only choose from the great masters. Who are we to improve upon them? We can only attempt, respectfully, to repeat."

"Why?" asked Howard Roark.

No, thought the Dean, no, he hasn't said anything else; it's a perfectly innocent word; he's not threatening me.

"But it's self-evident!" said the Dean.[39]

"You have worked on this alone?" asked International 1-5537.

"Yes," we answered.

"What is not done collectively cannot be good," said International 1-5537. (73)

The Dean and the scholar make essentially the same point.[40] But whereas the scholar goes straight to the essence in a short line of dialogue, the Dean argues at length (and the full conversation goes on for pages).

The Dean's fear at Roark's simple "Why?"—the fear of a man who has never looked at reality directly and who senses that his mind would now be impotent to do so—is equivalent to the scholars' terror of Equality's light in the scene from *Anthem* (see above, page 94). But while their running from the table is a naked, violent dramatization of the issue, the Dean's evasive "But it's self-evident!" is simply one conversational detail among many.

*Anthem* has no such details. As a psychological fantasy, it *cannot* have them.

Had *Anthem* presented a full re-creation of reality, the sheer force of accumulated material information would have displaced the focus from the hero's mind. To keep the *mental* focus, a psychological fantasy can re-create reality only in terms of bare essentials. Ayn Rand therefore has to build her edifice of bricks, but not with mortar.

The counterpart to *Anthem* is again *Peer Gynt*, which Ibsen tellingly called "a dramatic poem." Like a sketch, a poem is not a full re-creation of reality; it does not even have to tell a story (although it can); in Ayn Rand's words, "its basic attributes are theme and style."[41] For Ibsen, the poetic means of avoiding full-fledged realism were readily at hand: he was writing in rhymed verse.[42] Ayn Rand had to achieve the same sketch-like effect in prose; she had to present (to use her own description of *Anthem*) "a long series of incidents—in an abbreviated, essentialized, almost 'impressionistic' form."[43]

*Anthem*, as Ayn Rand herself said, is a prose poem.[44]

And also of interest, for the 1946 American edition of *Anthem*, Ayn Rand introduced the unconventional typographic device of putting a blank line between the paragraphs. (I have dispensed with these lines in quoting the novel.) This visual cue makes the paragraphs appear less as integral parts of a continuous fabric of representation and more as thematically separated units—precisely like the stanzas of a poem.

## CONCLUSION

In 1946, answering a fan letter about *Anthem,* Ayn Rand wrote: "I don't really think that you knew, while reading the book, how 'it would turn out' after the escape of the protagonists. Are you sure that you know it now? Read Chapter XI again."[45]

Presumably the fan had foreseen merely that Equality would in the end learn the word "I." But anyone would guess as much. We all know the *word* "I"; and Ayn Rand did not write *Anthem* just to remind us that it exists. She wrote the book to tell us that man's ego is sacred.

Writes Leonard Peikoff:

> There have been plenty of egoists in human history, and there have been plenty of worshipers, too. The egoists were generally cynical "realists" (à la Hobbes), who despised morality; the worshipers, by their own statement, were out of this world. . . . Ayn Rand's concept of an "anthem to the ego" throws out this vicious dichotomy. Her Objectivist philosophy integrates facts with values—in this instance, the actual nature of man with an exalted and secular admiration for it.[46]

This is the intellectual genius of *Anthem.*

Early in *Anthem,* Equality recalls an incident from when he was ten years old: the execution by burning of a man who had found and spoken the Unspeakable Word.

> There was a thin thread of blood running from the corner of their mouth, but their lips were smiling. And a monstrous thought came to us then, which has never left us. We had heard of Saints. There are the Saints of Labor, and the Saints of the Councils, and the Saints of the Great Rebirth. But we had never seen a Saint nor what the likeness of a Saint should be. And we thought then, standing in the square, that the likeness of a Saint was the face we saw before us in the flames, the face of the Transgressor of the Unspeakable Word. (50)

The word "saint" conveys an exalted moral perfection; and this incident is the first indication Equality gets (in the novel) that the true source of man's highest values is different from what he has been taught. But even at the age of ten, Equality must have had some implicit grasp of this fact, for him to see the likeness of a saint in the face of the transgressor. And the transgressor must have recognized this grasp in the young boy's face, to choose Equality as his heir.

> Perhaps it had only seemed to us. But it seemed to us that the eyes of the Transgressor had chosen us from the crowd and were looking straight upon us. . . . And it seemed as if these eyes were trying to tell us something through the flames, to send into our eyes some word without sound. And it seemed as if these eyes were begging us to gather that word and not to let it go from us and from the earth. (51)

In Russia, at the age of ten or less, Ayn Rand read a children's biography of Catherine the Great, and one scene in particular impressed her. The young Catherine attends a party given for the girls of the German nobility. The hostess brings in a fortune teller, points to the reigning favorite among the girls, a prominent young princess, and asks, "Can you foretell her future? Do you see a crown on her brow?" The fortune teller looks at the girl and says "No," then turns to the obscure Catherine and says, "But on this girl's forehead I see the mark of two crowns."

Ayn Rand did not need a fortune teller or the saint of the pyre to tell her she was a child of destiny. She later remembered thinking, "I am like Catherine. My forehead is marked in the same way, only they don't see it."[47]

We can see it now.

Like Equality, Ayn Rand escaped to freedom from a collectivist hell.

Like Equality, she discovered, and told the world, the meaning and glory of man's ego.

And like Equality, she told us in *Anthem*.[48]

## NOTES

1. Some have speculated about possible sources of inspiration for this idea of Ayn Rand's. The most likely source is the standard communist slogans of Soviet Russia in Ayn Rand's youth. In her first novel, *We the Living*, which accurately portrays life in early post-revolutionary Russia, a villain delivers a cliché-studded propaganda speech in which he says: "What, then, are the standards of our new humanity? The first and basic one is that we have lost a word from our language, the most dangerous, the most insidious, the most evil of human words: the word 'I.' We have outgrown it. 'We' is the slogan of the future. The Collective stands in our hearts where that old monster—'self'—had stood." Ayn Rand, *We the Living* (New York: Signet sixtieth anniversary paperback edition, 1996), 436.

2. Ayn Rand, *The Art of Fiction: A Guide for Writers and Readers*, ed. Tore Boeckmann (New York: Plume, 2000), 37.

3. On the collective's function being to explain the hero's predicament, see Rand, *Art of Fiction*, 37.

4. Leonard Peikoff, introduction to fiftieth anniversary American edition to *Anthem*, by Ayn Rand (New York: Signet fiftieth anniversary paperback edition, 1995), v.

5. I do not mean that the average person finds it hard to associate the word "I" with his own body and mental processes, as distinct from other people's. But this is not the same as forming a conceptual grasp of one's mind as an autonomous mental entity. Observe that many people lack even the inner *experience* of an enduring, autonomous self, which leads them to "identity crises." (If they do have an explicit concept of the ego, in the deeper meaning of the term, it is mainly because they have been told about the phenomenon.) A more superficial knowledge of one's

own individuality—the kind which Equality is shown to possess from the start—
*would* suffice for some kind of use of the word "I." But this would not constitute a
grasp of everything implied by that concept—which is what Equality reaches when
he does learn the word in the climax of *Anthem*. To say that he *could have* learned
the word more easily, with a more superficial understanding, is not to pose a valid
objection against the novel's superior dramatic structure.

6. Ayn Rand, *For the New Intellectual* (New York: Random House, 1961; Signet
paperback edition, 1963), 64.

7. Rand, *We the Living*, 89.

8. The paragraph is a compressed stylization of the depiction of life in Soviet Russia provided in *We the Living* and based on Ayn Rand's first-hand experience. See
also Dina Garmong, "*We the Living* and the Rosenbaum Family Letters," and Tara
Smith, "Forbidding Life to Those Still Living" in *Essays on Ayn Rand's* We the Living,
ed. Robert Mayhew (Lanham, MD: Lexington Books, 2004).

9. Ayn Rand, "Basic Principles of Literature," in her *The Romantic Manifesto: A
Philosophy of Literature*, revised edition (New York: Signet, 1975), 85.

10. On *Anthem* as plotless, see Rand, *Art of Fiction*, 36–37.

11. Aristotle [?], *Magna Moralia*, Book II, ch. 15, 1213a13–26. (Translation is from
Jonathan Barnes, ed. *The Complete Works of Aristotle: The Revised Oxford Translation*, vol. 2 [Princeton: Princeton University Press, 1984], 1920.) I owe this quote to Allan Gotthelf's lecture "Love and Philosophy: Aristotelian vs. Platonic" (audio cas-
settes, Second Renaissance, 1998). Gotthelf's excellent discussion contains much that
is relevant for understanding Equality and Liberty's love relationship, and any love relationship.

12. I call it the "main" rather than "only" conflict, since in chapter one there is a
brief dispute between Equality and his friend International 4-8818 about whether to
tell the councils about the tunnel. This dispute is resolved on the spot in Equality's
favor.

13. Quoted in Harry Binswanger, "Introduction," in *The Mysterious Valley*, by Maurice Champagne (Lafayette, CO: The Atlantean Press, 1994), xii.

14. The scholars are here reminiscent of the real-life scholars who refused to look
through Galileo's telescope.

15. Rand, *We the Living*, 42.

16. Ayn Rand, *Atlas Shrugged* (New York: Random House, 1957; Signet thirty-fifth
anniversary paperback edition, 1992), 619.

17. From the question period (in which Ayn Rand took part) following lecture 11
of Leonard Peikoff's 1976 "Philosophy of Objectivism" course. See also Rand, *Art of
Fiction*, 165; Ayn Rand, *The Art of Nonfiction: A Guide for Writers and Readers*,
Robert Mayhew, ed. (New York: Plume, 2001), 126; and Robert Mayhew, "Kira Ar-
gounova Laughed: Humor and Joy in *We the Living*" in Mayhew, *Essays on* We the
Living.

18. Mayhew, "Kira Argounova Laughed," 308.

19. Ayn Rand, "Of Living Death," in her *The Voice of Reason: Essays in Objectivist
Thought*, ed. Leonard Peikoff (New York: New American Library, 1989; Meridian paperback edition, 1990), 54. The phrase is italicized in the original.

20. Ayn Rand, *The Fountainhead* (New York: Bobbs-Merrill, 1943; Signet fiftieth
anniversary paperback edition, 1993), 377.

21. I am not implying that in writing *Anthem* Ayn Rand was influenced by *Peer Gynt*. But the comparison is nevertheless instructive.

22. My translation, as are all further quotes from *Peer Gynt*.

23. For a discussion of the primacy of consciousness—and its opposite, the primacy of existence—see Leonard Peikoff, *Objectivism: The Philosophy of Ayn Rand* (New York: Dutton, 1991), 17–23. On the connection between the primacy of consciousness and insanity, see Leonard Peikoff, "Madness and Modernism," *The Intellectual Activist* 8, no. 6 (November 1994): 1–15.

24. In Equality's statement in chapter eleven of *Anthem*, some lines could be taken to imply a primacy-of-consciousness premise, especially the following: "Whatever road I take, the guiding star is within me; the guiding star and the loadstone which point the way. They point in but one direction. They point to me" (95). In 1961, when Ayn Rand included Equality's statement in *For the New Intellectual*, these and some similar lines were omitted. Rand, *New Intellectual*, 64–65. However, the present discussion concerns how Equality's ego has been shaped by his *actions* in the novel—and in these, there is no hint of the primacy of consciousness.

25. Ayn Rand, *New Intellectual*, 68. The word "versus" is italicized in the original.

26. Rand, *Fountainhead*, 680.

27. Rand, *Fountainhead*, 683.

28. Rand, *Fountainhead*, 682.

29. Rand, *Fountainhead*, 679.

30. Or at least an Ayn Rand hero would not. The case might be different for someone whose metaphysical worldview celebrates conflict as such.

31. There are exceptions to this rule. For instance, in *The Fountainhead*, Ayn Rand describes Howard Roark and Dominique Francon's sexual encounters, which culminate in moments that "swept into a denial of all suffering, into its antithesis, into ecstasy." Later, Gail Wynand talks to Dominique about Steven Mallory's statue of her, and says, "It's startling to see the same elements used in two compositions with opposite themes. Everything about you in that statue is the theme of exaltation. But your own theme is suffering." Rand, *Fountainhead*, 283, 438–39. However, sex and art are by their nature metaphysical; they relate man to all of existence. Thus, the emotional content of a sex act or a sculpture is independent of any particular existential context. One may celebrate a benevolent universe through sex, or contemplate it in art, even in the midst of struggle. In fact, that is part of the purpose of sex and art.

32. Rand, *Atlas Shrugged*, 1073.

33. Michael S. Berliner, ed., *Letters of Ayn Rand* (New York: Dutton, 1995), 336.

34. Berliner, *Letters*, 314.

35. Thus Ayn Rand wrote in a letter: "Everything I said in *The Fountainhead* is in *Anthem*, though in a briefer, less detailed form." Berliner, *Letters*, 276.

36. Ayn Rand, "The Psycho-Epistemology of Art," *Romantic Manifesto*, 19.

37. Peikoff, "Introduction," viii.

38. Rand, *Fountainhead*, 20.

39. Rand, *Fountainhead*, 23.

40. Later in the Roark-Dean conversation, the Dean appeals even more directly to collectivism: "The proper creative process is a slow, gradual, anonymous, collective one, in which each man collaborates with all the others and subordinates himself to the standards of the majority." Rand, *Fountainhead*, 24.

41. Rand, "Basic Principles of Literature," 81.

42. The *scenography* of any production of *Peer Gynt* must similarly avoid a distracting realism. Before one production, at the Royal Theatre in Copenhagen, the scenographer said that *Peer Gynt* had to be "a journey through Norway," to which the director correctly replied, "*Peer Gynt* is no journey through Norway, but a journey through a man's mind." See Hans Jacob Nilsen, "*Peer Gynt*—eit anti-romantisk verk," in *Omkring* Peer Gynt, Otto Hageberg, ed. (Oslo: Gyldendal Norsk Forlag, 1967), 118.

43. Rand, *Art of Fiction*, 44.

44. Question period following the last lecture of Ayn Rand's 1969 course on non-fiction writing (transcripts of which are in the Ayn Rand Archives). Much earlier, in a 1946 letter to Rose Wilder Lane, Ayn Rand classified *Anthem* straightforwardly as "a poem." She did the same in a 1947 letter to Richard Mealand. Berliner, *Letters*, 293, 372.

45. Berliner, *Letters*, 351.

46. Peikoff, "Introduction," vii.

47. Biographical interviews (Ayn Rand Archives).

48. I wish to thank Robert Mayhew, Dina Schein Garmong, and Kristi Hall for their comments on earlier drafts of this chapter, and Michael Berliner of the Ayn Rand Archives for providing helpful information.

# 8

## *Anthem* in the Context of Related Literary Works: "We are not like our brothers"

*Shoshana Milgram*

Writers are often asked where they "get their ideas." When Ayn Rand was asked in 1960 how she decided, "out of the blue," to write *Anthem* in the summer of 1937, she replied that it was not exactly out of the blue, but out of her long-held convictions. "I had that idea for a long time, actually from Russia. Only then I thought of it as a play. A world of the future where they don't have the word 'I.'"[1] As she explained on another occasion: "I got the idea in my school days, in Soviet Russia, when I heard all the vicious attacks on individualism, and asked myself what the world would be like if men lost the word 'I.'"[2] Her ultimate literary expression of that idea, though, was not a play, but a novella (23,484 words in the 1938 edition; 19,190 in the 1946 edition), unique in her oeuvre not only in length, but in genre.

Ayn Rand is a Romantic Realist. *Anthem,* however, is based on a premise drawn from fantasy, and thus belongs to a non-realistic genre, more so than any of Ayn Rand's other fiction.[3] It invites a comparison with texts that are variously characterized as fantasy, anti-utopia, or dystopia—works whose setting is a future time that is neither a nice place to visit nor a place where anyone would choose to live. John J. Pierce distinguishes between the more general term, "dystopia," and a specific type of dystopia, the "anti-utopia." "A dystopia can be set in a future that is evil by neglect, rather than by intention; the anti-utopia is directed at a particular kind of evil—that of the planned society."[4] *Anthem* belongs both to the general category of the dystopia (the future gone wrong, in which important values have been lost—whether by design, catastrophe, or unspecified attrition) and the sub-category of the anti-utopia (in which social institutions are *directly* responsible for decline, decay, and ruin).

Ayn Rand, by her own account, decided to write this work when she did and as she did partly because she intended it to fit into a particular publication venue. One motive for the timing, to be sure, was her need for a break from the intense effort of constructing the plot of *The Fountainhead*,[5] but the need for a break did not determine the nature of the project. In writing this short, non-realistic text, she took advantage of what she deemed a promising opportunity to compose and publish a work she had long had in her mind.

In this essay, I will begin by considering the story that led her to write *Anthem* in the summer of 1937. I will then look at related literary works, mostly dystopias, and mostly written earlier. My purpose is to look more closely at significant aspects of *Anthem* by comparing *and* contrasting it with works that are in some respects similar to it, works she may have considered in planning and writing it. The key points of comparison will be the literary devices and patterns; the key point of contrast will be the various answers to the question of "Why?"—the respective reasons suggested by different writers for the degradation of the world. I will conclude by stating my best guess about the answer to the question of where she "got her ideas" for *Anthem*—and where she took these ideas after *Anthem*.


## STEPHEN VINCENT BENÉT


Ayn Rand recalled, more than twenty years later, her surprise at finding in the *Saturday Evening Post* "a fantastic story of the future," "an adventure story," with "no ideology," "no particular plot or theme"—only "the fact that some kind of war had destroyed civilization, and the last survivor in the ruins of New York." It was, she said, "the first time I saw a fantastic story—rather than those realistic, folks-next-door sort of serials. . . . And so I thought if they didn't mind fantasy, . . . I would like to try *Anthem*."[6]

What, specifically, surprised her? Not the publication of fantasy per se. She mentions, in passing, that she once planned a story about an airplane "caught in an interplanetary gravitational space" and pulled into orbit, but had decided not to write the lost-in-space story because she read, during her first year or two in Hollywood, a story in a "science fiction pulp magazine" that was based on a similar event. She was evidently familiar with publications that specialized in speculative fiction. But she was impressed to discover a work of fantasy in the unexpected setting of a popular mainstream magazine. The *Saturday Evening Post* could give her wide exposure and generous compensation; it was a desirable target. So in the summer of 1937, she decided to write a short piece of fiction, designed for the *Post* or a similar publication, based on the premise of a future world bereft of the word "I," with all that that word implies.

Although Ayn Rand did not name the story she read, the only *Post* story that fits her description was in fact published just before she wrote *Anthem*: Stephen Vincent Benét's "The Place of the Gods."[7] In this story, a priest's son named John journeys to the forbidden place across the river, to the east, where he expects to find spirits, demons, and the "ashes of the Great Burning." From his first-person account, we see that his civilization is relatively primitive; he takes pride in the fact that his people "are not ignorant like the Forest People—our women spin wool on the wheel. . . . We do not eat grubs from the tree." He has an inquiring mind: "my knowledge and my lack of knowledge burned in me—I wished to know more." He recognizes that his exploration defies the law, yet is not discouraged. He specifically contrasts his mental peace with his physical discomfort. After the ritual of purification: "My body hurt but my spirit was a cool stone." When he sets out on his journey, fasting: "My body hurt but not my heart."

On his way to the city, he encounters names and locations that are familiar to the reader, though not to John. He crosses the river "Ou-dis-sun," i.e., the Hudson River. He finds "the shattered image of a man or a god. It had been made of white stone and he wore his hair tied back like a woman's. His name was ASHING, as I read on the cracked half of a stone" (i.e., George Washington). He finds the food of the gods—sweet fruits in jars and strong drink in bottles of glass—in "the ruins of a great temple in mid-city," with a roof "painted like the sky at night with its stars" (i.e., Grand Central Station). He sees pictures on the wall of a "place of great riches": "I remember one of a bunch of flowers in a jar—if you came close to it, you could see nothing but bits of color, but if you stood away from it, the flowers might have been picked yesterday" (an Impressionist painting). He marvels at technology, and assumes it must be magic. "There was a washing-place but no water—perhaps the gods washed in air. There was a cooking place but no wood, and though there was a machine to cook food, there was no place to put fire in it."

At night, he awakens to a vision of "the city as it had been when the gods were alive." He sees that "their chariots blocked the streets," that they "turned night to day for their pleasure—they did not sleep with the sun," that "they burrowed tunnels under the rivers—they flew in the air."

> With unbelievable tools they did giant works—no part of the earth was safe from them, for, if they wished for a thing, they summoned it from the other side of the world. And always, as they labored and rested, as they feasted and made love, there was a drum in their ears—the pulse of the giant city, beating and beating like a man's heart.

He sees, too, "their fate come upon them." "When gods war with gods, they use weapons we do not know." He sees "the Great Burning and the Destruction," the falling of the towers, the deaths upon deaths, the poison "still in the ground" after many years.

He discovers, finally, a "dead god"—sitting in a chair, in a room that is "shut, hot and dry—no doubt that had kept him the way he was."

> He was sitting looking out over the city—he was dressed in the clothes of the gods. His age was neither young nor old—I could not tell his age. But there was wisdom in his face and great sadness. You could see that he would not have run away. He had sat at his window, watching his city die—then he himself had died. But it is better to lose one's life than one's spirit—and you could see from his face that his spirit had not been lost. I knew that, if I touched him, he would fall into dust—and yet, there was something unconquered in the face.

Seeing the "dead god," preserved in body as—during life—in spirit, John realizes that the gods of the past were men, and that, as a man, he too can aspire to the greatness made real in the city built by men. He promises to do so, with other men.

> It is not for the metal alone we go to the Dead Places now—there are the books and the writings. They are hard to learn. And the magic tools are broken—but we can look at them and wonder. At least we make a beginning. And when I am chief priest we shall go beyond the great river. We shall go to the Place of the Gods—the place new york—not one man but a company. We shall look for the images of the gods and find the god ASHING and the others—the gods Lincoln and Biltmore and Moses. But they were men who built the city, not gods or demons. They were men. I remember the dead man's face. They were men who were here before us. We must build again.

Ayn Rand's *Anthem* has several elements in common with Benét's story. Many of these derive from the basic premise: a future world that has lost the technology of our present. The cause of the loss is initially mysterious, known only in legends told of the "Old Days" and the "Great Burning" (in Benét) and hints whispered by the "Old Ones" of the "Unmentionable Times" before the "Great Rebirth" (in *Anthem*); both texts refer to fires and fierce conflict, but the cause does not emerge into full narrative clarity. Given the basic premise, both works develop on somewhat similar lines. In both, the culture forbids many activities and, in particular, constrains exploration. In both works, the first-person narrator is a young man who seeks knowledge and journeys bravely into the unknown (to the "Dead Places" and to the "Place of the Gods" in Benét, to the "Uncharted Forest" in *Anthem*), hunting with bow and arrow. Both works conclude with hope that what was lost can be rebuilt, and that the heroes, seeking information from special, secret books, can lead the way. Both works conclude by redefining the god as human: for Benét, the gods are men; for the hero of *Anthem*, the god is the "Ego." This redefinition is reflected in the titles: "The Places of the Gods" refers ultimately to the world as the places belonging to men, and "Ego" (the original title of Ayn Rand's novella) refers to the spirit of man. Perhaps most striking is the fact that

Benét's John sees in the face of the last survivor "something unconquered," and this very something is the quality the Golden One sees in the face of *Anthem*'s hero, a quality for which she names him "The Unconquered." Although, in Benét, it is the last survivor (rather than the hero) who is described as unconquered, both works underscore a *spiritual* invincibility that is unbreached by external circumstances—and unbreachable.

The sheer number of common elements is striking. Most of these elements, however, are characteristic of the quest narrative and the bildungsroman, i.e., fiction of exploration, spiritual crisis, and self-transformation. The parallels based on the premise of fantasy, however, are worth exploring, particularly because we as readers discover the premise in the same way in both works: through the narrative voice of a young man who does not understand the significance of the details he observes, because he lives in a time when such achievements as subways and electric lights—achievements that the readers take for granted—are no longer known, are no longer used, are no longer even whole, and thus are in danger of vanishing from existence as they have already vanished from consciousness.

It is not reasonable, though, to conclude that Ayn Rand owed this premise to Benét. He himself, indeed, would have been the last to assert originality for it. In August, 1937, he replied to a letter from another writer, Margaret Widdemer, who wrote to share with him her own "Ancient Lights":

> How very interesting! I've very much taken with "Ancient Lights" and, God knows, I wouldn't have thought "The Place of the Gods" had any influence on it, even if you hadn't told me. I don't see how that particular idea can help being at the back of a lot of our minds these days—it has suddenly come upon us that the works may blow up. I suppose Wells was the first to say it in our time—though it must go back to Macaulay's New Zealander brooding on the ruins of London Bridge.[8]

Invoking Macaulay's New Zealander, Benét is referring to an article in the *Edinburgh Review*, first published in October 1840, about Leopold von Ranke's *History of the Popes*. Thomas Babington Macaulay expressed his belief that the Roman Catholic Church might survive British civilization itself, and "still exist in undiminished vigour, when some traveler from New Zealand shall, in the midst of a vast solitude, take his stand on a broken arch of London Bridge to sketch the ruins of St. Paul's."[9]

The prospect of a future man looking at a world in ruins, writes Benét in his letter, is one that was at least a century old, but that had become more urgent to him in his own time. He comments that the story "began as a poem—it was going to be a fourth nightmare for the *New Yorker*. Then somehow I couldn't finish it, dropped it, picked it up again and made a short story instead."[10] The three nightmare poems published before "The Places of the Gods"— "Metropolitan Nightmare," "Nightmare with Angels," and "Nightmare Number

Three"—are visions of urban destruction due to, respectively, super-insects, gas pellets, and super-machines.[11] These poems, unlike "The Places of the Gods," are set close in time to the disaster, rather than many years after the fact. Later, Benét continued the series with "Nightmare for Future Reference" and "Nightmare at Noon."[12] The first blames the cessation of human births on a virus that arises during World War III (or on women's refusal to continue giving birth); the second, originally published in 1940, breaks the sequence by eliminating any fantasy premise and by expressing clearly a polemic purpose: to advocate the involvement of the United States in World War II.

Benét makes clear from the literary context of his related works that he is concerned with the general phenomenon of decline and destruction, not with any distinct cause. He assigns no reason, or he invokes a variety of reasons—which amounts to the same thing. One looks back at "The Places of the Gods," seeking some sort of explanation for the disaster. Yes, we are told that it followed a war, but what caused the war? Who fought, and why? The hero does not know how or why the world was lost, or how to prevent its being lost again if it is rebuilt. The only hint of a cause is a conversation between John and his father.

> I told and he listened. After that, I wished to tell the people, but he showed me otherwise. He said, "Truth is a hard deer to hunt. If you eat too much truth at once, you may die of the truth. It was not idly that our fathers forbade the Dead Places." He was right—it is better the truth should come little by little. I have learned that, being a priest. Perhaps in the old days, they ate knowledge too fast.

Is John (and Benét, through him) implying that the excessive pursuit of knowledge ruined the world? What does it mean to eat too much truth at once, or to eat knowledge too fast? The meaning is at best merely unclear, and at worst an attack on the mind (in the tradition of works such as Mary Shelley's *Frankenstein* and Nathaniel Hawthorne's "The Birthmark," for example, that decry scientific ambition as overweening and hence destructive). We cannot tell why the "Great Burning" came about, and the writer leaves us in a state of ominous puzzlement. Benét thus emphasizes the pain instead of the cause. When Ayn Rand commented that "The Places of the Gods" had "no ideology," "no particular theme," she was identifying what that story most prominently lacked, and what her own story most prominently possessed. Her own work—as I will later point out—was to make blazingly evident what ruined the world, and what must be reborn in order to rebuild that world. In examining the story that led her to write her novella in the summer of 1937, we see most obviously the key difference: Benét provides no distinct reason for the disaster he describes and deplores. But we note, too, that, in a letter about the story, he makes mention of H. G. Wells, "the first to say it in our time." His reference calls attention to a significant author.

in the genre to which both "The Places of the Gods" and *Anthem* belong, an author who forms part of the literary context of Ayn Rand's text.


## H. G. WELLS AND JOHN W. CAMPBELL

Ayn Rand was familiar with the science fiction of H. G. Wells;[13] it is likely that she first read his work in her youth, during her school days, when she first thought of the idea for *Anthem*. As Richard C. Borden observes: "H. G. Wells captured and held the Russian public's imagination in a way unequaled on his native soil. While his popularity and influence at the turn of the century was enormous, it was in the 1920s, when a generation of readers raised on his stories reached maturity, that his true impact was felt."[14] The science fiction of Wells was everywhere in Russia—not only in Russian translation but in the French adventure magazines that the young Ayn Rand read. She mentions, disparagingly, *The War of the Worlds*;[15] she may also have read additional works by Wells, including two that feature a portrait of the future gone wrong, a future looking back on a lost past: *The Time Machine* (1895) and *When the Sleeper Awakes* (1899).

*The Time Machine* contains the first-person account of the journey of an anonymous Time Traveller to the year 802,701 and to a still more distant future. He discovers a world in which the human race has become split into the grotesque, ugly Morlocks, who live below ground and are responsible for production, and the graceful, pretty Eloi, who live idly above ground, and whom the Morlocks kill and eat. It takes him some time to determine the state of affairs, and he is never in fact certain that he has completely understood. He contrasts his confusion with the clear exposition in "these visions of Utopias and the coming times which I have read" (by which he means such classic works as Thomas More's *Utopia* of 1516 and Francis Bacon's *The New Atlantis* of 1624, as well as more recent books, such as William Morris's *News from Nowhere* of 1891), which typically include a "convenient cicerone" who has the job of explaining to the visitor the rules and customs of the strange world.[16] What the Traveller most resents about the Eloi (whom he believes at first to be the sole descendants of humankind) is their intellectual weakness, which matches their physical weakness. When he realizes they are on the intellectual level of five-year-olds: "A flow of disappointment rushed across my mind. For a moment I felt that I had built the Time Machine in vain" (*Time Machine*, 36).

He notes their "lack of interest" in him or in anything else, their passivity, their indolence, the "brown and charred rags" he sees hanging from the sides of a gallery in the Palace of Green Porcelain, rags he soon recognizes as the "decaying vestiges of books" (*Time Machine*, 39, 80). Their buildings and furniture, although still attractive, are decaying, cracked, dilapidated. At first he attributes their decline to a perverse form of natural selection (according to which "security sets a premium upon feebleness" [*Time Machine*, 43]); when he learns of the existence of the Morlocks, he speculates that the situation may be the result of class division (according to which the idle aristocrats have become accustomed to pursuing "pleasure and comfort" above ground, while the workers toil below [*Time Machine*, 61]). Whatever the cause (and however confused his thinking about the possible cause), he clearly sees the Eloi as "humanity upon the wane," in a "slow movement of degeneration, . . . a general dwindling of size, strength, and intelligence" (*Time Machine*, 42, 62).

He eventually travels still further into the future, this time to a world of "steady twilight," pervaded by "the sense of abominable desolation," "bitter cold," devoid of human life, of sheep, of birds, of any animate beings with the exception of hideous monsters. "From the edge of the sea came a ripple and whisper. Beyond these lifeless sounds, the world was silent. Silent? It would be hard to convey the stillness of it" (*Time Machine*, 93, 95, 97). He escapes as soon as he can.

Wells, in his first "scientific romance," shows a future world from which the mind is vanishing, and then a further future from which all human life is gone. Ayn Rand's novella, too, evokes a future more backward than its present, and one that—but for the hero—would continue its decline. The world in *Anthem*, as in *The Time Machine*, is dying, and she uses the image of "twilight," as did Wells, to suggest that fact. The 1938 edition of *Anthem*, in a sentence cut for the 1946 edition, uses the image of twilight to convey the death of the mind: "When the twilight came, men wrote no longer, neither did they read."[17] The people of *Anthem*'s world, moreover, are largely complacent and cowed— as are Wells's Eloi. But if Ayn Rand read *The Time Machine*, she would have rejected—among other things—the idea that all the Eloi could be small, weak, stupid, and yet beautiful. In *Anthem*, the "brothers" and "sisters"—with a few exceptions—are characteristically unattractive in both body and soul. And she would have rejected the inevitability of the cold, silent end of the world. She does so, implicitly, in the following conversation between Dagny Taggart and Hank Rearden in her 1957 novel, *Atlas Shrugged*:

> "I keep thinking of what they told us in school about the sun losing energy, growing colder each year. I remember wondering, then, what it would be like in the last days of the world. I think it would be . . . like this. Growing colder and things stopping."
>
> "I never believed that story. I thought by the time the sun was exhausted, men would find a substitute."
>
> "You did? Funny, I thought that, too."[18]

But, as with Benét's "The Places of the Gods," the most significant contrast between Wells's vision and hers is found in the reason for the decline of the world. Benét barely offered one reason; Wells offers several, but without clarity. And if we do not know how the world was (or will be) lost, we cannot know how to save it. Whereas Benét's John promised to "build again," the Time Traveller offers no such hope, to the future or to the present that is on the path to that future. Whereas books help *Anthem*'s hero rediscover the "I," the books in *The Time Machine*—and the information they may have conveyed—are "decaying vestiges," too far gone to be of use to the Time Traveller. The Time Traveller's friend, who defies the Traveller's pessimism about the course of the world, serves as the frame narrator and delivers the summation: "If that is so, it remains for us to live as though it were not so" (*Time Machine*, 104). To live in defiance of knowledge is no answer, but *The Time Machine* does not clearly suggest anything better. Nonetheless, the narrative and visual qualities of this novella made it popular and influential, for its questions if not for its answers.

John W. Campbell's "Twilight," obviously a response to Wells, was published in 1934, a few years before "The Places of the Gods" and *Anthem*. (There is no evidence that either Benét or Ayn Rand knew it.) Its narrative structure is closer to that of Wells—with several narrators, a journey, and a return—than to those of "The Places of the Gods" or *Anthem*, but the dystopian vision is related to theirs.

Another time traveler visits a stagnant, depressing future in which a passive human race endures in ignorance, and will eventually die. What is responsible for the ongoing disaster? After some consideration of biological causes of sterility and decline, the traveler identifies what he sees as the essential cause: the loss of the mind, of the intellectual power to appreciate and pursue the achievements of the mind:

> Man had lost the instinct of curiosity.
> Oh, not entirely. They wondered at the machines, they wondered at the stars. But they did nothing about it. It was not wholly lost to them yet, but nearly. It was dying. . . .
> Can you appreciate the crushing loneliness it brought to me? I, who love science, who see in it, or have seen in it, the salvation, the raising of mankind—to see those wondrous machines, of man's triumphant maturity, forgotten and misunderstood. The wondrous, perfect machines that tended, protected, and cared for those gentle, kindly people who had—forgotten.
> They were lost among it. The city was a magnificent ruin to them, a thing that rose stupendous about them. Something not understood, a thing that was of the nature of the world. It was. It had not been made; it simply was. Just as the mountains and the deserts and the waters of the seas. . . .
> And all those people knew was to do a certain thing to a certain lever produced certain results. Just as men in the Middle Ages knew that to take a certain material, wood, and place it in contact with other pieces of wood heated red, would cause the wood to disappear, and become heat. They did not understand

that wood was being oxidized, with the release of the heat of formation of carbon dioxide and water. So those people did not understand the things that fed
and clothed and carried them.[19]

With considerable emotional power, Campbell evokes the loss of the
mind. Without it, the machines and cities built by human thought will eventually perish, and the lot of the "survivors" is tragic, a kind of living death.
His visual image of the doomed cities is also powerful, and, with the mention of "twilight" (its significance underlined by the story's title), an allusion
to the "steady twilight" of Wells:

> Twilight—the sun has set. The desert out beyond, in the mystic, changing col-
> ors. The great, metal city rising straight-walled to the human city above, broken
> by spires and towers and great trees with scented blossoms. The silvery-rose
> glow in the paradise of gardens above. . . .
> [The little men] wander through the vast cities their ancestors built, knowing
> less of them than the machines themselves. . . .
> I had been born in the first full light of man's day. I did not belong in the lin-
> gering, dying glow of man's twilight.[20]

The image of "twilight," as I have noted, appears with poignant effect in *Anthem*—and later, in the opening scene of *Atlas Shrugged*, Eddie Willers
thinks: "I hate the twilight."[21]

Campbell, unlike Benét and Wells, suggests a reason for the disintegration
of the world, and it is not a ridiculous reason. Without the active mind, there
is no human world. The active mind applied to science and technology,
moreover, is an honorable image of something to be cherished, something
the loss of which would be poignant and pervasive. But Campbell does not
even begin to explain how the mind could be lost, and his character's idea
of how to reverse the disaster is almost comic: Ares Sen Kenlin orders a machine "to make a machine which would have what man had lost. A curious
machine."[22] In "Night" (1935), a sequel to "Twilight," it is clear that the attempted rescue proved impossible.

Campbell's contribution to the genre is—from a philosophical stand-
point—an advance. Instead of muddled reasons or no reason at all, he offers
the beginnings of a good reason. He also makes the point—which, as we
shall see, comes up in the literary context of a future gone wrong—that it is
absurd to denigrate machines themselves.

Wells himself is ambiguous (and possibly ambivalent) regarding machines. Although the Morlocks' machines are as ugly as the Morlocks themselves, he celebrates, elsewhere, the achievements of technology. A few
years after *The Time Machine*, he published *When the Sleeper Wakes* (1899,
revised and reissued as *The Sleeper Awakes* in 1910 and again in 1921).[23] Graham, a Victorian gentleman who fell asleep in 1897, awakens in 2100 to find

glittering tall buildings, aqueducts, flying ships—as well as babies raised in crèches, "Babble Machines" broadcasting propaganda, and complete separation between the artificial world of the city and the "natural" world beyond the wall. He discovers that there is a split between the powerful, aristocratic tyrants (who aspire to rule by the right of their asserted superiority) and the powerless workers (who labor for their blue-canvas clothing and for all other needs, which are similarly uniform). As a wealthy man (whose investments have been drawing interest for two centuries), Graham is in fact virtually the owner of the world, and his aid is enlisted by both sides (either to rule with the tyrants, or to support the workers' revolution against the tyrants). The dichotomy reflects, to a large extent, Wells's socialistic ideas. The novel also reflects Wells's reading (and possible misreading) of Nietzsche. Ostrog, who represents the tyrants, proclaims:

> The hope of mankind—what is it? That some day the Over-man may come, that some day the inferior, the weak and the bestial may be subdued or eliminated. Subdued if not eliminated. The world is no place for the bad, the stupid, the enervated. Their duty—it's a fine duty too!—is to die. The death of the failure! That is the path by which the beast rose to manhood, by which man goes on to higher things. (*Sleeper* 1899, 200; 1910, 209)

Wells drew also on classical mythology. The Sleeper meets with a group of men in what is known as the "Atlas chamber," a room with a "gigantic white figure of Atlas, strong and strenuous" (*Sleeper* 1899, 47; 1910, 55). He is told: "*you* are the Atlas, Sire. The world is on your shoulders" (*Sleeper* 1899, 80; 1910, 93). He is invited, moreover, to fulfill this function by taking power: "Rule the world as it has never been ruled, for the good and happiness of men. For you might rule it—you could rule it" (*Sleeper* 1899, 192; 1910, 201). He chooses instead to side with the workers. In the final battle, though, Ostrog's plane flies to safety, and the sleeper's plane hurtles toward the ground, as he wishes, unrealistically, that he might wake and meet the woman he loves. In the 1899 edition of the novel, Graham reassures himself that his death is not in vain: "He was beaten but London was saved. London was saved!" (*Sleeper* 1899, 274); in the 1910 and 1921 versions, Wells removed even the hint of hope.

Although there is no evidence that Ayn Rand was familiar with this particular novel, it was, like *War of the Worlds*, one of those widely available in Russia in her youth. In 1927, not long after she arrived in Hollywood, she saw, twice, Fritz Lang's film *Metropolis*, which H. G. Wells considered an unauthorized borrowing of the premise of *When the Sleeper Wakes*.[24] In Thea von Harbou's screenplay, underground workers rebel against the idlers who reside in the glittering city above ground.[25]

Two features of *When the Sleeper Wakes* stand out. The first is that, as in *The Time Machine*, Wells offers some sort of explanation for the decline of the world, e.g., bad economic management over centuries, exacerbated by power-hungry, unscrupulous tyrants and enervated, passive "masses"—but that the explanation is neither clear nor stressed, nor is it unique. Years later, Wells wrote in the "Preface to the 1921 Edition":

> The present volume takes up certain ideas already very much discussed in the concluding years of the last century, the idea of the growth of the towns and the depopulation of the country-side and the degradation of labour through the higher organization of industrial production. "Suppose these forces to go on," that is the fundamental hypothesis of the story. (*Sleeper* 1910, xiii)

Are urbanization and industrialization, then, the key problems? Or should we, perhaps, consider this novel a preview of *The Time Machine*? The workers in *When the Sleeper Wakes*, who labor underground, may be on their way to becoming Morlocks, and the idle aristocrats, who holiday in Pleasure Cities, may be on their way to becoming Eloi.[26] What, though, motivates the transformation? Is it in any sense inevitable? Graham never really learns why his world has become a place of misery. That the end of the novel is abrupt and unresolved (it ends with a plane crash, which presumably he does not survive) is appropriate. When he awakened from his sleep, he did not awaken to knowledge or understanding; the mystery of the end of the novel matches the mystery of its middle. (*Anthem*, of course, has no such mystery at its heart.)

The second significant point about *When the Sleeper Wakes* is that technological splendor co-exists with wretchedness—wretchedness that is spiritual and in some places material as well. H. G. Wells appears to revel in the wondrous spectacle of the new city.

> [Graham's] first impression was of overwhelming architecture. The place into which he looked was an aisle of Titanic buildings, curving spaciously in either direction. Overhead mighty cantilevers sprang together across the huge width of the place, and a tracery of translucent material shut out the sky. Gigantic globes of cool white light shamed the pale sunbeams that filtered down through the girders and wires. Here and there a gossamer suspension bridge dotted with foot passengers flung across the chasm and the air was webbed with slender cables. A cliff of edifice hung above him, he perceived as he glanced upward, and the opposite façade was grey and dim and broken by great archings, circular perforations, balconies, buttresses, turret projections, myriads of vast windows, and an intricate system of architectural relief. (*Sleeper* 1899, 38; 1910, 45)

Through the amazed eyes of the Sleeper, Wells describes a vast array of new and efficient machines for transportation, communication, and agriculture. Yet he also suggests a darker side. The world of 2100 has hunger, censorship, and crèches of babies raised with no human contact.

Wells, then, not only shows technological advancement as being compatible with lack of freedom, but even seems to suggest that the progress itself may contribute to the specific misery of this world. Graham awakes to a world that is a semi-dystopia, a glass that can be viewed as half empty or half full. This is a departure from the works considered so far: *When the Sleeper Wakes* presents a future gone wrong that is better—as well as worse—than the present. Hence, if Wells were to address the question of what has gone wrong with the world and why, he might also address the corollary question of what has gone right, and why.

An additional, and seminal, work by Wells that is relevant to the literary context is *A Modern Utopia* (1905).[27] This work (which space does not permit me to analyze here) carries further the positive elements of the world of *When the Sleeper Wakes*, and omits or minimizes the negative elements. *A Modern Utopia*, unlike the other works so far treated, is unapologetically plotless: by "an act of imagination," the narrator and a companion are transported to, and from, a parallel world, in which human nature is unchanged, but unlimited changes with everything man-made. We read about

> a free hand with all the apparatus of existence that man has, so to speak, made for himself, with houses, roads, clothing, canals, machinery, with laws, boundaries, conventions, and traditions, with schools, with literature and religious organizations, with creeds and customs, with everything, in fact, that it lies within man's power to alter.[28]

The defining qualities of this utopia, as summarized by Mark Hillegas, are as follows: "Utopia as a World State; the voluntary nobility, the *samurai*;[29] the important role of science and technology; and Utopia seen as kinetic, not static."[30] Wells, in his text, invokes other utopian literature (from Plato's *Republic* to such recent works as William Dean Howells's *A Traveler from Altruria*, 1894), as if summing it all up in order to present his own work as the ultimate utopia. His attitude is unambiguously positive: he could be writing a travel brochure or real estate advertisement. This is not a future that has lost (or is on the verge of losing) what is precious in the present. This is a future made to order. Numerous later literary texts have analyzed, questioned, and rejected that "order," i.e., the planned society of *A Modern Utopia*—with special attention to the "modern" nature of his utopia, i.e., the scientific and technological achievements that make possible glittering cities, efficient transportation—and equally efficient regulation of land and production (for there is no private property), parenthood, and health (for there is no private life). *A Modern Utopia*—with the qualities Hillegas identifies as basic to it—is not primarily a point of reference for *Anthem* itself (and there is no evidence that Ayn Rand knew it). It stands, however, as the classic utopia against which several later fictional dystopias were framed. Some of these, as we shall see, bear fruitful comparison with *Anthem*.

## E. M. FORSTER

One such work is E. M. Forster's short story "The Machine Stops" (1909), described by its author as "a reaction to one of the earlier heavens of H. G. Wells."[31] Best known for his realistic novels (notably *A Passage to India* and *Howards End*) and his criticism (*Aspects of the Novel*), Forster also wrote several short stories with fantasy premises, collected in *The Celestial Omnibus* (1911) and *The Eternal Moment* (1928). In "The Machine Stops," people live secluded in their apartments in underground cities, ordering food, clothing, and entertainment by pushing buttons. They do not , for the most part, meet each other in the flesh; they interact by phototelephone. The hero, Kuno, yearns to see what he has rarely seen: the surface of the earth, the "curious stars," his mother's face. When he travels secretly to the surface of the city, he encounters the physical world and takes a stand for experience that is first-hand and self-chosen. As he tells his mother:

> Man is the measure. That was my first lesson. Man's feet are the measure for distance, his hands are the measure for ownership, his body is the measure for all this is lovable and desirable and strong. ("The Machine Stops," 125)[32]

When he climbs through levels of railway tunnels, he thinks of the workmen who built them, and climbs the ventilation shaft through which they breathed, in his quest to regain the lost world of the life above ground.

Forster's world has three of the characteristics of Wells's modern utopia, as identified by Hillegas: it is world-wide; it has a designated, non-hereditary noble class; and it uses modern technology. It may have the fourth quality as well—in that the machine "moves" until it "stops"—even though the society itself appears static. But Forster, unlike Benét and Wells, presents a clear reason for what has gone wrong with the world:

> We created the Machine, to do our will, but we cannot make it do our will now. It has robbed us of the sense of space and the sense of touch, it has blurred every human relation and narrowed down love to a carnal act, it has paralyzed our bodies and our wills, and now it compels us to worship it. The Machine develops—but not on our lines. The Machine proceeds—but not to our goal. . . . Oh, I have no remedy—or, at least, only one—to tell men again and again that I have seen the hills of Wessex as Aelfrid saw them when he overthrew the Danes. ("Machine Stops," 131)

His attack is not on the technology, but on the service for which it has been engaged. The world has declined because people have sacrificed their personal goals to an allegedly greater collective goal, and have done so by abandoning their first-hand experience for an allegedly superior second-hand experience.

The Machine . . . feeds us and clothes us and houses us; through it we speak to one another, through it we see one another, in it we have our being. The Machine . . . is omnipotent, eternal; blessed is the Machine. ("Machine Stops," 137)

At story's end, Kuno has ended the tyranny of the Machine. His life is the price. As he tells his mother, who is also dying, the world on the surface is still populated by men (those were expelled from society and presumed dead), and the Machine that has imprisoned him and his society will never be rebuilt.

"We have come back to our own. We die, but we have recaptured life, as it was in Wessex, when Aelfrid overthrew the Danes. We know what they know outside, they who dwelt in the cloud that is the colour of a pearl."
"But, Kuno, is it true? Are there still men on the surface of the earth? Is this—this tunnel, this poisoned darkness—really not the end?"
He replied:
"I have seen them, spoken to them, loved them. They are hiding in the mist and the ferns until our civilization stops. To-day they are the Homeless—to-morrow—:
"Oh, to-morrow—some fool will start the Machine again, to-morrow."
"Never," said Kuno, "never. Humanity has learnt its lesson." ("Machine Stops," 146)

Forster's story, framed as a response to Wells's utopias, depicts a society in which regimentation obviates individual choice, lectures substitute for learning, and direct sensory experience is regarded as dispensable. Although Forster does not explicitly name collectivism as the essence of the Machine's evil, the Machine society is in fact collectivist, built on enforced conformity. The narrative structure, like that of *Anthem*, follows a brave young man through his clandestine explorations to his eventual epiphany about his society's evil, and the need to destroy it, at any and all costs, in order to restore what has been lost (and what is in fact hiding, waiting to return, just beyond his world's borders).

The hero of "The Machine Stops," to be sure, expects the waiting army to rise and return without him; the hero of *Anthem* plans to be himself the agent of salvation, the leader of the outpost army (and in this, as we shall see, he resembles the hero of *Atlas Shrugged*). Forster's story, moreover, is different from *Anthem* in another important way: its very premise posits a Machine that continues to function effectively even after enervating the minds needed to create and maintain it. Forster's Machine is there until it is destroyed—rather than decaying for lack of the mind needed to sustain it. Forster's Machine is like the technological wonders of Wells's *When the Sleeper Wakes*: glittering and glorious in contrast with spiritual suffering. Most important, though, is Forster's inadequate—though valiant—attempt to explain what has gone wrong with the world. What exactly led to the diminishment of human life?

Although he comes close to identifying sensory experience as the key, does he mean to say that there is no legitimate use for anything bearing the name "idea" (which, in the story, is a pejorative term)? Are lectures never more than a substitute for learning? How did Man come to deny "the essence that is his soul, and the essence, equally divine, that is his body"? ("Machine Stops," 145).

Although Forster ultimately, like Campbell, does not provide a full reason for the world's downfall, we see that the atmosphere, the story line, and some of the evil of his invented world have parallels in *Anthem*. Richard De-Mille (son of Cecil B. DeMille, for whose production company Ayn Rand worked in her early years in Hollywood, and who will be discussed below in connection with Evgeny Zamyatin) commented, on reading *Anthem*, that it reminded him of "The Machine Stops"; he added: "But I do not confuse their meanings, which are different."[33] Ayn Rand's reply of November 27, 1946, does not mention Forster.[34] If she had read the story, before or after writing *Anthem*, it is likely that she would have agreed with Richard DeMille that the meanings of the works are different, but she might also have appreciated the hints of the emptiness of second-hand "knowledge"; she would, to be sure, have been wary of the risk involved in singling out the Machine as the symbol of evil—and thus implying that technology itself is guilty.

## EVGENY ZAMYATIN

This very issue—implicating technology in the evil of the future gone wrong—is key to another writer of speculative fiction. If Benét's story is the closest in time and place to the composition of *Anthem*, Zamyatin is the closest in time and place to the initial conception of *Anthem*. A Russian-born engineer who became a translator, editor, essayist, playwright, and novelist, Evgeny Zamyatin "was one of the very first writers to be silenced by Stalin."[35] In 1931, he left Russia for Berlin, and ultimately Paris; he died, still in exile, in 1937. Although he had initially identified himself as a Bolshevik, he "reported himself 'not one' shortly after the revolution."[36] His writings implicitly attacked the Soviet regime.[37] His specific political views are nowhere systematically articulated and developed—possibly because, as Edward J. Brown observes, explicitness on such subjects was dangerous.

For our purposes, his most significant fictional works are the novels *Islanders* [Ostrovitiane] and *We* [My]. *Islanders*—which he began writing while assigned to work in England on the icebreaker ship *Alexander Nevsky* and which he completed and published on his return to Petersburg in 1917—is set in contemporary England, and its events are within the bounds of realism. Several characters, however, express ideas that are expanded and formalized in the later novel, *We*. In *Islanders*, the Vicar Dooley, for example, organizes all of his activities—walks, meals, repentance, and sex—by a schedule. Lady Campbell maintains that all people should be alike, and O'Kelley, carrying this idea further, jokes about a parliamentary bill designed to remove the one remaining difference in people, the length of their noses (henceforth, by decree, to be the same).

*We* was composed in 1920–1921. It was circulated privately in Russia, published for the first time in English translation in the United States in 1924. It was not published in Russian until 1952 (and, then, in the United States), and not published in Russia until 1988.[38] Zamyatin envisioned a time, a millennium after his own time, in which, as *Islanders* had suggested, all activities (including sexual relations, organized by schedules and tickets) are regulated, and everything that can be made uniform about human beings has been made uniform—to the extent that names are no longer personal; neither clothing nor occupations nor recreations are a matter of choice, and differences between people are officially insignificant. This regulated future amounted to a fresh start; it was created following a long war and the deaths of most of the world's population. Regimentation has not restrained the growth of technology, which flourishes, with rockets, aeros, and a marvelous, mechanical, glass-roofed city separated by a glass wall from the surrounding uncivilized countryside. The main character, D-503, is an engineer whose private notebooks show that he is coming to resent and to oppose the "rationality" of his society, symbolized by the use of numbers. He is tempted, and confused by his awareness of a "soul" within him that is different from the machine-like identity he has accepted as a matter of course.[39] His incipient revolt—associated with his secret love for a woman unsanctioned by One State (a woman whose name is *I-330*, emphasis added)—is cut short when he is caught and "cured" by a conversation with the chief "Benefactor" [Blagodetel'] and by brain surgery.

*We*, like "The Machine Stops," fits within the general dystopian category and the more specific category of the anti-utopia: this bad future was created *on purpose*. The purpose is revealed in a climactic scene: the protagonist is told that what began as love can be cruelty, that human beings have always longed to escape freedom, and that, therefore, the chief tyrant is known as the "Benefactor."

> And this same Christian, all-merciful God—the one who slowly roasts in the fires of Hell all those who rebel against him—is he not to be called *executioner?* And those whom the Christians burned at the stake, are they fewer in number than the Christians who were burnt? But, all of this notwithstanding, you see, this is still the God who has been worshipped for centuries as the God of love. Absurd? No, on the contrary. It is the patent, signed in blood, of man's indelible good sense. Even then, in his savage, shaggy state, he understood: A true algebraic love of mankind will inevitably be inhuman, and the inevitable sign of the truth is its cruelty. . . . What is it that people beg for, dream about, torment themselves for, from the time they leave swaddling clothes? They want someone to

tell them, once and for all, what happiness is—and then to bind them to that happiness with a chain. What is it we're doing right now, if not that? The ancient dream of paradise.[40]

The "ancient dream of paradise," as made real in the world of *We*, is destructive in conception; although inconsistent in execution (as is apparent in the occurrence of physical and psychological aberrations, and in the need for measures to crush discontent and rebellion), the plan has achieved near-dominion.

Zamyatin's novel has parallels with the other works we have mentioned. *We* has the narrative pattern of "The Machine Stops" and *Anthem*—the protagonist faces and fights the evil of his society. *We* shares with *The Time Machine*, "The Places of the Gods," and *Anthem* the use of first-person narration as a guide to the contrast between the present and the past, as well as the examination of old books, old buildings, and other significant artifacts. In *We*, as in "The Machine Stops," "The Places of the Gods," and *Anthem*, there is a place outside the "city" that is an alternative to the city, a place the protagonist seeks to explore. But *We* is marked most strongly by its parallels with Wells. *We* possesses all four qualities identified by Hillegas. It is worldwide; it has a class of voluntary nobles; it uses technology; it is dynamic. It is, in other words, a form of Wells's *A Modern Utopia*.[41] Yet it suggests a negative attitude toward that utopia and, specifically, to its modernity. *We* shares with Wells's own *When the Sleeper Wakes* (which Zamyatin knew well[42]) and "The Machine Stops" (which he probably did not[43]) the contrast between the glittering towers and the depths of human suffering—even though in Zamyatin's world (as also in Forster's) the suffering is buried in the souls of people who have learned to dismiss their spiritual lives rather than (as in Wells) in the squalid daily lives of people who work underground.

The parallels with H. G. Wells are far from accidental. Zamyatin was familiar with the works of Wells. When he worked as an editor for the World Literature Publishing House (1919–1924), he edited and supervised the Russian publication of numerous volumes by Wells.[44] He also lectured on Wells at a St. Petersburg artists' union, and wrote "Herbert Wells" (published in 1922, revised in 1924), which discusses, along with Wells's realistic novels, such works as *The Time Machine*, *When the Sleeper Wakes*, *A Modern Utopia*, *Men Like Gods*, *In the Days of the Comet*, *The War in the Air*, and *The World Set Free*. Wells's scientific romances or "sociofantastic novels," he says, create a new form: they combine trenchant social commentary with the projection of a future that science has made imaginable in essence and in detail.[45] Zamyatin's project in *We* is—at least in part—Wellsian in inspiration.[46]

Yet a Wellsian "sociofantastic" novel, by its nature, draws on the time and place in which it is conceived—and Zamyatin's book was composed at the same time and place in which Ayn Rand first thought of her play about a

world without the word "I." Is there a reason to assert a particular link between *We* and *Anthem?* Did Ayn Rand ever meet Zamyatin? The evidence is
slender. No information has come to light regarding any contact between her
(or any friends or family members) and his various associations: the House
of the Arts, the House of Writers, or the World Literature Publishing House
and its studio for translators. Her family's situation during the early 1920s was
difficult. She attended only a few of her classes because it was hard to walk,
in worn-out shoes, three miles in the snow to the university. She remembered sitting on the floor of her family's apartment, too weak and hungry to
rise. In her first year at the university (1921–1922), she attended some student meetings and spoke her mind about politics; she then decided that it
was dangerous to speak, and she attended no more meetings. She was very
much aware that to read or write anti-Soviet ideas was to risk one's life; she
had burned her own diary before the family returned to Petersburg from the
Crimea in 1921.[47]

Did she read *Islanders* or *We*, while in Russia or after she left? It is possible.
More than thirty years after she came to the United States, she recalled her
reading during her college years: "There were a couple of modern novels by
Russian writers that were semi–anti-Soviet or thinly veiled anti-Soviet that I
liked for that reason, but that was minor. I don't even remember the authors'
names."[48] Zamyatin's *We* fits the general description, in that it was not openly
or explicitly anti-Soviet, but merely susceptible to an anti-Soviet reading by
those who wanted (or feared) such an approach. But this book, although read
aloud before many audiences, was not available in published form, and it was
clear that the book was considered "little short of treason" by the Soviet officials, and it had "the distinction of being the first novel banned by the Glavlit
(Chief Administration for Literary Affairs), established in 1922."[49] If she had
made the effort to find it or to attend a reading of it, it is likely that she would
have also made note of the name of the author or the work.[50]

One tantalizing coincidence is that both Ayn Rand and Zamyatin left Russia hoping to work in Hollywood. Both, moreover, had the same director in
mind. When Ayn Rand arrived in Hollywood, she had with her a letter of introduction to Cecil B. DeMille, and he became her first employer. Zamyatin,
too, was specifically interested in working for Cecil B. DeMille, whom he
had met in Moscow in August 1931. In February of 1932, DeMille in fact
wrote Zamyatin a letter of reference, to aid in his application in Berlin for an
American visa, and expressed his hope that Zamyatin would be able to come
to the States: "We are in need of good dramatic brains more than ever."[51]

Do the texts themselves suggest that Ayn Rand read Zamyatin? Salient similarities between *We* and *Anthem* include the regimentation of life, the world-
wide state, the replacement of names by numbers, and the first-person narration by a secretly rebellious protagonist. But these are not unique to *We*. The
regimentation of life and the world-wide state are features of Wells (as we

have seen), whom both Zamyatin and Rand read. The number-names and regimentation, as noted by Elizabeth Stenbock-Fermor, can be found in Jerome K. Jerome's "The New Utopia" (1891); Jerome's works were popular in Russia and easily available.[52] And whether or not Ayn Rand read the Jerome K. Jerome story, she did not simply adopt the number system used by him (consecutive numbers) or that used by Zamyatin (a single letter plus a three-digit number). In *Anthem*, the number-names include words ("Equality," "Liberty," "Solidarity," etc.) as well as numbers; as she explained in her answers to the students' questions: "I patterned the numbering after telephone numbers, with the prefixes consisting of statist slogans";[53] telephone numbers, at the time, consisted of a word—or the first two letters of that word—followed by a digit, a hyphen, and four more digits. The first-person narration by a malcontent is a staple of Russian literature, including two classics of the nineteenth century: Gogol's "Diary of a Madman" [Zapiski sumashedshego] of 1835 and Dostoevsky's *Notes from Underground* [Zapiski iz podpol'ia] of 1864 (to which I will return). There is nothing in *Anthem* that she could not have written without any knowledge of *We*.

The distinctions, moreover, are crucial. The prose of Zamyatin's D-503 is elliptical and cryptic; that of Equality 7-2521, even with the handicap of the absence of singular pronouns, is clear, as if to imply that clarity itself is a goal to be pursued. The contrast in styles becomes greater as the books progress: D-503 is progressively more disoriented, and Equality 7-2521 is progressively better equipped to describe his experiences and their significance. Zamyatin's world is one in which people build magnificent machines even when they are treated as if they were machines; in the world of *Anthem*, when people work together or not at all, the invention of the candle—by fifty men working together—is hailed as an achievement. In *We*, the tentative revolutionary actions of D-503 are alternatively encouraged and undercut by the women in his life, and he appears to be not even the hero of his own life story; in *Anthem*, the hero is dignified by his solitude, and his fate is in his hands. In *We*, D-503 ultimately loses his cause, his love, and his mind. The hero of *Anthem*, like Kuno in "The Machine Stops," expects that the value he fights for will triumph, whatever his own fate.

Zamyatin's title, nonetheless, is provocative, in our context. "We" is a direct contrast to Ayn Rand's original title for *Anthem*, "Ego." And, given that the word "we" is designated the essential "monster" in *Anthem* (96–97; 132–34 in 1938), as the symbol of the concept of collectivism, it is reasonable to speculate that, if she had heard of this work, and had known that it was in some way anti-Soviet, she might well have sought to read it. But *We* is, of course, not the source of her opposition to collectivism—she did not need to read a book in order to despise the Soviet state and everything it stood for—and, if she read it, she would not have found in it the inspiration for her own identification of the evil of collectivism (or, indeed, anything fundamentally like her idea). *We* has nothing to do with her idea for a play about the loss of the word "I." That a book happened to be "thinly veiled anti-Soviet" did not mean that it identified collectivism itself as evil—and in fact *We* does not do so, its title notwithstanding.

Zamyatin, who had little to say in public about this novel, did not identify any source for his title. Christopher Collins suggests that the title may have come from the manifesto of the "Smithy,"a proletarian culture movement: "*Kuznica*'s Nikolaj Ljashko (1884–1953) and others, in rejoicing that 'We' had driven out 'I,' may have furnished Zamjatin the title for the novel."[54]

One of these "others" who rejoiced in the defeat of the "I," according to Edward J. Brown, was Aleksandr Bezymensky:

> "The collective 'We' has driven out the personal 'I,'" shouted the youthful Bezymensky, and among the proletarian poets and novelists there developed a mystical belief in the collective as an entity in which the individual finds happiness by losing himself, like a Buddhist saint in nirvana.[55]

The alleged triumph of the "We" was accompanied, in proletarian art, by a vision of a "regimented paradise," described as follows by another "proletarian poet," Aleksei Gastaev:

> The mechanization, not only of gestures, not only of production methods, but of everyday thinking, coupled with extreme rationality, normalizes in a striking degree the psychology of the proletariat. . . . It is this that lends proletarian psychology such surprising anonymity, which permits the qualification of separate proletarian units as A, B, C, or as 325,075, or as O and the like. . . . In this psychology, from one end of the world to the other, flow potent massive streams, making for one world head in place of millions of heads. This tendency will next imperceptibly render individual thinking impossible, and thought will become the objective psychic process of a whole class, with systems of psychological switches and locks.[56]

This vision—the mechanization of thinking, the substitution of numbers for names, the impossibility of individual thought—finds literary form in *We*, but without the sort of enthusiastic endorsement Gastaev brings to his evocation "regimented paradise."

For writers who did not follow the path of proletarian culture, the abolition of the "I" was a target of ridicule. Vladimir Mayakovsky, mocking the proletarian poets, specifically called attention to their replacement of "I" by "We":

> The Proletcultists never speak / of "I" / or of the personality.
> They consider / the pronoun "I" / a kind of rascality. . . .
> But in my opinion / if you write petty stuff, you /
> will never crawl out of your lyrical slough /
> even if you substitute We for I.[57]

All of these references, whether or not they had any impact on Zamyatin's choice of title, fit well with what Ayn Rand said about hearing, in her school days in Russia, "all the vicious attacks on individualism, and [asking herself] what the world would be like if men lost the word 'I.'" After hearing poets and other propagandists saying that "we" can and must drive out "I," she planned a play, and ultimately a novella, that was an answer to that demand.

> What brought it to pass? What disaster took their reason away from men? What whip lashed them to their knees in shame and submission? The worship of the word "We." (102)

Zamyatin, too, considers the conflict between the "we" and the "I." His protagonist denies that the "I" could have any rights:

> So, take some scales and put on one side a gram, on the other a ton; on one side "I" and on the other "We," OneState. It's clear, isn't it?—to assert that "I" has certain "rights" with respect to the State is exactly the same as asserting that a gram weighs the same as a ton. That explains the way things are divided up: To the ton go the rights, to the gram the duties. And the natural path from nullity to greatness is this: Forget that you're a gram and feel yourself a millionth part of a ton." (*We*, 111)[58]

He cannot do so. He senses that he has a soul, and therefore concludes that he must be ill.

D-503 agrees with what "was understood by the Christians, our only (if very imperfect) predecessors: Humility is a virtue, pride a vice; *We* comes from God, *I* from the devil"; he holds his "self-consciousness" (his awareness of his separate identity, his "I") to be "a disease" and possibly "an epidemic" (*We*, 124, 88).

But although Zamyatin gives prominence to the word "we," he does not give the fact of collectivism an analogous prominence in his fictional world. He may have wanted to be clearer than he was about his target; to do so, though, would have meant taking even more of a chance. As one of his Soviet critics pointed out, the novel's polemic is a sort of package deal: "To oppose *grass*, human *willfulness*, and people covered with hair to communism means not to understand the essence of the question."[59] The reader knows which package is supposed to be preferred, but Zamyatin does not explain what ties the package together. Istvan Csicsery-Ronay goes so far as to say that the novel "does not represent freedom at all."[60] Collectivism is a feature of the world, but not the fundamental feature. Years after he wrote the novel, he remarked, in an interview, that this novel was based on "the relationship between the person and the collective . . . set within the framework of a utopian parody constructed out of a *reductio ad absurdum* of one possible solution."[61] It is, of course, true that his world nearly obliterates privacy and considers self-consciousness an illness. But the problem with the world he evokes is not only (or even primarily) the emphasis on "we" as opposed to "I," not collectivism *per se*, but the fact that the collectivist society is "mechanical," in that the use of machines has obliterated significant differences between men and machines. This aspect of his intention is evident in his statement in 1932: "This novel is a warning against the twofold danger which threatens humanity: the hypertrophic power of the machines and the hypertrophic power of the State."[62]

The phrase "twofold danger" places powerful machines on a level with the powerful State, as if the two are commensurate as threats. What is responsible for the decline of the world? The State—plus the machine. Part of the reason—it is implied—is reason itself. The character D-503, in effect, blames rationality, science, and technology—and holds these to be incompatible with what he takes to be genuine values: individuality and creative imagination.[63] His conception of reason, to be sure, is distorted: "The highest thing in Man is his reason, and what the work of reason comes down to is the continual limitation of infinity, dividing infinity into convenient, easily digestible portions" (*We*, 64). And he wrongly associates reason with the State, as if the two were the same thing (rather than—as in *Anthem*—bitter opponents). On the opening page, he writes of "the beneficial yoke of reason" (*We*, 3), and a sign refers to "the beneficent yoke of the State" (*We*, 36). In the final sentence of his notes, written after he has undergone an amputation of the imagination and has witnessed with indifference the torture of the woman he once loved, he states that the Numbers outside the wall have "betrayed reason," and that "we'll win. Because reason has to win" (*We*, 225). In context, this character's allegiance to reason amounts to an attack on reason—and thus invokes another major influence on Zamyatin: Dostoevsky.

## FYODOR DOSTOEVSKY

Zamyatin's *We*, as many critics have noted, is in part a response to Dostoevsky's *Notes from Underground*. Zamyatin's crystalline city—which expresses "this life of ours, this extremely transparent and permanent crystal" (*We*, 115)—is an imaginative projection of the Crystal Palace (itself a response to London's Exhibition of 1851 and Chernyshevsky's 1863 vision in *What Is to Be Done?* [Chto delat'?], at which Dostoevsky's Underground Man wanted to throw stones. The underground caves of Zamyatin's rebels are the counterpart of Dostoevsky's psychological underground. The regimentation of Zamyatin's society makes real the speculation of the Underground Man for a "mathematical table" to regulate all desires. The glorification of numbers in *We* stands as polar opposite to the attitude of the Underground

Man, who proposes to assert his freedom, his *self*, by rebelling against the equation "two times two is four."[64]

These familiar points carry weight. Whether or not the Underground Man speaks for Dostoevsky, and whether or not D-503 (or, for that matter, I-330) speaks for Zamyatin, both texts, as they stand, explore similar issues: freedom and the self—versus mathematics or reason. The Underground Man states that reason is the enemy of free will—and therefore assumes that only by defying reason can he assert his volition. The defiance of D-503 is parallel. Both characters consider opting out of the "rational" world that is supposed—but not by them—to be the epitome of human happiness. Both D-503 and the Underground Man associate selfhood with pain—and choose it nonetheless.

The Underground Man affirms his personal identity through toothache[65]: his discomfort makes him real, and he cherishes it for that reason. (He similarly enjoys his liver complaint, his psychological pain, and his social humiliation.) D-503 considers a parallel phenomenon, albeit with mixed emotions:

> I feel myself. But it's only the eye with a lash in it, the swollen finger, the infected tooth that feels itself, is conscious of its own individual being. The healthy eye or finger or tooth doesn't seem to exist. (*We*, 124)

To be an "I" is to feel pain, presented as the paradigm of the individual experience—and on this both characters agree.

Zamyatin's *We* has connections as well with several other works by Dostoevsky. The notion of an epidemic of self-consciousness, in *We*, recalls Raskolnikov's dream in Siberia, in the Epilogue of *Crime and Punishment* [Prestuplenie i nakazanie]:

> People who absorbed the [plague germs] became immediately like men wild and mad. But never, never did people consider themselves so wise and so unshakable in the truth as did those who were infected. Never had they considered their judgments, their scientific deductions, or their moral convictions and beliefs more unshakable. Whole villages, whole cities and peoples, were infected and went mad.[66]

Zamyatin, of course, does not mean to endorse the view (held by the society, and at times by D-503 himself) that the "soul" is a disease; he appears, however, to imply that the true plague is the certainty—or science—to which the future society (like the society in Raskolnikov's dream) adheres.[67]

The novel's title, moreover, may have Dostoevsky as one of its sources. In *Demons* ("Besy" in Russian, also translated as *The Possessed*), the villainous Verkhovensky tells Stavrogin, whom he is intending to recruit to help achieve a kind of socialist utopia:

the whole showhouse will collapse, and then we'll see how to build up an edifice of stone. For the first time! *We* will do the building, we, we alone![68]

The socialist utopia in question was also, perhaps, an inspiration to Zamyatin. A teacher summarizes as follows the system advocated by Shigalyov:

> One tenth is granted freedom of person and unlimited rights over the remaining nine tenths. These must lose their person and become something like a herd, and in unlimited obedience, through a series of regenerations, attain to primeval innocence, something like the primeval paradise. . . . The measures proposed by the author [Shigalyov] for removing the will from nine tenths of mankind and remaking them into a herd, by means of a re-educating of entire generations—are quite remarkable, based on natural facts, and extremely logical.[69]

Dostoevsky, to be sure, does not endorse this vision.

But he does not entirely repudiate it, either. Another striking parallel between Dostoevsky and *We* grows out of Shigalyov's vision of paradise at the expense of free will. The Benefactor's defense of the society, as Shane and others have noted, is reminiscent of Ivan's story about the Grand Inquisitor's confrontation with Jesus Christ in *The Brothers Karamazov* [Brat'ia Karamazovy]. The Inquisitor accuses Christ of burdening human beings with unbearable freedom, which they plead to exchange for passive security:

> No science will give them bread as long as they remain free, but in the end they will lay their freedom at our feet and say to us: "Better that you enslave us, but feed us." They will finally understand that freedom and earthly bread in plenty for everyone are inconceivable together, for never, never will they be able to share among themselves.[70]

He promises happiness:

> With us everyone will be happy, and they will no longer rebel or destroy each other, as in your freedom, everywhere.[71]

The Benefactor presents—as the same answer to a timeless prayer—happiness instead of freedom, the "ancient dream of paradise" (*We*, 207).

Dostoevsky and Zamyatin, as the numerous parallels show, ask some of the same questions, even if their answers are not necessarily the same (and even if it is not always possible to see clearly what their answers are). Both writers present characters who attack reason (and such related areas as science, knowledge, logic, and mathematics) as destroyers of the soul, as enemies of freedom—yet freedom (with such related entities as the soul and the self) is far from being an unequivocal good. Zamyatin's novel, in effect, makes real the implications of ideas expressed in Dostoevsky: Zamyatin describes—in physical detail—the Crystal Palace the Underground Man imagined, the plague Raskolnikov dreamed of, the socialist utopia Shigal-yov projected and Verkhovensky hoped to build, the end result pursued by the Grand Inquisitor.

Ayn Rand, too, was a reader of Dostoevsky. She read his major works in Russia. She named him repeatedly as a great writer, one she admired.[72] She knew the background of his work well enough to refer to his notes for the characterization of Stavrogin in *The Possessed* (or *Demons*).[73] While writing *Atlas Shrugged*, she purchased a Russian-language copy of that novel.[74] She planned—without "apology to Dostoevsky"—to use the title "Notes from the Underground" for one section of her introduction to the 1968 publication of *The Fountainhead*.[75] She considered, at one point, including in *Atlas Shrugged* a character she described as in the mode of Dostoevsky: "a man going insane in the attempt to live by the idea of charity, which he has accepted as a basic premise and axiom, accepted intelligently and consistently, i.e. with all its implications. That would be a kind of Dostoyevsky."[76]

Her literary response to Dostoevsky (a full account of which is beyond the scope of this article[77]) entailed considering the questions that concerned him. Ellsworth Toohey, for example, is in part a Dostoevskian character. He is—as Stavrogin said of Verkhovensky—a power-hungry criminal in the guise of a humanitarian socialist. Verkhovensky aims for a society of equality, with no room for ability, knowledge, or values:

> Each belongs to all, and all to each. They're all equal in their slavery. First the level of education, science, and talents is lowered. . . .
>     Listen, Stavrogin, to level the mountains is a good idea, not a ridiculous one. I'm for Shigalyov! No need for education, enough of science! . . . The thirst for education is already an aristocratic thirst. As soon as there's just a tiny bit of family or love, there's a desire for property. We'll extinguish desire; . . . we'll stifle every genius in infancy. Everything reduced to a common denominator, complete equality. . . . Slaves must have rulers.[78]

Ellsworth Toohey, who seeks to rule, intends to kill aspiration, integrity, the "capacity to recognize greatness or to achieve it. Great men can't be ruled. We don't want any great men" (*Fountainhead*, 635).[79] He intends to kill happiness.

> Happiness is self-contained and self-sufficient. Happy men have no time and no use for you. Happy men are free men. So kill their joy in living. Take away from them whatever is dear or important to them. Never let them have what they want. Make them feel that the mere fact of a personal desire is evil. Bring them to a state where saying '*I want*' is no longer a natural right, but a shameful admission. (*Fountainhead*, 636)

He expects people to be "glad to obey" (*Fountainhead*, 635)—as did Dostoevsky's Grand Inquisitor. His conclusion:

I want power. I want my world of the future. Let all live for all. Let all sacrifice and none profit. Let all suffer and none enjoy. Let progress stop. Let all stagnate. There's equality in stagnation. All subjugated to the will of all. Universal slavery— without even the dignity of a master. Slavery to slavery. A great circle—and total equality. The world of the future. (*Fountainhead*, 639)

And so—in anti-utopian fiction—it comes to pass. For all the talk of happiness in *We* and *Anthem*, authentic joy is fleeting and rare, among the "equal" slaves. Much of what Verkhovensky desired and what Toohey plotted is presented as achieved, in the joyless future worlds of *We* and *Anthem*. A key element of Toohey's vision illuminates a key difference between Ayn Rand's thinking and that implicit (and sometimes explicit) in Dostoevsky: Toohey expects progress to stop under conditions of equality—and it is clear that the novel would not want him to win. Dostoevsky's characters, by contrast, do not address the issue of progress—or see it as part of the problem; they do not, at any rate, consider material well-being to be incompatible with the projected "equality." Even Verkhovensky, who wants to "level the mountain," thinks that "there is sufficient material even without science for a thousand years to come."[80] In Zamyatin's world of the future, set approximately a millennium from his own time, the material has indeed "lasted"; in *Anthem*, deterioration is oppressively pervasive.

The Underground Man, of course, sees progress as symptomatic of the rational against which he wishes to exercise his freedom. Zamyatin's D-503 apparently agrees that freedom and selfhood are opposed to reason (the disorientation of his notes makes it hard to know exactly what he believes). The Underground Man singles out mathematics—as does Zamyatin—as the fundamental quality of the crystalline world (which the Underground Man wants to smash and which D-503 perhaps wants to flee). Ayn Rand utterly rejects the attack on reason and science: reason is an individual act, a volitional act, and is thus anything but the enemy of freedom. The hero of *Anthem*—who rebels against his society in the very act of engaging in scientific discovery—acts as an individual self for the free exercise of his mind. In *Atlas Shrugged*, where (contra the Underground Man's saying that twice-two can be five if he likes) Galt says "the noblest act you have ever performed is the act of your mind in the process of grasping that two and two make four."[81]

The Underground Man views his isolation as an illness (much as D-503 believes that having a soul is a disease). In his self-imposed psychological underground, he expresses his resentment of the solitude to which his social exclusion dooms him. Ayn Rand utterly rejects the idea that the self is a disease. In a *literalized* underground tunnel, *Anthem*'s hero cherishes his secret solitude.

And here is the heart of the matter: the "idea" of *Anthem* is individualism. The hero who exemplifies that idea is a man of reason in a society that has—to its manifest detriment—abandoned both reason and individualism.

Dostoevsky's Underground Man disparages reason—in the name of his version of individualism. Zamyatin's D-503 does the same—in a society that has not been materially damaged by its abandonment of individualism. In *Anthem*, to be an individual is to think; in Dostoevsky's Underground and in *We*, to be an individual is (frequently) to rave. The world of *We* can in fact get along, apparently, well enough without the "I"—as such Dostoevskian characters as Verkhovensky, Shigalyov, and Grand Inquisitor would expect.

Dostoevsky, speaking in his own voice, goes so far as to identity the "I" as the enemy of (Christian) love itself. At the time of the death of his first wife, not long before he ghost-wrote the notes of his Underground Man, he wrote in his own notebook:

> To love a person, *as oneself*, according to the commandment of Christ, is impossible. The law of the ego is binding on earth. *I* stands in the way. (emphasis in original)[82]

Dostoevsky, then, stands as the opposite of *Anthem*'s idea that the "I" is good—even if the "I" Dostoevsky attacks is not necessarily the same as the "I" the Underground Man asserts. Would Zamyatin agree? His D-503, as noted, dutifully points out that Christians connect the "I" with the devil, the "we" with God (*We*, 124)—but he does not appear tempted to regard his "soul" or self as an impediment to love. Hence, even when he fears that his awareness of self is a disease, he does not go so far as to condemn self entirely. But even though his novel does not clearly explain what he is for or against, his OneState suggests that he is presenting for contemplation the Crystal Palace against which the Underground Man railed—and implying that it might be time to gather some stones. He does not ask if machine-like slaves would be capable, after centuries of mandated collective life, of constructing the INTEGRAL rocket.

As a reader of Dostoevsky, Ayn Rand recognizes the fundamental difference between her idea and those expressed by his characters (and those expressed by himself). She rejects some of the elements that appear to have appealed to Zamyatin. Whereas Zamyatin and Dostoevsky present reason and science as the enemies of genuinely human life, *Anthem* shows what becomes of human life without them, and what becomes of science itself without the "I."

## ALDOUS HUXLEY

Another famous work in the anti-utopian genre is Aldous Huxley's *Brave New World* of 1932. It was, to begin with, an anti-Wellsian response to Wells's *Men Like Gods, When the Sleeper Wakes*, and *A Modern Utopia*.[83] He wrote it, he said, with no knowledge of Zamyatin's *We*[84]—but it is nonetheless a kind of imaginative sequel to it. Alexandra Aldridge sums up the situation as follows:

> *Brave New World* literally takes up where *We* left off—with the assumption that the creature must be altered in order to create a stable society. In *We*, worship of scientific rationalism had engendered a machine-like state inhabited by robotic human beings who nonetheless could be moved to rebel. Ten years later, after Pavlov and J. B. Watson, Huxley utilizes the behaviorist notion that mind and body are reducible to something like a machine, a hypothesis which in turn justifies the gene manipulation and conditioning that will insure smooth, continuous running of the human machine.[85]

The novel is not only a dystopia but an anti-utopia: it arrived by design at its present condition of mechanized misery. With the exception of the residents of what is known as the "Reservation," all inhabitants have been genetically engineered to possess various physical and intellectual attributes and "conditioned" (through recordings played while they are asleep) to be content with their assigned social roles, including their identities as Alphas, Betas, and so on, and the insistence that—sexually and in every other way as well—"everyone belongs to everyone else." *Brave New World* has three of the four criteria of the modern utopia, as listed by Hillegas: its scope is world-wide, it has an aristocracy, and it relies on technology. Huxley's world lacks the fourth criterion: it is static rather than dynamic. The inhabitants believe what they are told: that "stability" (i.e., the deliberate design of the human organism with minimal variation and virtually no decisions of consequence) is the prerequisite of "happiness." Only in the "Reservation" can one find such sources of instability as religion, Shakespeare, family ties, sexual exclusivity—and dirt and disease.

The story line reveals the discontent concealed by the routine proclamations of contentment. For example: Bernard Marx, attracted to Lenina Crowe, resents the very idea of her sexual involvement with others; meanwhile she herself is rebuked for the social indiscretion of seeing Henry Foster exclusively for four straight months. Helmholtz, a poet who has not been challenged by his official assignments, feels drawn to write "rhymes of Solitude," a kind of poetry he has never yet written: "I feel . . . as though I were just beginning to have something to write about. As though I were beginning to be able to use that power I feel I've got inside me—that extra, latent power. Something seems to be coming to me" (*Brave New World*, 123).[86] John Savage, who travels from the "Reservation" to the "modern" world, is unwilling to embrace the new world, but unable to escape it. In the end, he is responsible for the death of the one woman he cared for, and he takes his own life.

"Huxley's chief strategy," as Hillegas points out, "was to show that the conditioned happiness of *Brave New World* cuts men off from deep experience, keeps them from being fully human."[87] One of the best-known scenes in the novel is a dramatic confrontation: a sage but sinister spokesperson (Mustapha

Mond, the Controller) explains the principles behind the world to a resistant listener (John Savage). It is similar to the scenes that feature Zamyatin's Benefactor and Dostoevsky's Verkhovensky and Grand Inquisitor.

> "It would upset the whole social order if men started doing things on their own. . . ."
> "You can't have a lasting civilization without plenty of pleasant vices. . . ."
> "My dear young friend, " said Mustapha Mond, "civilization has absolutely no need of nobility or heroism. These things are symptoms of political inefficiency. In a properly organized society like ours, nobody has any opportunities for being noble. . . . The greatest care is taken to prevent you from loving anybody too much. There's no such thing as a divided allegiance; you're so conditioned that you can't help doing what you ought to do. . . . And if ever, by some unlucky chance, anything unpleasant should somehow happen, why, there's always [the drug] *soma* to give you a holiday from the facts."
> "But I don't want comfort. I want God, I want poetry, I want real danger, I want freedom, I want goodness. I want sin. . . ."
> "In fact," said Mustapha Mond, "you're claiming the right to be unhappy. . . . Not to mention the right to grow old and ugly and impotent; the right to have syphilis and cancer; the right to have too little to eat. . . ."
> "I claim them all," said the Savage at last.
> Mustapha Mond shrugged his shoulders. "You're welcome," he said. (*Brave New World*, 161–63)

The reference to pain makes this text parallel with the depictions of the Underground Man and D-503—as if feeling pain is the only way to experience the self.[88]

The universe of this novel is repugnant—and not only in the ways Huxley intended. Most literary works in the dystopian tradition—such as "The Places of the Gods," *The Time Machine*, "The Machine Stops," "Twilight," *We*, and *Anthem*—project another time or another place that is positively good. But there is no good in *Brave New World*, not in anything resembling reality. Reading Shakespeare (whose language stands for what the "modern" world lacks) does not improve John Savage's life. The portrayal of sexuality is particularly unpleasant. Everything is tainted and ugly—physically, morally, and often both.

There is no evidence that Ayn Rand read this work.[89] She would have agreed with designating totalitarian control as a target: life without freedom is not human life. She would have agreed with Savage that freedom is desirable whatever the price. An exchange in the play *Think Twice* (written in 1939, unproduced in her lifetime) expresses a sentiment similar to that of John Savage, above, speaking to the Controller.

> ADRIENNE. Let me go, Walter. Give me my freedom.
> BRECKENRIDGE. Freedom—for what? Freedom to hurt yourself.

ADRIENNE. Yes!—if necessary. To make mistakes. To fail. To be alone. To be rotten. To be selfish. But to be free.[90]

She would have disagreed with much else, including the dismal outlook on life. She would have detected at once the false alternative Huxley ultimately came to realize as "the most serious defect in the story, which is this. The Savage is offered only two alternatives, an insane life in Utopia, or the life of a primitive in an Indian village, a life more human in some respects, but in others hardly less queer and abnormal."[91] She would have observed that Huxley, like Zamyatin, sees technological advancement as compatible with political slavery, as if the mind could work just as well, if not better, without being free. She would not have seen in *Brave New World*—any more than in *When the Sleeper Wakes* or *We* or "The Places of the Gods"—the most important element in *Anthem*: her idea.

At one point, Bernard appears to be groping for his "I." He tells Lenina that he wants to look at the ocean without the "beastly noise" of the radio. When he does, he says: "It makes me feel as though . . . I were more *me*, if you see what I mean. More on my own, not so completely a part of something else. Not just a cell in the social body." He wishes to be "happy in some other way," i.e., "not in everybody else's way" (*Brave New World*, 60–61). But he never comes close to grasping what it would mean to think for himself and to live for his own sake; he craves the esteem of others, and relies on their judgment. Although he is "unstable" enough to be exiled to the islands for nonconformists, he is never intellectually independent. His quasi-rebellion, like the Savage's withdrawal to a lighthouse, is futile.

Huxley's world is like Wells's London of 2100 and Zamyatin's OneState: all have technological progress, political totalitarianism, and spiritual emptiness. His resolution has the gray drabness of resignation. Any rebellion is doomed. Any escape is temporary. Huxley implicitly blames—on equal terms—Vladimir Lenin and Henry Ford for the conditions (and conditioning) in his despicable "new" world—much as Zamyatin applied the word "yoke" to both reason and the State. Ayn Rand, as the Dark Ages of her collectivist future make clear, disagrees. And she is not alone.

## GEORGE ORWELL

George Orwell set out to write fiction in the mode of Zamyatin. Orwell was interested in reading *We* as soon as he heard of it; he commented that he himself was thinking of writing a dystopian novel, and that he was on the lookout for books of this type.[92] He read it in French translation somewhere between June 1944 and the end of 1945.[93] In 1946, when he reviewed *We* for the left-socialist *Tribune*, he remarked that "Aldous

Huxley's *Brave New World* must be partly derived from it. Both books deal with the rebellion of the primitive human spirit against a rationalised, mechanised, painless world, and both stories are supposed to take place about six hundred years hence."[94] Orwell describes not only the devices of *We*—the number-names, houses, uniforms, food, recreation, and sex arrangements—but the principle: "The Single State is ruled over by a personage known as The Benefactor, who is annually re-elected by the entire population, the vote being always unanimous. The guiding principle of the State is that happiness and freedom are incompatible. In the Garden of Eden man was happy, but in his folly he demanded freedom and was driven out into the wilderness. Now the Single State has restored his happiness by removing his freedom."[95]

Of the two books, Orwell prefers Zamyatin's. In *We*, there are unhappy dissenters tormented by "imagination," as well as those who plot rebellion and indulge in tobacco and alcohol. Huxley, by contrast, assumes that people will no longer have a "desire for liberty" or any other troublesome emotions or disturbing thoughts, because all troublesome aspects of the organism are controlled by drugs, pre-natal treatment, and hypnosis. He also notes, with favor, the implicit cruelty of Zamyatin's world. The machine of the Benefactor is the guillotine, an improved model. "The execution is, in fact, a human sacrifice, and the scene describing it is given deliberately the colour of the sinister slave civilisations of the ancient world. It is this intuitive grasp of irrational side of totalitarianism—human sacrifice, cruelty as an end in itself—the worship of a leader who is credited with divine attributes—that makes Zamyatin's book superior to Huxley's."[96]

Orwell, finally, speculates that Zamyatin's target may not be restricted to Soviet Russia. He observes that "conditions in Russia in 1923 were not such that anyone would revolt against them on the ground that life was becoming too safe and comfortable. What Zamyatin seems to be aiming at is not any particular country but the implied aims of industrial civilisation."[97]

Orwell's novel has features in common with *We*, notably the regimentation of human life and the secret rebellion against that regimentation.[98] But the two are also very different, as William Steinhoff points out:

> There is too much in *1984* that does not appear in *We*—the superstates, the direct attack on totalitarianism, permanent warfare, the dreary squalor, such novelties as doublethink and Newspeak, the disappearance of belief in objective reality, the substitution of "love" for law, the disaffected and defeated intellectual, the importance of history, tradition, and memory—and the ruling intellectuals of the Inner Party—to leave much ground for the claim that Orwell took *We* as his model.
>
> To sharpen the contrast, one might say that *We* exhibits in the Hour Tables the mathematical perfection of human reason and conduct—objectivity carried to its

utmost limits—and it is against the dominance of rationality that Zamyatin, like Dostoevsky, protests. But in *1984* human reason has turned into its opposite—pure subjectivity. What the Inner Party wants to create is a "collective solipsism" which destroys objective reality, including the reality of mathematics and the reality of common sense. Zamyatin revolts against the ideal of the machine; Orwell revolts against the ideal of ideology. In both books humanity is victimized, for in *We* the crime is to turn human beings into machines, and in *1984* the crime is to turn human beings into lunatics.[99]

Most of the features found in *1984* and not in *We* are (with the exception of constant war) found in some form in *Anthem*. Orwell's *1984*, in these areas, is much closer to Ayn Rand's *Anthem* than it is to Zamyatin's *We*.

Of the many other authors identified as important to Orwell (among them Swift, Kipling, Jack London, Cyril Connolly, G. K. Chesterton, and Arthur Koestler[100]) the most important in our context is Dostoevsky. Orwell knew Dostoevsky's fiction well.[101]

But Orwell has a quarrel with Dostoevsky, as he does with Zamyatin. Winston Smith's confrontation with O'Brien is, within the narrative structure, parallel to Christ's encounter with Dostoevsky's Grand Inquisitor, whose argument, as I have noted, is parallel with those of Huxley's Mustapha Mond and Zamyatin's Benefactor: all three say that freedom is the price of happiness, and that it is right for people to pay it. In the world of *1984*, by contrast, human happiness was never part of the plan. Winston Smith, assuming that O'Brien intends to use the same justification as the Grand Inquisitor, expects him to say that people cannot "endure liberty or face the truth . . . the choice for mankind lay between freedom and happiness . . . the Party was the eternal guardian of the weak" (*1984*, 216).[102] O'Brien stuns Winston with a simple statement of an unbearable fact: "Power is not a means; it is an end. The object of persecution is persecution. The object of torture is torture. The object of power is power. . . . Power is in tearing human minds to pieces and putting them together again in new shapes of your own choosing" (*1984*, 217, 220). As George Woodcock observes, "what distinguishes it [*1984*] even more strikingly from previous Utopias and even anti-Utopias is that the pretense of providing happiness as a compensation for the loss of freedom is not maintained. Even the synthetic pleasures and comforts promised by Zamyatin and Huxley no longer exist."[103]

The quarrel with Dostoevsky extends as well to the issue of reason. Mathematics, which stood for Dostoevsky and Zamyatin (and, implicitly, for Huxley as well) as the enemy, is the last bulwark of rationality in Orwell.

The Party told you to reject the evidence of your eyes and ears. It was their final, most essential command. . . . The solid world exists, its laws do not change. Stones are hard, water is wet, objects unsupported fall toward the earth's center. . . .

*Freedom is the freedom to say that two plus two make four. If that is granted, all else follows.* (*1984*, 69)

Such statements are in the spirit of *Anthem*—and contrary to the implications of *We*.

Orwell's hero not only attempts to uphold reason and reality, but identifies his independence as inviolable—in a way that would not be possible for Dostoevsky's Underground Man or Zamyatin's D-503. He agrees with what Julia tells him: "It's the one thing they can't do. They can make you say anything—*anything*—but they can't make you believe it. They can't get inside you" (*1984*, 137).

And whereas in *We* the engineers work well in harness for the building of the INTEGRAL rocket ship—and science is a bad thing—Orwell states, through the secret book of Goldstein, that progress (with minor exceptions) is not possible without freedom. The technological brilliance envisioned by Zamyatin, we are told, could never have come to be.

> The world of today is a bare, hungry, dilapidated place compared with the world that existed before 1914, and still more so if compared with the imaginary future to which the people of that period looked forward. In the early twentieth century, the vision of a future society unbelievably rich, leisured, orderly and efficient—a glittering antiseptic world of glass and steel and snow-white concrete—was part of the consciousness of nearly every literate person. Science and technology were developing at prodigious speed, and it seemed natural to assume that they would go on developing. This failed to happen, partly because of an impoverishment caused by a long series of wars and revolutions, partly because scientific and technical progress depended on the empirical habit of thought, which could not survive in a strictly regimented society. As a whole the world is more primitive today than it was fifty years ago. (*1984*, 155–56)

From the broken clock to the broken lift (both on the first page), the world is falling apart, and, we are told, is going backwards. *Anthem* shows a further regression to the primitive, and for a similar reason.

Orwell's *1984*—unlike *We*—shares with *Anthem* the observation that a decline in the quality of human life is accompanied by a decline in language. Although the word "I" has not (yet?) disappeared, the language of this world is being drained of dangerous words in order to eliminate the corresponding ideas. The principles of "Newspeak" will lead eventually to the obliteration of the first person, which will be deemed inessential. Perhaps the world of *1984* is similar to the "graceless years of transition" mentioned in *Anthem* (103), which would make Orwell's novel a sort of prequel to Ayn Rand's.

A full account of Orwell's politics is beyond my scope here. He was exceptionally concerned with the role of ideas in history and contemporary political life. He wrote—implicitly in *1984* and explicitly elsewhere—about the harm done by intellectuals (Catholics, Stalinists, and pacifist/Fascists) who sought or supported power and told lies.[104] He blames them for "the amputation of the soul."[105] He said, regarding his purpose in writing *1984*: "I believe also that totalitarian ideas have taken root in the minds of intellectuals everywhere, and I have tried to draw these ideas out to their logical consequences."[106]

Of all the books so far discussed, *1984* is the one that comes closest to the idea of *Anthem*—and to the related ideas of *The Fountainhead* as well. Although there is no evidence in his letters or published writings that Orwell read either, the same is true for other books that he is known to have read. He did not always credit his sources.[107] It is possible and likely that he read *Anthem*. Because he was on the lookout for books like *We*, he might have been interested in reading *Anthem* if he had run across it. Malcolm Muggeridge, his friend, reviewed *Anthem* favorably in 1938, when it was published in England.[108] And, if he read *Anthem* and recognized its merit, he might have read *The Fountainhead* as well when it was published in 1947 (while he was working on *1984*). O'Brien's speeches, in which all becomes clear, differ from Dostoevsky (and Zamyatin) on exactly the point that is the center of Toohey's speech. The purpose of power—as O'Brien says, chillingly—is power. Zamyatin's Benefactor would never have said that—but Ellsworth Toohey, who intends to rule, would and did. O'Brien tells Winston that "power is power over human beings. Over the body—but, above all, over the mind" (*1984*, 218). Toohey knows that "only mental control over others is true control."[109] Orwell's *1984* concretizes the future according to Ellsworth Toohey: "A world where the thought of each man will not be his own, but an attempt to guess the thought of the brain of his neighbor. . . . Since all must agree with all" (*Fountainhead*, 637).

Orwell's overall philosophy, of course, is not identical with Ayn Rand's— as both would have recognized. When she read his *Animal Farm* in 1946, it made her "sick"; she thought it was not anti-Communist (as it was alleged to be), but rather "the mushiest and most maudlin preachment of Communism . . . I have seen in a long time."[110] As for *1984*, she was familiar with it, and, according to her friend Edward Hunter, believed that it had been influenced by *Anthem*.[111]

Although Orwell's novel shows considerable understanding of the way totalitarian government and its fundamental principles threaten the mind, his conclusion speaks of despair: he believes that evil can win. As in *We* and Wells's *When the Sleeper Wakes*, the rebellion is doomed: Winston learns and struggles only to lose, and to lose in a sickening way. Winston (like D-503) betrays the woman he loves, and ends by capitulating to his destroyer. "He loved Big Brother" (245). No matter what is done to the hero of *Anthem*, he would never succumb in spirit. Hence Orwell's narrative line shows that the "I" is not in fact powerful enough to prevail.

Winston had said:" There is something in the universe—I don't know, some spirit, some principle—that you will never overcome. The spirit of Man." O'Brien replied: "If you are a man, Winston, you are the last man" (*1984*, 222). Orwell, ultimately, agrees with O'Brien. Orwell's original title for *1984* was "The Last Man in Europe"—which implies that the "I" could be killed. In his own last novel, written at the end of his life, Orwell viewed evil as metaphysically greater than even a man who has learned what it is to be a man.

In Ayn Rand's novels, by contrast, even a tragic ending shows that struggle is inspiring and makes life valuable, even if death is the end.[112] If Orwell's novel ends with the love of Big Brother, *Anthem* ends with the knowledge that the world of the "brothers" will never defeat him. The Spirit of Man that Orwell sees as doomed, is in *Anthem* the "word which will not die, should we all perish in battle. The word which can never die on this earth, for it is the heart of it and the meaning and the glory" (104–5). It is the "sacred word: Ego"—the idea of *Anthem*.

## *ANTHEM* AND AYN RAND'S OTHER FICTION

The uniqueness of *Anthem*—as distinct from such anti-utopias as *We* or such dystopias as "The Places of the Gods"—is the identification of the cause of the disaster. The idea of *Anthem*, the idea that Ayn Rand had from her youth in Soviet Russia, is the loss of the word "I," with all that that entails. The disappearance of the word "I"—the first-person singular—meant that the word "we"—the first-person plural—took its place (as, in contemporary English, "you" is both singular and plural). The significance of this disappearance is that it obliterates human life. For a man, life as a man means life as a single, individual man with a unique consciousness. If human beings are deemed interchangeable, so that any differences between one and the other are deemed trivial, then there is no human life. The "monster We" takes with it, when it destroys the "I," the "steel towers, the flying ships, the power wires" (102). No other work in the genre posited such a cause.

The key event, the climax, is an intellectual event: the hero's discovery of the word "I"; he recognizes that the concept it names is in fact what has disappeared from his world, and he resolves to fight to bring that concept back to the world. The heroes of "The Places of the Gods" and "The Machine Stops" make important discoveries about past or present circumstances, but their discoveries concern facts, not ideas. The intellectual event is entirely private. The hero discovers the word through his reading: he does not record the specific moment of his discovery, and he does not share his discovery with the woman he loves until he has taken several days to experience it on his own. None of the other works discussed presents an intellectual event as its key event.

The first-person narration, to be sure, may have been suggested to Ayn Rand by Benét's John (and by Zamyatin's D-503, Dostoevsky's Underground Man, and Wells's Time Traveller before him). It is not her usual choice. She had chosen first-person narration when she was learning to write in English, for the early short story "The Husband I Bought," but uses it only rarely in her full-length fiction (e.g., Jeff Allen's account of Starnesville in *Atlas Shrugged* and John Galt's first-person version of the start of the strike). Why would she choose it here? Perhaps because the use of the first-person-plural—where the first-person-singular is needed—shocks and annoys the reader into a state of anger with the world here presented. Because (perhaps) it allowed her to adapt to her own purposes the Russian literary device of the *skaz*, in which marked language conveys the point of view of a narrator who knows less than the author and thus functions simultaneously as narration and characterization. But most of all because the first person is exactly what she needs for a book about the discovery of individualism, of personhood itself.

*Anthem* is different from Ayn Rand's full-length novels in focusing on the intellectual event of the *discovery* of individualism. But, as she wrote in her open letter "To the Readers of *The Fountainhead*,"[113] she formed the intention to write about individualism at the same day and hour when she decided to become a writer. The very writing of this piece showed the importance for her of the first person singular. Her assignment was to produce a short biographical sketch. "After many tries, I found it impossible to do it in the third person, as an article about me written by somebody else."[114] Because all of her work deals with the theme of individualism itself, it is therefore right to see crucial links between this text and others, especially her novels. *Anthem*—in essence and even in details—is more like Ayn Rand's other fiction than it is like anything else in world literature.

In *We the Living*, Andrei's speech to the Party Club makes explicit this theme:

> Every man worth calling a man lives for himself. The one who doesn't—doesn't live at all. You cannot change it. You cannot change it because that's the way man is born, alone, complete, an end in himself. No laws, no Party, no G.P.U. will ever kill that thing in man which knows how to say 'I.' You cannot enslave man's mind, you can only destroy it. (408)[115]

The world we see in *Anthem* demonstrates the truth of Andrei's statement. The We-world has not enslaved the mind, only destroyed it, but a hero recovers the Unspeakable Word and expects to make it count again, because that which the earlier heroes thought was lost can never be lost. Andrei's formulation, drawn from the 1959 edition, is more explicit than the 1936 version, especially in referring to the knowledge of how to say "I"—the very subject of *Anthem*.

The idea, though, is present in Kira's speech to Andre: the idea that the distinct, individual consciousness is what makes one a living being:

> I was born and I knew I was alive and I knew what I wanted. What do you think is alive in me? Why do you think I'm alive? Because I have a stomach and eat and digest the food? Because I breathe and work and produce more food to digest? Or because I know what I want, and that something which knows how to want—isn't that life itself? (*We the Living*, 404)

*Anthem* is an extrapolation, in fantasy, of the ultimate purpose and nature of the collectivist state of Soviet Russia, in its denial of the value of the individual. The two are, of course, far apart regarding a primary literary attribute: *We the Living* is Ayn Rand's most tightly plotted novel, and *Anthem*, she comments, is plotless. But *Anthem*, in addition to sharing with *We the Living* an individualist theme and the specific reference to the "I," has some other parallels (not surprising, given that the two were written close in time).

One is that characters are described as understanding without words. Kira "had known something which no human words could ever tell and she knew it now" (*We the Living*, 464). When Liberty says "You are not one of our brothers, Equality 7-2751, for we do not wish you to be," he thinks: "We can not say what they meant, for there are no words for their meaning, but we know it without words and we knew it then" (43). In both cases, there are in fact words for the experiences—for the sanctity of life and for the glory of love—but it is also true that the characters reach their understanding without words, and are described as being conscious of that understanding at a particular moment.

Another is the description of the heroines' eyes. Liberty's eyes "were dark and hard and glowing" (39)—and in the manuscript, "as a storm cloud" (36A). Kira's are the "gray of storm clouds" (*We the Living*, 44); the description suggests intensity and barely-controlled passion. The heroines, moreover, have in common the willingness to forsake all else, to leave everything they know, in order to follow the heroes immediately and without question (in Liberty's case, without even being asked). *We the Living*, moreover, has a parallel to Liberty's yielding control of her actions and future to the hero's wishes, her begging him not to send her away—a submission and entreaty more explicit and extreme, especially in the 1938 edition, than in any other romantic relationship in Ayn Rand's fiction. The story of "Kira's Viking" (cut from the manuscript) ends with the queen-priestess of the sacred city at the feet of the conquering Viking, her hair sweeping the steps of the tower, her breasts touching the ground, her hands "still and helpless on the steps, the palms turned up, hungry in silent entreaty. But it was not mercy they were begging of him."[116] In the 1938 version of *Anthem*, Liberty is described as follows: "Then they knelt, and their golden head was bowed before us, and their hands lay at our feet, palms up, limp and pleading."[117] In both cases, the submitting women are shown elsewhere as strong and defiant.

"Kira's Viking" also includes another sentence that looks forward to *Anthem*: "And the earth lay still, tense in reverent waiting, as if its very heart and meaning were rising to the morning sky; and the morning was like a slow, triumphant overture for the song to come."[118]

In the 1938 version of *Anthem*, we see the motif of the "waiting" of the earth:

> Beyond the window, the moon is dripping silver upon the leaves, upon the peaks of mountains far away. The earth is still and blue and white. The earth seems waiting, waiting for some order which is to come from us. This earth is new, this world is ours to rule. We cannot know what word we are to give, nor what great deed this world expects of us. But it is waiting. We know that it is telling us it has great gifts to lay before us, but it wishes a greater gift from us. We are to bring the miracle that shall awaken life and give its heart, its aim, its highest meaning to all this silent beauty sleeping beyond the valley, beneath a cloudless sky.[119]

The passages just quoted, of course, also look forward to *The Fountainhead*, which Ayn Rand was planning during the summer when she wrote *Anthem*. In the opening scene of the novel, Roark looks at nature, as did *Anthem*'s hero, expecting to rule it.

> He looked at the granite. To be cut, he thought, and made into walls. He looked at a tree. To be split and made into rafters. He looked at a streak of rust on the stone and thought of iron ore under the ground. To be melted and to emerge as girders against the sky.
>
> These rocks, he thought, are here for me; waiting for the drill, the dynamite and my voice; waiting to be split, ripped, pounded, reborn; waiting for the shape my hands will give them. (16)

And the post-*Fountainhead* version of *Anthem*, not surprisingly, names—more clearly than did the 1938 version—the human function of shaping nature to our needs:

> And now we look upon the earth and sky. This spread of naked rock and peaks and moonlight is like a world ready to be born, a world that waits. It seems to us it asks a sign from us, a spark, a first commandment. We cannot know what word we are to give, nor what great deed this earth expects to witness. We know it waits. It seems to say it has great gifts to lay before us, but it wishes a greater gift from us. We are to speak. We are to give its goal, its highest meaning to all this glowing space of rock and sky. (92–93)

*Anthem*, like *The Fountainhead*, celebrates man's control of nature. The "meaning of life," as Roark says, is one's work: "The material the earth offers you and what you make of it" (*Fountainhead*, 551).

The connections between *Anthem* and *The Fountainhead* are intimate and fundamental. Ayn Rand frequently described these texts as alike, with *Anthem* as an "ancestor" of *The Fountainhead* , with the "same theme, though in an entirely different form and on a much smaller scale."[120] In 1944, she told her agent that *Anthem* was "too short a book, on the same theme" to be published right after *The Fountainhead*.[121] Roark's speech, surveying history as the record of the creators martyred for their discoveries, specifically names Prometheus "chained to a rock and torn by vultures—because he had stolen the fire of the gods" (*Fountainhead*, 678). "Prometheus" is the name chosen by the hero of *Anthem* when he names his nature.

Both heroes look back on the price paid by the martyrs. The hero of *Anthem* pays tribute to the discoverers ("every beam had come from the thought of some one man, each in his day down the ages" [102]), to those who fought the Councils of Scholars, to those who "perished with their banners smeared by their own blood" (103). He wishes he could tell them that "that which they died to save can never perish" (104). The hero of *The Fountainhead* pays tribute to the "self-sufficient, self-motivated, self-generated" creators who achieved "the things which are the glory of mankind," to their battle, to their suffering. He is willing to spend ten years in prison as an "act of loyalty" to "every creator who ever lived and was made to suffer"—but he expects to win, as he believes that all "men of unborrowed vision" have fought, suffered, paid—and won (*Fountainhead*, 678–79, 685, 678).

The enemy principle, too, is the same in both. The world we see in *Anthem* is the material form of Ellsworth Toohey's dream, which I quoted earlier: "Let progress stop. Let all stagnate. There's equality in stagnation. All subjugated to the will of all. Universal slavery—without even the dignity of a master. Slavery to slavery. A great circle—and a total equality. The world of the future" (*Fountainhead*, 639).

*The Fountainhead* also contains verbal parallels with *Anthem* and its central device: the word "I" as an expression of the concept of individualism. We hear it in Roark's reply to Dominique when she says that, if he asked, she would live only as his wife or property:

> If you married me now, I would become your whole existence. But I would not want you then. You would not want yourself—and so you would not love me long. To say "I love you" one must know first how to say the "I." (*Fountainhead*, 376)

We hear it again when Dominique allows Peter Keating to understand what is missing in their marriage, and in him, i.e., the "thing that thinks and values and makes decisions" (*Fountainhead*, 425). He tells her:

> "You're not here. You've never been here. If you'd tell me that the curtains in this room are ghastly and if you'd rip them off and put up some you like—

something of you would be real, here, in this room. But you never have. You've never told the cook what dessert you liked for dinner. You're not here, Dominique. You're not alive. Where's your I?"

"Where's yours, Peter?" she asked quietly. (*Fountainhead*, 425)

She continues:

"My real soul, Peter? It's real only when it's independent—you've discovered that, haven't you? It's real only when it chooses curtains and desserts—you're right about that—curtains, desserts and religions, Peter, and the shapes of buildings." (*Fountainhead*, 426)

Dominique, in speaking of the "I," refers to what amount to the Virtues of Preference, on whatever scale.

Another—and subtler—allusion to the "I" appears in the characterization of Gail Wynand. When he reads in Ellsworth Toohey's post-Cortlandt column an attack on Roark's "antisocial individualism," he hastens to his desk.

He had to write the editorial that would explain and counteract. He had to hurry. He felt no right to any minute that passed with the thing unwritten.

The pressure disappeared with the *first word* he put on paper. He thought—while his hand moved rapidly—what a power there was in words; later, for those who heard them, but first for *the one* who found them; a healing power, a solution, like the breaking of a barrier. He thought, perhaps the basic secret the scientists have never discovered, the first fount of life, is that which happens when *a thought takes shape in words*. (*Fountainhead*, 642, emphasis added)

This passage (which was further developed in the manuscript of the novel) underlines the significance of language.[122] Finding the words—even the first word—is a victory for Wynand, as losing the words—especially the Unspeakable Word—was, for the society in *Anthem*, a defeat.

But there is more. In his writing here, in his passion to express for the first time his own values in the pages of *The Banner*, the newspaper he had called his: "He had dropped his usual editorial 'we'" (*Fountainhead*, 642). To disown Toohey and to defend Roark, he needs a word—and a soul—that he has not had occasion to use before: he needs the "I."

But after he yields to the *Banner's* board of directors, after he tragically abandons his crusade, he buys a copy of the newspaper to read its editorial. "He thought: it is right that I should be the last to learn what I have said" (*Fountainhead*, 661). And, when he does, he reads an editorial signed "Gail Wynand"—beginning with the editorial "we." The "we" he tried to free himself from, is restored, and replaces his own voice. Literally and spiritually, Wynand has lost his "I."

Has he lost it permanently? After the trial, Roark writes in a letter: "What you think you've lost can neither be lost nor found" (*Fountainhead*, 664).

The letter is returned unopened. Roark's statement may reflect the passage from Nietzsche's *Beyond Good and Evil* that stood at the head of the manuscript of *The Fountainhead*:

> it is some fundamental certainty which a noble soul has about itself, something which is not to be sought, is not to be found, and perhaps, also, is not to be lost.—*The noble soul has reverence for itself*. (*Fountainhead*, x)

The hero of *Anthem*, in a similar spirit, contemplates the heroes who, as we recall, died with their *banners* smeared with their own blood; he wishes he could tell them that the battle they lost can never be lost.

And Roark—speaking for the last time to the man he loved best in the world, and speaking also of the world itself—tells Wynand the same thing:

> "Mankind will never destroy itself, Mr. Wynand. Nor should it think of itself as destroyed. Not so long as it does things such as this."
> "As what?"
> "As the Wynand Building." (*Fountainhead*, 691)

Wynand, in fact, has devoted some thought to himself as an entity, to his *self*. He imagines saying, to a "supreme judge":

> I am Gail Wynand, the man who has committed every crime except the foremost one: that of ascribing futility to the wonderful fact of existence and seeking justification beyond myself. This is my pride: that now, thinking of the end, I do not cry like all the men of my age: but what was the use and the meaning? *I* [emphasis his] was the use and meaning. I, Gail Wynand. That I lived and that I acted. (*Fountainhead*, 550)

His explicitness here recalls the discovery of the self on the part of the hero of *Anthem*.

> I wished to know the meaning of things. I am the meaning. I wished to find a warrant for being. I need no warrant for being, and no word of sanction upon my being. I am the warrant and the sanction. (94)

The 1938 version of this passage refers to "sanction," but not to "meaning." By the time she revised *Anthem* after writing *The Fountainhead*, she had found more of the words she needed, including the one she used for Wynand.

In the 1938 version of the following paragraph in the eleventh chapter of *Anthem*, the hero states:

> All things come to my judgment, and I weigh all things, and I seal upon them my "Yes" or my "No." (128)

This phrasing (which, as Robert Mayhew notes, has a parallel in Nietzsche) has a counterpart in *The Fountainhead*, where it is clearer than in the original *Anthem*. Roark tells Wynand:

> What you feel in the presence of the thing you admire is just one word—"Yes."
> . . . But the ability to say "Yes" or "No" is the essence of all ownership. It's your ownership of your own ego. Your soul, if you wish. Your soul has a single basic function—the act of valuing. "Yes" or "No," "I wish" or "I do not wish." You can't say "yes" without saying "I." (*Fountainhead*, 539)

The choice of "Yes" or "No," then, is tantamount—in *The Fountainhead* as in *Anthem*—to the "I." The same language appears, moreover, in Ayn Rand's notes of April 26, 1946, for *Atlas Shrugged*, written very close in time to the revision work on *Anthem*. Ayn Rand commented that the parasites, her villains, "will never say 'yes' nor 'no'—on anything."[123]

A further indication that *Anthem* is part of Ayn Rand's ongoing intellectual work appears in her journal during the earliest planning of *The Fountainhead*. In her notes of December 4, 1935, she writes:

> Returning to the immediate purpose of the book: A new set of values is needed to combat this modern dreariness, whether it be communism (which I may not include in the book), or the sterile, hopeless cynicism of the modern age. That new faith is *Individualism* in all its deepest meaning and implications, such as has never been preached before: individualism of the spirit, of ethics, or philosophy, not merely the good old "rugged individualism" of small shopkeepers. Individualism as a religion and a code, not merely as an economic practice. . . . A revival (or perhaps the first birth) of the word *"I"* as the holiest of holies and the reason of reasons.
> . . . We have developed technically—oh yes!—but spiritually we are far below Renaissance Italy. In fact, we *have no* spiritual life in the grand manner, in the sense it used to be understood.
> Is it the fault of machines? Is the twentieth century incapable and unfit for my spiritual exaltation? Or—is it only that little word "I," which, after twenty centuries of Christianity's efforts, has been erased from human consciousness, and along with it took everything that *was* human consciousness?[124]

Ayn Rand, at this point, did not state the incompatibility between collectivism and continued technological development. She did, however, underline the word "I" itself as a symbol, and as something that could be lost. She identified worship of the ego as the proper kind of reverence. She disagreed with the idea that machines (as Zamyatin or Huxley maintained) were responsible for the spiritual debasement of the modern age. Less than two years later, she took a "writer's vacation" from planning *The Fountainhead* to write about the loss of the "I," in an anthem to the sacredness of that word.

And, although Ayn Rand said that *Anthem* did not have a plot,[125] it is worth noting that the story contains a narrative element significant in the plots of the novels to follow, i.e., the double creative achievement. In all three works, the heroes begin by accomplishing feats of genius in the material world: the light bulb in *Anthem*, the buildings in *The Fountainhead*, the motor in *Atlas Shrugged*. They go on to identify life-or-death principles in the spiritual realm: the word "I," the principle of first-handedness, the morality of life. The principles are necessary to protect the feats of genius.

All three books, too, share an emphasis articulated in the description of Monadnock Valley, from the perspective of Steven Mallory:

> There is no glory in war, and no beauty in crusades of men. But this was a battle, this was an army and a war—and the highest experience in the life of every man who took part in it. Why? What was the root of the difference and the law to explain it? . . . The hills rose to the sky around them, as a wall of protection. And they had another protection—the architect who walked among them, down the snow or the grass of the hillsides, over the boulders and the piled planks, to the drafting tables, to the derricks, to the tops of rising walls—the man who had made this possible—the thought in the mind of that man—and not the content of that thought, nor the result, not the vision that had created Monadnock Valley, nor the will that had made it real—but the method of his thought, the rule of its function—the method and rule which were not like those of the world beyond the hills. That stood on guard over the valley and over the crusaders within it. (*Fountainhead*, 508)

The reference to a battle, an army, a war, and a crusade suggest the conclusion of *Anthem*. Although the hero's fort is located on a mountain rather than in a valley, other elements are the same: he plans to lead a crusade of men, he is prepared to fight, and he expects to win because of the power of his mind: "For they have nothing to fight me with, save the brute forces of their numbers. I have my mind" (100).

Monadnock Valley and the mountaintop, though, are significantly parallel to Atlantis, the valley of *Atlas Shrugged*. There too a group of chosen (and choosing) men are engaged in a war with everything on the outside, and again they are protected by "the method of [a man's] thought, the rule of its function." The hero of *Anthem* plans to "build a barrier of wires around my home, and across the paths which lead to my home; a barrier light as a cobweb, more impassable than granite; a barrier my brothers will never be able to cross" (100). Galt's Gulch was protected by the ray screen, a similarly light but impassable barrier.

There are additional parallels. John Galt, Francisco tells Dagny, is "Prometheus who changed his mind. After centuries of being torn by vultures in payment for having brought to men the fire of the gods, he broke his chains and he withdrew his fire—until the day when men withdraw their vultures."[126] The hero of *Anthem* takes the name of Prometheus, and pays tribute to the way the spirit of man broke through chains (101–2). Galt, like the hero of *Anthem*, undergoes torture, without surrender. The Prometheus of *Atlas Shrugged* does by design what the Prometheus of *Anthem* did under force: he works at a menial job, the equivalent of the position of street-sweeper in *Anthem*. The hero of *Anthem*—in saying "I ask none to live for me, nor do I live for any others" (96)—speaks virtually the words of Galt's oath: "I swear—by my life and my love of it—that I will never live for the sake of another man, nor ask another man to live for mine."[127]

From the perspective of the utopian, dystopian, and anti-utopian novels, *Atlas Shrugged* includes elements of all three. Starnesville is the anti-utopia: a planned community gone wrong. The world at large is a dystopia (but *not* an anti-utopia); it has disintegrated, but not by design, because of bad ideas—and because of the "Prometheus who changed his mind." And Atlantis is a genuine utopia, as a small-scale model, of proper human life based on a proper philosophy: the title for the second chapter of Part 3, accordingly, is "The Utopia of Greed." The chapters in which Dagny visits Atlantis are, in narrative approach, somewhat like the "tours" by which foreigners are introduced to utopian societies in such works as Thomas More's *Utopia*, Francis Bacon's *The New Atlantis*, and Edward Bellamy's *Looking Backward*.

*Anthem*, although uncharacteristic of Ayn Rand's fiction in both length and type, is nonetheless uniquely hers, and part of her ongoing progress toward her goal as a writer. She conceived of *Anthem* in Russia, before she wrote any of her novels. She wrote *Anthem* in 1937, while she was planning *The Fountainhead*; she revised *Anthem* for American publication in 1946, while she was planning *Atlas Shrugged*. Small in size, it is nonetheless large in scope. *Anthem* could have been written by no one but the author of *We the Living*, *The Fountainhead*, and *Atlas Shrugged*.

Ayn Rand, in between *We the Living* and *The Fountainhead*, wrote quickly for serial publication a novella she hoped to publish in the sort of magazine that had published Stephen Vincent Benét's "The Places of the Gods."[128] But *Anthem*, in essence, was no more like its literary brothers than Equality 7-2751 was like his. Ayn Rand knew, from her youth in Soviet Russia, that the collective as such was evil, that the individual as such was sacred, and that the former was out to destroy the latter, to control the individual—body and soul. In all of her writing, she made that point, and accordingly *Anthem* resembles her other fiction much more than it does the writings of anyone else. Not only that, but it is more different from several of its analogues than may at first appear. It is not only different, but opposite—specifically regarding the relation between the progress of scientific knowledge and the society's respect for life, liberty, and the pursuit of happiness. Rather than associating science with the means of enslavement, she presents a world in which the loss of knowledge accompanies the loss of freedom, and in which the rediscovery of the "I" is made by a scientist who first rediscovers electricity.

Within the genre of the dystopia, the future gone wrong, *Anthem* stands not as prophecy but as warning. In her novella as in her longest novel, Ayn Rand's purpose in writing the book was *"to prevent itself from becoming prophetic."*[129] As she wrote to Linda Jenkins, a high school senior:

> In regard to *Anthem*, I did not imply that future generations will necessarily collapse into collectivism. There is no pre-determined historical necessity. The course of history is determined by men's philosophical convictions. If men hold an altruist-collectivist philosophy, then they will reach a society on the order of the one presented in *Anthem*. If they choose a philosophy of reason-individualism-capitalism, then they will achieve a cultural renaissance.[130]

She added: "My novel *Atlas Shrugged* deals with these issues at much greater length." And so it does.

But *Anthem* also stands alone, uniquely valuable in its own right. As she wrote to Newman Flower, *Anthem*'s first publisher: "this story [is] more precious to me than anything I have ever considered writing. It is so very personally mine, it is, in a way, my manifesto, my profession of faith, the essence of my entire philosophy."[131]

## NOTES

1. Biographical interviews (Ayn Rand Archives).

2. "Questions and Answers on *Anthem*," in *The Ayn Rand Column*, second edition, ed. Peter Schwartz (New Milford, CT: Second Renaissance, 1998), 123.

3. For her comments on fantasy, see Ayn Rand, *The Art of Fiction: A Guide for Writers and Readers*, ed. Tore Boeckmann (New York: Plume, 2000), 169–72.

4. John J. Pierce, *Foundations of Science Fiction: A Study in Imagination and Evolution* (Westport, CT: Greenwood, 1987), 168.

5. Biographical interviews (Ayn Rand Archives).

6. Biographical interviews (Ayn Rand Archives).

7. July 31, 1937, CCX, 10–11, 59–60, reprinted as "By the Waters of Babylon" in Stephen Vincent Benét, *Thirteen O'Clock: Stories of Several Worlds* (New York: Farrar and Rinehart, 1937), 3–20. John J. Pierce, a science-fiction scholar, has independently identified this story as the one Ayn Rand read. After researching "The Places of the Gods" for my essay, I read his personal communication about this story to the Ayn Rand Institute, and contacted him. I have learned from his books and from wide-ranging conversations.

8. *Selected Letters of Stephen Vincent Benét*, ed. Charles A. Fenton (New Haven: Yale University Press, 1960), 301.

9. Thomas Babington Macaulay, *Essays* and *Lays of Ancient Rome* (London: Longman, 1909), 548. Regarding the cultural pervasiveness of this image, see Robert Dingley, "The Ruins of the Future: Macaulay's New Zealander and the Spirit of the Age."

*Histories of the Future: Studies in Fact, Fantasy and Science Fiction*, eds. Alan Sandison and Robert Dingley (Hampshire and New York: Palgrave, 2000), 17. The full article is 15–33.

10. Fenton, *Selected Letters*, 301–2. John J. Pierce pointed out, in a personal communication, that Benét's story, unlike Macaulay's prototype, is a post-holocaust quest story, a distinct sub-genre.

11. *Selected Works of Stephen Vincent Benét* (New York: Farrar and Rinehart, 1942), vol. 1, 448–54.

12. *Selected Works*, vol. 1 457–61, 464–68.

13. Ayn Rand, *The Romantic Manifesto: A Philosophy of Literature*, revised edition (New York: Signet, 1975), 109.

14. Richard C. Borden, "H. G. Wells' 'Door in the Wall' in Russian Literature." *Slavic and East European Journal* vol. 36, no. 3 (Fall 1992), 334. The full article is 323–38.

15. Rand, *Art of Fiction*, 170–71.

16. H. G. Wells, *The Time Machine. The War of the Worlds: Critical Edition*, edited by Frank D. McConnell (New York: Oxford University Press, 1977), 52, 62.

17. Ayn Rand, *Anthem* (London: Cassell and Co., 1938), 142.

18. Ayn Rand, *Atlas Shrugged* (New York: Random House, 1957; Signet thirty-fifth anniversary paperback edition, 1992), 162. John J. Pierce brought to my attention this passage, which he describes as "Wellsian." See his *When World Views Collide: A Study in Imagination and Evolution* (Westport, Conn.: Greenwood, 1989), 162.

19. John W. Campbell, "Twilight" in *Science Fiction Hall of Fame*, vol. 1, ed. Robert Silverberg (New York: Avon, 1971), 56–57. The full story is 39–61. The story was originally published in *Astounding Science Fiction*, November 1934, under the pseudonym "Don A. Stuart."

20. Campbell, "Twilight," 60–61.

21. Rand, *Atlas Shrugged*, 12.

22. Campbell, "Twilight," 61.

23. The versions of the novel differ in some details and episodes, but in few of the aspects discussed here. Gareth Davies-Morris analyzes the changes in "Afterword," *The Sleeper Awakes* (Lincoln: University of Nebraska Press, 1990). Hereafter this edition will be designated "*Sleeper* 1910." For the text of the 1899 version (to be designated "*Sleeper* 1899"), I refer to *When the Sleeper Wakes* (New York: Random, 2003).

24. "The Silliest Film: Will Machinery Make Robots of Men?" (1929), reprinted in *Authors on Film*, ed. Harry M. Geduld (Bloomington: Indiana University Press, 1992), 59–67.

25. Ayn Rand rated the film as a whole 5+ (her highest rating, and one consistent with her view that Lang was a great artist—cf. *Romantic Manifesto*, 72). Her low rating of the story (specifically, 0–) may reflect the fact that, in 1927, the only prints available for screening displayed a shortened version of the film, with a plot line reshaped by Channing Pollock, whom she was later to know as a co-crusader for individualism in the 1940s. See Ayn Rand, *Russian Writings on Hollywood*, ed. Michael S. Berliner (Marina del Rey, CA: Ayn Rand Institute Press, 1999), 207–9; Enno Patalas, *Making of* Metropolis, included in *Metropolis: Restored, Authorized Version*, King Video, 2002; Channing Pollock, *Harvest of My Years* (New York: Bobbs-Merrill, 1943), 232–33.

26. See Mark Hillegas, *The Future as Nightmare: H. G. Wells and the Anti-Utopians*, 1967, reprint edition (Carbondale, IL: Southern Illinois Univ. Press, 1974), 47 and *passim*. Hillegas also discusses two short stories by Wells that are part of the same imagined future history: "A Story of Days to Come" (1897) and "A Dream of Armageddon" (1901).

27. See Hillegas, *Future as Nightmare*, 63–81, for a thoughtful consideration of this book and a related text, *Men Like Gods* (New York: Macmillan, 1923).

28. H. G. Wells, *A Modern Utopia* (Lincoln: University of Nebraska Press, 1967), 8.

29. I.e., a designated, non-hereditary group of leaders, explicitly derived from Plato's Guardians, in the *Republic*.

30. Hillegas, *Future as Nightmare*, 70.

31. "Introduction" to *Collected Short Stories* (New York: Penguin, 1976). There are several candidates for this "earlier heaven." Hillegas suggests *A Modern Utopia* (*Future as Nightmare*, 86–87). Wilfred Stone nominates *The Time Machine* (*The Cave and the Mountain: A Study of E. M. Forster* [Stanford: Stanford University Press, 1966], 152). Pierce proposes "The Man of the Year Million" (Pierce, 1987, 98).

32. Pagination refers to E. M. Forster, *Collected Short Stories*. The full story is 109–46.

33. Richard DeMille to Ayn Rand, 22 November 1946 (Ayn Rand Archives).

34. Michael S. Berliner, ed., *Letters of Ayn Rand* (New York: Dutton, 1995), 350.

35. Christopher Collins, *Evgenij Zamjatin: An Interpretive Study* (The Hague and Paris: Mouton, 1973), 9. The name of the author can be transliterated as "Zamjatin," "Zamiatin," and "Zamyatin." Collins renders the writer's name "Zamjatin," according to a transliteration style that allows exact equivalents for Russian letters. For personal names in the text, I have used the most common English equivalents; for bibliographic identifications and for words as words, I have used the Library of Congress system for transliteration of modern Russian with the diacritical marks omitted. I have left unchanged the alternative transliterations used by other scholars.

36. Edward J. Brown, *The Proletarian Episode in Russian Literature 1928–1932* (New York: Octagon, 1971), 251.

37. For contemporary reminiscences of Zamyatin and information about Tsarist and Soviet literary cultures, see Iurii Annenkov, "Evgenii Zamiatin," reprinted in *Dnevnik moikh vstrech*, Iurii Annenkov (New York: Inter-Language Literary Associates, 1966), 246–286.

38. See Clarence Brown's introduction to his translation of Yevgeny Zamyatin, *We* (New York: Penguin, 1993), xi–xiv.

39. Although the novel associates mathematics with the basic values of the world of "We," Zamyatin—who surely knew better than to attack mathematics as such—is not unequivocally anti-math. As Brett Cooke observes: "For all the lip service it pays to mathematical concepts and great mathematicians, the Single State is mathematically naïve and often ignorant." See his *Human Nature in Utopia: Zamyatin's* We (Evanston: Northwestern University Press, 2002), 67.

40. Zamyatin, *We*, trans. Brown, 206–7. Clarence Brown's translation has been checked with the first full Russian edition, *My* (New York: Izdatel'stvo imeni Chekhova, 1952).

41. See Christopher Collins, "Zamyatin, Wells and the Utopian Literary Tradition," *Slavonic and East European Review* 44:103 (July 1966), 351–60.

42. Hillegas, *Future as Nightmare*, 106.

43. Hilllegas, *Future as Nightmare*, 109.

44. Alex M. Shane, *The Life and Works of Evgenij Zamjatin* (Berkeley: University of California Press, 1968), 31, 247–48.

45. The article "H. G. Wells" is available in Russian in *Litsa* (New York: Izdatel'stvo imeni Chekhova, 1955), 103–38 and, in English, in *A Soviet Heretic: Essays by Yevgeny Zamyatin*, ed. and trans. Mirra Ginsburg (Chicago: University of Chicago Press, 1970), 259–90.

46. Among the many treatments of *We* and Wells, the most useful are Hillegas, *Future as Nightmare*, Collins, "Zamyatin, Wells and the Utopian Literary Tradition," and Patrick Parrinder, "Imagining the Future: Zamyatin and Wells," *Science Fiction Studies* 1, 1 (1973), 17–26.

47. Biographical interviews (Ayn Rand Archives).

48. Biographical interviews (Ayn Rand Archives).

49. Gary Kern, "Introduction: The Ultimate Anti-Utopia," in *Zamyatin's We: A Collection of Critical Essays*, ed. Gary Kern (Ann Arbor: Ardis, 1988), 9. The full article is 9–21.

50. Discovering relevant information about any contact between the writers would require historical study—of Zamyatin's writing and teaching, of the Soviet literary milieu, and of the lives of both writers in Petersburg in the early 1920s. One might, for example, investigate the possibility that she might have attended Zamyatin's speech in late October, 1921, at an evening meeting of the House of Writers dedicated to the memory of Blok, her favorite poet (Shane, *Life and Works of Evgenij Zamjatin*, 35, 214). Such an inquiry would require Russian sources.

51. Shane, *Life and Works of Evgenij Zamjatin*, 83.

52. Elizabeth Stenbock-Fermor, "A Neglected Source of Zamyatin's *We*" and "Addendum: 'The New Utopia' by Jerome K. Jerome, 171–85, in Kern, *Zamyatin's* We. This source had not in fact been entirely "neglected"; Viktor Shklovsky, as indicated in Kern, *Zamyatin's* We, 49, had, as early as 1927, been reminded of Jerome K. Jerome's story.

53. Schwartz, *Ayn Rand Column*, 122.

54. Collins, *Zamjatin: An Interpretive Study*, 42. The original Russian text—"'my' v proletarskoi literature vytesniaet 'ia'" ["we" in proletarian literature squeezes out "I"]—appears in *Osnovnye otlichitel'nye priznaki proletarskoi literatury*, in *Literaturnye manifesty*, edited by N. L. Brodskii (Munich: Fink, 1969), vol. 1, 155. See also Kathleen Lewis and Harry Weber, "Zamyatin's *We*, the Proletarian Poets and Bogdanov's *Red Star*," in Kern, *Zamyatin's* We, 186–208; see especially 206 for references to additional poems featuring the Russian word "my" (we).

55. Edward J. Brown, *Russian Literature since the Revolution*, revised and enlarged edition (Cambridge: Harvard University Press, 1982), 54.

56. Quoted in English translation in Brown 1982, 54. The Russian text is in "O tendentsiax proletarskoi kul'tury" in *Literaturnye manifesty*, I, 132–133.

57. I am quoting from Edward J. Brown's translation in his *BRAVE NEW WORLD, 1984, and WE: An Essay on Anti-Utopia* (Ann Arbor, MI: Ardis, 1976), 42. The Russian text appears in Vladimir Maiakovskii, *Polnoe sobranie sochinenii* (Moscow: Khudozhestvennaja literatura, 1957), Vol. IV, 122.

58. References are to the Clarence Brown's Penguin translation.

59. Alexander Voronsky, "Evgeny Zamyatin," in Kern, *Zamyatin's* We, 45. The full article is 25–48.

60. "Zamyatin and the Strugatskys: The Representation of Freedom in *We* and *The Snail on the Slope*" in Kern, *Zamyatin's* We, 241. The full article is 236–59.

61. "Evgeny Zamyatin's Auto-Interview," in Kern, *Zamyatin's* We, 297. The full article is 295–99.

62. Quoted in Shane, *Life and Works of Evgenij Zamjatin*, 145, from F. Lefèvre, "Une heure avec Zamiatine," *Les Nouvelles littéraires*, no. 497 (April 23, 1932), 1. I have not been able to examine this text.

63. Cooke, *Human Nature in Utopia*, points out that the novel is not consistently anti-reason or anti-math, in that I-330 and her comrades make use of math (69).

64. For discussions of *We* in relation to Dostoevsky, see especially Richard A. Gregg, "Two Adams and Eve in the Crystal Palace: Dostoevsky, the Bible, and *We*" (1965), reprinted in Kern, *Zamyatin's* We, 61–69. Of the many other discussions of Dostoevsky and Zamyatin, see especially Shane, *Life and Works of Evgenij Zamjatin*, 142–43; Robert Louis Jackson, "Zamiatin's *We*" in *Dostoevskij's Underground Man in Russian Literature* (The Hague: Mouton, 1958), 150–57. Gary Saul Morson, *The Boundaries of Genre: Dostoevsky's Diary of a Writer and the Traditions of Literary Utopia* (Austin: University of Texas Press, 1981), especially 122–35.

65. *Notes from the Underground*, trans. David Magarshack, part I, chapter 4, in *Great Short Works of Fyodor Dostoevsky* (New York: Harper and Row, 1968), 273–75.

66. F. M. Dostoevskii, *Polnoe sobranie sochinenii* (Leningrad: Nauka, 1973), vol. 6, 419. Translation mine.

67. Shane, *Life and Works of Evgenij Zamjatin*, 143, notes the parallel.

68. Fyodor Dostoevsky, *Demons*, translated by Richard Pevear and Larissa Volokhonsky (New York: Knopf, 1994), 422. For the Russian text, see Dostoevskii, *Polnoe sobranie sochinenii*, vol. 10, 326. All passages from *Demons* have been compared with this Russian text. Gregg, 62–63 in Kern, *Zamyatin's* We, identified the possible connection between Zamyatin's title and Dostoevsky's text.

69. Dostoevsky, *Demons*, 403–4.

70. Fyodor Dostoevsky, *The Brothers Karamazov*, translated by Richard Pevear and Larissa Volokhonsky (New York: Vintage, 1991), 253. For the Russian text, see F. M. Dostoevskii, *Sobranie sochinenii* (Moscow: Khudozhestvennaya literatura, 1968), vol. 10, 325.

71. Dostoevsky, *Brothers Karamazov*, 258.

72. Rand, *Romantic Manifesto*, 43, 86–88, 107, 114–15; *Art of Fiction*, 103, 175, 176.

73. Rand, *Romantic Manifesto*, 114–15.

74. Letters to John Loos, October 20 and November 11, 1949 (Ayn Rand Archives).

75. David Harriman, ed. *Journals of Ayn Rand* (New York: Dutton, 1997), 693.

76. Harriman, *Journals*, 437.

77. The single article dealing with the two writers is Aleksei Tsvetkov, "Dostoevskii i Ein Rend," *Oktiabr* 3 (March 2002), 159–63. The article, which allots a few paragraphs to Ayn Rand, does not address her fiction in any detail.

78. Dostoevsky, *Demons*, 417–18.

79. Ayn Rand, *The Fountainhead* (New York: Bobbs-Merrill, 1943; Signet fiftieth anniversary paperback edition, 1993).

80. Dostoevsky, *Demons*, 418.

81. Ayn Rand, *Atlas Shrugged*, 973.

82. Dostoevskii, *Polnoe sobranie sochinenii*, vol. 20, 172. Translation mine.

83. Hillegas, *Future as Nightmare*, 110–20.

84. Shane, *Life and Works of Evgenij Zamjatin*, 140.

85. Alexandra Aldridge, *The Scientific World View in Dystopia* (Ann Arbor: UMI Research Press, 1984), 53.

86. Pagination refers to Aldous Huxley, *Brave New World* (New York: Perennial, 1969).

87. Hillegas, *Future as Nightmare*, 118.

88. For more on Huxley and Dostoevsky, see Andrew Hacker, "Dostoevsky's Disciples: Man and Sheep in Political Theory," *The Journal of Poltiics*, vol. 17, issue 4 (1955), 590–613.

89. Several people mentioned it to her, including Hugh MacLennan (letter, March 26, 1944) and Richard Mealand (letter, February 11, 1947) (Ayn Rand Archives). She did not respond in writing to their comments.

90. Leonard Peikoff, ed., *The Early Ayn Rand: A Selection from Her Unpublished Fiction* (New York: New American Library, 1984; paperback edition, Signet, 1986), 316.

91. "Foreword," Huxley, *Brave New World*, vii.

92. *Collected Essays: Journalism and Letters of George Orwell*, eds. Sonia Orwell and Ian Angus (New York: Harcourt, Brace and World 1968), vol. 3: *As I Please: 1943–1945*, 95. His letter to Gleb Struve is dated Feb. 17, 1944.

93. William Steinhoff, *George Orwell and the Origins of 1984* (Ann Arbor: University of Michigan Press, 1973), 226–27.

94. Orwell, *Collected Essays*, vol. 4: *In Front of Your Nose 1945–1950*, 72. The review, which occupies pp. 72–75 in this volume, was originally published in January 4, 1946.

95. Orwell, *Collected Essays,* vol. 4, 73.

96. Orwell, *Collected Essays*, vol. 4, 74–75.

97. Orwell, *Collected Essays*, vol. 4, 75.

98. For a vehement claim that Orwell was deeply indebted to Zamyatin, see Isaac Deutscher, "*1984*—The Mysticism of Cruelty" (1954), reprinted in *George Orwell: A Collection of Critical Essays*, edited by Raymond Williams (Englewood Cliffs, NJ; Prentice-Hall, 1974), 119–32. Orwell, according to Deutscher, borrowed the main elements—plot, characters, symbol, climate—from Zamyatin.

99. Steinhoff, *Orwell and the Origins of 1984*, 29.

100. For discussions of literary influences, see Steinhoff, *Orwell and the Origins of 1984*, and Jeffrey Meyers, *A Reader's Guide to George Orwell* (Totowa, NJ: Littlefield, Adams, 1977).

101. See Philip Rahv, "The Unfuture of Utopia" (1949) reprinted in *Modern Critical Views: George Orwell*, edited by Harold Bloom (New York: Chelsea, 1987), 13–20. Rahv says that O'Brien "simultaneously recalls and refutes the ideas of Dostoyevski's Grand Inquisitor" (17). See also Steinhoff, *Orwell and the Origins of 1984*, 137; Meyers, *Reader's Guide to George Orwell*, 88; Adrian Wanner, "The Underground Man as Big Brother: Dostoevsky's and Orwell's Anti-Utopia," *Utopian Studies*, vol. 8, no. 1 (1997), 77–88.

102. References are to George Orwell, *1984* (New York: New American Library, 1981).

103. George Woodcock, *The Crystal Spirit: A Study of George Orwell* (Boston: Little, Brown, 1966), 215–16.

104. Steinhoff, 57–71, 231–33.

105. "Notes on the Way," 1940, reprinted in Orwell, *The Collected Essays*, vol. 2: *My Country, Right or Left: 1940–1943*, 16.

106. Orwell, *Collected Essays*, vol. 4, 502.

107. Personal communication, Daphne Patai, July 13, 2002.

108. Review in *Daily Telegraph*, May 10, 1938, discussed in the present volume by Michael Berliner.

109. Harriman, *Journals*, 103. See also Rand, *Fountainhead*, 635.

110. Berliner, *Letters*, 310.

111. Edward Hunter, July 8, 1953 (Ayn Rand Archives).

112. Rand, *Art of Fiction*, 174.

113. 1946, reprinted in Berliner, *Letters*, 669–73.

114. Berliner, *Letters*, 233.

115. Ayn Rand, *We the Living*, sixtieth anniversary paperback edition (New York: Signet, 1996). The 1936 edition includes the same key statement: "No laws, no books, no G.P.U. will ever grow an extra nose on a human face. No Party will ever kill that thing in men which knows how to say 'I'" (New York: Macmillan, 1936), 501.

116. Peikoff, *Early Ayn Rand*, 203.

117. Rand, *Anthem*, 110.

118. Peikoff, *Early Ayn Rand*, 203.

119. Rand, *Anthem* (1938), 125.

120. Berliner, *Letters*, 315.

121. Letter to Margot Johnson, February 1, 1944 (Ayn Rand Archives).

122. For a discussion of the passage as it appears in the manuscript, see my "Artist at Work: Ayn Rand's Drafts for *The Fountainhead*," *The Intellectual Activist*, vol. 15, no. 9 (Sept. 2001), 30.

123. Harriman, *Journals*, 454.

124. Harriman, *Journals*, 80–81.

125. Rand, *Art of Fiction*, 37–38.

126. Rand, *Atlas Shrugged*, 480.

127. Rand, *Atlas Shrugged*, 984.

128. In a 1944 letter, Ayn Rand told Gerald Loeb: "I would never set out to write a story for *Harper's* or for *Click* or for anything. You don't write stories that way. . . . First you write, then you decide where to submit it. Never, never, never vice versa" (Berliner, *Letters*, 158). Her actions do not contradict that advice. In her letter to Loeb, she is expressing disagreement with his assumption that the intended audience determines the nature of the literary work, and she is doing so in very strong terms. She does not, after all, write in order to be published—any more than Roark builds in order to have clients. The fundamental "story"—in *Anthem* as everywhere in her work—is hers. The idea was hers. The fantasy premise was hers. The venue was relevant only with regard to the projected length and the timing of the composition.

129. "Is Atlas Shrugging?" in Ayn Rand, *Capitalism: The Unknown Ideal* (New York: New American Library, 1966; expanded Signet paperback edition, 1967), 150.

130. May 2, 1964 (Ayn Rand Archives).

131. January 2, 1938 (Ayn Rand Archives). I acknowledge the helpful comments and suggestions of Onkar Ghate, Robert Mayhew, and Gregory Salmieri, my fellow participants in a colloquium sponsored by the Ayn Rand Institute.

# 9

## "Sacrilege toward the Individual": The Anti-Pride of Thomas More's *Utopia* and *Anthem's* Radical Alternative

*John Lewis*

Ayn Rand understood early on that there could be no greater crime against man than to attack his sense of self. In a letter of 1936, thanking a writer for his praise of her novel *We the Living*, she wrote:

> I am particularly grateful to you for calling the public's attention to my book from an angle which is more important to me than any possible literary accomplishment of mine, namely for mentioning the fact that my book is not merely an argument against Communism, but against all forms of collectivism, against any manner of sacrilege toward the Individual. It would be easier for me to conceive of tolerance toward a theory preaching a wholesale execution of mankind by poison gas than to understand those who find any possible ethical excuse for destroying the only priceless possession of man—his individualism. After all, any form of swift physical annihilation is preferable to the inconceivable horror of a living death. And what but a rotting alive can human existence be when devoid of the pride and the joy of a man's right to his own spirit?[1]

Sacrilege is temple robbery—to take, for secular use, that which properly belongs to the divine.[2] For over two thousand years, man has been told that his refusal to grant God's supremacy over him is his greatest crime, that his unwillingness to keep to his place as a humble being is insubordination, and that his refusal to forsake ambition and to cringe before an omnipotent power is a sin. The ultimate sacrilege is pride, the queen of the seven deadly sins, a vicious monster in the soul and an affront to the almighty.[3] In the world of Thomas More, a powerful man of the church who projected his views into a literary *Utopia*, man's pride in himself must be annihilated, and his ambitions subordinated to a communist social system before he can achieve the nirvana of a happy Christian life.

172

Ayn Rand rejects all of this. Her radical conception is that man as a moral being is worthy of the reverence usually reserved for the divine—and that any attempt to strip him of his individualism is sacrilege. The proud man creates and affirms his own sacred value, and protects it from the prying hands of others. Prometheus, the hero of *Anthem*, guards his own ego as a sacred temple: "For in the temple of his spirit, each man is alone. Let each man keep his temple untouched and undefiled" (96). It is only by obliterating a man's sense of his own value—by effacing his pride of self as a thinking, loving, moral being—that he can be reduced to the nadir of living death that *Anthem* portrays. But *Anthem* is not about the political or economic subjugation of man. It goes far deeper into the moral sacrilege that makes physical slavery possible. In contrast to the medieval communism of More's *Utopia*—and the view of man promoted in Christianity generally—*Anthem* offers a radical re-affirmation of man's right to ambition, self-respect and pride.

Since the age of the ancient Greeks, the best of the utopian writers founded their visions upon some conception of man's moral nature. They then condemned man for possessing a nature that did not fit their ideals. Plato's *Republic* is such a world, one of rule by philosopher-kings claiming possession of a special knowledge of non-sensory, perfect, transcendent truths, and endowed with dictatorial powers over those inferior masses who cannot even grasp the nature of the good. This claim to philosophic perfection is a license to coerce and to lie, if they determine that this serves the good of all. But Plato took seriously man's inability to achieve this ideal in real life. In his last work, *The Laws*, he accepted mankind's failure to reach the ideal, and posited a mythical city founded on imperfect, humanly-created laws, imposed by force, as the "second best" way of organizing a political community.

Plato is both the intellectual founder of utopian writing and its most influential spokesman. He provided the basic split between the ideal and the real that has dominated western thought into the present day. To claim that a moral ideal has no reality on earth and is unknowable except to self-anointed leaders leaves no achievement and no pride possible to man. All he can do is obey the leaders without question. What the philosopher Aristotle called the "great-souled man," proud of himself and unwilling to subordinate the truth to the ruler's visions, would be a logjam in the social machine and a danger to the harmony of all.[4] To Ayn Rand, Plato committed the first, and greatest, sacrilege against the individual by robbing the individual of his mind and his freedom.

Augustine, in his *City of God*, took the Platonic *Republic* further, relying on God to provide the standards by which life should be lived. This earth is a vale of tears, life is sordid, man is depraved, and a proud man is a blasphemer. "'For pride is the start of every sin'" he wrote, quoting from the Old Testament; "what is pride but a perverse kind of exaltation?" A man's first step to virtue is to recognize his own worthlessness. There was no room for pride in Augustine's world, only humility and obedience before the unknowable. "God's instructions required obedience, and obedience is in a way the mother and guardian of all the other virtues in a rational creature."[5] Like Plato, Augustine begins his ethical and political thought with supernatural ideals, and has man take the blame for possessing a nature opposed to those ideals. Man's sin is his inability to change his nature, stifle his pride, subdue his mind, shrink his ambitions, and obey.

Thomas More's *Utopia*, published in 1516, was the first attempt since Plato to portray an ideal political community. It postulates both an idealized world—akin to Plato's *Republic* but based on Augustine's ideals—as well as a place that More claimed actually existed. There was a lively production of such literary works in the following century; Francis Bacon's *The New Atlantis*, Tomasso Campanella's *The City of the Sun*, and James Harrington's *The Commonwealth of Oceana*, among others, created political communities in the image of their authors' ideals. Despite the revolutionary nature of such works, there was no corresponding revolution in the Judeo-Christian values and virtues they embraced; humility and obedience continued to dominate the political thought of the day, and a proud man would be like sand ground between the gears of a smooth-running social order. Again, man is damned because he cannot change his nature to match the strictures of these ideals.[6]

To Ayn Rand, this is all sacrilege against the individual. The conflict in *Anthem* between the hero, Equality 7-2521, and his brothers epitomizes an age-old battle between every proud man and those who wish to stifle his self-esteem in favor of some alleged higher good. Ayn Rand's radical defense of pride is founded on her total rejection of the Augustinian view of man. It is man—his nature and identity as a thinking, working, proud being—who comes first. Pride returns to its rightful status as the crown of the virtues because man becomes the standard of perfection in a temple of his own making.

A comparison of *Anthem* to More's *Utopia* is a case study of two views of man, and correspondingly two views of pride. From the outset the styles of the two works reveal a fundamental difference in their authors' intellectual premises. More hides his message behind a veil of ambiguity. In contrast to the simple clarity of *Anthem*, he does not want to be understood precisely. On one level *Utopia* is humorous. The main speaker is Hythloday, from the Greek *hythlos* meaning "nonsense." "Utopia" itself is a new word based on Eutopia ("Good place") and Atopia ("No place"); it is impossible to know exactly what More means by his neologism. Its main city, Amaurot, is derived from the Greek for "dim."[7] This dearth of clarity is reflected in the status More claims for his creation. The island of Utopia is real, he asserts, and this is supposedly evidence for the truth of his ideals. Such literary devices are consistent with the views of Plato and Augustine, who thought that our knowledge was only a dim and imperfect reflection of a "higher," non-sensory world, which is real although beyond the range of human examination. Given this premise, clear correspondence to the truth is impossible, all writing is inherently ambiguous, and *Utopia* becomes a metaphor for an indescribable ideal. In contrast, Ayn Rand is able to write clearly, directly, and unambiguously, because she understands that our ideas are a human perspective on the only world that exists: the one we live in.

Although there are differences between the societies of *Utopia* and *Anthem,* there are also physical, social, and political parallels between the two works. In *Utopia,* as in the dictatorship of *Anthem,* each man's ambitions are chained to the requirements of a collectivist social order. More's paradise is an isolated island in the New World, a socialist nirvana devoid of both poverty and wealth, where travel is strictly controlled, freedom of religion is constrained by a mandatory belief in God, thought and action are allowed only if they serve the needs of society, and citizens have attained universal happiness. This new land is solidly in line with the ideals of the medieval Christian tradition, although the Utopians have followed those ideals without knowledge of Christ. The society of *Anthem* is likewise isolated, collectivistic, and bereft of freedom. The solution to man's alleged inability to grasp the truth is to immerse him in a world ordered by the superior knowledge of others.

Utopia itself is arranged in a precise geometrical order.[8] Like Plato and Augustine, More believes that each individual must accept a prescribed place in a greater whole. The basic social unit is the family homestead. Each has at least forty persons, not counting slaves, with a master and a mistress. Every year twenty persons from each rural household are selected by the authorities to move back to the city, and an equal number move from the city into the country. The ideal Utopian home is a cross between a slave plantation in the antebellum American south and a hippie commune under a guru. The houses are grouped under a hierarchy of political officials who elect a single prince, normally for life. A similar organizational rigidity is at work in the dictatorship of *Anthem,* from the enforced regularity of the work day to the arrangement of beds in the dorms.

But who is to design and enforce the ordering of the whole? Despite Hythloday's assertions, people are not equal in Utopia. Like Plato (who advocated the rule of philosopher-kings), Augustine (who was Bishop of Hippo), and Thomas More (the Chancellor of England), Utopia will have as rulers priests and politicians who control the population. Despite More's claims that the Utopians live as they do voluntarily, harsh penalties follow for those who violate the dictates of the rulers. The similarities to the dictatorship of *Anthem* are obvious; the primary means of maintaining the state is through indoctrination masked as education, but the whips come out when the propaganda fails. To get along in such a society a man must not aspire beyond the limits set by the rulers. Although the focus of *Anthem* is not on the leaders but on their victims, the various councils betray an organizational hierarchy that extends from Street Sweeper–Slaves to Council Leader–Masters.

Nor is there any alternative for those who do not submit. In Equality 7-2521's world, the very idea of travel brings to mind paralyzing fear of the Unmentionable Places; there is no need for laws against leaving, given this fear. What of the Utopians? All travel requires the permission of the leaders, and woe to those who wander off on their own:

> Anyone who takes it upon himself to leave his district without permission, and is caught without the prince's letter, is treated with contempt, brought back as a runaway, and severely punished. If he is bold enough to try it a second time, he is made a slave.[9]

Similar dictates govern the choice of careers. Upon coming of age, Equality 7-2521 is assigned to work; he has no choice in the matter. A Utopian rather inherits his trade from his father, and may change only if "father and authorities" approve.[10] What careers will be approved? Since money in other societies has led to "superfluous trades" and vicious luxury, workers in Utopia are "assigned" to "useful" tasks, primarily agricultural.[11] Utopia is designed to remain agriculturally-based and technologically-backward, to prevent the moral decay that More thinks will follow the production of excess wealth. Too much wealth, More thinks, will lead men away from piety and into sloth, another of the seven deadly sins.

What of privacy and love? For Equality 7-2521 and his brothers, these have been replaced by communal dining and the Palaces of Mating; it is a sin to be alone, and to prefer one person over another. The social hierarchy adopted by the Utopians is patriarchal, but attains the same result: the father is absolute head of the household, and "wives kneel before their husbands and children before their parents, to confess their various failures and negligences, and beg forgiveness for their offenses."[12] Does a Utopian wish to dine alone or with his spouse? Common meals are arranged by family, with fifteen chairs on one side, fifteen on the other. Women sit apart from men, so they will not disturb the men should they fall into pain from childbearing. What if a Utopian wants to use his spare time to simply relax? The leaders do not allow sloth. In such a society,

> there is no chance to loaf or kill time, no pretext for evading work; no taverns, or alehouses, or brothels; no chances for corruption; no hiding places; no spots for secret meetings. *Because they live in full view of all*, they are bound to be working at their usual trades, or enjoying their leisure in a respectable way.[13]

Similarly, in *Anthem*, "The laws say that none among men may be alone, ever and at any time, for this is the great transgression and the root of all evil"(17).

Further, throughout Utopia there are slaves who do the kinds of jobs that might corrupt virtuous citizens. Slaves work in slaughterhouses, for instance, and prepare meals.[14] Adulterers are made slaves, as are those who travel without a permit, who have been captured in wars, and who commit serious crimes.[15] More sees no problem in having multitudes of slaves—those who do not conform—do the menial work in his ideal state. They are the Street Sweepers of *Anthem*.

Economically, the crucial feature of Utopia is the communism of property. All things are held in common, and everyone has enough to live on because no one has more than enough. Hythloday asserts that without "drones," i.e., the idle rich who plague Europe, the Utopians attain universal prosperity by working six hours per day.[16] With everything free in Utopia, no one covets clothing beyond an undyed wool cloak, or material goods beyond the needs of survival. The Utopians invert the hierarchy of material values by turning iron into a valuable commodity, shackling slaves in golden chains and giving children precious gems as trinkets. They do not use locks. Because they do not value material things, there can be no rivalries—no conflicts—over things, and no misery derived from one man exploiting another. There are no heretics in Utopia; everyone—presumably even the slaves—is happy.

The society of *Anthem* might, to an external observer, appear to be just as happy. There are no wars, rivalries, or conflicts and no mass starvation. The society's apparently peaceful order is founded on the apparent happiness of its members, who are allowed to make no displays of unhappiness. Ayn Rand was asked why happiness was against the law in *Anthem*; her answer was: "Because the rulers wanted no complaints; they wanted the slaves to pretend to be satisfied with the conditions of their existence."[17] The societies of both *Anthem* and *Utopia* are built on appearances; the people appear to be happy, and the rulers appear to provide perfect sustenance for the people. But the purpose, in each case, is to maintain an order that is profoundly opposed to the nature of human life. Right down to the orderly arrangement of the beds in Equality 7-2521's dorm, and the lives organized by the clanging of a bell, the harmony of the social whole is the greatest value. Everyone is held in bondage by the ideas that underlie their world, although the whips and chains are ready for dissenters. But Ayn Rand's focus on the individual in *Anthem*—the very person missing in *Utopia*—allows her to penetrate beneath appearances, to see the society from an internal perspective and thus to expose the seething unhappiness in the souls of the best men that *Utopia* does not confront.[18]

All of this prevents a man of ambition and self-esteem from flourishing.

But the war against ambition goes far deeper than economics and the concerns of material wealth. What if a Utopian wishes to pursue scholarly work? There is a class of priests who function as guardians and teachers of public morality. These priests are above the law: "if one of them commits a crime, he is not brought into a court of law, but left to God and his own conscience."[19] If the priests recommend it, and the political leaders agree by a secret vote, a Utopian may be made a scholar, and freed from physical work.[20] But a scholar must always be on guard not to say, or think, the wrong things, since he is constantly under the threat of demotion by the priests. More replaces the wealthy nobility (the "drones") with a class of political and religious elites, who get their jobs through political pull and intellectual conformity. It is no accident that the Utopians, who take a delight in learning, have no accumulated literature. "Learning" here must be akin to medieval memorization and replication, not any expansion of knowledge; to learn is to give up all intellectual ambitions, to repeat and to obey.

In presenting the society of *Anthem* and its philosophical base, Ayn Rand takes this idea to its logical conclusion: there is no truth except that discovered by the collective, and no justice except that proclaimed by the group.[21] The man of independent intellect is enslaved. Equality 7-2521 is torn between his curse—his natural desire to learn and to understand, the intellectual parallels to his physical strength—and the dictates of society, which demand that he think only with the permission of the leaders. What might an ambitious Utopian feel, except the same pervasive fear that his sin might be discovered? And what might his reaction be when caught, except relief that he can now do penance for his sins? *Anthem* refuses to hide the private agony of the intellectually ambitious, which More fails to see or dares not discuss. Although there is no reason to think that More understood the truth about the collectivism of Utopia, a reader might wonder if Hythloday—like Americans who visited the USSR in the 1920s but were never shown the famines sweeping the countryside—was led around by guides who did not allow him to see the agonized individuals who cried out in the night, stifled in the nightmare of a living death.

Both *Utopia* and *Anthem* present statist political systems. Statism refers to any system in which the decrees of the state take precedence over the rights of individuals. As Ayn Rand wrote in her journals, "The essence of Statism is the idea that government must be all-powerful and must control the existence of men."[22] Under a statist system, there are no individual rights. Any "freedoms" that do exist are by permission; they are permitted if they support the regime, but forbidden if they do not. A statist-religious system (a theocracy) will control the lives of individuals according to religious ideals. A man is not free for his own sake in a statist system; he will be granted "freedoms" only to the extent that his "freedom" benefits the regime in power.

This is sacrilege against the individual. Ayn Rand later wrote about the nature and goals of statism:

> Politically, the goal of today's dominant trend is statism. Philosophically, the goal is the obliteration of reason; psychologically, it is the erosion of ambition.

The political goal presupposes the two others. The human characteristic required by statism is *docility,* which is the product of hopelessness and intellectual stagnation. Thinking men cannot be ruled; ambitious men do not stagnate. "Ambition" means the systematic pursuit of achievement and of constant improvement in respect to one's goal. Like the word "selfishness," and for the same reasons, the word "ambition" has been perverted to mean only the pursuit of dubious or evil goals, such as the pursuit of power; this left no concept to designate the pursuit of actual values. But "ambition" as such is a neutral concept: the evaluation of a given ambition as moral or immoral depends on the nature of the goal . . .

The common denominator [for every form of ambition] is the drive to improve the conditions of one's existence, however broadly or narrowly conceived. ("Improvement" is a moral term and depends on one's standard of values. An ambition guided by an irrational standard does not, in *fact,* lead to improvement, but to self-destruction.)[23]

Every word of this applies to the dictatorships of *Utopia* and *Anthem.* For More, reason means contemplation of the mysteries of God, and improvement is the affirmation of man's inferior status before Him. Given that the state is dominated by priests, who have the power to excommunicate, and political leaders, who can make a man into a slave, any Utopian who wished to improve himself independently through productive thought and work would immediately clash with the state. He would be tied to the same rack that brought suffering to Equality 7-2521, torn between his natural drive to improve himself and the demand of the state that he limit his ambitions. In either case, the state demands conformity and stagnation, and the individual must obey, lest he become a sinner and a criminal.

But More's war against ambition extends even deeper than economics, politics and education. His greatest concern is Christian virtue, and his political order is intended to subordinate every aspect of human life to his Christian ideals. Humility is his goal; the great enemies of virtue are ambition, pride and self-esteem. More limits ambition to make room for obedience. Although Hythloday claims that there is no organized religion (despite the priests with power above the law), and freedom of worship is given lip-service (despite the illegality of atheism), such "freedom" is set within strict limits. It is tolerated as long as it does not threaten the state, and may be withdrawn at any time.

The founder of Utopia, King Utopus, who seized power amidst religious strife, allowed each man the freedom

to choose what he would believe. The only exception he made was a positive and strict law against any person who should sink so far below the dignity of human nature as to think that the soul perishes with the body, or that the universe is ruled by mere chance, rather than divine providence.[24]

Such views have implications for any Utopian who might be tempted to rise above his ascetic lifestyle. To keep him in line, Utopia is governed by an all-encompassing emotion of terror. According to More, man's laws will be followed only under fear engendered by God. Terror of the afterlife allows the Utopians to hold onto their paradise, otherwise a person "would undoubtedly betray all the laws and customs of society, if not prevented by fear."[25] In More's mind, the threat of eternal hell-fire is the only foundation for law and morality. Because priests have the right to excommunicate those who do not follow their moral commandments, this fear must take the form of an immediate, personal terror of the religious hierarchy and the scholar-class from which they are chosen. This is More's solution to religious strife in England, a reaction which is poignant given More's own choice to be executed by the king rather than to disobey the dictates of the pope. When More said that we must subordinate ourselves to religious authorities, he meant it.

The dictatorship of *Anthem* is also dominated by a particular religion, "the worship of the state, of the collective."[26] A positive and strict law against questioning this religion was the foundation of Equality 7-2521's world. This society had its saints: the Saints of Labor, the Saints of the Council, and the Saints of the Great Rebirth (50). As in Utopia, there is also a pervasive atmosphere of fear, a characteristic of theocracies and communist dictatorships across history. Hythloday does not speak of dissidents, but this is not surprising, given that More never writes about individuals, and has no concern for heretics other than to enslave or kill them. His need to make his creatures happy behooves him to silence malcontents. In *Anthem*, the façade of compliance with the inhuman demands of society falls away to reveal the internal turmoil of victims who have been told to deny their own natures in deference to an ideal that is in mortal conflict with their own lives.

Hythloday's insistence that the Utopians favor the pleasures of the mind over those of the body requires them to follow the ideology of the Utopian state without exception. This means accepting the same level of material survival granted to Equality 7-2521—who, More might observe, did have enough to eat, and did not have to work *that* hard. To More, "happiness" is possible only after a war against ambition and achievement—an internal *jihad* in which a person pushes his own spirit down to the level of physical survival and ties his mind to the prescribed ideas. Attaining a victory over one's own ambitions is a precondition of happiness. And if a potential heretic falters in his war against his self, he can remember the threats of the whip, slavery, and eternal damnation. This is the rack that nearly tears Equality 7-2521 in two—until he rejects the ideals, flees into the Unmentionable Places, and affirms his own nature. As Hythloday concludes:

> Now that they have rooted up the seeds of ambition and faction at home, along
> with most other vices, they are in no danger from internal strife, which among

us has been the ruin of many other states that seemed secure. As long as they preserve harmony at home, and keep their institutions healthy, the Utopians can never be overcome or shaken by envious neighbors, who have often attempted their ruin, but always in vain.[27]

Imagine a Utopian who fails to deny his desire to achieve, and who undertakes to invent something, but without permission. How would the priests and leaders react to him? Their response could be taken from *Anthem*:

> We have much to say to a wretch who have broken all the laws and who boast of their infamy! . . . And if the Councils had decreed that you should be a Street Sweeper, how dared you think that you could be of greater use to men than to sweep the streets! (71–72)

In her 1961 essay "For the New Intellectual," Ayn Rand recognized the presence in history of those who claim to rule by commanding physical reality (the Attilas, the "mystics of muscle"), and those who claim a special form of knowledge (the Witchdoctors, the "mystics of the spirit"). Utopia is ruled by such men, the Prince and the Priests, who are designated by a sheaf of grain for the Prince, and a candle for the Priest.[28] The symbols are appropriate; the one controls the material wealth of the island, which he divides up as if he were the patriarch of an extended family; the second claims possession of the special knowledge required of a moral and intellectual censor. Each is supported by the Producers, those victims who work and sustain the rulers. Although we are not given the details of how *Anthem* is ruled—a necessary consequence of Ayn Rand's focus on the individual hero—a similar material and spiritual regime is behind the control held by the various councils over every aspect of life, and in the special class of "Leader" for those selected to rule.

The result:

> The damnation of this earth as a realm where nothing is possible to man but pain, disaster and defeat, a realm inferior to another, "higher," reality; the damnation of any values, enjoyment, achievement and success on earth as a proof of depravity; the damnation of man's mind as a source of *pride,* and the damnation of reason as a "limited," deceptive, unreliable, impotent faculty, incapable of perceiving the "real" reality and the "true" truth; the split of man in two, setting his consciousness (his soul) against his body, and his moral values against his own interest; the damnation of man's nature, body and *self* as evil; the commandment of self-sacrifice, renunciation, suffering, obedience, humility and faith, as the good; the damnation of life and the worship of death, with the promise of rewards beyond the grave—*these* are the necessary tenets of the Witch Doctor's view of existence, as they have been in every variant of Witch Doctor philosophy throughout the course of mankind's history.[29]

Thomas More was a persecutor of Protestants, a burner of heretics who also wrote treatises on heresies. He professed to hating the vices of the heretics more than the heretics themselves, and destroyed them only after trying to get them to see the error of their ways. Like the heretics who refused to repent, he was willing to lose his own life rather than betray what he saw as a principle—the authority of the pope to forbid a divorce to King Henry VIII of England. This is a power that the priests would have in More's ideal commonwealth. The absolutism with which he held his ideals has no better expression than in his own willingness to kill, and to be killed, for them. This is a Witchdoctor, in the service of Attila.

As to the fate of a man who refused to deny his own individual nature in deference to the rulers of a collectivist universe, consider the Saint of the pyre (as Equality 7-2521 calls him) in *Anthem*:

> As the flames rose, a thing happened which no eyes saw but ours, else we would not be living today. Perhaps it had only seemed to us. But it seemed to us that the eyes of the Transgressor had chosen us from the crowd and were looking straight upon us. There was no pain in their eyes and no knowledge of the agony of their body. There was only joy in them, and pride, a pride holier than it is fit for human pride to be. And it seemed as if these eyes were trying to tell us something through the flames, to send into our eyes some word without sound. And it seemed as if these eyes were begging us to gather that word and not to let it go from us and from the earth. But the flames rose and we could not guess the word. (51)

It is Equality 7-2521's pride that brought him into conflict with the regime, and forged a connection with the Saint of the pyre. It is Equality 7-2521's pride that must be beaten down to the level of the mob, if the state and its collectivist creed is to survive. There is no middle ground—no possibility of compromise—between the totalitarian state and "I." So it is in Utopia. The Utopians—and More's readers—must hold no pride in themselves or their work, if More's ideal is to become real. More makes this easy for them, by caricaturing pride as the basest opponent of human life:

> And in fact I have no doubt that every man's perception of where his true interest lies, along with the authority of Christ our Saviour (whose wisdom would not fail to recognize the best, and whose goodness would not fail to counsel it), would long ago have brought the entire world to adopt Utopian laws, if it were not for a single monster, the prime plague and begetter of all others—I mean Pride (*Superbia*).
>
> Pride measures her advantages not by what she has, but by what other people lack. Pride would not condescend even to be made a goddess, if there were no wretches for her to sneer at and domineer over. Her good fortune is dazzling only by contrast with miseries of others, her riches are valuable only as they torment and tantalize the poverty of others. Pride is a serpent from hell which

twines itself around the hearts of men; and it acts like the suckfish in holding them back from choosing a better way of life.[30]

As More describes it here, the Latin *superbia* means arrogance or haughtiness towards others. *Superbia* in this sense is not an emotion related to the achievement of positive values; it rather rejoices in superiority achieved by destroying the values of others. *Superbia* wishes not to increase its own wealth through productive activity, but rather to destroy the wealth of others. It is a *dependent*, not an *independent*, concept; it evaluates every person *relative* to others, not in terms of an independent standard. Its closest English equivalent is *envy*: a desire that others lose what they have. But as we shall see, More's description of *superbia* as "envy" in *Utopia* does not express his deepest view of what constitutes this "suckfish" that prevents men from achieving virtue.

More's description of *superbia* in *Utopia* is a way to convince his readers to forego material prosperity in order to achieve the positive consequences of the Utopian system. But for More, pride has a deeper tie to vice than greed or sloth, and it is bad for reasons much deeper than its alleged social consequences. The worst of man's sins is a positive view of himself. This is the suckfish that must be purged from man's soul. In his *Treatise of the Passion,* More is direct about this deeper view of pride. To achieve a deeper reverence towards God, a "pestilent pryde," implanted into man by the devil, must be expunged:

Let us here now good readers before we proceed further, consider well this matter, and ponder well this fearful point, what horrible peril there is in this pestilent sin of pride, what abominable sin it is in the sight of god, *when any creature falls into the delight and liking of itself:* as the thing whereupon continued, inevitably fails not to follow, first the neglecting and after the condemning and finally with disobedience and rebelling, the very full forsaking of God.[31]

More continues in his *Passion,* laying out the social consequences of this pestilence of self-esteem:

And if it be a thing detestable for any creature to rise in pride, *upon the respect and regard of beauty, strength, wit or learning of one's person,* or other such manner of thing as by nature and grace are properly their own; how much more foolish perversion is there in that pride, by which we worldly folk look up on height, and solemnly set by our self, with deep disdain for other far better men, only for very vain worldly trifles that properly be not our own?[32]

More is well aware that people can hold their own persons in high regard without hurting others—and he rejects this as the basest sin. The social concerns of *Utopia* are used to smuggle in a deeper agenda: to denigrate the prosperity—and self-esteem—rising in England, and to return to the medieval ideals championed by Augustine. This is an end in itself. Deeper than ambition, it is pride—in the sense of self-esteem and moral ambitiousness—that must be destroyed, before men can live devout, austere, Christian lives. To convince the readers of *Utopia* to follow this path, he buries his deepest view of pride beneath a social construct that equates pride with the destruction of others, and creates a package deal of envy and pride. This conceptual redefinition leaves men with a false alternative: between the sin of unlimited rapacity and the virtue of abject humility. This destroys all "respect and regard of beauty, strength, wit or learning of one's person."

To lower man's head before God, every man's estimation of himself must be lowered before those who claim to know God's will. The communism, the rules, even the claim that the Utopians are really happy—all of it is intended to break any elevated sense of self in More's readers. To help his readers along this path, More arms them with Newspeak ideas that make it impossible to express thoughts that do not conform to the demands of the Utopian state: prosperity is subsistence; achievement is usefulness to others; lawfulness is fear; thinking is following the orthodoxy; freedom is asking permission; happiness is humble conformity; virtue is subordinating oneself to the group; self-esteem is self-abnegation.

The translators buy into this sacrilege against the individual by translating *superbia* as "pride," thus equating a positive view of oneself with attempts to denigrate others. This historic error is reflected in the *Oxford English Dictionary* definition of pride, which conflates it with envy:

> The quality of being proud.
> I.1.a. A high or overweening opinion of one's own qualities, attainments, or estate, which gives rise to a feeling and attitude of superiority over and contempt for others; inordinate self-esteem.

The lack of an independent concept of pride in More's *Utopia*—and in western thought for centuries—left human beings no way to even conceive of, let alone achieve, earned self-esteem and non-sacrificial rewards. This concept of "pride"—similar to the "vain-glory" of Thomas Hobbes—engenders warfare, since it can only be expressed in terms of contemptuously beating another person.[33] It leads to tyranny, since the "proud" man demands absolute power.[34] It brings economic exploitation, since it claims that one can become rich only by unjustly seizing the property of others. This kind of "proud" man acts as a rapacious beast, destroying others before they have a chance to destroy him. He then feels superior given his ability to dominate others. It should be obvious that this perverse equation of "pride" with "envy" has nothing to do with the self-sufficient and rational egoism of Prometheus, who does not measure his own value in relation to others. His pride blossoms fully only after he flees alone into the woods, and sees his own image for the first time.

The war against ambition and pride is a moral war against the mind. As Ayn Rand wrote in her introduction to *The Fountainhead*:

> Just as religion has pre-empted the field of ethics, turning morality *against* man, so it has usurped the highest moral concepts of our language, placing them outside this earth and beyond man's reach. "Exaltation" is usually taken to mean an emotional state evoked by contemplating the supernatural. "Worship" means the emotional experience of loyalty and dedication to something higher than man. "Reverence" means the emotion of a sacred respect, to be experienced on one's knees. "Sacred" means superior to and not-to-be-touched-by any concerns of man or of this earth.

Ayn Rand's great achievement in *Anthem* is to smash the false dichotomy between rapacity and humility in matter and in spirit, and to regain the proper sense of man's highest abstractions. She re-establishes pride as the crown of the virtues by providing an objective means for a man to evaluate, improve, and honor his own life. Her break with the Judeo-Christian condemnation of ambition and pride removes the stigma of otherism—either of one's neighbor, or of a higher transcendent reality—from moral evaluations, and leaves man free to understand and value this world and his own person by an independent moral standard. As she later elaborated in her essay "The Objectivist Ethics":

> The virtue of Pride can best be described by the term: "moral ambitiousness." It means that one must earn the right to hold oneself as one's own highest value by achieving one's own moral perfection—which one achieves by never accepting any code of irrational virtues impossible to practice and by never failing to practice the virtues one knows to be rational—by never accepting an unearned guilt and never earning any, or, if one has earned it, never leaving it uncorrected—by never resigning oneself passively to any flaws in one's character—by never placing any concern, wish, fear or mood of the moment above the reality of one's own self-esteem. And, above all, it means one's rejection of the role of a sacrificial animal, the rejection of any doctrine that preaches self-immolation as a moral virtue or duty.[35]

This is the central ambition possible to man: a self-created moral character, achieved according to an objective standard. As philosopher Leonard Peikoff elaborated, the virtue of pride has both existential and intellectual aspects. Existentially, to be proud one must actually do something worthy of praise. The society of *Utopia* is designed to eliminate any possibility of actually achieving anything to be proud of. Equality 7-2521 is in just such a position. But, when he breaks free of his prison and runs into the woods, he proclaims, for himself and for his readers, that he can achieve his values. In his transformation into Prometheus, he discovers the existential aspect of pride as a moral virtue, in the act of procuring a meal for himself:

> We stopped when we felt hunger. We saw birds in the tree branches, and flying from under our footsteps. We picked a stone and we sent it as an arrow at a bird. It fell before us. We made a fire, we cooked the bird, and we ate it, and no meal had ever tasted better to us. And we thought suddenly that there was a great satisfaction to be found in the food which we need and obtain by our own hand. And we wished to be hungry again and soon, that we might know again this strange new pride in eating. (79)

This discovery of his own efficacy is his gateway to the discovery of the intellectual aspect of pride. His implicit recognition of the value of his own self is precisely what he vaguely felt earlier as a sin. His prior acceptance that his brothers had an unimpeachable claim on what "we" do left him no means of achieving pride—as it would be impossible for the Utopians to achieve. By condemning the products of ambition, Utopia roots out the existential basis for pride. By debasing human nature and substituting the good of the community and reverence for God, *Utopia* uproots the intellectual basis by which pride can be achieved. The only people in *Utopia* who can tolerate the misery are those who bow their heads and accept the substitution. (It is More's fervent wish that the entire world do so.) Prometheus follows a different road: he takes his own achievements—his light bulb, and his sense of self—and he learns to live by his own actions.

The vision of Prometheus, triumphant after producing his own meal and in awe of his own image, is Ayn Rand's vision of what is possible to each one of us. Her radical return to Aristotle's conception of pride as the crown of the virtues is a deep challenge to the views of man held by Plato, Augustine, More, and a long line of western thinkers. Her scope extends far beyond the other utopian—and anti-utopian—writers of the twentieth century. She corrects the sacrilege of the ages by placing man at the center of her thought, and deriving her ideals from his nature as a moral being. No longer needing the warrant and the sanction of either medieval ascetics or modern socialists, man can now take his place as "this god who will grant them joy and peace and pride" (97). The sacrilege ends when each man's sacred temple, and the values it holds, are placed off-limits to others. In Ayn Rand's thought, pride is no longer a "perverse kind of exaltation" but the only kind of exaltation truly possible: man-worship.

By focusing her efforts on what is truly the highest and noblest, Ayn Rand provides a truly revolutionary Eutopian vision. Her world is based not on Platonic idealism and a doomed struggle by each victim to shape his nature into the form of unreal ideals, but rather on an Aristotelian vision in which one recognizes as ideals those standards that conform to man's true, elevated nature. Each man can rise ambitiously to the height of his own perfection, and can exalt in his own achievement. In her world, as in that of Aristotle, man can truly become good, and then see himself as good—the reward of pride. "It is truly hard to be proud," said Aristotle, "since it is not possible without being fine and good."[36] But the ideal is possible, for it is real, and of this earth. As Equality 7-2521 says, anticipating the rebirth of man: "our son will be raised as a man. He will be taught to say 'I' and to bear the pride of it" (100).

## NOTES

1. Michael S. Berliner, *Letters of Ayn Rand* (New York: Dutton, 1995), 33–34; letter dated July 5, 1936.

2. "Sacrilege" is a combination of the Latin *sacer*, "sacred" and *legere*, "to gather up or take away."

3. *The Compact Oxford English Dictionary*, second edition (Oxford: Clarendon, 1991): "pride" (B.I.1.d) reckoned the first of the deadly sins; see also "deadly" (5).

4. Aristotle, *Nicomachean Ethics*, trans. Terence Irwin (Indianapolis: Hackett, 1985), 101 (4.3, 1124.a1).

5. St. Augustine, *City of God*, trans. Henry Bettenson (New York: Penguin, 1984), 571 (14.12–13, citing *Ecclesiastes* 10.13).

6. That More was concerned to extend the communism of Plato's *Republic* even to wives is stated by Desiderius Erasmus; see David Wootton's introduction to Thomas More, *Utopia with Erasmus's The Sileni of Alcibiades*, ed. and trans. by David Wootton (Indianapolis: Hackett, 1999), 5.

7. More is consistent with other writers of the Northern European Renaissance, such as his friend Erasmus, whose own book, *Praise of Folly*, plays on More's name (in Latin, the book is titled *Encomium Moriae*, "Praise of More") and uses a character, Folly, to hide Erasmus's own views. It is impossible to know whether the "Praise" is Erasmus's praise of Folly, or Folly's praise of the things that Erasmus is attacking.

8. "*Utopia*" refers to the book; "Utopia" to the island portrayed in the book.

9. Thomas More, *Utopia*, trans. Robert M. Adams (New York and London: Norton, 1975), 49.

10. More, *Utopia*, 40. Normally this requires adoption into another family.

11. More, *Utopia*, 42.

12. More, *Utopia*, 86. The Utopians oppose attempts at physical beauty by women. They "consider cosmetics a detestable affectation. From experience they have learned that no physical beauty recommends a wife to her husband so effectually as truthfulness and reverence," 68.

13. More, *Utopia*, 49, emphasis added.

14. More, *Utopia*, 46, 47, 58. Given that slaves are often criminals being punished for crimes, and given that the purpose of punishment is to lead men to virtue (19) to place slaves in vicious conditions is contradictory. Perhaps these particular slaves are

foreigners, captured in war. In any case, Utopia is a slave society, and the Utopians must fear being turned into slaves.

15. More, *Utopia,* 61, 64–65, 67.

16. The idle rich are a feature of many utopian works of the time; Campanella's *City* has an idle and avaricious majority. See Henry Morley, *Ideal Commonwealths* (New York: Hippocrene, 1988), 158.

17. Ayn Rand, "Questions and Answers on *Anthem,*" in *The Ayn Rand Column,* ed. Peter Schwartz (New Milford, CT: Second Renaissance Books, 1991), 118.

18. *The Sileni of Alcibiades* by Erasmus deals with an ugly sculpture that has a beautiful figure inside it. This contrast between internal and external viewpoints is, to Wootton, needed to understand *Utopia.* See Wootton's introduction to his translation of More's *Utopia.*

19. More, *Utopia,* 84. Priests get preferential treatment in hospitals, 46. More's solution to conflicts between church and state is to establish a class of church officials with their own laws.

20. More, *Utopia,* 43. More stresses, more than once, that scholarship is "assigned" in a "class" (or "order") of learned men, e.g., 53.

21. Ayn Rand, *Anthem:* "the Councils are the voice of all justice, for they are the voice of all men" (22); "What is not thought by all men cannot be true" (73).

22. Ayn Rand, "An Analysis of the Proper Approach to a Picture on the Atomic Bomb," in *Journals of Ayn Rand,* ed. David Harriman (New York: Dutton, 1997), 314.

23. Ayn Rand, "Tax-Credits for Education," in her *The Voice of Reason: Essays in Objectivist Thought* (New York: paperback edition, Meridian, 1989), 247.

24. More, *Utopia,* 80.

25. More, *Utopia,* 80.

26. Schwartz, *Ayn Rand Column,* 118.

27. More, *Utopia,* 90–91.

28. More, *Utopia,* 68, including Adams's note 2: "The grain (prosperity) and the candle (vision) obviously symbolize the special function of each ruler."

29. Ayn Rand, *For the New Intellectual* (New York: Random House, 1961; Signet paperback edition, 1963), 18.

30. More, *Utopia,* 90. English translator Ralph Robynson (1551) emphasized "pride" by repeating the word several times; More only says *superbia* once, and makes further references in the form "she."

31. Thomas More, *The Complete Works of St. Thomas More,* vol. 13., ed. Garry E Haupt (New Haven: Yale University Press, 1976), 7, 14 (language modernized, emphasis added). The *Treatise on the Passion* was written late in More's life, probably during his imprisonment in the Tower, from April 17, 1534, to July 6, 1535, and immediately before his execution. More had earlier acknowledged his debt to Augustine for the phrase "wicked . . . pryde"; see 246, note to sec. 14/3.

32. More, *Complete Works,* vol. 13, 8 (emphasis added).

33. Thus the poet Vergil, in his epic *Aeneid,* charts Rome's destiny as follows: "Roman, these will be your arts: to teach the ways of peace to those you conquer, to spare defeated peoples. Tame the proud (*superbos*)." *The Aeneid of Vergil,* trans. Allen Mandelbaum (New York: Bantam Books, 1981), 160 (6.850–53).

34. The name of the last King of Rome, Tarquinius Superbus, is commonly translated as "Tarquin the Proud." Livy, *The Early History of Rome,* trans. A. de Sélincourt

(New York: Penguin, 1971), 101, 105. He was overthrown for his tyranny and debauchery.

35. Ayn Rand, "The Objectivist Ethics," in her *The Virtue of Selfishness: A New Concept of Egoism* (New York: New American Library, 1964), 27.

36. Aristotle, *Ethics*, 101 (4.3, 1124.a3–4). Irwin's translation "magnanimous" is here altered to "proud" for clarity.

# 10

## Needs of the *Psyche* in Ayn Rand's Early Ethical Thought

*Darryl Wright*

> *After all, any form of swift physical annihilation is preferable to the inconceivable horror of a living death. And what but a rotting alive can human existence be when devoid of the pride and the joy of a man's right to his own spirit?*
>
> —Ayn Rand, Letter to John Temple Graves, July 5, 1936[1]

In her 1964 essay collection *The Virtue of Selfishness*, as well as in her 1957 novel *Atlas Shrugged*, Ayn Rand presents the ethical theory for which she is today well-known.[2] The theory developed in stages over several decades, as Rand worked through a range of questions concerning the foundations and substantive content of ethics. My interest here is in the earliest stages in this process of development, from shortly after she immigrated to the United States from the Soviet Union, in 1926, through the publication in Great Britain of the first edition of *Anthem,* in 1938.

This period offers a wealth of material to consider, and one can see many key aspects of Rand's mature ethical thought beginning to take shape. I will concentrate on one main issue: the earliest antecedents of her innovative later views regarding the foundations of ethics. Rand later held that values, in the broadest sense of the term, were grounded in the survival needs of living organisms, and that specifically *ethical* values were grounded in a distinctive (survival-related) need of human beings for a framework of abstract principles by which to guide their action. Even in the late 1930s, Rand remains many steps away from a complete formulation of this theory and its supporting arguments, for which she will have to rely on views about the epistemology of ethics that she does not reach until the 1940s and 1950s. But from very early on, she is convinced that human life gives rise to needs—in particular, to what might be called needs of the *psyche* or *spiritual needs*—that form the basis of ethical norms. I will chart the emergence of this view in Rand's writings prior to *Anthem,* and then explore her use of it, in *Anthem,* to structure the course by which her protagonist, Equality 7-2521, gradually re-orients himself toward an ethics of egoism from one of collectivist self-denial.

The discussion that follows is selective and somewhat episodic. I omit much of Rand's early corpus, including much that a full account of the development of her ethical thought would have to cover. I also make almost no attempt to relate her thought to that of other philosophers, although there is much to be said here, especially in regard to her relation to Greek ethics and to Nietzsche. I do, however, bring into focus aspects of Rand's early ethical thought that may not be apparent at first but that can help us better understand both the ethical vision of *Anthem* and Rand's mature views. I deal with the latter briefly at the conclusion of the essay.

## NORMS FOR LIVING: *THE SKYSCRAPER,*
## *THE LITTLE STREET,* AND "THE HUSBAND I BOUGHT"

Let us start by looking at three early fiction-writing projects undertaken by Ayn Rand in the late 1920s. My aim is to elicit from these an initial conception of the nature and source of ethical norms, a conception whose development I then follow, in schematic form, up through the publication of the first edition of *Anthem.*

One of the first projects Rand worked on in America (as a screen writer for Cecil B. DeMille) was a scenario for a movie about the construction of a skyscraper. In her working notes for the scenario (entitled *The Skyscraper*), which date from 1927, she describes what the movie should show:

> The *effort* of the building, the construction—all the details of that effort. The types, what they do, what happens to them and so on. . . .
> *"Achievement is the aim of life."*
> Life is achievement. . . .
> Achievement—give yourself an aim, something you *want* to do, then go after it, breaking through everything, with nothing in mind but your aim, all will, all concentration—*and get it.*[3]

From an ethical perspective, what is of particular interest here is the statement that "Achievement is the aim of life." How should we understand this? Taken as a description of how people live, it is false, for clearly achievement is not everyone's aim, nor even necessarily *most* people's aim. Rand would have acknowledged as much; her view, during the period when she wrote the above notes, was that people rarely had achievement as their aim.[4] At best, we would have to say that achievement is an aim that some people have and others lack, but "some people seek achievement—therefore achievement is the aim of life" hardly seems a promising inference. It is not immediately clear, therefore, what to make of Rand's claim about achievement. How can it be the case that the aim of life is achievement, if achievement may well be the farthest thing from most people's minds most of the time?

The possibility is not as anomalous as it might seem. There are many things that are true of "human life" that are not true of every individual human life or even necessarily of most human lives. Consider the statement "Man ingests food through his mouth and walks on two legs." The statement is true, even though not every human being can do these things; and even if a great many people could not do these things, it would not *thereby* follow that the statement was false. When we generalize about human life in these instances, we set aside cases of defect and disease. "Man walks on two legs" does not mean "All men walk on two legs" with the quantifier "all" ranging over every member of the species. It is a statement about human life in its non-defective and non-diseased instantiations, about human life *as such*. Thus we can say that it is in the nature of human life that man walks on two legs, even though some men do not. Seemingly paradoxically, in cases of this kind, we generalize about "human life"—and can only do so—by deliberately excluding some instances of that life from consideration. The same is true throughout the biological study of human life, and throughout all biological study, insofar as it is concerned to characterize the human or any other life form.[5] There is a precedent, therefore, for the idea of generalizing about human life *as such* from a restricted class of cases.

The analogy to biological generalization suggests that Rand's claim about achievement has a *normative* dimension, because biological generalizations themselves have a normative dimension. The statement "Man ingests food through his mouth and walks on two legs" tells us how things are when they are as they *ought to be* with a member of the human species. If a particular person is unable to do these things, we conclude that things are not right with him; that there is some defect preventing him from functioning properly. If we were to adopt a parallel understanding of the statement about achievement, we would take it to entail similar conclusions about someone who did not seek to achieve anything.[6] We would understand the statement about achievement as a *normative* claim, presenting achievement as the *proper* (or, at least, as *a* proper) aim of life. This, I think, is how the statement should be understood, notwithstanding its descriptive-looking surface grammar. Rand is describing how a person ought to live, not how people actually live[7]; a human life, she is saying, ought to be a life dedicated to the concentrated, determined pursuit of self-chosen goals.

What, then, is the basis of Rand's normative claim? What is the source of the norm she advances here? She restates the claim to read that "Life is achievement." This suggests that the norm about achievement is grounded in the nature of human life itself; that in some sense life by its very nature "demands to be" a process of achievement.[8] On this view, it is possible to derive norms for what a human life should be—for how such a life should go—from facts about what it is. There is no need to suppose that such norms are imposed on life from the outside, as it were, by some distinct source of normative authority such as the will of God, the Form of the Good, or the conventions of society.[9] But the nature of such norms seems puzzling. How could an examination of human life itself lead to the conclusion that achievement is its proper aim, or one of its proper aims? One can certainly find individuals in real life who—like the heroes of *The Skyscraper*—do make achievement their aim. However, it is not immediately clear what pointing to such individuals accomplishes, beyond confirming an unsurprising fact—that some people seek achievement. What we are looking for is a norm concerning what everyone should seek, and the identification of a sub-class of achievement-oriented human beings would seem to put us no closer to establishing any such norm. In order to establish that "achievement is the aim of life," we would need grounds for regarding the lives of these achievement-seekers as normative for all human lives. Moreover, our grounds for so regarding them would need to be drawn from facts about the human life process itself, rather than from anything external to that process, if the norm about achievement were to have the requisite sort of "internal" justification.

Our previous examples are again instructive, as a model of the kind of norms we need and how they might be grounded. When we say that there is something the matter with a person who cannot ingest food through his mouth—something the matter with the person's health—our reason is neither that ingestion by mouth is what God wills, what society expects, nor what is good in some abstract, Platonic sense, but rather that the impairment of this capacity impairs a person's ability to live at all. It is in this sense that our reasoning appeals to the nature of the human life process itself; the process, we say, is of such a nature that its continuation is hampered or threatened when the capacity for oral ingestion of food is impaired. Similar points would apply to other norms of physical health. Broadly speaking, these norms have the same sort of foundation in the nature of human life that Rand appears to be claiming for the norm about achievement.[10]

How, then, might an attempt to ground the norm about achievement in facts about human life go? As in the preceding examples, there would have to be facts about human nature in virtue of which a life not focused on achievement was hampered or threatened. Presumably these would be facts of a rather different kind from the facts about human physiology on which our judgments in the preceding examples would be based. Even if there were some kind of connection between the lack of a commitment to achievement and ill-health, Rand's point in the above passage is surely not that those who do not seek to achieve anything suffer from ill health. She is presenting achievement not as a means to health but, in some sense, as what life is all about. If there is some defect in those who do not seek to achieve anything, it is not (as far as Rand is concerned) a health defect but a defect in the way they view and conduct their lives. We might call it a defect within the *psyche* or the *soul,* a defect that is *spiritual* rather than physical, in a wholly naturalistic sense of all three of these terms. Rand (who was an atheist) uses the term "spiritual" throughout her writings, to refer to that which concerns our conscious lives, and so I will follow that usage here in characterizing her views.[11] In order to ground the norm about achievement in facts about human nature, then, we would have to show that features of our conscious lives can either facilitate or hamper our ability to go on living and, on that basis, draw a distinction between (as I will say) spiritual well-being and deficiency. Spiritual well-being might then turn out to depend on, or to be partly constituted by, a commitment to seeking achievement, and the condition of the spiritually well-off individual (this commitment included) could be taken as normative for the species as a whole.[12]

The passage on achievement gives us Rand's view of the general form that a spiritually well-off human life will take, in one aspect at least. It will be a life characterized by the concentrated and determined pursuit of self-chosen goals. We can take this passage as Rand's first pass at characterizing spiritual well-being. In later writings, she will enrich and refine this characterization, and she will make her reliance on an analogue of the distinction between health and disease more explicit. For evidence of both trends, we can turn to one of her next projects.

In 1928, Ayn Rand made notes for a novel (never completed) that was to be entitled *The Little Street*.[13] The novel's theme was to be "The tragedy of a man with the consciousness of a god, among a bunch of snickering, giggling, dirty-story-telling, good-timing, jolly, regular fellows." Here is part of her description of the "regular fellows," that is, average people:

> Show *that humanity is utterly illogical,* like an animal that cannot connect together the things it observes. Man realizes and connects much more than an animal, but who can declare that his ability to connect things is perfect? The future, higher type of man will have to perfect just this ability [to achieve] the clear vision. A clear mind sees things *and* the connections between them. Humanity is stumbling helplessly in a chaos of inconsistent ideas, actions, and feelings that can't be put together, without even realizing the contradictions between them or their ultimate logical results.[14]

In part, this passage describes average people as they seemed to Rand in this period.[15] But it also does something more, as the reference to "the higher type of man" indicates. The passage provides further elaboration of Rand's conception of (what I have called) spiritual well-being and deficiency and, thus, expresses a norm for human life. The spiritually deficient individual gropes around in an intellectual chaos produced by his failure or inability to make connections among the things he observes. By contrast, the spiritually well-off individual is concerned to make logical connections, to eliminate contradictions from his thinking, and to act on the basis of a clear understanding of the "ultimate logical results" of his "ideas, actions, and feelings." This adds to the previous characterization of spiritual well-being in terms of the commitment to achievement. Spiritual well-being now depends both on the commitment to achievement and on the formation and maintenance of an integrated worldview.[16]

But what shows that this is what spiritual well-being involves, or that there is any objective distinction between well-being and deficiency in this area? It is easy enough to draw distinctions between "higher" and "lower" modes of life. But it is not sufficient merely to draw such distinctions; the *way* in which we draw them needs to be justified, if the norms we expect the distinctions to support are to have any claim to objectivity. For all we have said so far, the distinction between spiritual well-being and deficiency might be arbitrary or based only on an esthetic preference for certain modes of life over others. If this distinction is to support norms whose objectivity rivals that of the norms of physical health, there must be something in the nature of human life that requires us to consider certain instances of that life to be diseased or defective. I have already suggested what this is, drawing on the analogy to health. What must be shown is that there can be features of a person's conscious life that hamper or threaten his ability to go on living. Does Rand hold such a view of the characteristics she regards as forms of spiritual deficiency? She does, beginning in the notes for *The Little Street* and continuing, with various additions and modifications, throughout all her subsequent fiction and much of her nonfiction. In this essay, I can canvass only a small selection of this material, mostly restricted to Rand's early writings. I begin by looking further at the notes for *The Little Street*.

Let us consider two passages describing, respectively, the protagonist of the novel, Danny Renahan, and the majority of people (in the novel and in real life). Here is Rand's description of Danny Renahan:

> He realizes that he is living, he appreciates every minute of it, he wants to *live* every second, he is unable to *exist* as other men do. He doesn't take life for granted and live as he happens to be living—just calm, satisfied, normal. For him, life [must be] strong, high emotion; he has to live "on top," "breathing" life, tense, exalted, *active.* He cannot spend eight hours each day on work he despises and does not need. He cannot understand men spending their lives on some work and not liking that work, not doing with it what they please. . . .
>
> He doesn't have people's attitude toward life, that is, the general way of existing calmly day to day and [experiencing] something strong and exalting only once in a while, as an exception. "*Everyday life*" *does not exist for him.*

His normal state is to be exalted, all the time; he wants *all* of his life to be high, supreme, full of meaning.[17]

There follows a description of the majority of people:

They do not hold anything to be very serious or profound. There is nothing that is sacred or immensely important to them. There is nothing—no idea, object, work, or person—that can inspire them with a profound, intense, and all-absorbing passion that reaches to the roots of their souls. They do not know how to value or desire. . . . They are too small and low for a loyal, profound reverence—and they disapprove of all such reverence.[18]

The first of these passages gives us a new way of characterizing the difference between the "higher type of man" and other men. The higher types *live,* whereas the others merely *exist.* What does this distinction come to? As the two passages together show, the general contrast is between activity and passivity. Those who merely "exist" fail to become fully engaged in life; though they presumably take some action, they are inactive in important respects. The second passage sums up the essential nature of their inactivity in the statement that such people "do not know how to value or desire." "Valuing" suggests a conceptual appraisal whereas "desiring" suggests an affective response, and Rand's description suggests that both are involved in the state of being she calls "living." "Living" involves *holding* things sacred—whether an "idea, object, work, or person"—and being inspired with *passion.*[19]

Rand has now further expanded her conception of spiritual well-being and spiritual needs. Spiritual well-being now involves "knowing how to value and desire," as well as seeking achievement and maintaining an integrated worldview. Values and desires, in turn, are a spiritual need; those who lack them are spiritually deprived. Thus, as Rand now says, they "exist" but do not "live."

Rand's use of the distinction between "living" and "existing", in the first of the passages we have been considering, suggests that she does indeed believe that there can be features of a person's conscious life that hamper or threaten his ability to live, and that she does indeed mean to base her judgments of spiritual deficiency on the requirements of sustaining life. But let us be careful. To read Rand in this way requires us to ascribe literal content to the distinction between "living" and "existing"; it requires us to view this distinction as more than a metaphor. Can the distinction be viewed in this way? It seems to me that it can. The "life" of any living organism consists in a (generally variegated, multifaceted) process of action performed by and/or occurring within the organism. In the short run, at least, the process is not an all-or-nothing proposition: it can be carried on incompletely, with some of its elements either not occurring or occurring in a weakened form. Where the process is significantly impaired, there is a literal sense in which, to the extent of its impairment, the organism is "not living," even though it is also not yet dead. And this, I suggest, is how we should read Rand's statement above. Her point is that there is a significant gap in the life-functions of the non-valuing, non-desiring types of people. They drag on, like a drooping plant deprived of water, but the life process has been compromised.

Understood in this way, the living-existing distinction suggests a structural analysis of spiritual deficiency in terms of the suspension or impairment of certain necessary life-functions. The life-functions in question must be ones that we carry on through our conscious lives—that is to say, through thought, affect, and action—rather than functions performed automatically by our bodies, such as cell nutrition or blood circulation. The suspension or impairment of any of these needed life-functions would constitute a form of spiritual deficiency.[20] This account implies that what would have to be shown, in order to justify a distinction between spiritual well-being and de-fect, is that there are certain life-functions—beyond those in terms of which we conceptualize health and disease—that are *necessary* for us. How, then, might this be shown? What kind of necessity are we dealing with here?

The life-functions that sustain health are necessary in the sense that their impairment has costs for a living organism's ability to function at all, that is, to remain in existence as a living thing. For example, the prolonged absence of liver function in human beings will eventually shut down all the other physiological systems and processes that, at the physiological level, make up the life of a human being. Liver function is necessary because its prolonged absence results in physical collapse and death. For humans and some other animal species, physical malfunctions also generally carry, at some point or other, the more immediate cost of physical pain. Now we have already said that Rand is not advancing the norm about achievement, or by parallel other norms of spiritual well-being, as norms of health. So we should not expect to find physical pain or physiological breakdown among the direct costs of spiritual deficiency. But if forming an integrated worldview, valuing and de-siring, and striving for achievement are necessary life-functions for a human being, then there should be *some* clear costs to our lives in neglecting these activities. Spiritual deficiency should have some negative bearing on our ability to live.

One kind of cost might involve our ability to satisfy *material* needs, needs for food, shelter, transportation, and so forth. The disorientation and passiv-ity of "existing" without "living" would assuredly make the satisfaction of these needs vastly more difficult (if not impossible), especially if writ large on a broad social scale, since it would deprive us of most of the discoveries and innovations on which we rely in order to satisfy them. Scientific knowledge and technological advancement require just the sort of active-mindedness, dedication to values, and commitment to achieve that Rand associates with "living" and with spiritual well-being. The material costs of spiritual decline will be a central theme of *Atlas Shrugged* and a prominent theme in *We the Living* and in *Anthem*. In her earliest work, however, Rand stresses not the material but the psychological costs of spiritual deficiency. Her notes for *The Little Street* suggest that, at the limit, the destruction of spiritual well-being is marked by emotional suffering and what we might call "spiritual collapse," that is, the psychological collapse of one's ability to think, choose, and act.

Let us consider, in this connection, two passages from the notes. The first describes one of the minor characters in the novel:

> A genius gone wrong. A handsome, brilliant young actor with a fine mind and a beautiful soul. Famous and successful, but gone wrong in that he is genuinely unhappy; his life is empty of desires or interests; he is cynical, tired, disgusted with everything—inside. Outside—he leads a wild life full of vice. He is not clear to himself, there is a continual chaos in his mind, regarding himself and the world. He does not know what he lives for or why he lives. *He does not care*— in an immense sense. An example of a fine frame that the little street has filled with its rotten content. Instinctively, he does not accept [the little street's view of life], he revolts against it—but he has no other. And it is too late for another. He shows how empty the little street's ideals are and what a wreck they make of an exceptional being. For they can't fill such a soul and they do not permit the [ideals] that could fill it. He is utterly cynical and does not believe in anything. He could not accept the little street's beliefs; they only killed in him all belief in believing.[21]

The second passage describes Hetty, the woman in love with Danny. By the end of the story, Danny has been convicted of the murder of a famous pastor, apparently a kind of Nietzschean ascetic priest who, motivated by a hatred of strength and happiness, had used his influence to ruin Danny's life and career.[22] Here is the description of Hetty, both in general and in the aftermath of Danny's conviction:

> A clear, *straight* soul. . . . Very sensitive. Lonely. Not a strong, ambitious career woman, but—a woman. Bewildered by life. Unable to adapt herself to things as they are. In the end, left aimless, with nothing to live for and a terror of living— showing how empty a place this world is for one who does not and cannot share its vices and vicious virtues.[23]

Hetty and the actor both have attributes of spiritual well-being, but they both also lack the strength of mind to resist the spiritually destructive effects of their social environment—an environment dominated by the types of people described earlier, who hold no meaningful values, take nothing seriously, and, in some cases (such as that of the pastor whom Danny kills) are motivated by a desire to destroy greatness. We consequently see both in Hetty and in the actor evidence not just of spiritual deficiency but of spiritual collapse, the inability to go on functioning as thinkers and agents. The actor is unhappy, has no desires or interests, is tired and cynical, outwardly wild and out of control, inwardly in a state of mental chaos. He has lost all concern for his life. Hetty, left without Danny, is aimless and terrified, with no further values to live for. These examples show that, for Rand, the etiology of spiritual collapse can have a social component; Hetty's and the actor's problems are not self-made but derive from the social conditions in which they find themselves. The social world has made it impossible for them to make sense of their lives and to sustain the deep reverence for values that each had inwardly been capable of. The examples show, also, the kinds of costs Rand would point to in order to justify the view that the lack of values, the failure to seek achievement, and the failure to bring order to one's observations and experiences are human defects. The costs Hetty and the actor bear are extreme; Rand need not claim that every spiritual defect unavoidably brings on spiritual collapse, any more than we would expect every physical ailment to cause death.[24] Presumably, however, she would also want to count less extreme forms of stultification and suffering as evidence that a mode of life was spiritually deficient.

The cases of Hetty and the actor presage more complex portrayals in Rand's later writings of tragic spiritual collapse, notably the collapses of Leo Kovalensky in *We the Living* and of Gail Wynand in *The Fountainhead*.[25] Not all spiritual collapse is tragic, in Rand's view; sometimes it is self-made and deserved, as in the case of Peter Keating in *The Fountainhead,* who lives to please and impress others, and whose lack of authentic values disables him in the end. Rand's most chilling fictional portrayal of deserved spiritual collapse is that of James Taggart toward the end of *Atlas Shrugged;* Taggart, when we last see him, is at the edge of insanity. Whatever the differences among these cases, as to the causes of collapse and the agent's own level of responsibility for it, what stands out in Rand's portrayals of the ends met by these various characters is that the individuals in question undergo the psychological destruction of their capacity to function as thinkers and agents. In that sense, their capacity to live is damaged. By contrast, the characters in Rand's fiction who are able to achieve and sustain spiritual well-being are able to sustain themselves as thinkers and agents, even in the most oppressive of circumstances. Kira Argounova, for instance—Rand's protagonist in *We the Living*—remains clear-sighted and intensely active right up to (and even briefly beyond) the moment when she is shot by a Soviet border guard in the attempt to escape from the USSR.

I am going to call the view that the nature of human life generates norms not just for man's physiological systems but for thought, choice, and action as well "the normative view of human life," or, for short, just "the normative view of life." We can find this view, in an attenuated form at least, in Rand's writings even before her notes for *The Skyscraper* and *The Little Street.* Here is a passage from a short story written in 1926, entitled "The Husband I

Bought." In this passage, the protagonist, Irene Wilmer, describes her feelings in the aftermath of losing the husband she had deeply loved:

> One has to live, as long as one is not dead. I live on. But I know that it will not be long, now. I feel that the end is approaching. I am not ill. But I know that my strength is going and that life simply and softly is dying away in me. It has burned out. It is well.[26]

Rand has not yet made the living-existing distinction that she introduces in *The Little Street*. But this passage relies on the same implicit contrast. Irene says previously that without her husband, "All was finished. . . . I had done my work. . . . Life was over."[27] She lives on, then, even though her life is over. There is no contradiction in what she says here since two different senses of "living" are in play. Irene is not dead, but she moves through her days in a state of loneliness, isolation, and lethargy; in Rand's subsequent terminology, she exists but does not truly live.[28] It is even clearer here than in Rand's descriptions of Hetty and the actor, in the notes for *The Little Street,* that Irene is unable to go on in this state. Although there is nothing physically the matter with her, she has reached a point where she is incapable of sustaining herself spiritually.

The normative view of life also pervades Rand's later writings. Although my main interest in this essay is Rand's early work, I want to cite one (lengthy) later passage that is closely related in content to those we have considered so far. The passage, from a 1966 article entitled "Our Cultural Value Deprivation," presents some of Rand's mature perspective on the same issue of spiritual well-being and deficiency that I have been tracing in her early writings:

> Man's emotional mechanism works as the barometer of the efficacy or impotence of his actions. If severe and prolonged enough, the absence of a normal, active flow of *value experiences* may disintegrate and paralyze man's consciousness—by telling him that no action is possible. . . .
>
> A chronic lack of pleasure, of any enjoyable, rewarding or stimulating experiences, produces a slow, gradual, day-by-day erosion of man's emotional vitality, which he may ignore or repress, but which is recorded by the relentless computer of his subconscious mechanism that registers an ebbing flow, then a trickle, then a few last drops of fuel—until the day when his inner motor stops and he wonders desperately why he has no desire to go on, unable to find any definable cause of his hopeless, chronic sense of exhaustion.
>
> Yes, there are a few giants of spiritual self-sufficiency who can withstand even this. But this is too much to ask or to expect of most people, who are unable to generate and to maintain their own emotional fuel—their love of life—in the midst of a dead planet or a dead culture. And it is not an accident that *this* is the kind of agony—death by value-strangulation—that a culture dominated by alleged humanitarians imposes on the millions of men who need its help.

A peculiarity of certain types of asphyxiation—such as death from carbon monoxide—is that the victims do not notice it: the fumes leave them no awareness of their need of fresh air. The specific symptom of value-deprivation is a gradual lowering of one's expectations. We have already absorbed so much of our cultural fumes that we take the constant pressure of irrationality, injustice, corruption and hooligan tactics for granted, as if nothing better could be expected of life. It is only in the privacy of their own mind that men scream in protest at times—and promptly stifle the scream as "unrealistic" or "impractical." The man to whom values have no reality any longer—the man or the society that regards the pursuit of values, of *the good,* as impractical—is finished psychologically.[29]

"Death by value strangulation" is death by a *spiritual affliction.* It is what Irene is in the process of undergoing when, shortly after the passage cited earlier, "The Husband I Bought" ends. Similarly, in *The Little Street,* it is the path that Hetty and the actor—who are trapped in a society that does not take the pursuit of values seriously—find themselves on.

Rand's notes for *The Little Street* criticize conventional views of ethics. The criticism implies that she intends the normative view of life as a *replacement* for conventional morality:

> *Morals* (as connected with religion) the real reason for all hypocrisy. The wrecking of man by teaching him ideals that are contrary to his nature; ideals he has to accept as his highest ambition, even though they are organically hateful and repulsive to him. And when he can't doubt them, he doubts himself. He becomes low, sinful, imperfect in his own eyes. He does not aspire to anything high, when he knows that the high is inaccessible and alien to him. Humanity's morals and ideals, its ideology, are the greatest of all its crimes. ("Unselfishness" first of all.)[30]

Rand believes that the acceptance of conventional moral ideals, such as the belief that it is admirable to be selfless, is spiritually damaging. She does not yet explain why selflessness and other conventional ideals are harmful, but her rejection of conventional morality is predicated on the normative view of life. Later in the same set of notes, her character description of Danny Renahan tells us that he reflects "the perfect egoism and will to live,"[31] which similarly suggests that the normative view of life will underwrite a defense of egoism.

But if Rand is proposing to replace conventional moral ideals, is she proposing to replace them with a new *morality* or with some *alternative* to morality? Norms of spiritual well-being are fundamentally egoistic: what they require of a person, they require for the person's own sake. But on some views of morality, moral norms are by definition non-egoistic.[32] Rand, however, rejects such views.[33] Holders of these views would see Rand as wanting to replace morality with something else. Although I think that there are decisive objections to such views, to engage the debate over the definition of morality would take us too far afield. In any event, the above passage shows that *Rand*, at least, thinks of morality simply as a system of ideals to live by. Since *this* conception of morality (which, if less widespread, is hardly idiosyncratic) leaves the content of moral ideals open, it would have us see Rand as wanting to replace conventional morality with a new set of moral ideals rooted in the normative view of life. This is certainly how she viewed her own aims; she meant to champion a new morality, not to advocate amoralism.


## THE NORMATIVE VIEW OF LIFE IN *WE THE LIVING* AND *IDEAL*

The distinction between living and existing—and with it the entire normative framework we have uncovered in *The Skyscraper, The Little Street,* and "The Husband I Bought"—carries over into Ayn Rand's ethical thought during the early 1930s. Nowhere is this more evident than in her first (completed) novel, *We the Living,* which invokes the living-existing distinction right in its title. The title refers primarily to the novel's three central characters, Kira Argounova, Leo Kovalensky, and Andrei Taganov. They are among the "living," not because they have survived some great pestilence or holocaust, but because they are among those who "know how to value or desire," in Rand's words from *The Little Street.* In this section, I explore Rand's use of the normative view of life in *We the Living* to undergird a political argument. I then discuss, much more briefly, the rather different use she makes of the normative view of life in her play *Ideal.* My general aim in this section is to illustrate the continuing importance of the normative view of life in Rand's ethical thought during the period in which she wrote these two works, both of which were completed in 1934.

*We the Living,*[34] which is set in Russia during the years following the Bolshevik revolution, has a moral-political theme; it is a defense, on moral grounds, of political individualism and a critique of all forms of collectivism. Rand frames the opposition between individualism and collectivism in terms of an individual's right to pursue personal values. Individualism affirms such a right; collectivism denies it, requiring that the pursuit of personal values be subordinated to the pursuit of social goals and values. But if personal values are a spiritual need, then so, Rand believes, is the political freedom to pursue them; and if there is a spiritual need for political freedom, and collectivism deprives us of such freedom, then collectivism stands condemned by the normative view of life. This is *We the Living*'s central moral argument for political individualism and against collectivism.[35]

Rand's expansive sense of "living" is explicit in a scene from late in the novel, in which Kira confronts Andrei—who has been a Communist Party member and an officer of the G.P.U.—about what the communist system has done to her life. She says, in part:

> Now look at me! Take a good look! I was born and I knew I was alive and I knew what I wanted. What do you think is living in me? Why do you think I'm alive? Because I have a stomach and eat and digest the food? Because I breathe and work and produce more food to digest? Or because I know what I want and that something which knows how to want—isn't that life itself? And who—in this damned endless universe—can tell me why I should live for anything but for that which I want? Who can answer that in human sounds that speak for human reason?[36]

What Kira wants, fundamentally, are a career in engineering and a life with Leo, whom she loves. (That her chief wants are for two of the items on Rand's list in the earlier passage on "valuing and desiring" suggests, I think, that "wanting" has substantially the same meaning here as "valuing and desiring" has in that passage.) Both have been closed off to her for political reasons (she has been prevented from pursuing her career on account of her bourgeois lineage, and Leo has been sent to prison on account of his aristocratic lineage). The communist system thus destroys life not only through the material hardships it imposes, which *We the Living* depicts in ample detail, but by seeking to contain and control the process of valuing and desiring that is integral to living. Kira describes the system's spiritual toll in the same scene with Andrei:

> you've tried to tell us what we should want. You came as a solemn army to bring a new life to men. You tore that life you knew nothing about, quivering, out of their very guts and you told them what it had to be. You took their every hour, their every minute, every nerve, every thought in the farthest corners of their souls, and you told them what it had to be. You came and you forbade life to the living. You've driven us all into an iron cellar and you've closed all doors, and you've locked us airtight, airtight till the blood vessels of our spirits burst! Then you stare and wonder what it's doing to us. Well, then, look! All of you who have eyes left—look![37]

The analogy between spiritual and physical deprivation and damage places this passage squarely within the framework of the normative view of life. The freedom to set one's own ends is presented here as a spiritual need, and the metaphor of being locked airtight anticipates Rand's later concept of "death by value strangulation."

*We the Living* is a detailed account of the spiritual costs of collectivism. Rand's most dramatic case study in the novel is Leo, and so I focus on him here.[38] Leo—who, as the son of a prominent counter-revolutionary, has been forced into hiding when the novel begins—is presented as having had latently the same passion for life as Danny Renahan has actually. But the first time we see him, there are signs that he has already been spiritually broken—or very nearly so. He advises Kira to run from people and warns her that it is his habit to "drink like a sponge."[39] They have met along a street in Petrograd, as Kira (lacking carfare) was making her way home and Leo was halfheartedly wandering in search of a prostitute. As they talk, "her face was a mirror for the beauty of his. Her face reflected no admiration, but an incredulous, reverent fear."[40] But Leo remains cynical, telling her, "I want to drink. I want a woman like you. I want to go down, as far down as you can drag me."[41] Kira replies, "You know, you're very much afraid that you can't be dragged down"[42]—and this is true. Leo, like Danny, "wants . . . life to be high, supreme, full of meaning."[43] If Rand believes that those who do *not* want this are spiritually deficient and suffer as a result, she believes that those who *do* want it, but are precluded from acting to achieve it, suffer that much more intensely. Leo makes this point explicitly the second time he and Kira meet:

> I don't want to believe anything. I don't want to see too much. Who suffers in this world? Those who lack something? No. Those who have something they should lack. A blind man can't see, but it's more impossible not to see for one whose eyes are too sharp. More impossible and more of a torture. If only one could lose sight and come down, down to the level of those who never want it, never miss it.[44]

In seeking to "drag himself down," Leo is seeking to obliterate his desire for a life "full of meaning." From Rand's perspective he has reason to be afraid that he cannot succeed at this—it means that his intense suffering will go un-relieved. Later, he tells Kira, "I thought you'd do it for me [that is, help him to degrade himself spiritually]. Now I'm afraid you'll be the one who'll save me from it. But I don't know whether I'll thank you."[45]

At their first meeting, Leo marvels at Kira's "appetite for life." "If one no longer has that appetite," she tells him, "why sit at the table?" He replies, "Perhaps to collect under the table a few little crumbs of refuse—like you—that can still be amusing."[46] As they part—planning to meet again in a month if Leo, who is about to leave Petrograd, is able to re-enter the city—he says that he will see her again "If I'm still alive . . . and if I don't forget."[47] But Kira becomes an unexpected source of spiritual renewal for him. At the end of their second meeting, as they again make plans to meet in another month, Kira tries to anticipate him by stipulating that they will meet "If you're still alive—and if you don't. . . ." But Leo interrupts with, "No. I'll be alive—because I won't forget."[48] Kira has become for him a reason and an incentive to live. Nevertheless, Leo is hardly optimistic. He tells Kira that he has no de-sires except "to learn to desire something," and that he has little expectation of success in this regard.[49]

If Leo's capacity to desire has been crippled, then, from the perspective of the normative view of life, so has his capacity to live. Why, however, does Leo lack the ability to desire anything? He seems inwardly stronger than Hetty or the actor in *The Little Street*. Rand first describes him as fol-lows: "His mouth, calm, severe, contemptuous, was that of an ancient chieftain who could order men to die, and his eyes were such as could watch it."[50] It is therefore not clear that a cultural atmosphere of indiffer-ence to values would be sufficient to debilitate him, although his initial ad-vice to Kira does suggest that he suffers from the sight of people who have no deep concerns and no enthusiasm for living. During their second meet-ing, Leo focuses on the political causes of his spiritual incapacitation. Kira, who at eighteen remains intensely optimistic, describes to him the engi-neering projects she sees in her future, including a glass skyscraper and an aluminum bridge. "Is it worth while, Kira?" Leo asks her. The exchange continues:

"What?"
"Effort. Creation. Your glass skyscraper. It might have been worth while—a hundred years ago. It may be worth while again—a hundred years from now—though I doubt it. But if I were given a choice—of all the centuries past—I'd se-lect last the curse of being born in the one we're living [in]."[51]

After telling Kira that the only desire he has is to learn to desire something, Leo gives a concise explanation of why he believes that effort and creation are not worth it: "It's a curse, you know, to be able to look higher than you're allowed to reach. One's safest looking down, the farther down the safest—these days."[52] This explanation implies that the reason why Leo is incapable of desiring is that he will not be allowed to fulfill whatever desires he might form. And this makes sense: it is psychologically plausible that a belief that one will be precluded from achieving what one wants would undermine one's ability to find anything to want.

It is clearly the political conditions of Soviet society (and perhaps other parts of the world) that Leo sees as the impediment here. Kira suggests that the system can be fought. But Leo finds the prospect of having to fight the communists itself degrading. "Sure," he says, "you can muster the most heroic in you to fight lions. But to whip your soul to a sacred white heat to fight lice . . . ! No, that's not good construction, comrade engineer. The equi-librium's all wrong."[53] In his mind as in Rand's, the communists are moti-vated only by envy for life that is strong and successful; there is no grandeur, no idealism even of a misplaced kind, in their cause.[54] To accept the need to fight them, Leo believes, would be to degrade himself in a way that would render him spiritually unfit for victory.

Notwithstanding his love for Kira, Leo is unable to overcome the spiritual damage he suffers. An attempt (with Kira) to escape from the country fails, so he and Kira must try to function within the confines of the Soviet system. After a bout with tuberculosis and a stay at a Crimean sanatorium, Leo returns to Petrograd physically well but spiritually devastated. Here is part of his exchange with Kira when she meets him at the train station on his arrival home (Kira speaks first):

> "And you're well? Quite, quite completely well? Free to live again?"
>
> "I am well—yes. As to living again . . ."
>
> He shrugged. His face was tanned, his arms were strong, his cheeks were not hollow any more; but she noticed something in his eyes that had not been cured; something that, perhaps, had grown beyond cure.
>
> She said:
>
> "Leo, isn't the worst of it over? Aren't we ready now to begin. . . ."
>
> "Begin with what? I've nothing to bring back to you—but a healthy body."[55]

Kira does not yet appreciate the way in which her own inner strength surpasses Leo's. She is one of what Rand would later call the "giants of spiritual self-sufficiency,"[56] whereas Leo is not. What saves Kira, spiritually, is a heroic refusal to accept her present conditions of life as permanent and unalterable, and, consequently, a refusal to make terms with the society around her. "I'll be afraid only on a day that will never come," she tells her cousin, Irina. "The day when I give up."[57] But Leo does give up, descending into alcoholism and increasingly risky behavior as an illegal speculator, in collaboration with the most cynical and corrupt elements of the Party. Just as Leo's doubts about his ability to live again, despite his restored health, express the normative view of life, so, too, does Kira's urgent warning to him, late in the novel, about the course he is pursuing:

> Leo, the bootlicking and all those things—that's nothing. There's something much worse that it's done to Victor, underneath, deeper, more final, and the bootlicking—it's only a consequence. It does that. It kills something. Have you ever seen plants grown without sunlight, without air? It can't do that to you. Let it take a hundred and fifty million living creatures. But not you, Leo! Not you, my highest reverence.[58]

Kira now sees, as she did not in the scene at the train station, that Leo's life remains endangered.

In the end it is Andrei who makes the political conclusions of *We the Living* explicit, in a speech at his Party Club that was to have been a routine report but becomes a critique of the Party itself. Andrei had initially seen the revolution and the ascendancy of the Bolsheviks as an opportunity to work against political and social oppression. Fired by idealism and consumed with his own work within the Party, he is slow to recognize the oppressive character of the revolution itself. Kira, whom he befriends and falls in love with, becomes the catalyst for that recognition. For although the revolution's operating principles require the near-total absorption of the private sphere of life into the public, Andrei cannot help but see his relationship with Kira as a purely private matter, and his joy in that relationship as a justification for it that no public considerations (including Kira's family background and conspicuous lack of interest in the Party) could override. Through his (ultimately unrequited) love for Kira, he grasps "what it is to feel things that have no reason but yourself [i.e., oneself]" and "how sacred a reason that can be" and that "a life is possible whose only justification is your [i.e., one's] own joy."[59] Contrary to the collectivist ideals of the Party, which call for the abolition of private purposes and private joys, Andrei now sees his own well-being and happiness as the proper purpose[60] and justification of his actions.

Andrei's speech at the Party Club invokes the normative view of life as a justification for egoism and political individualism:

> Every honest man lives for himself. Every man worth calling a man lives for himself. The one who doesn't—doesn't live at all. You cannot change it. You cannot change it because that's the way man is born, alone, complete, an end in himself. You cannot change it any more than you can cause men to be born with one eye instead of two, with three legs or two hearts. No laws, no books, no G.P.U. will ever grow an extra nose on a human face.[61]

The man who does not live for himself "doesn't live at all," that is to say, he merely "exists," his way of functioning is defective, with all that this implies for his ability to go on as a thinker and an agent. Once again, the reason why man must live for himself is grounded in human nature; man's essential nature—"the way man is born"—is such that he cannot function successfully if he lives any other way. Andrei's last sentence makes it clear that, for Rand, it is *nature* rather than convention that grounds the principles of ethics; these principles are no more alterable by human choice than are the biological principles of human physical development.[62]

What is the relation between the form of egoism described here and the normative view of life? I noted in the last section that the normative view is implicitly egoistic in regard to the justification of norms: it issues prescriptions for action in the interest of the agent's *own* well-being. From the perspective of the normative view of life, the requirements of the agent's own well-being are sufficient justification for action. What Andrei's statement now suggests is that a person's spiritual well-being depends in part on his *adopting this perspective on himself,* that is, on his regarding himself as the normative view of life regards him (or his well-being), namely, as a stopping point in the process of justifying how he should live.

Andrei's statement introduces the idea that human beings are *ends in themselves*. The phrase is a familiar one in Kantian ethics, but Rand gives it a different meaning from the one Kant attached to it. It would not fit with Kant's interpretation of this phrase to say that one should "live for oneself," that is, for one's own chosen ends, since this would be to neglect the duty Kant believes we all have to embrace and further the ends of others.[63] Andrei uses the thesis that human beings are ends in themselves to challenge the Communist Party's right to impose totalitarian rule. If individuals are ends in themselves, the state must leave them free to pursue their own self-chosen aims. For Rand, the thesis that human beings are ends in themselves also has a foundation in the normative view of life. When Andrei says that man is "born . . . an end in himself," he is plainly not referring to the actual social conditions into which men are born, since it is not true that men are always born into societies that allow them to set their own ends. He is saying, rather, that the freedom to set one's own ends is characteristic of human life in its non-defective forms and, therefore, is a norm for human life in general. The spiritually depleted condition of the masses under Soviet rule, as well as of their leaders, would be Rand's evidence that a political regime that treats individual human beings as means to social ends promotes spiritual defect and decay.[64]

The view that human life has spiritual needs, as well as physical and material ones, is also central to Rand's play *Ideal*. In this connection, the play deserves much more extensive analysis than I can give it here; two brief points will have to suffice. The protagonist is a revered actress named Kay Gonda, a Garbo-esque figure at the peak of her fame. Rand's career choice for Gonda is a brilliant stroke, for the play dramatizes *her* need for just the sort of heroic inspiration that her screen performances have provided for her fans. Late in the action, Gonda explains what it is that she longs for:

> Johnnie. If all of you who look at me on the screen hear the things I say and worship me for them—where do I hear them? Where can I hear them, so that I might go on? I want to see real, living, and in the hours of my own days that glory I create as an illusion! I want it real! I want to know that there is someone, somewhere who wants it, too! Or else what is the use of seeing it, and working, and burning oneself for an impossible vision. A spirit, too, needs fuel. It can run dry.[65]

This passage refers to (or implies) three distinct kinds of spiritual need. There are the needs satisfied by artistic representations, such as a screen performance (but by implication any form of art). There is the need to see artistic ideals made real in the world around us (for example, to see real achievements, or real acts of heroism or justice, similar in significance to those that might be dramatized in a work of fiction). And there is the need for *other persons* who take inspiration from the same ideals or values as oneself. In an earlier scene, involving a character whom she briefly views as a soul mate, Gonda calls this last the need for an "answering voice":

> One can do it just so long. One can keep going on one's own power, and wring dry every drop of hope—but then one has to find help. One has to find an answering voice, an answering hymn, an echo. I am very grateful to you.[66]

I will not attempt to analyze Rand's treatment of each of these three kinds of spiritual need here. For present purposes, I simply want to stress that what is at stake, for Gonda, in the satisfaction of these needs, is *her ability to go on with her life.* This is explicit in both passages, and it reflects the continuing prevalence in Rand's thought of the normative view of life.

## NORMS AND BIOLOGY

In *We the Living* and *Ideal,* Rand uses metaphors involving physical harm or deficiency to convey the point that there are forms of spiritual deprivation that can be as devastating for a human being, in the long run, as any purely physical deprivation or malfunction, such as the a lack of air or the breaking of a blood vessel or, in the case of plants, a lack of sunlight. The metaphors are literarily striking but, philosophically, just what one would expect to see in Rand's fiction, since the normative view of life depends precisely on an analogy between physical and spiritual needs. Rand's clearest, most explicit formulation of this analogy comes in a set of philosophical notes made in 1934, the same year in which she completed both *We the Living* and *Ideal.*

At one point, the notes discuss the will and freedom of the will. Rand writes:

> And if, as according to Mencken, the question of "freedom of the will" has to be studied on the basis of psychology with all its dark complexes—then what are we actually studying? Will as it is expressed in subnormal cases? Or in normal, average cases? Or in the highest types of human mentality?
>
> Are we studying will as *it is* actually in the majority of cases—or as *it can be essentially,* as a human attribute?
>
> Do we judge all human terms as applied to existing humanity or to humanity's highest possibility?
>
> If we are trying to form a general conception of a "stomach"—do we study a hundred diseased stomachs—and form our general conception from that—so that "stomach" as such is something with a number of diseases attached to it—or do we find the healthy stomach first, in order to learn what it is, and *then* judge the others by comparison?[67]

It is not clear what, in H. L. Mencken's writings, this passage refers to, but this is not particularly important for eliciting the point of the passage. Rand ascribes to Mencken the view that to consider the problem of free will it is necessary to study psychology "with all its dark complexes." Whether it is Mencken who sees psychological study as focusing on "dark complexes" or Rand who does (perhaps due to the impact of Freud on the field at that time)—and so whether Rand is challenging a particular conception of psychological inquiry (held by Mencken among others) or the relevance of psychology *per se* in a study of the will—is uncertain. Nevertheless, her view is that a method of inquiry focusing on "dark complexes" gives *defective* cases of willing undue influence on our overall understanding of the will. Rand maintains instead that study of the will should be broadly analogous to study of the stomach or of any other biological organ or system. It should be predicated, therefore, on some analogue of the distinction between a healthy and a diseased organ, and it should take the "healthy" will as its point of departure. The failure to proceed in this way will lead to a distorted conception of the will, according to Rand, just as the failure to distinguish between healthy and diseased stomachs, or to take the healthy stomach as a point of departure for biological study of the digestive system, would lead to a distorted conception of the stomach.[68]

Rand clearly views the biological sciences as normative rather than merely descriptive or statistical disciplines. We are to "find the healthy stomach first," study its nature and functioning, and then "judge the others by comparison." She is surely right about this. The normative approach is indispensable in biology. The stomach, for example, could not be understood apart from the concepts of health and disease. But health and disease are *normative* concepts: "health" is not the state of the majority of the members of a species or of any statistically defined subgroup; it is a state characterized by the *proper* operation of an organism's various systems (such as the respiratory system, the nervous system, and so forth). To distinguish healthy from diseased stomachs is to make a normative judgment about them. But it is only on the basis of such judgments that we can come to understand what the stomach *is*. For to understand what the stomach is, is *not* to know a set of statistics about stomachs. To understand what the stomach is, is to understand *what it ought to be*—what its proper operation consists in and requires. If we tried to exclude any normative perspective on the subject matter from biological inquiry, we would risk falling into the absurd sort of procedure that Rand lampoons in the above passage: the procedure of generalizing from a series of defective cases, and concluding that an organ or system is *by nature* in a condition that a normative perspective would identify as subnormal and diseased. The risk would remain even if we based our generalizations on what is statistically typical among a given population, since it is possible for a diseased or unhealthy state to be statistically typical (consider the incidence of myopia among humans or the growing incidence of obesity and of adult-onset diabetes among Americans). Anything we did learn about healthy stomachs (or what have you) would be purely accidental, and there would be nothing in our conceptual framework to flag such knowledge as having any significance beyond whatever statistical significance it might have.

In the above passage, Rand seems to be suggesting that the method of in-quiry used in biology can serve as a model for philosophical or psycholog-ical inquiry concerning the will. The reasoning seems to be that *since* we study the stomach (for example) normatively in biology, so, too, should we study the will normatively in philosophy or psychology. What might have led Rand to think that biology should be the model here? I suspect that she is *antecedently convinced* that there is a distinction to be made between the "highest instances" of the will and various levels of lesser instances. The question is then how to account for this distinction and determine its prin-ciple. What we are dealing with is a distinction in value, and Rand, as an atheist, would have rejected out of hand any theological basis for such dis-tinctions. She is also too empirical-minded to accept a non-naturalist ac-count of value along the lines of Plato's or G. E. Moore's,[69] and too contrary in her judgments of "higher" and "lower" to prevailing standards of value to take seriously the possibility that value-distinctions are rooted in culture or convention. Nor, clearly, is she willing to consider the distinction between higher and lower instances of the will an arbitrary one or a mere reflection of her own preferences in people. The distinction, as she sees it, is neither personally nor socially constructed, nor is it supernatural in origin. But then the same is true of biological norms (or so I would argue). What makes it true that a stomach in a certain condition is healthy—that it is as it ought to be—is neither that it is individually or socially approved of; that it is ap-proved of by God; that it instantiates a non-natural property of "health"; nor that we simply call stomachs like that "healthy." Biology, then, offers a model for norms that are objective but non-supernatural, norms with just the features Rand would have wanted to ascribe to the distinction she draws between the higher and lower instances of the will. As we have already seen, Rand deploys just such a model widely in her early writings, and she may have concluded, from repeated applications, that it helps make sense of a range of observations she had made about human life, for instance, that certain kinds of social conditions incapacitate us spiritually, or that having an integrated worldview helps us gather and sustain the initiative for de-manding forms of action.

## VALUES AND THE SELF: NOTES FOR *THE FOUNTAINHEAD*

In the mid-1930s, Ayn Rand began to work on her novel *The Fountainhead*. Her earliest working notes for the novel show her exploring further two is-sues we have seen her raise previously: the importance of values in human life and the justification of egoism. I will not discuss *The Fountainhead* in this essay, nor much from these notes, but I want to briefly document the continuing influence of the normative view of life on Rand's view of the nature of values.

In a passage dated December 4, 1935, she writes:

> are morals, or ethics, or all higher values a thing outside, god's law or society's prescription, something related not to a man, but to others around him, an ultimatum forced upon man and essentially selfless and *un*selfish? Or—a man's very own, his sacred, highest right, his best inspiration, his real life and real self? . . . . If, then, the higher values of life (such as all ethics, all philosophy, all esthetics, everything in short that results from a *sense of valuation* in the mental life of man) come from within, from man's own spirit—then they are a right, a privilege and a necessity—*not a duty.* They are that, which constitutes a man's life—and he, therefore, if he is an egoist in the best sense of the word, will choose these higher values *for himself* and for himself alone, that is, for his own sake and satisfaction, not because of a duty to god, fellow-men, the state or any other fool abstraction outside of himself. If a man has a certain code of ethics it is primarily for his own sake, not for anyone else's.[70]

The subject of the passage is the nature of the "highest" or most abstract sorts of values. Rand describes such values as "a right, a privilege and a necessity." I take it that what she means in calling them a "right" is not that these values should in some way be guaranteed to one—Rand never accepted the concept of "positive" rights, rights to be furnished with various goods or services—but that one has a right to pursue values unhindered by interference from others. She is thus re-affirming the political individualism defended in *We the Living.* Given this interpretation of the idea that values are "a right," Rand's next point, that values are "a privilege," cannot be taken to mean that having or pursuing values is a privilege granted to us by others (and so potentially revocable by them). She is using "privilege" more loosely, to refer to something one takes pleasure in, as opposed to something one endures grudgingly or with difficulty. In Rand's view, then, we have a right to pursue values and it is a pleasure, not a burden, to do so. Her next claim is even stronger: values, she writes, are "a necessity"—they are something we cannot do without. The claims that values are a "privilege" and a necessity are readily understandable in light of the normative view of life. The need for values and desires, as a guide and inspiration to action, has been central to her elaboration of that view all along; and pursuing or upholding what we value should benefit us spiritually and, consequently, be a pleasure, not a burden, according to the framework that the normative view of life provides.

Rand goes on to say that values are "that which constitutes a man's life." Here she rejects what might be called a *materialistic* conception of living, by which I mean a view that conceives of living exclusively in terms of physical self-maintenance. If holding values partially constitutes the life of a human being, then a human being's life comprises more than physical self-maintenance, and keeping oneself *alive* will involve more than just attending to physical needs. In effect, what Rand is doing here is reaffirming the distinction between "living" and "existing" presented in the notes for *The Little Street.* She is construing the holding of values as a necessary life-function for a human being. This makes it explicit that the standard of need being invoked in the statement that values are "a necessity" is the same as in Rand's earlier elaborations of the normative view of life, namely, the life-needs of a human being.

## THE ETHICAL VISION OF *ANTHEM*

Like *We the Living, Anthem* is a defense of individualism, this time against the backdrop of a mythic society of the remote future, rather than a real society from Ayn Rand's recent past. The society is so thoroughly collectivized that even proper names and singular pronouns have vanished. The populace is so thoroughly obedient and demoralized that Rand's protagonist, Equality 7-2521, unlike Kira in *We the Living,* has no trouble escaping across an un-patrolled border, once he decides that this is what he must do. The difference here is emblematic of a more general shift of focus, from Kira's struggle against a collectivist society to an inner struggle, on Equality's part, to understand his own rebellious nature.

Does the normative view of life survive into *Anthem?* Several features of the story show that it does. The clearest indication that the normative view is still operative comes after Equality has broken from his society and fled into a deserted area known as the Uncharted Forest. At one point, Equality reflects on the ethical teachings of his society:

> There is no life for men, save in the useful toil for the good of all of their brothers. But we lived not, when we toiled for our brothers, we were only weary. There is no joy for men, save the joy shared with all their brothers. But the only two things which set our soul on fire are the power we created in our glass box and the Golden One. And both these joys belong to us alone and concern not our brothers in any way. Thus do we wonder. (114/220)[71]

This passage relies on the living-existing distinction. Toiling for his brothers, Equality was unable to sustain that active vitality which, as we saw from her description of Danny Renahan, in Rand's view characterizes those who are fully engaged with life; he existed but did not live. By the terms of the normative view of life, therefore, the life of toil for one's brothers must be regarded as a defective form of human life, which is exactly how Equality is here in the process of coming to view it. "If that which we have found is the corruption of solitude," he wonders, "then what can men wish save corruption? If this is the great evil of being alone, then what is good and what is evil?" (113-114/219-20).

Similarly, according to the normative view of life, a life well lived will be joyous, whereas suffering and the absence of joy are indications that a way of life is defective.[72] The leaders of Equality's former society claimed that the only possible forms of joy are those which a person shares with all his fellow men. Equality's own experience, however, has suggested that this is not the case. He found no joy in the life he shared with his "brothers," but his secret and unauthorized construction of an electric light and his experiences with Gaea, a young woman he meets, have been the private, unshared sources of the deepest joy he has known. This implies that the rules of his former society, which forbid private human relationships and private work and study, mandate a defective way of life, and that Equality's violations of those rules have made his life more ideal.

Other evidence that Equality acquires supports the same conclusions. His life and his society are shot through with ethical inversions, in which the good looks like evil and the evil looks like good. International 4-8818, who conspires with Equality to violate the rules prohibiting private undertakings and private enjoyments, "are a tall, strong youth and their eyes are like fireflies, for they twinkle and there is laughter in them. We cannot look upon International 4-8814 and not smile in answer" (26/132). Although Equality believes that "The depth of our crime is not for the human mind to probe" (37/143), he finds that

> there is no shame in us and no regret. We say to ourselves that we are a wretch and a traitor. But we feel no burden upon our spirit and no fear in our heart. And it seems to us that our spirit is clear as a lake troubled by no eyes save those of the sun. And in our heart—strange are the ways of evil!—in our heart is the first peace we have known in twenty years. (37–38/143–44)

To have a personal friend or lover is called the "Transgression of Preference" and is against the rules of Equality's society. Yet when Equality commits this transgression for the second time, by taking an interest in Gaea, he "know[s] not why, when we think of them, we feel of a sudden that the earth is good and that it is not a burden to live" (44/150), and he finds himself singing after walking home from meeting her (51/157). One of the society's worst transgressors of the rules, who is burned at the stake, is so fully at peace with himself that there is "no pain in their eyes and no knowledge of the agony of their body. There was only joy in them, a joy holier than it is fit for human joy to be" (59/165).

By contrast, those who do live by the rules have bowed heads and "eyes that are not clear, but veiled and lusterless, and never do they look one another in the eyes" (52/158). In addition,

[t]he shoulders of our brothers are hunched and weary, and their muscles drawn, as if their bodies were shrinking and wished to shrink out of sight. And a word steals into our mind, as we look upon our brothers, and that word is fear. (52/158)

Equality adds:

There is fear hanging in the air of the sleeping halls, and in the air of the streets. Fear walks through the City. . . . All men feel it and none dare to speak.

We feel it also when we are in the Home of the Street Sweepers. But here, in our tunnel we feel it no longer. The air is pure under the earth. There is no odor of men here. And we feel clean, clean as if we had stepped out of a bath. (52–53/158–59)

Although the ethical code of his society specifies that "it must not matter to us whether we live or die" because "we matter not," Equality "rejoice[s] to be living" (53/159). But his "brothers" are seen to "cry without reason" or to scream "Help us!" in their sleep (53–54/159–60), and the leaders of the society evince terror at the sight of Equality's new invention when he presents them with his electric light and demonstrates its workings (90–91/196–97).

In terms of the ethical standards of Equality's society, one would have to say that moral goodness leads to fear and desperation, whereas moral evil produces feelings of joy, cleanliness, and inner peace. This seems highly paradoxical, to say the least, and it is a paradox that Equality ultimately cannot accept. But he does not resolve the paradox until he has lived in the Uncharted Forest and discovered that the "corruption of solitude" is a myth. Before that time, the paradox festers, as Equality's damnation of himself becomes ever more complete. Noticing that he cares less and less whether he violates society's rules, he writes,

It cannot be, we cannot be as evil as this. But we are. If only, we pray, if only we could suffer as we say this. Could we but suffer remorse, we would know that there is a spark of good left in us. But we suffer not. Our hand is light. Our hand and the thought which drives our hand to write, laugh at us and know no shame. (66/172)

Upon entering the Uncharted Forest, he believes that "We have torn ourselves away from the truth which is our brother men, and there is no road back for us, and no redemption" (98/204). The final stage of his self-excoriation comes when he acknowledges his true motives for producing his electric light. It had been possible for him to consider the light good without challenging his society's ethical standards by thinking of the ways in which the light could benefit mankind. However, Equality confesses, "We have lied to ourselves. We have not built this box for the good of our brothers. We built it for its own sake. It is above all our brothers to us, and its truth above their truth" (99/205). That realization leads Equality to pronounce himself "one of the Damned" (99/205), and, expecting that he will never see Gaea again, to conclude that "It is best if the Golden One forget our name and the body which bore that name" (99/205).

Taking the normative view of life as the basis for ethical judgments would require Equality to re-assess the standards by which he has judged himself, in light of the fact that violating these standards has brought him joy rather than suffering. It need not be denied that a person can feel good, for a time, about doing wrong. But if moral evil is a form of spiritual defect, with the criterion of defectiveness being the requirements of spiritual or psychological self-sustenance, then moral evil must be linked with emotional suffering in a manner broadly analogous to the way in which ill-health is linked to physical pain. At the time when he enters the Uncharted Forest, Equality is not ready for a re-assessment of his ethical standards. He takes his lack of remorse as proof that he lacks any spark of goodness, on the premise that a person who felt no remorse over wrongdoing would have to be unremittingly evil; he does not yet view his lack of remorse as grounds for challenging the standards of wrongdoing that he is applying. Why is this? The reason, it seems to me, is that at this point, he believes that he shortly *will* begin to suffer for his many transgressions and expects that, in the end, he *will* regret how he has lived. In entering the Uncharted Forest, he believes, he is beginning his descent into the ultimate form of moral corruption, the "corruption of solitude." In the moral universe of Equality's former society, the Uncharted Forest is the earthly equivalent of Hell, and the corruption of solitude—the corruption of a life wholly separate from that of the mass of men—is a penalty of equivalent severity to consumption by fire. Implicitly, therefore, Equality *does* accept the normative view of life; he believes that human nature is a source of norms concerning the overall form that a human life must take, and that the attempt to live in a manner at odds with these norms must ultimately be self-destructive. However, he believes that the norms warranted by human nature are precisely those of his former society. Because those norms have continued to govern significant aspects of his life, even if he has varied from them significantly as well, he has not yet had an opportunity to test them fully. Thus, from his perspective, upon entering the Uncharted Forest, the likeliest explanation for his lack of remorse over his "evil" is not that he has judged himself by the wrong standards, but that evil has so thoroughly permeated the depths of his soul that only the corruption of solitude could stir him to remorse—by which time it will be too late.[73]

The passages with which we began this section show Equality in the process of revising his moral outlook. "We have broken the law," he writes just before the first of these passages, "but we have never doubted it. Yet now, now as we walk through the forest, a great doubt rises in our heart" (114/220). It is his experience of life in the Uncharted Forest—the life that was to have exposed him to the greatest physical dangers and to have brought him to the deepest, most final state of moral corruption—that fuels this doubt. Equality discovers that he is capable of sustaining himself independently; the rumors of terrifying beasts and insurmountable perils turn out to have been unfounded. Moreover, there are forms of joy accessible to him that were impossible in his former society. Not only is he able to supply his own food, without having to rely on his brothers to provide it, but the process of feeding himself now acquires spiritual significance for him. Equality tells of killing a bird with a stone:

> We made a fire and we cooked the bird and we ate it, and no meal had ever tasted better to us. And we thought suddenly that there was a great satisfaction to be found in the food which we need and obtain by our own hand. And we wished to be hungry again and soon, that we might know again this strange new pride in eating. (103/209)

What converts Equality's doubts about his former society's moral code into certainty that this code must be rejected is his discovery that an entire culture, highly advanced both in its intellectual and material achievements, had flourished in the same environment in which he himself has found his greatest sense of fulfillment and well-being. In chapter X, he and Gaea discover a house from the Unmentionable Times—the remote (and individualistic) past—abundantly stocked with artifacts of that culture, and at the conclusion of their exploration of this house, Equality declares,

> This moment is a warning and an omen. This moment is a sacrament which calls us and dedicates our body to the service of some unknown duty we shall know. Old laws are dead. Old tablets have been broken. A clean, unwritten slate is now lying before our hands. Our fingers are to write. (125–26/231–32)

Equality now believes that he has grasped the ultimate results of the transgressions he has committed. The house he and Gaea explore is a private residence, equipped for only two people, as evidenced by the fact that it contains only two beds (120-21/226-27). He therefore recognizes it as an artifact of a culture that sanctioned and protected an individual's right to a private life, a culture whose moral code was the opposite of his own society's moral code. The code of his society has produced stagnation and misery. The rejection of that code, Equality is now in a position to conclude, opens the way not to some extreme of suffering and corruption but to intellectual advancement, material abundance, and joy. From the evidence of his own case and of the culture of the Unmentionable Times, he is now certain that he must reject the moral code of his former society and revise his judgments of himself.

In the above passage, Equality recognizes that he needs to find a new moral code to live by; the blank slate must not remain blank. And just as the normative view of life implicitly drives his rejection of his society's moral code, so too does it provide the implicit framework for a new code. Equality now believes that

> my joy needs no reason and no questions and no higher aim to vindicate it. My joy is not the means to any end. It is the end. It is the reason of reasons. This earth is mine. This earth exists but as a field for my desires and for the choice of my will. I am upon this earth but for the joy I wrest from it. What blind vanity, what folly can command me to live for pain? (130/236)

To allow a higher aim to constrain one's pursuit of happiness is to view one's own spiritual needs as providing insufficient justification for decisions about how to live. But that, in turn, is to accept that suffering and the frustration of those needs is endemic to the *proper* way to live, which, from the perspective of the normative view of life is an inversion of the truth. Equality thus dismisses the thought that he should put any other end above his own happiness as a "folly."

Equality intends in time to "call to me all the men and the women whose spirits have not been killed within them and who suffer under the yoke of their brothers" (141/247). Like Kay Gonda, he knows he needs an "answering voice" (and more than one), as well as partners in the construction of a new society. The satisfaction of both these needs will depend on the ability of those around him to preserve *their own* spiritual well-being. Equality therefore resolves that he will "ask none to live for me, nor [will] I live for any others. I covet no man's soul, nor is my soul theirs to covet" (131/237). He adds that he "shall choose companions from among my brothers, but neither slaves nor masters" (132/238). His need *for* others gives him a reason to respect the spiritual needs (and so the autonomy) *of* others.

## CONCLUSION

When Ayn Rand discussed the need for values in her notes for *The Little Street,* her examples of values were both particular (an individual person) and abstract (an idea). Later, in her *Fountainhead* working notes, she stresses the need for abstract ethical values, which she saw as defining a person's identity and giving shape to his life. She does not yet attempt to settle what ethical values a person should hold, other than those associated with egoism and individualism. In the 1940s and 1950s, however, she fills this gap, arguing that human beings need a specific code of moral values and virtues. In this period she argues explicitly, in terms only foreshadowed in her writings of the 1930s, that this moral code is a prerequisite of a human being's long-range physical and material survival.

There is no over-emphasizing the significance Rand placed on this last point, which is dramatized vividly and extensively in *Atlas Shrugged*. But if she is concerned there to show the material benefits of morality, she is equally concerned to show that the process of satisfying material needs has spiritual and moral meaning—a point that returns us to Equality's killing of the bird and to his "strange new pride in eating." Rand was serious in what she wrote to John Temple Graves; she did regard a spiritually empty life as a form of "living death" worse than "swift physical annihilation." If one reads her later writings carelessly or too selectively, one can miss the importance she attaches to needs of the *psyche* and matters of spiritual well-being. I hope the present discussion has illustrated that one thereby misses something of crucial importance in her thought.

## NOTES

1. Michael S. Berliner, ed., *Letters of Ayn Rand* (New York: Dutton, 1995), 33–34.

2. See Ayn Rand, *The Virtue of Selfishness: A New Concept of Egoism* (New York: New American Library, 1964), and *Atlas Shrugged* (New York: Random House, 1957; Signet thirty-fifth anniversary paperback edition, 1992). These are the two main sources for Rand's mature ethical views, although there are a number of important ancillary sources, including the essays "Causality Versus Duty" (in Ayn Rand, *Philosophy: Who Needs It* [New York: Bobbs-Merrill, 1982; Signet paperback edition, 1984]) and "Who is the Final Authority in Ethics?" (in Ayn Rand, *The Voice of Reason: Essays in Objectivist Thought*, ed. Leonard Peikoff [New York: New American Library, 1989; Meridian paperback edition, 1990); and Rand's book on esthetics, *The Romantic Manifesto: A Philosophy of Literature*, revised edition (New York: Signet, 1975).

3. Undated composition book from the 1920s, pages 18–20. Ayn Rand Archives. Safe #2, item 62. Reprinted in David Harriman, ed., *Journals of Ayn Rand* (New York: Dutton, 1997), 8.

4. See, for instance, the description below of how most people live their lives, drawn from her notes for the planned (but never written) novel *The Little Street.*

5. Which is not to say that there is nothing more to biology than this, but only that to the extent that biology seeks to characterize the way in which a given species lives or a given organic system operates, it must set aside cases of defect and disease.

6. This way of understanding the statement about achievement should not be taken to imply that a person could not be responsible for his failure to seek achievement, any more than the parallel claims about healthy functioning would imply that a person could not be responsible for being in poor health.

7. Neither, of course, is she foreclosing the possibility that some people will live as they ought to.

8. Or more precisely, perhaps, the idea seems to be that life "demands to be" a process of *seeking* achievement, since the norm Rand presents tells us to *aim* for achievement. I take it that if external circumstances frustrated one's efforts to achieve, one would still have adhered to this norm as long as one has done what one reasonably could to make one's efforts successful.

9. Another view that seeks an internal source for norms would be the Kantian view that *rational nature* gives rise to norms binding on every *rational* being. This view also rejects the attempt to ground norms in social convention, divine will, or any other "external" source of authority. But it contrasts with the view that *human* nature generates norms applicable only to *human* life, because it abstracts away from every human attribute except rationality. Since there is nothing to suggest that Rand was following this latter procedure, I read her as seeking to ground norms for human life in (the whole of) human nature. Although, as far as I am aware, Rand did not explicitly discuss the alternative, Kantian view, it is clear from her later epistemological writings that she would have rejected Kant's appeal to a priori concepts, including the (putatively) a priori concept of a rational being, without which the Kantian approach cannot get off the ground. See Ayn Rand, *Introduction to Objectivist Epistemology,* expanded second edition, edited by Harry Binswanger and Leonard Peikoff (New York: Meridian, 1990). (Rand did express strenuous objections to other aspects of Kant's ethics, related to its focus on the concept of "duty," in her article, "Causality Versus Duty.")

10. The concept of "health," and the nature of norms of health, have been subjects of philosophic controversy. I am presupposing a certain kind of account of these matters, which I believe is both common-sensical and philosophically supportable. But I cannot argue this point here. For a defense of the general sort of view I am assuming, see James G. Lennox, "Health as an Objective Value," *Journal of Medicine and Philosophy* 20 (1995): 499–511.

11. For instance, in *Introduction to Objectivist Epistemology,* discussing the formation of concepts having to do with "moral or spiritual values," she notes parenthetically that she is using the term "spiritual" to mean "pertaining to consciousness." See Rand, *Objectivist Epistemology,* 33. In some early notes that I will discuss below, she writes of someone being "wrecked spiritually," where the meaning is simply that the person has been psychologically damaged, rather than anything mystical, so the usage I propose in the text seems to be one that she adopted early on.

12. For purposes of this article, I am going to set aside the question of whether a commitment to achievement, and the other attitudes and practices that Rand will link with spiritual well-being, should be understood (on her view) as conditions of spiritual well-being or as helping to constitute spiritual well-being. This would be an important question to address in a fuller discussion, but as far as I can see nothing hangs on it here.

13. These notes are not part of the collections of the Ayn Rand Archives, and I have been unable to examine them directly. I rely, therefore, on an edited version of the notes contained in Harriman, *Journals of Ayn Rand.* Square brackets within the passages quoted from these notes reflect Harriman's interpolations.

14. Harriman, *Journals,* 24.

15. For a more positive later assessment, at least of ordinary Americans, see Rand's article "Don't Let it Go," in *Philosophy: Who Needs It,* 250–62.

16. Though Rand is not explicit about this, I assume that she means to expand rather than replace her earlier characterization of spiritual well-being, since there is nothing to suggest a retraction of that characterization, and since her later writings continue to stress the importance of achievement.

17. Harriman, *Journals,* 28.

18. Harriman, *Journals,* 28.

19. Presumably those who "exist" but do not "live" have some minimal concerns and incentives, if only to find food for their next meal or to go out to a movie. What they lack are the more-than-minimal values and desires that give shape and meaning to one's life—that give one something to live for. I will assume this qualification in subsequent discussion of the need for values and desires.

20. Deficiency here does not entail responsibility. Rand's early writings suggest two factors that would mitigate a person's responsibility for spiritual deficiency: the possibility that spiritual well-being is partly a function of innate predispositions and the possibility that it depends in part on the social environment. In her later writings, Rand abandons the idea that individuals can be innately predisposed toward or away from spiritual well-being. But, as I will indicate briefly below, she retains the idea that spiritual well-being depends in part on one's social environment. (For the idea that spiritual well-being depends on innate predispositions, see Harriman, *Journals,* 28.)

21. Harriman, *Journals,* 33–34.

22. That, at any rate, was the tentative story line. Like Howard Roark's dynamiting of the Cortlandt Homes housing project in *The Fountainhead,* and Steve Ingalls's murder of Walter Breckenridge in *Think Twice,* Danny's crime is intended as a symbolic, literary representation of his refusal to be victimized by injustice. (For Rand's play *Think Twice,* see Leonard Peikoff, ed., *The Early Ayn Rand: Selections From Her Unpublished Fiction* [New York: New American Library, 1984; Signet paperback edition, 1986], 296–377.)

23. Harriman, *Journals,* 30.

24. In one respect, one would expect even small degrees of spiritual defect to be more dangerous. The human body has automatic responses to physical impairments (think of the responses triggered within the immune system, or of what happens when one gets a small cut or scrape). These are sometimes sufficient to correct the problem. Is there a similar kind of automatic corrective mechanism at the spiritual level? Rand's eventual view will be that there is not (although she will hold that our emotional responses can warn us of problems, if we understand what those responses mean). Impairments to spiritual well-being will all have to be corrected by individual choice (at least where the social environment is not implicated in the problem). That presents the risk of their going uncorrected and continuing to do damage.

25. See Ayn Rand, *We the Living* (New York: Signet sixtieth anniversary paperback edition, 1996), and *The Fountainhead* (New York: Bobbs-Merrill, 1943; Signet fiftieth anniversary paperback edition, 1993).

26. Ayn Rand, "The Husband I Bought," in *Early Ayn Rand,* 35.

27. Rand, "Husband I Bought," 34.

28. Once again, since in Rand's view external conditions beyond a person's control can affect whether one is able to live, rather than merely exist, it does not follow that Irene is to blame for her problems. The story makes it clear that Rand considers her blameless and, indeed, heroic in the face of the circumstances she has faced (she

has had to decide whether to encourage her husband's love for another woman, a love her husband's sense of marital fidelity has made him unwilling to acknowledge). Irene reproaches herself for loving "beyond all consciousness." It is not clear whether Rand, at this time, would have considered it a mistake (albeit a non-culpable one) to love another person "too deeply." The love story in *We the Living* is far more tragic than that presented here, but there is no sign of such a view there, and later on Rand would assuredly have regarded such a view as evincing what she called the "malevolent universe premise," the view that our most important values will always be defeated.

29. Ayn Rand, "Our Cultural Value Deprivation," in *The Voice of Reason,* 100–14; see 103–4.

30. Harriman, *Journals,* 25.

31. Harriman, *Journals,* 31.

32. See, for example, Kurt Baier, *The Moral Point of View* (Ithaca: Cornell University Press, 1958), and Peter Singer, *Practical Ethics* (Cambridge: Cambridge University Press, 1993).

33. Later on, in a 1963 essay entitled "Collective Ethics," she critizes views of this kind for "substituting a specific ethics . . . for the wider abstraction of 'ethics'" (*Virtue of Selfishness,* 103–11; see 105).

34. Since my focus, in this article, is on Rand's ethical thought in the 1920s and 1930s, I rely on the 1936 first edition of *We the Living* (New York: Macmillan, 1936) rather than on the revised edition, which was published in 1959 and contains significant changes, including changes in the wording of certain important philosophical passages. For an analysis of these changes, see Robert Mayhew, "We the Living: '36 and '59" and Shoshana Milgram, "From *Airtight* to *We the Living:* The Drafts of Ayn Rand's First Novel," both in *Essays on Ayn Rand's* We the Living, ed. Robert Mayhew (Lanham, MD: Lexington Books, 2004), 185-219 and 3–45, respectively. For ease of reference, I will give page references to the revised edition (cited in note 25, above) parenthetically after each reference to the first edition.

35. It does not seem, at this point, that Rand has worked out what precise role the state should have in an individualistic social system. In *We the Living,* Kira describes the state as "a necessity and a convenience" for individuals, rather than something for which individuals must sacrifice themselves, but in her early writings (published and otherwise) Rand's remarks on the state tend to be rather indefinite. See Rand, *We the Living,* 94 (revised edition, 90).

36. Rand, *We the Living,* 496 (revised edition, 404).

37. Rand, *We the Living,* 496 (revised edition, 404–5).

38. For further analysis of *We the Living,* in this regard, see Tara Smith, "Forbidding Life to Those Still Living," in Mayhew, *Essays on Ayn Rand's* We the Living, 317–34.

39. Rand, *We the Living,* 59 (revised edition, 62).

40. Rand, *We the Living,* 58 (revised edition, 62). In the revised edition, Rand changes "fear" to "awe."

41. Rand, *We the Living,* 59-60 (revised edition, 63).

42. Rand, *We the Living,* 60 (revised edition, 63).

43. Harriman, *Journals,* 28.

44. Rand, *We the Living,* 86 (revised edition, 83). I take it that the statement that "[t]hose who lack something" do not suffer is an exaggeration intended to highlight

Leo's point that those who "have something they should lack" suffer far more. For he goes on to say that life is "more impossible and more of a torture" for those in the latter group than for those in the former, implying that those in the former do suffer to some extent. Similarly, even if those in the former group "never want" and "never miss" what they lack, it would not follow that their deficiency causes them no suffering, but only that they would have difficulty grasping the cause of whatever suffering they had to endure, whereas people such as Leo understand why they suffer.

45. Rand, *We the Living,* 86 (revised edition, 84).

46. Rand, *We the Living,* 60 (revised edition, 63).

47. Rand, *We the Living,* 64 (revised edition, 66).

48. Rand, *We the Living,* 87 (revised edition, 84).

49. Rand, *We the Living,* 85 (revised edition, 83).

50. Rand, *We the Living,* 56 (revised edition, 61).

51. Rand, *We the Living,* 85 (revised edition, 83).

52. Rand, *We the Living,* 86 (revised edition, 83).

53. Rand, *We the Living,* 86 (revised edition, 83).

54. Rand's view of the communists is epitomized by her portrayal of the scheming, thoroughly corrupt Pavel Syerov. For detailed discussion of Syerov, see Onkar Ghate, "The Death Premise in *We the Living* and *Atlas Shrugged,"* in Mayhew, *Essays on Ayn Rand's* We the Living, 335–56.

55. Rand, *We the Living,* 314 (revised edition, 263).

56. Rand, "Our Cultural Value Deprivation," 104.

57. Rand, *We the Living,* 427 (revised edition, 350).

58. Rand, *We the Living,* 445 (revised edition, 364).

59. Rand, *We the Living,* 335 (revised edition, 277).

60. The 1959 edition of the text changes "reason" to "purpose," clarifying, in light of Rand's more nuanced command of the language, what must have been the intended meaning all along. See Rand, *We the Living,* sixtieth anniversary edition, 277.

61. Rand, *We the Living,* 501 (revised edition, 408).

62. Perhaps advances in genetic engineering could bring the gruesome scenarios Andrei projects as impossible into the realm of possibility. Even so, Rand's point, I take it, would be that there are *some* underlying principles of human biological development that are immutable, and that would govern even the possibilities for the genetic alteration of human beings.

63. See Immanuel Kant, *Grounding for the Metaphysics of Morals,* third edition, translated by James W. Ellington (Indianapolis: Hackett, 1993), 37. (The material appears on page 430 of the standard, Prussian Academy Edition of Kant's works, the pagination of which is given in the margins of most English translations of Kant.)

64. I have discussed the issue of the spiritual costs of collectivism in the context of Rand's fiction, but Rand drew the background for *We the Living* according to her own experience of life under the Soviet regime, so, in this regard, the novel's critique of collectivism has a factual basis. See, in this connection, Rand's letters to her literary agent at the time, Jean Wick, dated March 23 and October 27, 1934, in Berliner, *Letters* 4–6 and 17–19.

65. Ayn Rand, *Ideal,* in *Early Ayn Rand,* 209–90; see 280.

66. Rand, *Ideal,* 246.

67. Composition book from 1934. Entry dated May 9, 1934. Ayn Rand Archives. Safe #2, item #64. See also Harriman, *Journals,* 69.

68. I do not mean to suggest that we learn all there is to know about healthy stomachs before we learn anything about diseased ones. Clearly, our knowledge of health and our knowledge of disease develop in tandem. Rather, the point is that disease can only be conceptualized as a departure from health, and so we must have at least some minimal conception of health in place, in a given area of study, before we can begin to conceptualize any of the various forms of disease.

69. For Plato's account, see the discussion of the Form of the Good in Book VI of the *Republic;* and for Moore's, see G. E. Moore, *Principa Ethica* (Cambridge: Cambridge University Press, 1903), chapter 1.

70. Notebook, "Second Hand Lives," pp. 2–4. Ayn Rand Collection of the Ayn Rand Archives. Box 457. S.2-66A/A.

71. As with *We the Living,* I rely here on the first edition of *Anthem* (London: Cassell and Co., 1938). The novelette was published in the United States, with significant revisions, in 1946. The current edition of the work contains the 1946 edition, followed by a facsimile of the 1938 edition with Rand's handwritten changes. I will give page references for *Anthem* parenthetically in the text, showing first the relevant page(s) in the 1938 edition and then, following a slash, the page(s) in the current edition where the 1938 material is reprinted. Thus (5/111) would refer to page 5 of the 1938 edition, which appears at page 111 of the current edition.

72. That is to say, if a way of life *itself* results in suffering and lack of joy, this indicates a defect in that way of life. The normative view of life would not entitle us to conclude that a person's way of life was defective merely because the person had suffered, since some suffering is caused by "accidental" circumstances, such as the death of a loved one, rather than by anything inherent in the way in which one has chosen to live or in the social conditions in which one lives. And, of course, it may be difficult in particular cases to untangle the different effects on a person's overall emotional state of accidental factors, social conditions, and his own choices concerning how to live. But in principle the normative view of life tells us that, accidental factors aside, proper individual choices and proper social conditions will be conducive to happiness rather than suffering.

73. Why does Equality's observation of the suffering endured by his more obedient "brothers" not cause him to question the moral code of his society? He is aware that "[a]ll is not well with our brothers" (53/159) early on, and seems to see a connection between their problems and the rules of the society, which require everyone to agree with one another (54/160). Perhaps at this point the evidence is not sufficient for him to conclude that there is any *basic* problem with the way his society is structured, especially given the distorted picture of history the leaders of his society have inculcated.

# 11

## Breaking the Metaphysical Chains of Dictatorship: Free Will and Determinism in *Anthem*

*Onkar Ghate*

*Dictatorship and determinism are reciprocally reinforcing corollaries: if one seeks to enslave men, one has to destroy their reliance on the validity of their own judgments and choices—if one believes that reason and volition are impotent, one has to accept the rule of force.*

—Ayn Rand, "Representation Without Authorization" (1972)

*Anthem* tells the story of a man who breaks free from an all-encompassing collectivist society. It is the novel in which Ayn Rand most heavily emphasizes the importance of the individual's will. To understand why, I think one must understand the connection between determinism and dictatorship—and between free will and political freedom. A collectivist society is necessarily at war with individual judgment and choice. And if one realizes that the chains holding down the members of society in *Anthem* are not just moral (the preaching of the idea that the individual should serve the group) and epistemological (the absence of the word "I"), but also metaphysical, one gains a fuller appreciation of the enormous intellectual feat Equality 7-2521 performs to liberate himself from his society.

### DETERMINISM AND DICTATORSHIP

One of the startling aspects of the dictatorial society in *Anthem* is how seldom its rulers must resort to the outright use of force. The members of society do as they are told. With no voices raised in protest, people live in whatever buildings they are told to live in, sleep in a row of beds beside whomever they are told to sleep beside, rise when the big bell in the tower rings and go back to bed when it rings again, accept whatever occupation is prescribed to them, and report for procreation duties whenever they are told to report. No soldiers or secret police are needed to roam the streets, because no one thinks of stepping out of bounds. The meetings of the Councils are unguarded; the leaders do not fear for their lives. When members of society break one of the City's oppressive laws, they lack the self-assertion to consider escaping. The cell in which Equality 7-2521 (hereafter "Equality") is placed after he refuses to divulge his whereabouts during a performance at the City Theater has old locks on its doors and no prison guards. The only cries one hears from the populace are cries not of protest but of despair: among Equality's fellow street sweepers, Fraternity 2-5503 sobs "suddenly, without reason," and Solidarity 9-6347 screams in his sleep, "Help us!" (47).

Why are there almost no instances of self-assertion in the society of *Anthem*? Why do the citizens not shout that their own lives and choices count?

Part of the answer, no doubt, is that the citizens are taught that it is wrong—evil—to assert any element of individuality. They are told that it is a sin to prefer one subject in school more than the others, one classmate over others, one career more than another, one man or woman more than any other.

But this is only part of the answer. If it were the full answer, it would imply that a citizen is an impassioned moralist, personally striving to enact what he recognizes to be the good. But individual understanding, including of morality, is unwelcome in society. Imagine if a citizen viewed himself as competent to discern good and evil, and as acting properly only when he first understands clearly why the action demanded of him is right. If that were the case, more citizens would rebel. The more intelligent ones would grasp the contradiction: their society demands firsthand understanding and choice of collectivist morality—a morality which declares that firsthand understanding and choice are wrong. The more intelligent ones would be able to realize that their society's morality strangles an important element of themselves: their individual understanding, interests, and choices. Thus more overt force would be needed to control the populace: soldiers would march people off to the mating halls and guards would be posted outside the doors of the prison cells. That this does not occur indicates that collectivist morality is not the only force pacifying the populace; as we shall see, collectivist morality plays a crucial role in controlling the subjects, but it is a secondary role.

The corruption of man's ideas by collectivism runs deeper than morality. Morality—the knowledge to distinguish good from evil and the dedication to achieve the good and abide by it in action—presupposes an individual who knows that he is self-governing and that he must select his course of action wisely. To enter the field of morality presupposes that one knows that one is free to judge and to choose one's path (which is why moral concepts are not applied to lower animals). But the citizens have great difficulty conceiving of this precondition of moral understanding and action. Their indoctrination is meant to preclude them from grasping that they are beings who possess free will.

This deeper corruption of course is most eloquently dramatized in *Anthem* by the fact that the rulers of society have expunged the word "I" from the language.[1] Men and women can no longer conceptualize themselves as separate, distinct individuals. They cannot identify themselves as acting on their own power and motive toward a goal, much less conceive of themselves as choosing a goal to pursue, one not shared by others and with which others might even disagree. In their minds, they are inextricably tied to the group, unable, mentally or physically, to detach themselves or carve themselves apart.

When a reader picks up *Anthem* for the first time, and reads through the first few pages of Equality's journal, what strikes him is not that something is askew morally in the world of *Anthem*, but that something is askew *metaphysically*. It is a nightmare universe not because the individual acting alone is regarded as evil, but because the individual acting alone has, seemingly, been wiped out of existence.

If, however, a subject does not regard himself as a self-governing being, able to forge his own soul and character, he still needs an account of where his identity comes from. The only alternative left to fill the void is some version of determinism.[2]

The subjects in *Anthem* are bombarded with determinist propaganda. They are told repeatedly not that it is evil to separate one's own life from the lives of other people, but that it is *impossible*; one is unavoidably tied to the group. For instance, over the portals of the Palace of the World Council is carved in marble (in part): "There are no men but only the great WE, one, indivisible and forever" (19). Five-year-old children are required to chant each night, "We exist through, by and for our brothers who are the State" (21). Though it is whispered that occasionally someone physically separates from the collective by entering the Uncharted Forest, only to find himself powerless to fend for himself and at the mercy of hunger and wild beasts, the rulers deny that this even occurs (48). The rulers go so far as to claim that inanimate actions, not just human actions, are dictated by the group. "[W]ithout the Plans of the World Council," Unanimity 2-9913 declares to Equality, "the sun cannot rise" (74).

But it is not just physical actions that are said to be determined by the group. The subjects are told that there is no such thing as a single mind thinking or judging or reaching knowledge, only a committee of minds. "What is not thought by all men cannot be true," states "the oldest and wisest" member of the World Council of Scholars, Collective 0-0009 (73, 69).

In short, the "Great Truth" is "that all men are one and that there is no will save the will of all men together" (20).

Of course, admonishments that free, individual thought and action are impossible imply that they are possible. The attempt to spread the theory of determinism by persuasion implies that man is free to judge and choose; this is a contradiction inherent in the theory's advocacy.[3] But this does not change the fact that the goal of the rulers is to get the subjects to view themselves as determined beings. Thus, already crippled by the elimination of any concept that refers to the ego—to a mind that possesses free will and chooses its own direction—the individual subject faces a barrage of metaphysical propaganda instructing him how to misconceptualize the facts. You are but a part of a super-organism—his indoctrination goes—able to exist only by permission of the whole, able to know only when the group decrees, and able to act only when the group wills. Unable to conceive of himself as a being capable of independent thought, independent action, and independent existence, the individual subject cannot even wonder whether this kind of life is good, let alone grasp that it is.

Because this metaphysical corruption is the principal method by which the dictatorial power in the City is maintained, the authorities must remove opportunities for willful self-exertion. To permit acts of individual judgment and choice, however minor, would be to leave out in the open the raw data from which an opposing metaphysical view could be developed. Any individual act of discrimination or selection—of saying "Yes" to some thing and "No" to other things—must be stamped out or, better still, eliminated before it has had a chance to begin.[4]

There are, for example, no varied colors or individualized garments; these would afford the opportunity for personal selection and discrimination (90–91). Questions—which imply that something interests one, that one wants to know something more than other things, or that one wants to understand something that one has not understood—are forbidden; group recitation is the method of instruction (23–24, 21). Fighting at school "for any cause whatsoever" is punished severely; to fight with someone could indicate that one regards one's own position as superior to the other person's, that one considers oneself in the right and the other person in the wrong (20). Friendships and love interests are not permitted; emotions of friendship and love require and encourage the formation of individual values. One responds to and chooses the other person because that individual embodies personal qualities which one values (30, 38).[5] Any desire to choose work that brings one joy is squashed: the Council of Vocations sentences Equality, who passionately wants to be a scholar, to the Home of the Street Sweepers and sentences International 4-8818, a budding artist, to the same fate (22–26, 29–30).

Just as, physically, the authorities strive to prevent a subject from seeing his own individual face and body (61–62), so, spiritually, they strive to prevent him from seeing the operation of his own will.

Thus indoctrinated, the citizens are docile and obedient. Believing themselves to be determined beings, devoid of the power of independent judgment and free choice, they unquestioningly submit to orders. They live where they are told to live, they work at what they are told to work at, and they sleep with whom they are told to sleep. For the authorities, therefore, the overt use of force is rarely necessary.

Even when overt force is needed, it is rarely resisted by the subjects. Believing themselves to be appendages of a super-organism or intertwined parts of a large machine, they accept the use of force as natural and as sometimes required. If someone deviates from the course set for him by the collective, what alternative do the authorities have but coercion? If one has crooked teeth, one does not argue with one's teeth to persuade them to *choose* to return to proper alignment; one simply clamps them with a brace. If a cable from the battery of one's car becomes loose, one does not reason with the cable to persuade it to *choose* to reattach itself; one simply screws it back on. So when a citizen inexplicably strays from his path, he is forcibly realigned or reattached to the whole. And the person subjected to such treatment regards it as proper. Some inexplicable defect about himself has caused him to depart from the group; for his own sake he needs to be coercively oriented back to the collective. With such an indoctrinated populace, the authorities need not fear for their lives, and the prison cells will not require secure locks or human guards.

In short, the citizens resemble automatons more than individual human beings. In their indoctrinated minds there is no such experience as: "*I* accept this idea because *I* have followed the chain of evidence that makes it true" or "*I* choose to take this action because *I* have followed the reasoning that shows it will be good for me." There is only: "outside forces have determined this idea to be 'true' or this action to be 'good.'" To swallow determinism is to lobotomize oneself. A lack of conviction is the consequence.

There is little moral fire left in the subjects for what their society proclaims as the good. Morality presupposes choice; moral passion presupposes an unswerving dedication to that which one knows is good. But knowledge, dedication, and choice are concepts alien to the populace. A mind relieved of the responsibility to reach truths and form values is an empty shell, devoid of ego. The citizens are thus like the living dead; going to and fro, they perform their duties with stony, expressionless faces and lifeless movements.

Consider for example how Equality describes the five members of the Council of Vocations, who sentence him to be a street sweeper. "They sat before us and they did not move. And we saw no breath to stir the folds of their white togas. But we knew that they were alive, for a finger of the hand of the oldest rose, pointed to us, and fell down again. This was the only thing which moved, for the lips of the oldest did not move as they said:

'Street Sweeper'" (26). Or consider Equality's description of his fellow subjects: they have bowed heads, dull eyes, hunched shoulders and drawn muscles, "as if their bodies were shrinking and wished to shrink out of sight" (46). They dare not speak to one another and instead "are glad when the candles are blown for the night" (47). Or consider when Equality is finally caught sneaking back from the tunnel: even when a law has been broken, the members of the Council of the Home question him without curiosity or anger; then the oldest member, in a bored voice, orders Equality to be lashed at the Palace of Corrective Detention (63–64).

The only moral fervor one observes in the City is directed not toward promoting what is considered good, but toward eradicating any obviously threatening element, any element that could awaken a sense of personal knowledge and values. In the case of the subjects, we witness this when the Saint of the pyre is set aflame for discovering the Unspeakable Word. The citizens in the crowd do not try to shrink out of sight: they collectively shriek and scream and spit curses at him (50). They do so *not* because they know he is evil or guilty: they do not know what the Unspeakable World is or why it is destructive, let alone that the Saint uttered it. Nor is he the image of a monster. But his posture and countenance do suggest independence and pride, and this could make the subjects wonder whether their status as automatons is self-made. Their mass, vehement, ungrounded denunciations of him obliterate in their minds the need to face the issue.

We witness similar behavior on the part of the rulers. Equality first describes the members of the World Council of Scholars, for example, as sitting around a long table, "shapeless clouds huddled at the rise of the great sky" (68). But when they learn of Equality's invention, they vehemently denounce it, unanimously crying out that his electric light "must be destroyed!" (74). The rulers are more conscious of the forces that enable them to retain their power. Their concern is not the well-being of the citizens, to whom the electric light would be an enormous boon, but rather the eradication of anything or anyone that provides evidence for the existence of their enemy: independent judgment and choice.

Such moral denunciations on the part of the subjects and the rulers are a clue to why a moral code still exists in society. Insofar as the inculcation of determinism is successful, a morality is not actually needed to control the citizens. The indoctrinated citizen does not need guidance on the "correct" choices to make, since he believes he functions without choice: he believes his course is set inexorably by outside forces, i.e., by the group. And so he does not judge or choose but obeys and follows. Should an individual, however, succeed in overcoming the obstacles placed in front of him: the elimination of the word "I," the constant determinist propaganda, and the campaign to stamp out any evidence of his own will—should he somehow remain on the path toward conceptualizing the fact that he has a self which thinks, chooses, and desires—the forces of collectivist morality are unleashed against him.

Part of the purpose of collectivist morality is to warn such developing individuals that any move toward living for self and away from living for others is evil. Since these individuals have a glimmer of the fact that they possess choice, the warning carries some meaning. "Everything which comes from the many is good. Everything which comes from one is evil. Thus have we been taught with our first breath," Equality writes (85). But this instruction presupposes the existence of a single, individual valuer. It presupposes someone facing a choice, wondering to himself down which road lies good and which evil (as Equality is beginning to wonder). For the rulers, the need to offer such counsel actually represents defeat.

The more insidious purpose of collectivist morality is to tell a developing individual that his very question—What do I think is true and false, right and wrong?—is *morally* wrong, that this *question* should be barred from his mind as depraved. To ask what is true and good, to personally want to understand the world and select the proper course of action in it—in other words, the existence of a thinker and valuer—is evil. The goal is to prevent the developing individual from fully discovering the sphere of judgment, choice and morality—by using his nascent sense of morality against itself.

"How dared you think that your mind held greater wisdom than the minds of your brothers?" Collective 0-0009 asks Equality (71). "How dared you, gutter cleaner, to hold yourself as one alone and with the thoughts of the one and not of the many?" Fraternity 9-3452 asks him (72). "What is not thought by all men cannot be true," Collective 0-0009 informs him (73). Regardless of the content of the thought, "there is no transgression blacker than to . . . think alone," Equality has been told all his life (17).

In this regard (as in many others), a parallel with *The Fountainhead*, which Rand was working on at the time of writing *Anthem*, is striking. Ellsworth Toohey destroys souls struggling to become valuers, like that of Catherine Halsey, by the same type of inner corruption. Catherine enters Toohey's study to voice the convulsions of her dying soul. She regards herself as vicious because she has always wanted to do what is right, but, having done so by becoming a social worker, now finds herself miserable and starting to detest the person she is becoming. Uncertain from the start of her ability to judge issues of morality—"I knew that I'm not a brilliant person and that it's a very big subject, good and evil"—she accepted and tried to live up to what Toohey and all the great moralists of history say: selfishness is evil and that "one can find true happiness only in dedicating oneself to others."[6] Now, facing her own unhappiness and struggling to retain the conviction that she should want to do what is right, she is beginning to glimpse the perversion in what she has been taught and, haltingly, to question accepted notions of right and wrong. She tells Toohey:

> Don't you see what it is that I must understand? Why is it that I set out honestly to do what I thought was right and it's making me rotten? I think it's probably because I'm vicious by nature and incapable of leading a good life. That seems to be the only explanation. But . . . but sometimes I think it doesn't make sense that a human being is completely sincere in good will and yet the good is not for him to achieve. I can't be as rotten as that.[7]

In delivering his death blow, Toohey uses Catherine's sense of morality against itself. He counsels her that it is selfish and thus vicious for her to want to know or do what is right, that if "your first concern is for what you are or think or feel or have or haven't got—you're still a common egotist." If this idea is difficult for her to accept because she does not, personally, understand it—that is the very proof of her corruption. One must abandon the quest for understanding as selfish; to be good, one "must stop wanting *anything*," Toohey tells her. "We are poisoned by the superstition of the ego. . . . We must destroy the ego first. . . . We must not think. We must *believe*. Believe, Katie, even if your mind objects. Don't think. Believe. Trust your heart, not your brain. Don't think. Feel. Believe."[8]

She obeys him: "I always thought that I must think. . . . But you're right, that is, if right is the word I mean, if there is a word. . . . Yes, I will believe. . . . I'll try to understand. . . . No, not to understand. To feel. To believe." This submission is an act of spiritual self-destruction; it is described in the novel thus: "She sat still, composed, but somehow she looked like something run over by a tank."[9] When we last meet Catherine in the novel, she is remarkably like the "brothers" in *Anthem*: a lifeless, mindless body moved not by personal thoughts or values but by outside opinions, interpreting the world in deterministic terms.[10]

A necessary condition of morally valuing something is choosing to pursue it because one understands that it is good; it requires an act of thought and of will, and for this reason must be eliminated in the society in *Anthem*. To ban it as immoral is a master stroke of deviousness—and a reason why all totalitarian dictatorships strive to hold a monopoly on morality. Just as in the physical realm the subjects in *Anthem* are told not to venture forth into the Uncharted Forest, because there lies only destruction, so in the spiritual realm the general prohibition against thought warns them in effect not to venture forth into the uncharted world of morality, because there lies only evil. And so, like Catherine in *The Fountainhead*, in the name of the *good* the budding moralist will slash away the questions from his mind, and merge back into the unthinking collective.

For a dictatorship the inculcation of metaphysics, not morality, is the final, fundamental way of maintaining power. Every dictatorship in history has relied on some version of determinism, some version of the idea that human life is controlled by outside forces—from the doctrines of a caste system to a supernaturally-favored priestly class to racism to a divinely-appointed nation to an historical progression of economic forces. The slave society in *Anthem* is no exception; it also maintains its dictatorial power by preaching determinism. Should anyone be able to resist its metaphysical indoctrination—to retain a glimpse of the fact that he has a will which is free and to question the tenets of his society—collectivist morality descends upon him. It is evil to be self-programming, it is evil to demand to be convinced before one accepts an idea, it is evil to think—collectivist morality declares. Instead, one must let outside forces (i.e., the group) dictate one's convictions and actions. If the resistor succumbs to this litany, he commits spiritual suicide by drowning himself in the collective. He becomes, like those who did not resist, a cog in the machine (as Catherine becomes in *The Fountainhead*).

But to appreciate why there are so few resistors in the first place even though the truth is on their side, why those like Equality and Liberty 5-3000 and International 4-8818 are such rare exceptions, it is important to understand fully Rand's point that dictatorship and determinism are reciprocally reinforcing (see the quotation that heads this chapter). For one can observe in *Anthem* how day-to-day existence in a dictatorship reinforces the inculcation of determinism.

In the actions that comprise his daily life, a subject functions only on orders from others. Men do not work at a job unless they have been ordered to do so (25); "men may not write unless the Council of Vocations bid them so" (17); men do not walk through the city streets unless they have been told to do so (35). In brief, "everything which is not permitted by law is forbidden" (31).

Physically, the citizens are tied to one another, never allowed space to be alone or a moment's time to think alone. Equality's life as a street sweeper vividly illustrates this (27–28). He sleeps in a hall with a hundred other street sweepers. They rise together when the bell rings, dress, and then eat on tables which each seat twenty people. They work in teams. After dinner, they march together to one of the "City Halls," to attend a "Social Meeting." There they listen to speeches about their duties and the day's business at the City Council. Afterward, they sing hymns together. They are then afforded three hours of recreation—"Social Recreation." This consists of watching, in a crowded theater, plays about toil, performed without actors, only choruses. Then they return to their hall to sleep, to regain the energy to repeat the ordeal the next day.[11]

A person brought up in this kind of society will have great difficulty envisioning a human mind that generates its own thoughts and content, a mind filled not by the speeches, songs, and stories of others. And he will have great difficulty envisioning a human life that can exist apart from the collective.

It is thus not surprising if a citizen should find the collectivist, deterministic slogans of his society tempting. For in his society, a person's existence *is* (as far as is possible) determined by outside forces: his mind is filled by the voices of other people and his actions are dictated by the group. Moreover, awareness of any alternative mode of existence has been wiped from his mind. The riches of the Unmentionable Times have been destroyed, the books burned, the language expunged of any trace of individualism. It is not absurd—although still an error—for someone subjected to these conditions to believe that determinism is an inexorable, metaphysical fact about human nature. In his mind, the existence of his dictatorship confirms the "truth" of the theory of determinism—and so reaffirms the appropriateness of his dictatorship.

Determinism and dictatorship thus create a vicious circle, one exceedingly difficult to break free from. The theory of determinism preaches that man exists without thought, judgment, and choice. This leads people to accept obedience and force as the appropriate ways to govern human relationships. The actual existence of a dictatorship, of a society demanding obedience and ruled by force, leaves people feeling personally helpless and out of control. This can lead them to believe that they are in fact determined beings who would be doomed if separated from the collective that controls them.

How does Equality break free from this vicious circle?

## FREE WILL AND POLITICAL FREEDOM

The key to the answer is that Equality is, in the most exalted sense, a thinker. This provides him simultaneously with the data necessary to grasp that he is a sovereign being and the means by which to grasp it.

From the dawn of his mind, Equality "wished to know" (23). He develops a probing mind, a mind keen to observe and categorize what it has seen, a mind striving to connect its ideas together, and a mind which takes its own ideas seriously. Questions, Equality tells us, give him no rest; from a young age he asks so many "that the Teachers forbade it" (23–24). He has an active, insatiable curiosity, which makes him think "that there are mysteries in the sky and under the water and in the plants which grow" (23). To learn more about these mysteries, he collects discards from the Home of the Scholars— glass vials, scraps of metal, and dried bones—and wishes he had a place to hide them (29). In the tunnel, he meticulously collects whatever he can find from the Unmentionable Times (53–54).

But Equality is not content to rest with questions and mysteries; he attempts to answer and solve them. He does this by careful examination, by cataloging what he observes, by testing, by paying close attention to similarities and differences, and then by trying to *identify*, to put into words, what he has seen and discovered. In the tunnel, for instance, Equality experiments with strange metals, mixes acids, and dissects animals in order to contrast and compare aspects of the physical world and thereby learn "secrets of which the Scholars have no knowledge" (35–36). For whatever new phenomenon he encounters or new discovery he makes, Equality seeks to *name* it. After seeing the leg of a dead frog move unexpectedly, he tries to identify the cause and learns that copper and zinc immersed in brine produce a new power. He investigates this new power, catalogs its properties, and discovers that it causes lightning. He christens the new power, "the power of the sky" (52). When we first meet Equality, as he writes the opening pages of his journal, he is trying to name this strange new activity of his: "It is as if we were speaking alone to no ears but our own" (17). When Equality sees Liberty 5-3000 (hereafter "Liberty") for the first time, he names to himself what is distinct about her, different from the other women he has seen: "Their body was straight and thin as a blade of iron. Their eyes were dark and hard and glowing, with no fear in them, no kindness and no guilt. Their . . . hair flew in the wind, shining and wild, as if it defied men to restrain it. They threw seeds from their hand as if they deigned to fling a scornful gift, and the earth was as a beggar under their feet" (38–39). The new, intense, personal feeling of longing that he experiences for the first time at the sight of her he classifies as "pain more precious than pleasure" (39). When he creates his electric light, he attempts to explicitly identify what made the invention possible: "We made it. We created it. We brought it forth from the night of the ages. We alone. Our hands. Our mind. Ours alone and only" (57). Later, he struggles to understand his new life in the forest on its own terms and to find his own words to describe it, undistorted by the lies of his teachers (78–80). Even when Equality cannot find the words by which to understand his experiences, such as when he is wondering what concepts have been lost from the Unmentionable Times (48–49), he remains on the premise of always seeking to expand the range of his awareness.

Nor is Equality content to rest with a splintered set of ideas. He tries to connect his conclusions together, to relate them to one another, to make them fit into a whole. He connects his discovery of the tunnel to the whispered tales of the Unmentionable Times, and grasps that the tunnel is evidence confirming that those times did in fact exist (19, 32). As he thinks more about the tunnel and the pleasures it has brought him, he tries to figure out why the discoveries and inventions from the Unmentionable Times have been destroyed and what words have been lost. When he identifies a new feeling of pain more precious than pleasure upon seeing Liberty, he does not stop there; he relates his experience to what he feels when he is among his "brothers" and what his "brothers" seem to feel—unhappiness and fear (45–46). And of course over a period of two years he slowly pieces together evidence for the existence of a new force of nature, electricity.

As a result of all this firsthand mental activity and effort, Equality takes the conclusions of his mind seriously. Even as a youngster, he opposes and fights with his brothers.[12] Later, he ignores the orders of the Councils and pursues instead his interest in science. When the World Council of Scholars threatens to destroy his electric light, he knows its value and so flees to the Uncharted Forest.

Clearly, to say that Equality is a thinker is not simply to say that he is a scientist, intent upon studying electricity. His field of vision is *all* of reality. He wants to understand his world and thereby successfully chart his journey through it. Equality is what Rand would later describe as a conceptualizer:

> The process of concept-formation does not consist merely of grasping a few simple abstractions, such as "chair," "table," "hot," "cold," and of learning to speak. It consists of a method of using one's consciousness, best designated by the term "conceptualizing." It is not a passive state of registering random impressions. It is an actively sustained process of identifying one's impressions in conceptual terms, of integrating every event and every observation into a conceptual context, of grasping relationships, differences, similarities in one's perceptual material and of abstracting them into new concepts, of drawing inferences, of making deductions, of reaching conclusions, of asking new questions and discovering new answers and expanding one's knowledge into an ever-growing sum. The faculty that directs this process, the faculty that works by means of concepts, is: *reason*. The process is *thinking*.[13]

But granted that Equality is a thinker, a conceptualizer, what does this fact have to do with the existence and discovery of his free will?

To think is an act of choice—the primary act of will, according to Rand. At the latest by the time of completing *Atlas Shrugged*, Rand had concluded that man's (only) volitional faculty is reason. According to her philosophy, "will" is not a separate faculty, in addition to man's rational faculty. The power of choice is an aspect of reason. "The key to what you so recklessly call 'human nature,' . . . is the fact that *man is a being of volitional consciousness*. Reason does not work automatically; thinking is not a mechanical process; the connections of logic are not made by instinct. The function of your stomach, lungs or heart is automatic; the function of your mind is not."[14] One's primary choice, the area in which each individual is sovereign, is whether he chooses to think or not.

> In any hour and issue of his life, man is free to think or to evade that effort. Thinking requires a state of full, focused awareness. The act of focusing one's consciousness is volitional. Man can focus his mind to a full, active, purposefully directed awareness of reality—or he can unfocus it and let himself drift in a semiconscious daze, merely reacting to any chance stimulus of the immediate moment, at the mercy of his undirected sensory-perceptual mechanism and of any random, associational connections it might happen to make.[15]

Although Equality's depiction as a volitional being is not made in terms of the primary choice, which Rand grasped only later,[16] essential to Equality's characterization is a crucial aspect of this choice. Equality will never surrender control of his mind to others; he will never let others program the content or direction of his thought; he will follow the evidence wherever it leads, not where others say it leads. Made consistently, this choice is, like Howard Roark's in *The Fountainhead*, the root of Equality's independence. Since one has total power to set one's mind in purposeful motion or to leave it adrift, to deploy one's intelligence and mental resources or to leave them idle, one has complete control over whether or not an idea will pass beyond the threshold of one's mind. For any idea advanced in one's society, one retains the power to bring it before the tribunal of one's conscious mind and ask "Do I see that it is true?"—and to allow it to pass only if the answer is "Yes." This sovereign power Equality never relinquishes. In the terms of *Atlas Shrugged*, Equality never places a "they say" above an "I know": a "mystic is a man who surrendered his mind at its first encounter with the minds of others. . . . At the crossroads of the choice between 'I know' and 'They say,' he chose the authority of others, he chose to submit rather than to understand, to *believe* rather than to think." Equality makes the opposite choice.[17]

Equality chooses "I know" over "they say" from his birth as a conceptual being. As I have suggested, the fact that at an early age he fights with his "brothers" in the Home of Infants indicates that he will not place others' views above his own. Even more clearly, at the age of ten Equality witnesses a Transgressor, tongue cut out, being burned alive for discovering the Unspeakable Word. Observe Equality's thought process as he is forced to behold this horrifying event. The discovery of the Unspeakable Word is a great evil, the leaders of his society say, the only crime punishable by death. The Transgressor, they say, is the devil incarnate. The other members of the crowd shriek and scream and spit curses at the Transgressor. In contrast, Equality observes the scene firsthand and arrives at his own conclusions. He notices that as the Transgressor walks toward the pyre, blood running from the corner of his mouth, he does not falter; his face is calm and happy, his lips smiling. As the Transgressor is being burned alive, there is no pain in his eyes, "only joy in them, and pride, a pride holier than it is fit for human pride to be" (51). However forbidden the idea may be—"a monstrous thought came to us then, which has never left us" (50)—Equality concludes that the man before him is not the image of a sinner but of a saint.

What gains standing and permanence in the young Equality's mind is not a baseless "they say," but only that which he actually grasps. Equality knows on what factual basis he evaluates the image of the Transgressor as that of a saint not a sinner, and he is offered no understandable reason for the opposing conclusion held by society. The two ideas therefore do not compete in his mind. The first connects to what he sees and to his other knowledge, such as the meaning and potential causes of joy; the second is disconnected both from what he observes and from other things he knows. The two mental states are different and are experienced as different. The first is what it means to know, to be aware conceptually; the second is not.

One might maintain, however, that there is one area in which the young Equality accepts, at least to some extent and for a period of time, what "they say": the realm of morality. But to maintain this I think would be a mistake. There is a sense in which Equality, for a time, accepts his society's view of good and evil. But he accepts it firsthand, not simply because others say it; he accepts it cognitively, as a thinker. His error, therefore, remains open to later correction.

In the Home of the Students, Equality masters his lessons too quickly; his teachers disapprove and deprecate him for being different from his "brothers" (21). Bored and frustrated at school, Equality is unable to figure out why he is unhappy; but the fact that he is, is evidence that something is wrong and that a change in course might be warranted. In such a situation, it is not unreasonable for a child to think that the elders he respects possess wisdom greater than his, that they grasp that certain things are good and bad which he is not yet in a position to grasp. They may know the cause of his frustration as well as a cure. But if their advice proves wrongheaded, he will quickly abandon it as the counter-evidence presents itself. Thus Equality does briefly try to emulate a student whom his teachers approve of, Union 5-3992, "a pale boy with only half a brain" (21). But it does not work (because it cannot work, as I discuss later); Equality's lashings continue, and he abandons the attempt.[18]

Later, as a result of his devotion to knowing, Equality develops a passionate interest in science. But he abandons his interest (temporarily) because the leaders of his society brand such a desire as evil. To understand Equality's action here, it is again important to appreciate the context. As a budding chooser and self-programmer, Equality is forming a genuine sense of personal values and interests. But he is given no conceptual tools to understand this fact. Like Catherine in *The Fountainhead*, Equality takes morality seriously and wants to be good, but even more so than for Catherine in *The Fountainhead*, Equality's only notions of good and evil are the collectivist ones advanced in his society. Equality does not yet possess the evidence— which he will garner from his own later life—to explicitly challenge these notions. Further, an element of what his teachers say about the good makes sense to him, namely, that the good lies in the happiness of himself and his "brothers." At this point he has no reason to suspect that his leaders and teachers are monsters, and some reason to think that they know things that he does not yet know and do in fact seek the happiness of all. So for his personal desire to be sent to the Home of the Scholars, Equality is ready to accept, proudly, his punishment as street sweeper.

The crucial point here is that in the process of accepting his punishment, he never discards his mind. Unlike Catherine in *The Fountainhead*, Equality does not doubt his ability to understand issues of good and evil; he does not think that, somehow, others can grasp things that must forever remain a mystery to him. Since he is doing what is good, he expects happiness to result; he expects to learn why the Council of Vocations was right to think that he should be a street sweeper and not a scholar. But what does Equality observe in the ensuing months? The mind-crushing routine of a street sweeper's life, when he is capable of so much more; a life which leaves him bored and, along with his fellow street sweepers, unhappy. So again the promises of his leaders fail to materialize. And given the counter-evidence (his actual unhappiness), Equality's suppressed desire to be a scholar reemerges, and he begins collecting discarded scientific materials from the Home of the Scholars. There is here no mindless following of what "they say."

The refusal to allow a "they say" to rule his thoughts, born in Equality's youth, characterizes his mature mind as well. For instance, he tells us in the tunnel that when he is tempted, he repeats to himself the slogans carved over the portals of the Palace of the World Council, but the slogans do not enable him to resist. Dogma has no power in his mind. But most eloquent in this regard is his discovery of (and subsequent stealing away to) the tunnel. It marks Equality's transition from childhood to adulthood and is an important turning point in the story. Let us see why.

Equality stumbles upon the entrance to the tunnel when he is looking to dispose of the scientific materials he has collected but is unable to hide. He goes in, against International 4-8818's counsel. He enters the tunnel with the same attitude that he collects discards from the Home of the Scholars: not with defiance but, simply, with insatiable curiosity. He is an explorer and investigator, who wants to know. But when Equality emerges from the tunnel, he declares to International 4-8818, in a voice that is hard and without mercy, his face white: "We shall not report our find to the City Council. We shall not report it to any men" (33). Why the dramatic change?

When Equality goes into the tunnel, he certainly is not paying any attention to what "they say." International 4-8818 reminds him that what is not permitted is forbidden, but Equality, who sees no reason for this rule that stifles knowledge, says he is going in nevertheless. What does Equality discover when he enters? Concretely, a tunnel. But his mind does not stop there. He connects what he sees to his other knowledge, and realizes that he has discovered a place beyond the ability of any men of his day to construct. Connecting his discovery still further, he realizes that he has found a remnant from the Unmentionable Times, evidence which confirms that those times existed and contained wondrous things. Thus what Equality discovers is evidence that the authorities likely have been deceiving the citizens, concealing facts from them. Given this discovery, he is now much less likely to put credence in what the authorities say, as he did occasionally in his youth, on the premise that they have reached knowledge that he has yet to reach. He is much less likely to give them the benefit of the doubt, even for a short period of time, that he is ignorant while they know. And further, from a positive perspective his discovery confirms his sense that, contrary to what the Scholars say, there are indeed "mysteries in the sky and under the water and in the plants which grow," mysteries that need to be (and can be) solved (23).

From this point forward, there is on Equality's part growing defiance and rejection of what his society says—or, more precisely, Equality pays less and less cognitive attention to what the authorities maintain. From this point in time, he will follow only his expanding knowledge and convictions. For over two years after discovering the tunnel, he ignores what they say in their plays about the virtues of toil (28) and instead escapes to the tunnel to study alone for three hours each day. When he catches his first glimpse of Liberty while sweeping the streets, he pauses to admire her, the two later exchanging furtive glances and silent greetings (39–40). Observe that Equality does "not wonder at this new sin of ours" and takes "no heed of the law which says that men may not think of women, save at the Time of Mating" (41). His leaders say that it is wrong "to feel too much joy" or to be glad to be living, but Equality is glad to be alive. "If this is a vice," Equality writes, "then we wish no virtue" (46–47).

True, Equality does struggle with himself when thinking about the words that have been lost from the Unmentionable Times and, later, when naming the fact that he discovered a new power of nature (electricity) alone. But he struggles with himself not because he believes that what the authorities say might be true: he fears what they might do to him for stating truths. He does not want to think of the "words of the Evil Ones," not because this might mire him in error, but because he does not want to "call death upon our head" (49). And through his resolve to know, he overcomes the fear; he ends this journal entry by writing "What—even if we have to burn for it like the Saint of the pyre—what is the Unspeakable Word?" (51) Similarly, when Equality soon afterward discovers the power of electricity, he is reluctant to name the fact that he discovered it alone and that the Council of Scholars is "blind." He is reluctant not because he thinks the opposing views of his leaders might be true, but because he does not want to be punished. "It is said," he writes after naming the facts about his discovery. "Now let us be lashed for it, if we must" (52).

Thus in choosing both as a child and as an adult to follow what he knows, not what "they say," Equality constantly exercises his will. And to exercise his will is a precondition of discovering it explicitly. But it is only a precondition. By repeated acts of choice, Equality makes himself into an independent thinker. But how does he come to identify this fact? Equality, I have said, is a conceptualizer, but by what specific steps does he put himself on the path toward conceptualizing his free will? Other members of his society could have read the books that Equality found in the house from the Unmentionable Times—and been unchanged by them. But because Equality has paved the road to them not only physically but also intellectually, he is enlightened: he grasps the books' truths. This is a remarkable achievement, especially since Equality must overcome the obstacles that his collectivist society deliberately erects to prevent an individual from identifying the fact that he has a will which is free. How does Equality accomplish this feat?

To begin, Equality must find the time and privacy to think. Prior to discovering the tunnel, Equality can think only in brief snatches, such as late at night, before he drifts off to sleep (24). The tunnel affords him opportunity to study and concentrate for long, uninterrupted stretches of time. The tunnel, of course, is not the cause of his thinking but, if anything, the effect. Equality is able to carve himself out physically, below the surface of the City, only because he has already carved himself out spiritually from society. He finds and enters the tunnel only because in his personal quest to know, he ignores what "they say." The point here is that the tunnel offers indispensable time for his thought to develop further.

Once in the haven of his tunnel, Equality must continue to exercise his will: he must continue to think. This he does, with materials he has collected and stolen throughout the city. Early on in his studies, he notices the leg of a dead frog jerking for some unknown reason. For over two years, he pursues the cause relentlessly (52–53).

But if this were the only thinking that Equality did, as great as it is, he would not become the liberator of mankind. If his were a compartmentalized mind, exerting prodigious effort to investigate scientific phenomena but proceeding uncritically and conventionally when dealing with matters of morality and human nature, he would never have discovered his free will (or the tunnel, for that matter). Equality's mind, as I have indicated, is on the premise of understanding *all* of reality. Within his field of vision, Equality seeks to identify what he observes—and thereby to expand that field continually, "to feel as if with each day our sight were growing sharper than the hawk's and clearer than rock crystal" (36). For both the outer world and the inner world, Equality desires to know. He extrospects *and* introspects—as he must, if he is to discover his free will.

Thus the fact that Equality keeps a journal is much more than a fiction writer's device employed by Rand. His journal writing, Equality tells us, takes valuable time away from his scientific studies (18); that he still decides to write shows how vital it is to him to understand himself and his society. Maintaining a journal is a crucial step in his self-liberation. It is at once a physical manifestation of and an aid to his introspection. Equality wants to understand himself, his society, and human nature. And therefore, as in the case of material phenomena, he carefully records his observations and tries to piece the facts together into a conceptual whole.

Equality's quest, however, would be doomed if he felt a sense of personal, profound guilt for his actions. Collectivist morality preys on guilt. It counts on one's self-esteem being impaired, but one not understanding why or knowing how to restore oneself to health. It then offers a spurious and deadly explanation of one's lack of self-esteem. You are feeling self-reproach, collectivist morality declares, because you are too concerned with your self, your ego, your thoughts, your personal understanding of good and evil. This is precisely how Toohey poisons Catherine, who with reason is beginning to dislike herself. Because of his commitment to thought and his fierce intellectual honesty, Equality maintains a soul fundamentally untouched by guilt—and therefore renders himself immune to such poison. This point requires some elaboration.[19]

In regard to the world, as we have seen, Equality maintains an active mind whose purpose is not to impress or defy others, but simply to know. "We must know that we may know," Equality writes (24). The ruling question in his mind is always "What *is* it?"—and over the answer neither the words nor the actions of others can take precedence. This same intellectual honesty is evident when Equality thinks about his own life and mind.

There is no attempt at self-deception as Equality tries to understand the differences between himself and his "brothers"—no attempt to paint himself in an unwarranted light—to excuse his crimes on the grounds that he did not really know what he was doing—to rationalize his sins against society as actions his rulers would actually approve of if only they understood his full context—or to pretend that the meaning of his actions is other than what it in fact is. In the effort to understand himself, and in the terms he possesses at the time, Equality carefully identifies his own actions: both their nature and their consequences. To take one of many examples, Equality openly admits at the beginning of *Anthem* that it is a sin to write down one's thoughts on paper: it is "base and evil" to act "as if we were speaking alone to no ears but our own" (17). But he also observes that this sort of action has brought him the first peace he has known in his life (37).

Precisely because of such ruthless intellectual honesty, Equality preserves a clean soul. He experiences no fundamental guilt for his "sins." Since Equality is committed to know the truth about himself and to do what he actually sees to be right, he has no reason to feel guilty. He never consciously indulges in that which he grasps firsthand to be false or evil.

Absence of guilt characterizes Equality's soul whether he is rejecting or (momentarily) accepting the tenets of his society. Sitting alone in the tunnel writing his journal, Equality catalogs his sins and transgressions. This explicit categorization is of course in the only terms of good and evil that Equality possesses, his society's. But he also knows, at least implicitly, that he has never been given much reason to think that what is branded as evil is in fact destructive of happiness, a value his society claims to work toward. Further,

Equality has positive evidence to think that there is something suspect in the views he has been taught. The Saint of the pyre is classified as the height of evil, yet the Saint's posture and countenance suggested otherwise to Equality. Most important, his own life and inner experiences do not integrate with his explicit categories of good and evil. Emulating Union 5-3992, for instance, brought Equality not contentment but further lashes, and abandoning his desire to be a scholar brought him not happiness but ignorance and boredom; whereas the "evil" of deciding to enter the tunnel has brought him much knowledge unknown to his teachers (36).

So at one level Equality struggles with himself when he wants to do that which is forbidden as evil. But at a deeper level, he is not actually convinced that the action is evil and has reason to think that it might be a path to pleasure, knowledge, joy. And therefore when he does that which is forbidden, he does not experience guilt. This is why at the conclusion of his first journal entry, after stating that the "evil of our crime is not for the human mind to probe," Equality can accurately write:

> And yet there is no shame in us and no regret. We say to ourselves that we are a wretch and a traitor. But we feel no burden upon our spirit and no fear in our heart. And it seems to us that our spirit is clear as a lake troubled by no eyes save those of the sun. And in our heart—strange are the ways of evil!—in our heart there is the first peace we have known in twenty years. (37)

Even when Equality followed the claims of his society in his youth, he did not earn guilt. As a child, he momentarily accepts the idea that he should be like Union 5-3992. But, as discussed, there are reasons for his action: he is miserable and his teachers might possess wisdom he lacks; his action does not occasion guilt because it did not require the suspension of thought. Later, when Equality accepts his sentence as street sweeper, he does so not because he had felt guilt. Granted, he does write "We knew we had been guilty" (26)—but this is not the same thing as having experienced guilt. Equality is here viewing his action from a third-person perspective: he acknowledges that the wish to be placed in a particular profession is declared to be evil and something that should be suppressed. To identify himself as guilty here is but another example of Equality's intellectual honesty—of stating openly, as best he can, the nature of his actions. But the desire itself is not experienced as corrupt; there exists no genuine cause for self-reproach. And notice that what Equality feels when sentenced is pride. What he is in fact experiencing is a child's step toward adulthood: the pride of learning (from adults' advice) to put what he thinks are his long-term interests ahead of his short-term desires, the pride of mastering oneself. When Equality learns that this is not what he has done—when he begins to sense that he has actually stifled his self—his interest in science returns.

Thus the key to understanding Equality's intact self-esteem is his profound intellectual honesty—his choice to place nothing above his attempt to know the facts. But despite his intellectual honesty, Equality at first misconceptualizes the introspective data when he reflects on his own life and mind. Initially, he thinks that the reason he is different from his "brothers" is that he is cursed: "We were born with a curse. It has always driven us to thoughts which are forbidden. . . . We know that we are evil, but there is no will in us and no power to resist it" (18). There is, in other words, some unknown, deterministic element within him that controls his mind and pushes him forward, an element that he possesses and which others seem to lack, an element he cannot resist. Equality's error here is not surprising—and contains the seeds by which he will learn to correct it.

Remember, first, that Equality has no concept of a mind or will that is free and self-governing. He is beginning to grasp firsthand that there is some causal difference between the functions of his mind and those of his brothers. To the extent that any causes are known in his society, they are instances of physical, deterministic causality, which he would have learned while studying the Science of Things. It would be natural for Equality at first to accord a new, unidentified cause the same status. Moreover, his society explicitly and deliberately accounts for human action in deterministic terms, so when Equality observes a difference between his mental life and that of his "brothers," it would again be natural to explain this difference in deterministic terms. There must, he thinks, exist some causal difference between himself and others that *makes* him act in a different way.

Second, there can appear to be an element of compulsion in thought, something easily mistaken as deterministic, especially if determinism is the only theoretical framework one has for interpreting one's mental life. This compulsive element is particularly salient when one faces a demand to accept the unsupported or the unintelligible—as Equality constantly faces. So long as one continues to make the basic and solemn choice to think, to make awareness of reality one's goal, one *must* implement this goal by unwaveringly choosing to follow the evidence wherever it leads. To choose otherwise, to accord anything precedence over truth, is to abandon thought. If one continually chooses to think, no command to oneself to accept what others believe will affect one's mind. There is no way for one to inject a "they say" into one's thought process without derailing it.

Equality experiences this fact repeatedly. Alone in his tunnel, he writes that his curse is that he sees his actions to be evil, but performs them nevertheless. "This is our wonder and our secret fear, that we know and do not resist" (18). But as we have seen, he has little reason to think that what he is doing is evil, and he is accumulating evidence that his actions bring positives—and thus he cannot resist. For what could he do to prevent himself from acting? Equality tries repeating to himself the words inscribed over the portals of the Palace of the World Council: "We are one in all and all in one. There are no men but only the great WE, one, indivisible and forever" (19). But it has no effect. This empty slogan cannot convince him that his actions are wrong or obliterate from his mind the evidence that his actions are in fact yielding values. A mind that is choosing to think cannot command itself to be deflected by an unsupported, even unintelligible, "they say." To obey such a command would be to choose to abandon awareness of reality as one's ruling goal—but setting awareness as his ruling goal is precisely the choice Equality is making. Yet if one has not conceptualized one's sovereign choice, this situation can be easily mistaken for one of compulsion. Equality orders himself to stop his "evil," but for some unfathomable reason his order is not obeyed.

In actual fact, Equality's observation that "there is no will in us and no power to resist it" is, misconceptualized, his first explicit grasp of his free will (18). He has caught a glimpse of the fact that his mind and will are free—he self-consciously tries to resist his "curse"—but this freedom seems ephemeral and causally impotent: it does not enable him to resist. And thus he still conceptualizes the essence of his mental life not as free but as determined.

Consider the other instances where Equality views himself as cursed. He says that his curse makes him understand his school lessons too easily (21), which his teachers frown upon. He decides to try to emulate Union 5-3992, but finds that he cannot. So his mind again seems unruly. But of course it is not: so long as one continues to choose to think, to deploy fully one's intelligence, one cannot *not* understand. Deliberate, thoughtful mindlessness is impossible. To have succeeded in emulating Union 5-3992, Equality would have had to have chosen to let go of the reins of his mind—something his teachers hope for but a choice he will not make. Or: Equality's curse makes him prefer the Science of Things to his other school lessons (22). But if Equality chooses to maintain his commitment to know, it is understandable that he would prefer a subject in which he encounters (some) factual grounds for the claims being made to subjects in which no such grounds are offered. Or: Equality's curse makes him ceaselessly ask questions (24). But so long as one is choosing to think, to ask questions is unavoidable. To choose to stop asking questions Equality would have to choose to stop thinking. Or: through a long process of thought Equality comes to ask himself what the words are that have been lost from the Unmentionable Times. He castigates himself for this question, viewing himself still in some way as a victim of an outside power: "We had no wish to write such a question, and we knew not what we were doing till we had written it. We shall not ask this question and we shall not think it. We shall not call death upon our head" (49). But as we have seen, to implement the choice to think one must choose to follow the evidence wherever it leads, no matter others' commands or threats. And so Equality's next words are

"And yet . . . And yet . . ." (49)—and he returns to thinking about the lost words from the Unmentionable Times (49-51).

From such inner experiences as these we can understand Equality's error in conceptualizing his will as determined.[20] But precisely because Equality preserves his commitment to thought and because his own mental life actually provides the introspective counter-evidence to his erroneous conclusion, he will correct his error. Given the opportunity to think, given his considerable intelligence, and given his commitment to using it, Equality will grasp that his mind is not determined but free.

I think the moment Equality first grasps this fact is when he discovers the power of electricity (52). Why does he grasp that his mind and will are free at this point? Two interrelated conditions are I think crucial. First, he needs to engage in a process of thought in which he is not constantly ordering himself to stop and finding that, mysteriously, his order is disobeyed; he needs to see his will not as causally impotent but as potent. His two-year quest for the power that made the leg of the dead frog move is such a process of thought.

Second and perhaps more important, he needs to be engaged in a sustained process of thought that ends successfully. When the terminus is reached, he can look back on the journey and ask himself what caused it and made it possible. What does Equality see when he looks back at his discovery of electricity? He sees months of prodigious effort, of active experimentation—"we melt strange metals, and we mix acids, and we cut open the bodies of animals" (35)—of trial and error—"we tested it in more ways that we can describe" (53)—all of which would have involved making false starts, asking innumerable questions, hitting dead-ends and starting over, etc.[21] The result of the process is new knowledge. The conclusion to draw, Equality sees when looking back on his journey, is that a process of thought (and so its product) is not determined outwardly by the group or inwardly by a "curse." It is not determined at all; it is *self*-initiated and *self*-governed. Knowledge is reached by choice, by willful self-exertion. In his journal Equality writes: "We, Equality 7-2521, have discovered a new power of nature. . . . The secrets of this earth are not for all men to see, but only for those who will *seek* them" (52, emphasis added).

Although he does not yet have the exact words to identify his discovery, at this point Equality has broken the basic chain of his dictatorship. From this point forward, he no longer views himself as cursed. From this point forward, he no longer describes his mind as though it were controlled by some outside power or force. He knows that it is he who controls and directs his mind.[22] The metaphysics of collectivism, which declares that the individual's mind and will are governed by the group—the Great Truth, which states "that all men are one and that there is no will save the will of all men together" (20)—has lost any hold on Equality.

But this does not mean that Equality is ready to flee the City. As we have seen, the dictatorship inculcates not just the view that the individual's mind is controlled by the group, but that his whole life is. Any attempt to exist apart from the group, the subjects are told, spells death. To grasp (implicitly) that his mind is not determined but free is not yet for Equality to grasp that he can live alone. To complete the job of liberating himself from the nightmare universe in which the individual has, seemingly, been obliterated, Equality must come to see himself not simply as a free mind and will, but as an individual *being*, capable (and worthy) of independent existence.

To break this chain is difficult, because a dictatorship drives a wedge between mind and body. Even if a subject in the society in *Anthem* is able to preserve some small realm of private thought, that thought is irrelevant to his existence. Down to almost every detail, a subject's daily actions are prescribed by his rulers. What goes on in his head has no bearing on what goes on in his life. Equality must grasp the perversity of this. He must see his body not as a deterministic, interchangeable hunk of matter—as it is regarded in his society—but as a living thing animated by his will. He must see that his mind and will are eminently practical faculties, and that his body is the tool indispensable to fulfilling their edicts. He must grasp that his body deserves the same respect as his will. He must grasp that his mind and body form a unity.

This he does by observing his interactions with Liberty, his time alone in the tunnel, and his life alone in the forest. Equality's admiration of Liberty stirs in him a passionate physical desire, which he does not understand but which he endeavors to. At first, he sees no connection between the judgment of his mind and the response of his body. He admires her because she shares his independent soul—her eyes are "dark and hard and glowing, with not fear in them, no kindness and no guilt" (39). The result is a violent physical desire for her, a "pain more precious than pleasure" (39). Equality's realization that he has singled her out because of her unique character—she is "not like the others" (41) and is someone who he hopes also thinks forbidden thoughts (56)—grows concurrently with his knowledge that he wants to be in physical contact with her. He waits painfully for an hour each day to catch sight of her, then exchanges physical greetings with her from afar, then speaks to her, then touches her lips with his hands. Finally, in the forest when they sleep together, Equality learns "the one ecstasy granted to the race of men" (84); he learns that his evaluation of her (and hers of him) demands physical expression.

Perhaps even more important to Equality's discovery of the connection between mind and body is his invention of the electric light, a device revolutionary in its practical consequences. Equality's discovery of a new power of nature does not remain at a theoretical level; he uses it to create something that will radically improve his life and the lives of everyone in his society. And for the creation of the light, he now realizes, his body was the instrument. "We made it. We created it," Equality declares. "We alone. *Our hands. Our mind.* Ours alone and only" (59, emphasis added). And so at this precise moment, he comes to value his body and desires to know what he looks like:

> For the first time do we care about our body. For this wire is a part of our body, as a vein torn from us, glowing with our blood. Are we proud of this thread of metal, or of our hands which made it, or is there a line to divide these two?
> We stretch out our arms. For the first time do we know how strong our arms are. And a strange thought comes to us: we wonder, for the first time in our life, what we look like. (61)

This connection between the thought of his mind and the value-oriented action of his body is confirmed and expanded by his experiences in the Uncharted Forest. At first he is in despair because he was not ready to flee the City but had to because his electric light was threatened. He does not think he can survive alone in the forest and expects to be devoured by wild beasts. But then he learns the pleasures of deciding when to rise and act, the joy of exerting his body, the satisfaction of using his mind to gain food by his "own hand" (79). He is learning that life alone, chosen and directed by himself, apart from the collective, is possible. When he sees his own reflection for the first time, he gains a visual record of the fact that he is not just a free mind or will, but an independent being capable of independent existence. "Our body was not like the bodies of our brothers, for our limbs were straight and thin and hard and strong. And we thought that we could trust this being who looked upon us from the stream, and that we had nothing to fear with this being" (80). The next day, when the Golden One joins him in the forest, he tells her not to be afraid because "There is no danger in solitude" (83).[23]

In the quotation that heads this chapter, Rand observes that a human being who does not trust himself will welcome dictatorship. Equality is not such a human being—and at this point, he *knows* it. Against his dictatorship's attempt to inculcate the metaphysical theory of determinism in regard to both man's thought and action, Equality has broken free. Just as he knows that he is capable of individual, successful thought apart from the collective, so he now knows that he is also capable of individual, successful life apart from the collective. He is ready to learn the words for his discoveries from the books of the Unmentionable Times.

Remember, however, that in the society in *Anthem* a secondary force suppresses the burgeoning individual: collectivist morality. Equality, as we have seen, does not succumb to its only lethal weapon: the command to stop thinking. So essentially he is beyond its reach. But to conclude, let me briefly indicate how Equality frees himself fully from this chain as well.[24]

The more Equality sees himself as a self-governing mind and then a self-governing being, the more he sees his need to choose his own actions and select his own goals. He will question and reject what his society considers virtuous action before he questions and rejects what it considers noble goals.

At first, Equality has no quarrel with the idea that the good is to achieve the prosperity and happiness of all, including his own. Of course he is happy, a member of the Council of the Home tells Equality, "How else can men be when they live for their brothers?" (45). Equality accepts his sentence as street sweeper in part because he thinks it is proper to "work for our brothers" (26). When he decides later to bring his invention to the Scholars, whom at that point he still regards as fellow thinkers, he is ready to work with them to "give our brothers a new light" (60). But the means to achieve the happiness of all, his teachers declare, is to tie men together into a superorganism. This is the first moral "truth" Equality will question.

From the exercise of virtue, his society declares, the good must result. But what is considered vice and virtue in his society? It is vicious to think or act alone (17), virtuous to horde together, everyone equally afraid of speaking his mind (47)—vicious to ask questions, virtuous to mindlessly swallow one's lessons (23)—vicious to take any action that is not expressly permitted, virtuous to do as one is told (23)—vicious to wish something for oneself, virtuous to think of others (24)—vicious to engage in work which has no purpose "save that we wish to do it," virtuous to toil for one's brothers (36)—vicious to take notice of an individual of the opposite sex, virtuous to regard them all as interchangeable (38)—vicious to care whether one lives or dies, virtuous to regard oneself as a cog in the machine (46–47).

Equality's ruthless commitment to thought, however, leads him to take vicious action. And what he gradually discovers is that his "vicious" actions bring values. By taking an action that is not permitted, he discovers the tunnel. By thinking alone and asking questions, he learns things "not in the scripts" and solves "secrets of which the Scholars have no knowledge" (36). By admiring and pursuing Liberty, he experiences a profound pleasure. By following his own desire to be a scientist and to study for no other purpose than to know, he discovers electricity and invents an electric light. Personally, the overall result of his "vicious" actions is joy. He sings aloud, happy to be alive—and is looked at suspiciously by his leaders. "If this is a vice," Equality concludes, "then we wish no virtue" (47).

In stark contrast to his own life, the lives of his "brothers" who follow the path of virtue are desolate. The normal state of his "brothers," Equality comes to grasp, is fear and suffering (47). There is something wrong, Equality is beginning to see, with what his society says about virtue and vice. At the very least, other roads also lead to happiness.

When Equality decides to bring his electric light before the World Council of Scholars, he expects that they will understand and forgive (61). As fellow thinkers, they will understand his wayward path even if they themselves do not take it. Even if Equality has found a different means to the noble goal of happiness for all, they will welcome him as one of their own since the gift he has to offer for the well-being of his fellow citizens is so great. The Council's hostility shocks Equality. The Scholars, faced with the choice of progress and happiness, or stagnation and misery—and at this point Equality knows implicitly that it is a choice—choose the latter. They demand that the electric light be destroyed. Even though he cannot put into words his feeling when he hears their verdict, Equality senses immediately that their goal is monstrous. So in protection of the supreme value that is his electric light, he seizes his invention, smashes the windowpane, and runs.[25]

Wandering through the forest with Liberty, thinking about his life and the issue of good and evil, Equality realizes that he reached values only when *both* his means and end were individual and solitary: "the only things which taught us joy were the power we created in our wires, and the Golden One. And both these joys belong to us alone, they come from us alone, they bear no relation to our brothers, and they do not concern our brothers in any way" (86). By contrast, when his end was collective, he was miserable. "There is no life for men, save in useful toil for the good of all their brothers. But we lived not, when we toiled for our brothers, we were only weary" (86). If that which actually brings knowledge, invention, joy, and happiness is labeled evil, and that which actually brings ignorance, stagnation, suffering, and misery is labeled good, then perhaps the goal—the standard for determining virtue and vice—is misguided, even inverted. Thus for the first time Equality asks himself: "what is good and what is evil?" (85).

Equality has now freed himself from the metaphysical and moral chains of his dictatorship; he is ready to learn the words for his discovery of individualism. The books from the Unmentionable Times help Equality conceptualize what he is on the verge of grasping: that he is a being whose thought and will are free, a being who is individual and independent and should live for himself. To such a being, Equality sees, political freedom is an indispensable value. If one's mind is not free to judge and follow the evidence wherever it leads but is instead shackled to the beliefs of others, blindness results. If one's will is not free to choose one's own good but is instead subordinated to the wishes and needs of others, misery results.[26]

The goal of his collectivist society, Equality now sees, is not to raise men up to happiness but to grind them down to the level of chained animals. This is why it destroyed the concept of "I"—of a self which possesses free will. This is why it turned virtues into vices and vices into virtues. This is why it permits no political freedom.

But Equality is done with the vicious circle of determinism and dictatorship. The free society that he will erect will replace this vicious circle with a virtuous one. First created by the minds and actions of individuals, a free society in turn demands independent judgment and choice from its members. Because success in a free society requires exercise of an individual's thought and will, Equality knows that "the roads of the world will become as veins which will carry the best of the world's blood to my threshold" (104).[27]

Given the metaphysical discovery that made possible both the escape from his society's vicious circle and the envisioning of a new society, it is only fitting that in his penultimate chapter Equality declares: "Many words have been granted me, and some are wise, and some are false, but only three are holy: 'I will it!'" (94–95).[28]

## NOTES

1. For a discussion of the steps Equality must perform to recapture the concept "I," see Gregory Salmieri, "Prometheus' Discovery: Individualism and the Meaning of the Concept 'I' in *Anthem*," in the present volume.

2. In this context I regard indeterminism not as a separate theory but as a version of determinism: whether a person thinks that his life, mind, and actions are necessitated by outside forces or "ruled by chance" matters not.

3. Rand later argued that the theory of determinism is self-contradictory. For a conceptual, fallible being to know that the theory is true (and then to argue for its truth), he would have to be exempt from the theory. He would have to accept the theory *not* because he was determined to do so—irrespective of the evidence—but because he had the freedom, and actually did choose, to follow the evidence where it leads. But this means that, in logic, the evidence cannot lead to the theory of determinism. See Leonard Peikoff, *Objectivism: The Philosophy of Ayn Rand* (New York: paperback, New Meridian, 1993), 69–72. Another way of stating the contradiction inherent in the theory of determinism is that it "steals" the concept of truth: in denying the concept of free will it has no logical right to use the concept of truth (or falsity). For more on how the collectivist language in *Anthem* is replete with stolen concepts, see Salmieri, "Prometheus' Discovery," in the present volume, p. 260–62.

4. Rand used the language of "Yes" and "No" in the 1938 edition of *Anthem* but cut it from the 1946 edition (234). She also used it in *The Fountainhead*: see Ayn Rand, *The Fountainhead* (New York: Bobbs-Merrill, 1943; Signet fiftieth anniversary edition paperback, 1993), 503; and in her journals: see David Harriman, ed. *Journals of Ayn Rand* (New York: Dutton, 1997), 80 and 252–54. The language may have been suggested to her from reading Nietzsche: see Robert Mayhew, "*Anthem*: '38 & '46," in the present volume, p. 39.

5. As Howard Roark states in *The Fountainhead*, "To say 'I love you' one must know first how to say the 'I'" (Rand, *Fountainhead*, 366).

6. Rand, *Fountainhead*, 362.

7. Rand, *Fountainhead*, 364.

8. Rand, *Fountainhead*, 365–66.

9. Rand, *Fountainhead*, 366.

10. Rand, *Fountainhead*, 595–601. In this final scene between Catherine and Peter Keating, her last scene, Catherine claims that economic factors determine the course of the world, she explains human actions in terms of reflexes and conditioning, and

she compares her pain from Peter having failed to go through with his marriage proposal to her to a physical, deterministic response: contracting measles.

11. In this regard the society in *Anthem* obviously resembles actual totalitarian dictatorships, like that of Soviet Russia, where a citizen's life is made almost completely social. And of course Rand was aware of this fact and depicted this aspect of communist life in Ayn Rand, *We the Living* (New York: MacMillan, 1936; Signet sixtieth anniversary paperback edition, 1996).

12. It is not explicitly stated in *Anthem* why Equality fights with others as a young boy; though fighting at this age can often be the result of impulse, I think the rest of the story suggests why the young Equality would be fighting with his "brothers." Interestingly, Rand wrote many years later about the evil of Progressive nursery schools and the "problem children" who reject the schools' conditioning; some of these "problem children," she wrote, are "violently rebellious." See Ayn Rand, "The Comprachicos," in *Return of the Primitive: The Anti-Industrial Revolution*, ed. Peter Schwartz (New York: Meridian, 1999), 51–95.

13. Ayn Rand, *The Virtue of Selfishness: A New Concept of Egoism* (New York: New American Library, 1964), 21–22.

14. Ayn Rand, *Atlas Shrugged* (New York: Random House 1957; Signet thirty-fifth anniversary paperback edition, 1992), 930. At the time of writing *Anthem*, I do not think Rand regarded will as only an aspect of reason. This is more clear in the 1938 edition of *Anthem*, where thought and will seem to be treated as separate and equal powers, or even faculties; see especially 234–37. In the 1946 edition, thought and will are brought closer together, but still seem separable (if not separate). Crucially, however, even if, when writing and editing *Anthem*, Rand viewed reason and will as separate faculties of the mind, she viewed them as in metaphysical harmony. This of course makes sense if the conclusion she was progressively moving toward is that the faculty of reason is volitional. Note also that in her nonfiction writing after *Atlas Shrugged*, Rand continued to speak of the faculty of volition while simultaneously stating that volition is but an aspect of man's rational faculty. See for instance Ayn Rand, "The Metaphysical Versus the Man-Made," in her *Philosophy: Who Needs It* (New York: Bobbs-Merrill, 1982; Signet paperback edition, 1984), 23–34.

15. Rand, *Virtue of Selfishness*, 22. The life-or-death meaning of this primary choice is dramatized fully in *Atlas Shrugged*. For a discussion of one aspect of this dramatization, see Onkar Ghate, "The Death Premise in *We the Living* and *Atlas Shrugged*," in *Essays on Ayn Rand's* We The Living, ed. Robert Mayhew (Lanham, MD: Lexington Books, 2004), 335–56.

16. I think the closest Rand comes in *Anthem* to naming the primary choice is the passage where Equality asks why he must know—and finds no answer: "We must know that we may know" (24). One's primary choice is to activate one's faculty of reason or not, and about this choice one cannot legitimately ask "Why?" The need and value of being conscious at the conceptual level of awareness is known to anyone; there is no competing mode of awareness to entice one with the promise of greater rewards; the only alternative to choosing the conceptual level of awareness is to relegate one's mind to emptiness. To ask *why* one must know—to ask for a *reason* to be conscious at the conceptual level—already presupposes the activation and value of one's rational faculty. For more on this last point, see Peikoff, *Objectivism*, 59–60, 153, and 211–12.

17. Rand, *Atlas Shrugged*, 960–61. The heroes in *Atlas Shrugged* also make the opposite choice. When a childhood Dagny Taggart faces what "they say," namely, that she is unbearably conceited and selfish, but receives no answer when she asks what is meant—she dismisses their claims and wonders to herself "how they could imagine that she would feel guilt from an undefined accusation" (Rand, *Atlas Shrugged*, 54). In this respect Dagny is Equality's heir.

18. To tell a child to "be like Mike"—basketball superstar Michael Jordan—may make sense to him; to tell him to be like Union 5-3392 will likely not. A thinking child will try to be like Union 5-3392 only if he is miserable, which Equality is at this point in his life.

19. There is an interesting parallel between one of the heroes in *Atlas Shrugged*, Hank Rearden, and Equality. Both accept tenets of altruist-collectivist morality, tenets meant to engender guilt and enable society to harness Rearden and Equality. Early in the novel, for instance, Rearden calls himself (and Dagny) "a couple of blackguards"; he says this "indifferently, as a statement of fact." But fundamentally Rearden, like Equality, remains immune to the poison of altruism-collectivism because as a thinker and achiever he feels not guilt but its opposite. In the same scene where he calls himself a blackguard, he is described as "looking at his mills beyond the window; there was no guilt in his face, no doubt, nothing but the calm of an inviolate self-confidence." Rand, *Atlas Shrugged*, 87–88. And in time Rearden is able to grasp the error in his ideas because of his intellectual honesty.

20. For more of Rand's observations on this "compulsive" element in thought, I suggest reading her haunting article "The 'Inexplicable Personal Alchemy,'" *Return of the Primitive*, 119–29. Rand discusses the plight of some young dissidents trapped in the Soviet Union, who had for a few moments, seemingly against their will, spoken openly on Red Square about their country's invasion of Czechoslovakia. For another, fictional treatment of the issue, see Ayn Rand, "The Simplest Thing in the World," in her *The Romantic Manifesto: A Philosophy of Literature*, revised edition (New York: Signet, 1975), 173–85. In this short story a serious fiction-writer who is struggling financially orders himself to accept a baseless view of what "good," sales-deserving fiction is. He discovers that his mind will not obey, that he cannot write under such an order.

21. Compare this to Rand's description of Hank Rearden's invention of Rearden Metal in *Atlas Shrugged*, 35–36.

22. Equality refers to himself as cursed only in Chapter I and, looking back on his life, in Chapter XII. The last time he regards his thought process as outside of his (full) control is when he starts thinking about the words from the Unmentionable Times in Chapter II. From Chapter III on, he knows that he is in control of his mind.

23. For more on Equality's intellectual development in the forest, including why it is important that he see himself as the selector of his values, see Gregory Salmieri, "Prometheus' Discovery: Individualism and the Meaning of the Concept 'I' in *Anthem*," in the present volume.

24. For more on Equality's development of the morality of individualism, see Salmieri, "Prometheus' Discovery," in the present volume.

25. I do not mean to suggest that prior to this event Equality has no reason to question the goal of living for the happiness of all. He does, for instance, feel a violent hatred toward his brothers when he thinks of Liberty being sent to the Palace of Mating

(44–45). He does not yet understand his reaction, but it is initial evidence that there might be a profound conflict between his own happiness and the "needs" of the collective.

26. In the 1938 edition of *Anthem* Equality states: "And so I guard my will before I guard my life. Let no man covet my will and the freedom of my will" (237). Rand cut this passage from the 1946 edition, probably because it is too strong and the language is more appropriate for a nonfiction treatise. In her own later nonfiction, Rand said that there are "two activities which an actually selfish man would defend with his life: judgment and choice" (Ayn Rand, "Selfishness Without a Self," *Philosophy: Who Needs It*, 50).

27. Rand discusses the virtuous circle of a free society in Ayn Rand, "What is Capitalism?" *Capitalism: The Unknown Ideal* (New York: New American Library, 1966; Signet expanded paperback edition, 1967), 11–34.

28. I wish to thank Robert Mayhew, Shoshana Milgram, and Gregory Salmieri for comments on an earlier version of this paper.

# 12

## Prometheus' Discovery: Individualism and the Meaning of the Concept "I" in *Anthem*

*Gregory Salmieri*

> *The theme is the word "I." The whole story is built around one idea: what would happen if a man lost the concept "I," and how would he regain it? . . . It is a psychological issue that I have to dramatize only on the discoveries of that man—on how he recaptures the concept.*
>
> —Ayn Rand, 1969 nonfiction writing course[1]

*Anthem*'s theme is the meaning of the concept "I."[2] Ayn Rand dramatizes this meaning by showing what happens when the concept is expunged. By recounting the steps by which Prometheus re-forms the concept, Rand shows why it is needed. The facts that give rise to the need for the concept, and the implications of these facts, constitute the philosophy of individualism that Prometheus expounds in the novel's final two chapters.

In this essay I discuss the relationship between "I" and individualism, and I detail the steps by which Prometheus discovers both. My aim is to highlight the argument for individualism contained in the steps by which Prometheus reaches it. Throughout I draw heavily on Rand's theory of concepts. Rand would not develop this theory until the early 1940s,[3] but elements of it are anticipated in her earlier thought, and the theory articulates the way she (and her characters) formed and used concepts throughout her career. Indeed, Rand developed the theory by asking herself: "What is it that my mind does when I use concepts? To what do I refer and how do I learn new concepts?" (*Introduction to Objectivist Epistemology* [*ITOE*], 307).

## INDIVIDUALISM AND THE CONCEPT "I"

In a 1936 letter, Ayn Rand wrote: "That one word—individualism—is to be the theme song, the goal, the only aim of all my writing."[4] It is certainly the theme song and aim of *Anthem*, but what precisely is it? In its most general sense, individualism is an emphasis on or endorsement of the individual as opposed to the collective. This attitude finds expression in a series of interconnected philosophical theses which are captured nicely by the *Oxford English Dictionary*'s (*OED*) three definitions of the term:

1. Self-centred feeling or conduct as a principle; a mode of life in which the individual pursues his own ends or follows out his own ideas; free and independent individual action or thought; egoism.
2. The social theory which advocates the free and independent action of the individual, as opposed to communistic methods of organization and state interference. Opposed to Communism and Socialism.
3. In metaphysics the doctrine that the individual is a self-determined whole, and that any larger whole is merely an aggregate of individuals, which, if they act upon each other at all do so only externally.[5]

The doctrines specified in these definitions stand in a certain logical relationship. The first definition presents an ethical theory (henceforth "egoism") advocating the principle of selfish action. Following the *OED*'s entry on egoism, we can elaborate this principle as follows: "Self-interest is the foundation of morality" such that one should hold "one's own interest as the supreme guiding principle of [one's] action." Egoism presupposes the doctrine espoused in the third definition of individualism, which we can call "metaphysical individualism."[6] "Independent individual action or thought" cannot be proper unless it is possible, and it is not possible if men are mere fragments of some larger social organism. Only if each man is a metaphysically distinct, self-determining creature can he have ideas, ends, or interests *of his own* to act on. If metaphysical individualism is a premise for egoism, then the doctrine described in the remaining definition is a consequence of it. We can call this doctrine "political individualism." If each man ought to pursue his own ends on the basis of his own thinking, then the proper political system is the one that leaves him free to do so.

Individualism can thus be seen as egoism along with its metaphysical presuppositions and political implications. It is this complex doctrine that Prometheus discovers over the course of *Anthem*. The climax of the progression is his rediscovery of the concept "I." In order to understand why this is the crucial step, we need to consider the meaning of the concept.

We can begin by asking why we need the concept. Or, to put the question in the context of the novel: What exactly is it that Prometheus lacks before he learns the concept "I"? Certainly he is aware of himself as a distinct physical entity. He is aware that he is referring to only one man when he tells us that his name is Equality 7-2521, that this name is written on a bracelet around his left wrist, that he is twenty-one years old, six feet tall, and so on. In Prometheus' first journal entry it is clear that he is also aware of himself as spiritually distinct from his "brothers." He contrasts his moral character to theirs:

> All men are good and wise. It is only we, Equality 7-2521, we alone who were born with a curse. For we are not like out brothers. (20)[7]

Two years prior to writing this entry, Prometheus was even capable of asserting an individual claim to property:

> This place is ours. This place belongs to us, Equality 7-2521, and to no other men on earth. And if we ever surrender it, we shall surrender our life with it also. (34)

Prometheus self-consciously had distinctive preferences throughout his years in the Home of the Students. He preferred the Science of Things to his other studies, and likely already preferred International 4-8818 to his other classmates. So what exactly does Prometheus lack before rediscovering the concept "I"?

For the beginning of an answer, recall the awkward, wordy form that his language requires for the expression of individual judgments and preferences. Singular pronouns facilitate the isolation of one person from others in thought. Without them it is still possible to think of people individually, but not without special effort. This effort is most eloquently dramatized in Gaea's profession of love:

> "We are one . . . alone . . . and only . . . and we love you who are one . . . alone . . . and only." (87)

Each qualification of "we" and "you," and the pauses between them, represent a distinct mental action that Gaea needs to perform to achieve the thought that we can fluently express with the words "I love you."[8]

The first person singular pronoun, "I," allows a man effortlessly to maintain an awareness of himself in distinction from others. The grammatical policy of referring to oneself by this pronoun exclusively makes this view of oneself omnipresent in thought. But why is it necessary to maintain this perspective on oneself? Why does a man need a concept, denoted by a special word, to keep himself differentiated from others in his thoughts? A brief discussion of the general function of concepts will be useful in answering this question.

The difference between Gaea's lengthy statement and "I love you" points to what Rand would later identify as the cognitive role of all concepts. They are devices for achieving what she called "unit economy." In making even the most rudimentary decisions we need to deal with massive quantities of information. Yet we are only able to hold a small number of distinct items (or "units") in mind at once. This gives rise to a need "to reduce a vast amount of information to a minimal number of units" (*ITOE*, 63). The need is fulfilled by concepts.[9] Each concept is a single unit of thought, held in mind by means of a single word denoting it, but it represents a potentially vast body of knowledge.

To borrow one of Rand's examples, consider the case of a juror who reminds himself of his responsibilities by thinking "I must be just." The concept "justice" is a unitary grasp[10] of a complex phenomenon: "the act of judging a man's character and/or actions exclusively on the basis of all the factual evidence available, and of evaluating it by means of an objective moral criterion" (*ITOE*, 51). "If that concept did not exist," Rand asks, "*what number* of considerations would a man have to bear in mind simultaneously, at every step of the process of judging another man?" (*ITOE*, 70).

The point of the example is not simply that the concept "justice" saves time, making the juror's job less taxing. Rather, without the concept it would be *impossible* for the juror to do his job at all. In order to formulate his intention to be just, he would need to hold so many considerations in mind that he would have no mental space left to consider the evidence of the case. By condensing our knowledge into a manageable form, concepts enable us to take actions (e.g., judging) that would not otherwise be possible. They also make possible new knowledge (e.g., the verdict in the court case). This knowledge can, in turn, be condensed by further concepts which would not have been possible without the initial ones. For example, concepts like "verdict" and "mistrial" would not be possible without the concept "justice."

The need for unit-economy thus gives rise to the need for concepts, and it mandates that we form concepts in specific cases where there is a wealth of data to be made available for use (in thought and action) by conceptual condensation. But we do not need to form concepts for every sort of thing we can distinguish; we designate many things by descriptive phrases. To form concepts in most of these cases would be cognitively stultifying. Rand discusses the case of "beautiful blondes with blue eyes, 5'5" tall and 24 years old":

> If such a special concept [for these women] existed, it would lead to senseless duplication of cognitive effort (and to conceptual chaos): everything of significance discovered about the group would apply to all other young women as well. There would be no cognitive justification for such a concept. (*ITOE*, 71)

The promiscuous formation of concepts to denote such things as Rand's blue-eyed blondes would frustrate our need for unit-economy by burdening us with extraneous considerations. The standards for when to form concepts are determined by "the requirements of cognition (and the principle of unit-economy)" (*ITOE*, 69), and on this basis, the mere fact that we *can* make a differentiation does not mean that a special concept is necessary or even permissible.

The concept "I" denotes an individual man from his own perspective.[11] The fact that we can take such a perspective on ourselves does not by itself establish that we need a special concept for this purpose. As I noted earlier, the concept "I" makes the distinction between self and others a constant motif of our mental lives.[12] Why is such a policy necessary? Why is the distinction between self and others *so* important that it must *always* be present in thought?

A man needs the concept "I" because "the mind is an attribute of the individual,"[13] so that, if a man is to think at all, he must do it as "one . . . alone . . . and only." Rand makes this point in terms of valuing in a 1935 journal entry:

> How can there be valuing without those who value? A verb does not exist in a vacuum. A verb presupposes a noun. There is no such thing as an action without the one who acts. And who can do the valuing except a man?
>
> A collective valuing would amount to this: one believes what others believe, *because* others believe it. If we have ten people and each one of them chooses to believe only what the nine others believe—just exactly who establishes the belief, and how? . . . There has to be a cause of causes, a determining factor, a basic initiative. If it is not taken by a man—by whom, then, is it taken? If a man is not the one to weigh, value and decide—who decides?[14]

Weighing, valuing, and deciding are not automatic. They require an effort on which men can default. Indeed Rand identifies the thing that is most "wrong with the world" as the absence of "the act and habit of valuing and selecting in one's mental life."[15] Consider the process by which Prometheus discovers the "power of the sky" (52–53). He decides to pursue the study of electricity in preference to his other studies. He sustains this decision over the course of two years, during which time he devises and performs innumerable tests. At each step he specifies what he knows (e.g., metal draws the power forth), how he knows it (because he saw lightning repeatedly hit a tall iron rod), and what he does not yet know ("what this power is," "whence it comes," how it relates to the artifacts from the Unmentionable Times). He then continues working to answer the remaining questions. Every component of this process is *self-consciously chosen* as part of the larger project of understanding the strange new power. The process requires an awareness of what *he* knows, and how *he* knows it.

This need for self-awareness is especially acute when Prometheus' conclusions come into conflict with the conventional opinions that he has been taught. Conventional wisdom has it that the loadstone always points North and that this cannot be changed, yet Prometheus has seen the power of the sky make the needle on the compass move (53). Without distinguishing himself from others, it would be impossible for Prometheus to decide whether his observation or the generalization which forbids it is more authoritative.[16]

In general, "thought is a process that must be initiated and directed at each step by the choice of one man, the thinker."[17] The self-direction in this process requires a constant cognizance of the self as distinct both from the objects of study and from other consciousnesses. The concept "I" makes this perspective on oneself second nature, and it is the constant need for this perspective that makes the concept mandatory.[18]

In short, it is because of *metaphysical individualism* that we need the concept "I." In the words of the *OED*, men are "self-determined wholes" who "if they act upon each other at all do so only externally." But to say that a man is self-determined is to say that he is the "cause of causes," "determining factor," or "basic initiative" of his thoughts and actions. And, if men act on each other "only externally," then, in the words of Howard Roark:

> No man can use his brain to think for another. All the functions of body and spirit are private. They cannot be shared or transferred.
>
> We inherit the products of the thought of other men. . . . But all through the process what we receive from others is only the end product of their thinking. The moving force is the creative faculty which takes this product as material, uses it and originates the next step. This creative faculty cannot be given or received, shared or borrowed. It belongs to single, individual men.[19]

*This* is the metaphysics of individualism. It tells us that thinking can only be performed by men as individuals. And, since thinking is a complex activity, to perform it a man needs a pervasive self-consciousness; he needs to be constantly aware of himself as an individual; he needs the concept "I."[20]

The perverse language of the City is founded on the opposite, collectivist premise. It forces the thinker to consider himself primarily a part of some larger whole, and it inculcates the view of consciousness that would be necessary if the mind were inherently social. But collectivism is false. The only alternative to *individual* thinking and valuing is the sort of passive demurral from judgment that we saw Rand discuss in her journals, and this is not a form of thinking or valuing at all. A man whose mind works this way is a passive nothing moved at random by accidental influences.

The mind is an attribute of the individual and operates by self-direction. Its proper functioning thus requires the constant self-awareness provided by the concept "I." A man needs this concept to think and to value just as he needs the concept "justice" to render a just verdict. Indeed the very concepts "thought" and "value" depend on the vocabulary of individualism, just as the concepts "verdict" and "mistrial" depend on the concept "justice."

Collectivism (and the City's language in particular) is guilty of the fallacy Rand called "concept stealing": it uses concepts while ignoring or denying the antecedent knowledge on which they depend.[21] Earlier we saw Rand note that actions are impossible without entities to act—that verbs presuppose nouns. At the time we were concerned with a metaphysical point: there cannot be actions without (individual) entities to carry them out. But there is an epistemological point here as well: there cannot be knowledge of actions without knowledge of entities capable of performing them. In order to learn about walking, for example, one must know about animals with legs. Not only do we need to know about legged animals to know about walking, we need to have conceptualized them. Imagine trying to understand what it means to walk without using any concepts denoting legged animals; the mind would boggle. Thus the concept "walk" presupposes concepts denoting legged animals, and, in general, "a verb presupposes a noun."

But the City dwellers use verbs denoting mental actions while negating the noun these verbs presuppose. All our concepts of consciousness were formed by self-conscious individuals introspecting the actions of their own minds.[22] (And, as we saw earlier, many of these actions would not even be possible without the concept "I.") Thus all our concepts of consciousness presuppose metaphysical individualism, and so these concepts lose their meaning when this presupposition is denied. But the City dwellers appropriate concepts of consciousness while denying the existence of the individual mind and censoring the concepts by means of which a man can be aware of himself.

The fact that one concept presupposes another does not mean that every man who uses the later concept understands the earlier one.[23] It is possible to use a word without grasping its meaning. Starting from a habit of doing so,

> people find it impossible to grasp higher abstractions, and their conceptual development consists of condensing fog into fog into thicker fog—until the hierarchical structure of concepts breaks down in their minds, losing all ties to reality; and, as they lose the capacity to understand, their education becomes a process of memorizing and imitating.
>
> Words, as such people use them, denote unidentified feelings, unadmitted motives, subconscious urges, chance associations, memorized sounds, ritualistic formulas, second-hand cues—all of it hung, like barnacles, on some swimming suggestion of some existential referent. (*ITOE*, 75–76)

This sort of confusion makes possible every sort of conceptual fallacy, including the most evil:

> the destruction of language—and, therefore, of thought and, therefore, of communication—by means of anti-concepts. An anti-concept is an unnecessary and

rationally unusable term designed to replace and obliterate some legitimate concept.[24]

The City's language is the end result of this practice.[25] "We", as used by the City dwellers, is a stolen concept. "We" denotes a group of people including one-self. Without a prior distinction between self and others this would be impos-sible—without "I" it would be impossible to distinguish between "we" and "they." Sometimes honest error can result in stolen concepts and other "ra-tionally unusable terms," but this is not the case with "the great WE" (19). It is an anti-concept devised expressly to replace "I," and to destroy individualism.

Thus the City's language hampers Prometheus by forcing him to go through contortions in order think of himself as an individual. But concepts cannot be obliterated without leaving traces. All of the concepts that the City dwellers steal depend for their meaning on a recognition of the individual mind. Insofar as the Councils succeed in censoring such a recognition, they render the concepts meaningless. But an active mind can recapture the con-cepts. It will be focused on reality, and so will be able to reconstruct the logic behind the empty words rehearsed by others. The Councils can destroy con-cepts, but they cannot destroy the facts they name. These facts remain and can be discovered, but they "are not for all men to see . . . only for those who will seek them" (52).

## PROMETHEUS' DISCOVERY OF HIMSELF AS A VALUER

Readers of *Anthem* have access to Prometheus' most private thoughts "put down upon a paper no others are to see" (17). Every sentence is evidence of an active mind that wills to seek facts—of an author who strives for full clar-ity, never contenting himself with the vague or approximate. For example, consider how Prometheus describes steel when he first encounters it in his tunnel: "On the ground there were long thin tracks of iron, but it was not iron; it felt smooth and cold as glass" (32). He does not rest content with his initial identification of the metal as iron, nor even with a vague differentia-tion of it from iron; he specifies how it differs.

For a more striking example, consider Prometheus' reaction when he re-alizes that the tunnel is left from the Unmentionable Times:

> [W]e thought "This is a foul place. They are damned who touch the things of the Unmentionable Times." But our hand which followed the track, as we crawled, clung to the iron as if it would not leave it, as if the skin of our hand were thirsty and begging of the metal some secret fluid beating in its coldness. (33)

The specter of damnation must create an impulse to evade either the origin of the metal or his attraction to it. Prometheus could leave these facts unnamed or rationalize away his feelings. Instead he identifies and records the whole truth. He will allow nothing—certainly no emotion—to stand between his mind and reality. For the same reason, when he takes an action he regards as a sin, he acknowledges it as such. In the words of another Ayn Rand hero: he wants "no pretense, no evasion, no silent indulgence, with the nature of [his] actions left unnamed."[26] His first allegiance always is to reality.

According to Objectivism, such a commitment to truth is the essence of morality. It consists in a choice that must be renewed in every moment. Indeed, it is man's basic choice:

> [T]hat which you call "free will" is your mind's freedom to think or not, the only will you have, your only freedom, the choice that controls all the choices you make and determines your life and your character.[27]

This choice confronts us in the form of the alternative between *focusing* our minds to "a full, active, purposefully directed awareness of reality" or drifting in a "semi-conscious daze." A man out of focus is passive and moved by chance; his consciousness, such as it is, is not the author of any thoughts. Such a man holds no convictions and no values, but merely reacts to stimuli "at the mercy of his undirected sensory-perceptual mechanism and of any random, associational connections it might happen to make."[28] If a man is habitually out of focus, his mind serves as a repository for stale dogmas and rote behaviors, picked up at random from others. To paraphrase from *The Fountainhead*: "such a man is not there, he's not alive, he has no I."[29]

We have already discussed how the individual consciousness (the I) is the noun presupposed as the subject of mental verbs such as "think" and "value." We can now see that this consciousness must *will itself into existence*.[30] Prometheus is a man who constantly does this. He wills to seek knowledge and then to act on it. It is this activity—the very essence of human life—that creates the basis and the need for the concept "I."

It is primarily by introspection on his own functioning and observation of its consequences that Prometheus recaptures the concept "I" and discovers individualism. But the collectivism with which he has been indoctrinated skews the way he initially conceptualizes and evaluates the introspective data: "We were born with a curse. It has always driven us to thoughts which are forbidden. It has always given us wishes which men may not wish" (18). In fact this curse is just a subconscious habituated to the demands of a focused mind. Well stocked with values and brimming with fresh connections, it is the result of a constant *willing* to seek the facts.[31] The curse "whispers . . . that there are great things on this earth of ours, and that we can know them if we try, and that we must know them" (24).

Prometheus loves the Science of Things and wants to be a scholar, thus committing the Transgression of Preference, and he believes that there are mysteries, despite the Councils' claim that there are none. These preferences and beliefs are not causeless. Prometheus longs to be sent to the Home of the Scholars because "all the great modern inventions" come from it and because these inventions have their origin in the scientific study that Prometheus loves. His belief that there are mysteries and great things to be discovered is based on his own observations of nature. His claim that there are mysteries "in the sky and under the water and in the plants that grow" suggests that he has specific mysteries in mind based on specific observations. That Prometheus is continually making such observations is clear from his descriptions of twilight and evening respectively: "The shadows are blue on the pavements, and the sky is blue with a deep brightness which is not bright"; "The sky is like a black sieve pierced by silver drops that tremble, ready to burst through. The moths beat against the street lanterns" (27–28). Such careful observation will suggest questions: What causes the peculiar look of twilight? What is the "brightness that is not bright"? In what way is it different from a normal brightness? Why do the stars tremble? Why are moths attracted to flame? If Prometheus chooses to keep his mind active and to attend to nature, then these sorts of mysteries will necessarily occur to him. If he notices his aptitude for this sort of thought, the joy he takes in it, and its practical value (in leading to "modern inventions"), then it is no surprise that he develops a passion for science. Prometheus' "curse" is just a habit of being *mentally active.*[32]

Notice how Prometheus' mental activity is evident in the way he deals with his "curse." He conceptualizes it, inquires into its nature, and works to combat it. Rather than passively accepting a vague sense of discomfort during his years in the Home of the Students, he *concludes* that the quickness of his mind is evil and he *devises* and *enacts* a plan to correct it (viz., emulating Union 5-3992, "they of the half-brain" [29].) When his curse whispers that he must know the answers to the mysteries, he *asks* why he must know. When he accepts his disappointing Life Mandate his "voice was the clearest, the steadiest voice in the hall" (26) because he has *identified* the mandate as a way to atone for his "sins" and has *chosen* to accept it as such. Prometheus is consistently active even in his attempts to conform to the passivity demanded by his society.

Prometheus' values and conclusions—the consequences of his mental activity—put him in constant conflict with his society. He has questions, but the teachers forbid them. He has reason to believe that there are mysteries but the Councils say that there are none. He wants to be a Scholar, so that he can "ask questions of [the rivers, sands, winds, and rocks], for they do not forbid questions" (24). But the Teachers tell him not to choose a profession, and the Council of Vocations determines that he is most needed as a street sweeper. He notices Gaea's dark, hard, glowing eyes and her wild golden hair, but "men are forbidden to take notice of women" (38). When he sees the Transgressor of the Unspeakable Word, he notices the calmness, joy, and pride on his face, and thinks of him as a saint, but this is a "monstrous thought" (50). In every way, Prometheus is in constant conflict with others from his days in the Home of the Infants onward. These conflicts all derive from the distinctive *thoughts* and *values* of a mind that chooses to think. They serve as a constant sign that Prometheus is "one . . . alone . . . and only."

Prometheus has two core values: his scientific career and Gaea. It is reflection on these values which brings him ultimately to grasp individualism. The first step in his progression is noticing that *he* chooses these values because they have a special significance *to him*.

The intensity of Prometheus' love for science is directly introspectable; he desires to be sent to the Home of the Scholars so much that his "hands trembled under the blankets in the night" and he experiences this desire in the form of an unendurable pain (24). The teachers' warnings against choosing a career serve to underscore what Prometheus is doing in wishing to be a scholar, and the unusual circumstances in which he is finally able to study make it especially clear that this activity is *chosen by him*. Already in his first journal entry, Prometheus writes: "We alone, of all the thousands that walk this earth, we alone in this hour are doing a work that has no purpose save that we wish to do it" (36). Prometheus is aware too of the emotional rewards of this work. It makes him "feel as if with each day our sight were growing sharper than the hawk's and clearer than rock crystal" (36), and it brings peace to his heart.

The theme of an intense personal response prompting self-consciously distinctive choices is present too in Prometheus' love for Gaea. At first sight of her he knows fear for the first time and feels a "pain more precious than pleasure" (39). It is his love for her that makes him "feel of a sudden that the earth is good and that it is not a burden to live" (41). This leads him to be glad to be alive, and to endorse this emotion in self-conscious defiance of the City's moral code. He writes: "If this is vice, then we wish no virtue" (47). The positive emotions Prometheus experiences as a result of pursuing science and meeting Gaea are new to him. He will later observe that "the only things which taught us joy were the power we created in our wires, and the Golden One" (86).

This new-found joy raises questions and makes possible a new observation about his brothers. It is a dogma of the City that all men are happy, but it is now evident to Prometheus that this is not so. His brothers have dull, evasive eyes, hunched shoulders, and bowed heads,

> and their muscles are drawn as if their bodies were shrinking and wished to shrink out of sight. And a word steals into our minds, as we look upon our brothers, and that word is fear. (46)

Prior to learning joy from his love for Gaea, Prometheus knows of no state with which to contrast the miserable fear "hanging in the air of the sleeping halls and in the streets" (46). It is his own happiness that allows him to see that "our brothers are not like us. All is not well with our brothers" (47).

The City dwellers have no values and so they have none of the emotions that stem from the pursuit and attainment of values, nor do they really understand the concepts for values and the emotions that flow from them.[33] (If they did, they would not be able to maintain that all men are happy.) All of their evaluative concepts are stolen. This is why Prometheus' evaluations of his own actions in terms of the code of the City have no motivational force—repeating the city's laws to himself has no effect, and he does not feel guilty when he breaks them. It is only the values that *he chooses* that give meaning to evaluative concepts. For example, notice how the idea of a saint becomes meaningful to him only through the image of the Transgressor of the Unspeakable Word, an individual who has chosen and achieved real values and in whom Prometheus (the incipient valuer) can recognize real virtue.

Once his chosen values have breathed life into his evaluative concepts, Prometheus can see how unhappy his brothers are. Although he is not yet ready to break with the City, he begins to contemplate alternatives to it. His mind is drawn to the Uncharted Forest and the Unmentionable Times, and he recalls the Saint of the pyre.[34]

We have discussed how valuing depends on a mental activity—on selecting and judging. But these mental actions are not sufficient for valuing. A value isn't something that one merely *evaluates* as worth having, it is something one *pursues* as a result of such an evaluation. An unpursued value is not a value at all, but an empty wish.

Prometheus' values demand specific existential actions from him. In order to study he must *claim* the tunnel, *sneak* out to it night after night, and *steal* candles, knives, manuscripts, and other supplies. In order to understand the power of the sky he must take all the actions we discussed earlier. Even in cases where it is not clear how he can achieve or protect his values, Prometheus operates on the premise of acting to attain and defend his values. Thus he resolves to prevent Gaea from going to the Palace of Mating though he does not know "How to prevent it, how to bar the will of the Councils," and when telling Gaea that sweeping the road by her Home is his regular assignment, he adds a resolution that "no one will take this road away from us" (44–45).

So Prometheus chooses his values and he acts to realize them. From his successes in his scientific work, he comes to see himself as the achiever of his values. In his third entry, he writes that he knows things that the council does not because he seeks knowledge. In particular he knows about the power of the sky because he took the specific actions necessary to discover it. The emphasis in this entry is on the fact that he is alone in his knowledge because "the secrets of this earth are not for all men to see, but only for those who will seek them" (52). He alone knows because he alone sought. This realization runs counter to the City's dogma that "we all know the things which exist" (52), but it is undeniable. It leads Prometheus to renew his dedication to the study of the power, forgetting "all men, all laws, and all things save our metal and our wires" (54). This in turn leads to a greater achievement: the invention of the light.

The entry discussing the invention is pervaded by a euphoric self-confidence. It begins: "We made it. We created it. We brought it forth from the night of the ages. We alone. Our hands. Our mind. Ours alone and only" (59). In the previous entry on electricity, his solitude was acknowledged and accepted. Now it is celebrated.

Prometheus goes on to discuss the meaning of his achievement. He proceeds from its immediate practical applications of lighting his tunnel and then his and other cities to its wider significance:

> The power of the sky can be used to do men's bidding. There are no limits to its secrets and its might, and it can be made to grant us anything if we but choose to ask. (60)

This gives him a profound sense of himself as an achiever. In appreciating the power and value of the light, he is also appreciating the power and value of its *producer*—of himself. Thus in valuing the light he comes to value himself, to care about what happens to his body. And in wondering at the light's power, he comes to wonder about his own strength and appearance. The wire is a part of him, "as a vein torn from us, glowing with our blood" (61).

The analogy is apt. It is glowing with his blood in that its glow is due to his self-generated effort. He has spent part of *his life* animating it. There is a second, related sense in which the wire is like one of Prometheus' veins. A vein is an organ that contributes to the life of the organism, and its meaning and value lie in this fact. The light is a part of Prometheus in this sense as well. The light's meaning and value lie in the contribution it can make to his life. The box is a part of Prometheus' life. It was created by *his energy* to serve *his ends*. It would not exist without his efforts, and it is worthless outside of the context of his life and his values.

Prometheus does not immediately grasp this second sense of his analogy. Just as the corrupt concepts and values he learned from the City cause him initially to misidentify his mind as a curse, they lead him to misidentify the nature of the light's value and his motives in inventing it. He conceives of the light's value in terms of its use to his brothers, and he thinks he invented it for their sake. This is understandable. Without the concept "I" to keep himself clearly differentiated from his brothers, it would be impossible for Prometheus to evaluate the light in terms of its meaning for *his* life.

Prometheus does not even distinguish between his life and that of the group's. He is aware that he pursues clandestine evening studies in a tunnel, but three hours a night in isolation does not make for a *life of one's own*. It is only later, when he finds himself alone in the Forest, that he begins to contemplate solitude as such. Even then he thinks that a solitary life is both impossible and corrupt (76). Thus Prometheus cannot yet conceive of his life as distinct from that of his Brothers. Consequently, though he can recognize the light as *his* invention, he cannot see its meaning in terms of *his own life*. Also, Prometheus knows no code of values other than the one taught him by his society. By this point in the novel he has formed and achieved values of his own, but he has not discovered how they fit together into a whole, and he does not understand what makes them values. Yet he needs such an integrated perspective on values—he needs a code of values—in order to assess the significance of such a profound value as the light.

The moral code Prometheus needs will elude him until he learns the concept "I." However, the Scholars' rejection of the light explodes his altruistic misconception of the light's value. It makes him realize that the light is of no value to his brothers and that he did not make it for their sake. This realization is a crucial step towards rediscovering "I" and grasping egoism. In his evaluation of the light Prometheus assumes a standard of value alien to the Scholars. The light is good because it can be made to do man's bidding, because it can be used to ease the toil of men and to flood the cities with light, because it is "the key to the earth" (71). In *Atlas Shrugged*, Rand identifies Man's Life—the specific type of life required by man's nature for his survival—as the standard of value, and she shows that men do not value their lives automatically. In *Anthem* she has not yet formulated this standard, but all of Prometheus' evaluations presuppose a valuing of life on earth. He sees all his values as contributing either to life itself or to its enjoyment. The analogy between his light and a vein is particularly striking in this regard.

Prometheus has specific values, and he values the successful life that is their sum. Therefore *he* evaluates the light as a profound value. This makes it a great value *to him*. But the Scholars do not value their lives. They do not even care whether they live or die, "which is to be as our brothers will it" (47). Nor do they have any other actual values. If the value of the light resides in its ability to increase one's standard of living, it will be of no value to men who do not wish to live. If the value of the power of the sky is that it can grant men anything they ask for, the power will be of no value to those who seek nothing. Prometheus expects the Scholars to appreciate the value of the light and his value as its creator, but neither Prometheus nor his light is of any value to the Scholars. Both are threats to their mindless, valueless routine. Thus the Scholars respond with fear, and they seek to destroy the light and its creator.

To protect the light, Prometheus flees the City. The encounter with the Scholars has made it clear to him that he did not design the light for his brothers:

> We have lied to ourselves. We have not built this box for the good of our brothers. We built it for its own sake. It is above all our brothers to us, and its truth is above their truth. (76)

When it was clear that his brothers did not value the box, he did not seek a more appropriate way to serve them, as he would have if the box were really *for them*. Rather he protected the box from them by taking it into the Uncharted Forest. If the box were made for their good, this action would be incomprehensible. Perhaps on an altruistic premise Prometheus could resent the Scholars and think they were foolish not to see the value of the box, but he could not flee the City removing the box from the very conditions that make it a value—the needs of his brothers.

If Prometheus were to remain in the City, abandoning the box and seeking a more appropriate way to serve his brothers, he would have to surrender his mind. Service to others and independent thought are incompatible. Prometheus cannot *make* his brothers value the box or benefit from it. He cannot force the City to adopt the new technology. (Even if he could, the light would not be a value to his brothers; they would adopt it in the fearful, joyless manner in which they do everything else.) Thus to remain in the City, Prometheus would have to sacrifice the light. In doing so, he would be sacrificing his greatest achievement *and his judgment*. Leonard Peikoff explains the relevant principle:

> If you know enough to see the tie between cognition (knowledge) and your choice and ability to act and achieve, then you know that your mind is a function in both choosing and achieving these values. An assault on your action is an assault also on the conclusions which lead you to that [action], which is an assault on your mind.[35]

If Prometheus accepted the Scholars' decision to destroy the light, he would be renouncing his mind by placing "his brothers' truth" above what he knows to be true. The Scholars claim that there are no mysteries, that individual men are impotent, and therefore, that the light Prometheus created on his own is impossible, unreal, and worthless. But Prometheus has discovered that there are such mysteries, and he knows that the light is good and that he produced it on his own.

Prometheus' whole method of functioning—his seeking the truth and his selecting and achieving values—is inconsistent with an ethics that demands service to his brothers. Yet it is only this method of functioning that gives rise to values and to evaluative concepts. Values as such only exist for *valuers*—individuals who select and produce. Thus the facts that give rise to values are incompatible with the altruistic morality of the City. An egoistic ethics is inherent in individual valuing, and this is the only sort of valuing there is. But Prometheus does not see all this immediately; describing his state of mind when leaving the Home of the Scholars, he writes: "We knew only that we must run" (75).

## PROMETHEUS' DISCOVERY OF INDIVIDUALISM

When Prometheus first arrives in the Forest, he has not yet explicitly rejected the collectivist philosophy of the City, much less formulated the individualistic alternative he espouses in his final two journal entries. His deepest value has just come into conflict with the only morality he has ever known. To save it he abandoned the City and its standards. But he knows no other way to live. He wants no part of the City—of the "truth which is our brother men"—but he knows no alternative (76). As far as he knows, life apart from the collective is impossible. He has learned of the possibility of discrete private values and achievements, but only as an exception to a collectivized life. Thus when he arrives in the Forest he expects to die. He is dejected, so much so that he is disinterested even in answering the moral questions raised by his encounter with the Scholars. Thinking of the way he values the box ahead of his brothers, he asks: "Why wonder about this? We have not many days to live" (76–77). Before he can progress philosophically, he needs to see that the pattern he observed in his invention of the light applies to values more generally. In particular, he needs to see that it applies to values most immediately relevant to survival.

When he awakes the next day his mood is lighter. He suddenly realizes his new freedom and it makes him giddy. Yet he still lacks direction and perspective. If the first day in the Forest is a "day of wonder," it is still a collection of discrete wonderful experiences not yet seen as components of a new life. The day contains an event crucial to Prometheus' philosophical development.

> We stopped when we felt hunger. We saw birds in the tree branches, and flying from under our footsteps. We picked a stone and we sent it as an arrow at a bird. It fell before us. We made a fire, we cooked the bird, and we ate it, and no meal had ever tasted better to us. And we thought suddenly that there was a great satisfaction to be found in the food which we need and obtain by our own hand. And we wished to be hungry again and soon, that we might know again this strange new pride in eating. (79)

The significance of this event should be clear. It shows both that on his own Prometheus is competent to produce the basic values necessary for his survival and that these values acquire an added meaning when he produces them for himself. Notice that the satisfaction Prometheus takes in eating stems not just from his obtaining the food by his own hand, but also from his satisfying his own need. Prior to this point, the relationship between his values and his own person was not clear to him. Prometheus knew since childhood that he had his own wishes, but he did not understand the relationship between the objects of these wishes and himself. In his discussion of the power of the sky, he mentions how great the power is, that it can be made to do men's bidding, and that it is the key to the earth, but he never mentions its specific effects on him. He does see the glowing wire as a part of him, comparing it to a vein, but he does not grasp the full significance of this. He sees it as his vein in the sense that it carries his blood, but not in the sense that it carries it in service of his needs. In the past when he has experienced personal needs (the unendurable pain of wishing for a career as a Scholar, and the longing for Gaea) he was unaware of their source and their connection to the rest of his life. The case of the bird is different. The role and source of hunger is obvious. And it is to serve this need that he finds and kills his dinner. The value and the achievement are self-evidently and self-consciously in the service of a *need* of his *own*.

The significance of this new observation is marked in the tenth journal entry in the way Prometheus explains why the house they discover is theirs alone:

> This is your house, Golden One, and ours, and it belongs to no other men whatever as far as the earth may stretch. We shall not share it with others, as we share not our joy with them, nor our love, nor our hunger. (105)

Where love is a form of valuing and joy is an emotional response to values, hunger is an indication of a need. Its place at the end of the list is significant. The list goes from effect to (partial) cause. They share joy because they value each other. But now Prometheus is beginning to see that values are in response to needs, and that these needs are *private*. It is in part because of this that values and their emotional consequences are private, and that property should be privately owned.[36]

Before entering the Forest, Prometheus had grasped two ways in which he as an individual was responsible for his values: he chose them and he achieved them. It is only with the killing of the bird that he begins to grasp a third way in which he is responsible for his values: they are necessary because of *his needs*. The role of his own needs in his values and actions is evident in every element of his life in the Forest. He needs to make arrows to kill birds, and he needs to find clearings to sleep in and to build fires around the clearings to provide for his safety. Eventually he will need to build a house.

The killing of the bird and the strange new pride in eating it are the beginning of Prometheus' realization of the role of his needs in his values. This realization is the completion of the thought he glimpsed when he analogized the wire to one of his veins. *He is the achiever of his values and these values serve his needs.* It is fitting then that Prometheus uses the word "pride"[37] when discussing both his creation of the light and his killing of the bird. Notice also that immediately after each achievement he takes an interest in his own body. In his tunnel after creating the light, he notices the strength of his arms and wonders what he looks like. He finds out immediately after eating the bird when he comes upon a stream and sees his reflection in it for the first time. Unlike his brothers he is beautiful and strong.

By the time Gaea finds Prometheus on his second day in the Forest, he has not yet processed all of his new observations, but he now sees the possibility of an independent life in the Forest and invites Gaea to discover such a life with him:

> Our dearest one. Fear nothing of the forest. There is no danger in solitude. We have no need of our brothers. Let us forget their good and our evil, let us forget all things save that we are together and that there is joy as a bond between us. Give us your hand. Look ahead. It is our own world, Golden One, a strange, unknown world, but our own. (83–84)

It is in the context of this new, self-sufficient, joyous life that he begins to reflect explicitly on morality for the first time. His thinking begins with reflection on the code of the City that "Everything which comes from the many is good" and "Everything which comes from one is evil." "We have broken the law," he writes, "but we have never doubted it. Yet now, as we walk through the forest, we are learning to doubt" (85–86). The questions abound:

> If that which we have found is the corruption of solitude, then what can men wish for save corruption? If this is the great evil of being alone, then what is good and what is evil? (85)
>
> There is no life for men, save in useful toil for the good of all their brothers. But we lived not, when we toiled for our brothers, we were only weary. There is no joy for men, save the joy shared with all their brothers. But the only things which taught us joy were the power we created in our wires, and the Golden One. And both these joys belong to us alone, they come from us alone, they bear no relation to our brothers, and they do not concern our brothers in any way. Thus do we wonder.
>
> There is some error, one frightful error, in the thinking of men. What is that error? We do not know, but the knowledge struggles within us, struggles to be born. (86)

There is an inner contradiction in the code of the City. In denying the individual and demanding that one live for others, the City dwellers undercut the roots of valuing. Thus they destroy values and the emotions that stem from them. They make life meaningless. Prometheus *lived* only insofar as he broke this code, insofar as he pursued, achieved, and enjoyed values that did not concern his brothers in any way. Prometheus sees this, yet he is unable to articulate it. The knowledge struggles within him to be born. It is in the context of this struggle that Prometheus tells us of Gaea's halting attempt to express her love for him.

> Today, the Golden One stopped suddenly and said:
> "We love you."
> But then they frowned and shook their head and looked at us helplessly.
> "No," they whispered, "that is not what we wished to say."
> They were silent, then they spoke slowly, and their words were halting, like the words of a child learning to speak for the first time:
> "We are one . . . alone . . . and only . . . and we love you who are one . . . alone . . . and only."
> We looked into each other's eyes and we knew that the breath of a miracle had touched us, and fled, and left us groping vainly.
> And we felt torn, torn for some word we could not find. (86–87)

It is the vain groping that connects Gaea's attempted profession of love with Prometheus' attempt to identify the frightful error in the thinking of men. And it is here that it becomes clear to Prometheus that what he is missing is a word, that there is some defect in the way he and Gaea have been taught to think of themselves, and that there is a need to conceptualize themselves as each "one . . . alone . . . and only." Had Prometheus not found the word "I" in manuscripts from the Unmentionable Times, he would have soon formed the concept on his own, because he sees the need for it and he sees that need in relation to his moral questions.

Prometheus shows us in his eleventh entry that he has grasped the concept "I" and answered his moral questions. Fittingly, his need for the concept and for an answer to these questions is most evident in the conclusion of the tenth entry. He writes sitting at a table in the new house where he and Gaea have resolved to spend the rest of their lives. He is free and well equipped to provide for his needs and to continue his studies. Yet something is still missing:

> And now we look upon the earth and sky. This spread of naked rock and peaks and moonlight is like a world ready to be born, a world that waits. It seems to us it asks a sign from us, a spark, a first commandment. We cannot know what word we are to give, nor what great deed this earth expects to witness. We know it waits. It seems to say it has great gifts to lay before us, but it wishes a greater gift from us. We are to speak. We are to give its goal, its highest meaning to all this glowing space of rock and sky. (92–93)

Prometheus sees that value comes from him in all the senses discussed above. He sees the earth as raw material for his values. He plans to spend his life in his own house, providing for his own needs, pursuing values that bring him joy, with the woman he loves. Yet each of these observations and intentions is a discrete unit in his thought. He can notice connections between them and, with work, he can name and retain these connections. But they do not comprise a unity. Thus Prometheus' world, like his knowledge, *waits to be born*. In particular, it waits for a certain *word* from him. It is only with the advent of the concept "I" that Prometheus' knowledge and values are integrated into a whole in which each observation and value reinforces the others.

> I stand here on the summit of the mountain. I lift my head and I spread my arms. This, my body and spirit, this is the end of the quest. I wished to know the meaning of things. I am the meaning. I wished to find a warrant for being. I need no warrant for being, and no word of sanction upon my being. I am the warrant and the sanction. (94)

The basic facts expressed in Prometheus' eleventh journal entry, his anthem to individualism, are all things he had already observed. But the concept "I" allows him to see their interconnection and their implications.

He begins with the assertion that *he* exists, thinks, and wills. He knew all of this before; what is new is the individualistic emphasis provided by the concept "I." He continues with a personal claim to *his* hand, spirit, sky, forest, and earth. When Gaea first found him in the forest, he had told her that the world belonged to them. Again, what is new in the eleventh entry is the emphasis provided by the first person singular.

From at least the time of his third journal entry he grasps that he discovers the truth by the independent exercise of his own mind, and in the subsequent entries he gradually grasps how the meaning of his values is also a result of his own thought and choice. But the concept "I" automatizes the self-emphasis, freeing Prometheus to carry the thought further than he was able to before.

> It is my eyes which see, and the sight of my eyes grants beauty to the earth. It is my ears which hear, and the hearing of my ears gives its song to the world. It is my mind which thinks, and the judgment of my mind is the only searchlight that can find the truth. It is my will which *chooses,* and the choice of my will is the only edict I must respect. (94)

He can now draw a conclusion from the facts that his consciousness makes values possible, his judgment identifies truths, and his will chooses values based on these truths: he is the warrant for his own being, and the choice of his will (based on his judgment of truth) is the only edict he must respect. Thus he sees *his will* as holy.

Before the eleventh entry he had found happiness and he had resolved not to surrender it. Only now can he formulate the principle involved: that *his* happiness is an end in itself. "It is *the* end. It is its own goal. It is its own purpose" (95, emphasis added). Thus Prometheus grasps *egoism*. Increasingly Prometheus has been living from himself and for himself, but now he can identify this fact, celebrate it, and self-consciously dedicate himself to it: "This miracle of me is mine to own and keep, and mine to guard, and mine to use, and mine to kneel before" (95).

The concept "I" inaugurates a frenzy of new integrations. From his grasp of egoism, he proceeds immediately to its social and political implications. If his happiness is an end in itself, then he is not "the means to any ends others may wish to accomplish" (95). Thus he neither lives for his brothers nor asks them to live for him. As he chooses all his values, he chooses his friends, and the nature of the relationships he chooses with them is set by the principle that each man is an end in himself free to associate or not with others as he wishes.

> For in the temple of his spirit, each man is alone. Let each man keep his temple untouched and undefiled. Then let him join hands with others if he wishes, but only beyond his holy threshold. (96)

While walking through the Forest, he knew that there was a fearful error in the thought of man, an error that results in the living death of toiling for one's brothers, but now he can identify this error as a violation of the principle that forms the basis of proper human relationships. Relationships are a value when based on the judgment and choice of the individuals—they are a value only when "we" is spoken "as a second thought" after "I." But the City dwellers reverse this by demanding that "we" be "placed first within man's soul." This is the error which he had struggled to grasp. Now with the concept "I" he can identify this "creed of corruption" and repudiate it (96–97).

In the twelfth entry, Prometheus relates his new philosophical knowledge with what he has just learned of world history. He grasps that "the structure of the centuries" was the result of *egoism*. Its "every beam had come from the thought of some one man, each in his day down the ages, from the depth of some one spirit, such spirit as existed but for its own sake." Just as he created his light for his own sake and his brothers sought to destroy it, so other individualists had produced the wonders of the Unmentionable Times—"the steel towers, the flying ships, the power wires"—and it was the "worship of the word 'We'" that destroyed these achievements (102).

The difference between the tenth and eleventh entries—between an inchoate mass of judgments and a philosophy—is the condensation and integration provided by the concept "I." The concept is necessary because of man's need to think and act self-consciously as an individual. It enables him to see himself as the locus of thoughts and values and thus to *direct* his life. The doctrine of egoism is the culmination of the self-conscious direction demanded by metaphysical individualism and made possible by the concept "I."

## *ANTHEM'S* ARGUMENT

As part of a 1997 series of lectures entitled *Objectivism Through Induction*, Leonard Peikoff discusses the steps by which a thinker would initially discover and justify egoism.[38] The progression he sketches is essentially the same as the one Prometheus follows, and reviewing it will give us a more abstract perspective on the argument traced in the steps of Prometheus' discovery.

Peikoff argues that in order for a thinker to discover that his own interest should be the supreme end of his actions, he would first need to grasp the concept of self-interest, which itself depends on the concept "value." A value is "that which one acts to gain and/or keep."[39] To grasp the concept, as it applies in the human case, one needs to grasp that men *act* to achieve goals that they have *chosen* in accordance with some *standard*. Peikoff projects that a thinker would first grasp that all the things that he pursues and treasures are things that he *chose* (as opposed to passively accepted). He would then grasp that his values must be achieved by him in action and subsequently would formulate a standard of value.

Peikoff points out that the act of choosing is directly introspectable and that the role of choice in a man's values is especially evident to him in cases of conflict between his values and those of others. "There's a self-assertion in choosing values that has to strike you, or you won't get to egoism, and most people don't [get to egoism], because they don't choose their values." Prometheus does choose, and his choices do bring him into conflict with others. Even if he initially misidentifies his chosen values as the result of a "curse," by the time he writes his third journal entry he is certainly aware of the self-assertion involved in choosing values.

The second stage of the progression is realizing that each of one's values must be attained by one's own action, so that one thinks of himself as the "chooser and achiever of all [his] values." The dictatorial rule of the Councils severely limits Prometheus' opportunities to act in pursuit of his values,[40] but wherever there are such opportunities Prometheus takes them. Most importantly, he claims the tunnel and conducts his scientific research there. Thus he comes to recognize himself as the achiever of his values. (See especially chapters 3 and 5.)

After completing this second stage, a thinker has a clear concept of value, but it lacks content. To proceed, he needs "a whole series of values, a common denominator that makes them values—the standard—therefore giving [him] the idea of [his] own welfare or interest." The thinker would arrive at a standard of value by reflecting on a wide range of values and considering the pre-philosophical reasons he has for pursuing them. He would look for a common denominator that can unite them into an integrated conception of his interest.[41] Peikoff argues that an intelligent, first-handed thinker would be able to grasp that all of his values contribute to his life and his enjoyment of it.

Prometheus never formulates a standard of value. In his ecstatic eleventh journal entry he writes that *his happiness* is its own purpose. But as Rand explains in "The Objectivist Ethics," there is a difference between a standard and a purpose. "[A] 'standard' is an abstract principle that serves as a measurement or gauge to guide a man's choices in the achievement of a concrete, specific purpose."[42] If happiness is Prometheus' purpose, a standard would be a principle by which he can gauge what will actually promote his happiness.

> To take "whatever makes one happy" as a guide to action means: to be guided by nothing but one's emotional whims. Emotions are not tools of cognition; to be guided by whims—by desires whose source, nature and meaning one does not know—is to turn oneself into a blind robot, operated by unknowable demons (by one's stale evasions), a robot knocking its stagnant brains out against the walls of reality which it refuses to see.[43]

In her later writings Rand advocates Man's Life a the standard of value. The joyous life standard which Peikoff discusses in his lectures is considerably more primitive, but it is not subjective like "whatever makes one happy." Instead of judging goals in isolation by the feelings they evoke, it judges them by how they would fit into a holistic, if imprecise, conception of a happy life. Many of the values are seen as contributing to the preservation of life as such, others are seen as harmonizing with and enhancing these.[44]

Though Prometheus never articulates such a standard, it is clear from the context of the novel that he is not a hedonist pursuing "whatever makes him happy." Rather the germs of the joyous life standard are implicit even in his earliest evaluations, and more elements of this standard emerge as he develops. Even as a child Prometheus sees that science is good in part because of its contribution to survival through such modern inventions as "glass, which is put in our windows to protect us from the rain" (24). When he masters electricity he assesses its meaning in terms of its potential to aid in production, and later he plans to use it to defend his home (100). Throughout the novel he is cognizant of the joy associated with each of his values. As he progresses, he begins to see connections between this joy and his survival needs. This is evident in his fascination with hunger in the Forest. So, while he never reaches a fully explicit standard of value, he is operating on the joyous life standard and the basis of his evaluations is self-conscious enough for him to progress to the final step of the progression Peikoff outlines.

A thinker who has reached the joyous life standard of value will understand values as "things I choose and achieve that foster life and the enjoyment of life." Such a thinker would be in a position to grasp egoism, the doctrine that each person should aim in all his actions at achieving such values *for himself*. What egoism advocates is "the pursuit in action by your own creative effort of objects chosen by you as necessary to your own life or happiness." It can be validated by seeing that this principle is inherent in the concept "value." One sees this by noticing in a range of cases that he *is* the intended beneficiary of his own values and by recognizing that the values could not be values if he pursued them for anyone else.

This is what Prometheus does. In the Forest he realizes that he created the light for its own sake, and for the joy it brought him. He sees too that he killed the bird to satisfy his own hunger, and that he wants Gaea because she is essential to his happiness. These values would be impossible if Prometheus lived for his brothers. Consider the case of the light: Prometheus chooses his scientific career and he chooses to study the power of the sky in particular. His brothers forbid this. Prometheus invests his time, his life, his thought, his blood, into creating and defending the light. It is the result of his passionate commitment, yet on the premise of altruism he must be indifferent to its fate—he must be willing to give it up to his brothers to use or to destroy. It is the requirements of Prometheus' life and happiness that make the light valuable. It would lessen labor leaving men more leisure time, it would enable new discoveries, it would unlock the earth. But it is only for Prometheus (and for those like him) that these things are values. His brothers do not want to unlock the earth and so the light is of no use to them. Moreover, they want to deprive Prometheus of its benefits.

Altruism, as Peikoff argues, is a "triple assault": "it's an assault on your choice, it's an assault on your achievement, and it's an assault on your life or enjoyment of it. In other words it's an all out destruction."

> In effect, altruism says: "You shouldn't get the consequences of your choices, the results of your actions, you shouldn't enjoy your life or even, perhaps, keep it.
>
> So we could summarize [the argument for egoism and against altruism] like this: You, in effect, created the values that we're talking about in three different ways. Your choice made it possible for them to be values. Your action brought them into existence. Your life and happiness made it necessary for you to choose and act. All of that is inherent in the pattern of establishing what it was to value and to pursue a value. . . . The essence of altruism is to say: "Value something and then throw it away." It wouldn't be a value to anybody else if it isn't a value, so it wouldn't profit any beneficiary. So you're supposed to: choose it [and] create it, [because] there's a reason for it to be a value, and then

annihilate it, get rid of it, abandon it. That is in the nature of the principle of altruism.

What we can say at this point is: "Egoism is an affirmation of all of the conditions of value and therefore of values as such. Altruism is the negation of all of the conditions of valuing while demanding that you pursue values."

Altruism steals the concept "value," but a thinker would not initially see it in these terms. Rather, by considering many cases, he would see that, in each instance, the factors that make the value *valuable* are undermined by the principle of altruism. From here he would generalize that inherent in something's being a value is that *someone* chooses and achieves it because it enhances *his own* life. It is by this inductive argument that Prometheus reaches his philosophical conclusion.[45]

Thus *Anthem* tells us that values presuppose metaphysical individualism and can only exist for some *individual* who *selects* and *achieves* them in pursuit of *his life and happiness.* In *Atlas Shrugged* Ayn Rand presents a full validation of egoism based "on an argument that the concept 'value' depends on the concept 'life' and so is only meaningful in the context of an organism pursuing its life as its ultimate value."[46] *Anthem's* argument is more preliminary, but it has a parallel structure. Both arguments work by showing that the facts presupposed by the concept "value" have implications for valuing. *Anthem's* argument is that values are an inherently individualistic phenomenon, conceived by individual thought and choice, achieved by individual action, and meaningful only in the context of an individual's life. It is these facts about value (and the related facts about thought) that make the concept "I" necessary. They constitute its meaning, which is *Anthem's* theme. And they imply egoism and, through it, political individualism.[47]

## NOTES

1. This passage was not included in the book based on the course (Ayn Rand, *The Art of Nonfiction: A Guide for Writers and Readers*, ed. Robert Mayhew [New York: Plume, 2001]). Part of it appeared in Ayn Rand, *The Art of Fiction: A Guide for Writers and Readers*, edited by Tore Boeckmann (New York: Plume, 2000), 36.

2. In *For the New Intellectual* Rand states *Anthem's* theme as "the meaning of man's ego" (New York: Random House, 1961; paperback edition, Signet, 1963), 64. Interestingly, in a 1946 letter she writes that *Anthem* "has the same theme, spirit and intention" as *The Fountainhead* (New York: Bobbs-Merrill, 1943; Signet fiftieth anniversary paperback edition, 1993). See Michael S. Berliner, ed., *Letters of Ayn Rand* (New York: Dutton, 1995; paperback edition, Plume, 1997), 314, cf. 276. She identifies *The Fountainhead's* theme as "individualism versus collectivism, not in politics, but in man's soul; the psychological motivations and the basic premises that produce the character of an individualist or a collectivist" (*For the New Intellectual*, 68). As will be clear from what follows, there is no contradiction between these different statements of the theme.

3. The theory was not published until significantly later. Rand presents it in *Introduction to Objectivist Epistemology* (henceforth *ITOE*), which was published first as a multi-part series in *The Objectivist* in 1966–1967, and then as a monograph in 1967. There is a more recent expanded second edition: Ayn Rand, *Introduction to Objectivist Epistemology*, ed. Harry Binswanger and Leonard Peikoff (New York: Meridian, 1990).

4. Berliner, *Letters of Ayn Rand*, 33.

5. *Oxford English Dictionary*, Oxford University Press, 1971 (henceforth "*OED*").

6. I borrow this term from Allan Gotthelf, *On Ayn Rand* (Belmont, CA: Wadsworth, 2000), 76.

7. On Prometheus' assessment of his own character at different points in the novel, see Onkar Ghate's "Breaking the Metaphysical Chains of Dictatorship: Free Will and Determinism in *Anthem*," in this volume.

8. Interestingly, the English "you" is ambiguous between singular and plural. In the 1938 addition of Anthem, Gaea eventually learns to say "I love thee" (137). "Thee" is unambiguously singular. In the 1946 edition Gaea says "I love you" (98). The change was part of a larger program of eliminating archaic language. (See Robert Mayhew's "*Anthem*: '38 & '46," in this volume, p. 33–35.) Notice that, despite the ambiguity of "you," Gaea's modernized profession of love is at least as powerful and personal as the archaic version. The ambiguity of "you" doesn't seem to cause the problems that *Anthem*'s "We" does. "You" is naturally assumed to denote a singular listener. (This is why dialects tend to evolve alternative second-person plurals, like "y'all," "youse," and "yins," rather than second-person singulars.) I think this is because of a difference between the purposes of first- and second-person pronouns. The first-person pronoun allows the speaker to keep himself distinguished from others in his own thought. As I discuss later, this is a crucial need. Without maintaining such a perspective on oneself, thought would be impossible. The second-person pronoun respects the listener's need to think of himself as distinct from all other men, and thus makes possible communication and co-operative thinking. Since people can only hear and evaluate speech as individuals, each listener can normally take the second-person pronoun to refer to himself individually. So, by speaking to a group in the second person, one respects *each listener's* individual need to think of himself as distinct. Thus there is not a constant need for a distinction between singular and plural in the second person.

9. Rand presents her theory of concepts primarily as a solution to the Problem of Universals. The core of the theory is an original account of how men form universal concepts on the basis of knowledge of a handful of concrete instances. These universal concepts, denoted by words, serve the function of unit economy by allowing us to think in one unit (the concept) of an unlimited number of existents (the many referents).

10. I borrow this phrase from Allan Gotthelf, who uses it in "Ayn Rand on Concepts, Definitions, and Essences," *Review of Metaphysics*, forthcoming.

11. Rand never wrote about the concept "I" from the perspective of her theory of concepts, but she did discuss it twice during a series of workshops on the theory conducted between 1969 and 1971. (The transcripts of these workshops are in the Ayn Rand Archives and portions of them have been published as an appendix to the expanded second edition of *ITOE*.) In the workshops she said that a pronoun is "the

same form of concept as a noun but from a specific perspective." Personal pronouns, she explained, denote men from specialized perspectives. "I" denotes a man, "as against all other men," from his own perspective. Because a pronoun conceptualizes entities from a specialized perspective involving their relationship to the speaker, it "involves concepts of consciousness." In a separate discussion from the workshops, Rand said "I," "self, "and "consciousness" all denote the same fact (though, again, from different perspectives). In this same discussion she agrees to another participant's claim that "I" refers to the whole man, not just to his consciousness. So her position seems to be that "I" refers to the man from his own perspective, i.e., as a conscious being aware of himself as distinct from other men.

12. Like all other concepts, pronouns are justified only when they aid in cognition by unit-economizing. Multiplying them beyond necessity would hamper cognition. When we distinguish between categories of things with different pronouns, the distinction becomes a constant feature of our thought. The distinctions we make with our pronouns mark the most important and pervasive distinctions in our thinking: one versus many, conscious versus inanimate, self versus others, male vs. female. (This last distinction acquires a special importance because of the significance of sex.)

13. Rand, *The Fountainhead*, 679.

14. David Harriman, ed., *Journals of Ayn Rand* (New York: Dutton, 1997; paperback edition, Plume, 1999), 86.

15. Harriman, *Journals*, 80. Significantly, she blames this problem on the lack of "that little word 'I', which after centuries of Christianity's efforts, has been erased from human consciousness, and along with it took everything that *was* human consciousness."

16. The generalization that the loadstone always points north, as a rational scientist would hold it, is not contradicted by the discovery of the effects of electric current. (For discussion of a similar case, see Leonard Peikoff, *Objectivism: The Philosophy of Ayn Rand* [New York: Dutton, 1991; paperback edition, New Meridian, 1993], 173ff.) The proper way of holding such generalization requires a self-conscious method that makes provisions for how one will deal with new evidence as it becomes available.

17. Peikoff, *Objectivism*, 198.

18. It may be possible, with effort, to maintain this perspective to some extent without the concept "I." Clearly Prometheus does so, or else it would be impossible for him to do his scientific work. But, as we will see, there are limits to how much Prometheus can accomplish intellectually before he learns the concept.

19. Rand, *Fountainhead*, 679.

20. In note 11 I discussed the relationship between the concepts "I" and "consciousness." "Consciousness" is one of three axiomatic concepts Rand discusses in *ITOE*. She writes that

although they designate a fundamental *metaphysical* fact, axiomatic concepts are the products of an *epistemological* need—the need of a volitional, conceptual consciousness which is capable of error and doubt. . . . It is only a man's consciousness, a consciousness capable of conceptual errors that needs a special identification of the directly given. . . . Axiomatic concepts are epistemological guidelines. They sum up the existence of all human cognition: something *exists* of which I am *conscious*; I must discover its *identity*. (58–59)

The concept "I" also denotes a directly given metaphysical fact and it denotes it in the service of an epistemological need. It denotes oneself, *one's own consciousness*, in a way that underscores its individuality and so facilitates self-direction.

21. Rand introduces the idea of stolen concepts in Galt's Speech, from *Atlas Shrugged* (New York: Random House, 1957; thirty-fifth anniversary paperback edition, Signet, 1992), 951–52. There are elaborations on this fallacy in Nathaniel Branden, "The Stolen Concept," *The Objectivist Newsletter*, January 1963, and in Peikoff, *Objectivism*, 136.

22. We know that metaphysical individualism is true in the same way that we know that consciousness exists. We can know that we are conscious and that human consciousness is self-directed by introspection, but what each of us knows by introspection is *his own* consciousness. We learn that other people and animals are conscious by observing their behaviors, but this too only gives us evidence of *individual* consciousnesses. Metaphysical individualism is self-evident and is presupposed by all concepts of consciousness.

23. Similarly, the fact that metaphysical individualism is self-evident does not mean that it is universally accepted or that there can be no confusion about it. Self-evident truths are contained implicitly in sense-perception, but thought is required to make them explicit and to remain true to them in one's thinking. Mistaken or dishonest philosophical doctrines can hinder us from conceptualizing self-evidencies and prevent them from playing their proper role in our thought. A frequent theme in Rand's writing is the way men deny or evade the self-evident facts of identity and causality. For example, in "Causality vs. Duty," in *Philosophy: Who Needs It* (New York: Bobbs-Merrill, 1982; paperback edition, Signet, 1984), she argues that the anti-concept "duty" obliterates "causality," an axiomatic concept, from a man's mind.

24. Ayn Rand, "Credibility and Polarization," *The Ayn Rand Letter*, October 11, 1971, p. 1. Some anti-concepts are "stolen concepts," others are "unnecessary and rationally unusable" for other reasons. Some originate in mysticism; many are "package deals" which group things by nonessential resemblances, obscuring more significant differences.

25. It is questionable whether anti-conceptualization could actually be carried as far as it is in *Anthem*. Anti-concepts are parasitical on valid concepts. If they totally succeeded in destroying the valid concepts, they would lose all semblance of meaning. It is not clear that Rand intended the City's language to be possible. In her journals Rand described the strike in *Atlas Shrugged* as a fantasy premise, an exaggeration of an actual phenomenon. (See Harriman, *Journals of Ayn Rand*, 398.) Similarly, I think, the City's language is a fantastic exaggeration of the conceptual fallacies inherent in collectivism.

26. Rand, *Atlas Shrugged*, 238. The comment is made by Rearden who, like Prometheus, has accepted and violated a false and vicious moral code.

27. Rand, *Atlas Shrugged*, 931.

28. Ayn Rand, *The Virtue of Selfishness: A New Concept of Egoism* (New York: New American Library, 1964), 22.

29. Rand, *Fountainhead*, 425.

30. In a sense, a man is conscious prior to choosing to focus, but in the distinctively human sense—the sense that gives rise to the need for the concept "I"—a man is not conscious until he focuses his mind. As Rand puts the point in "The Objectivist Ethics":

When man unfocuses his mind, he may be said to be conscious in a subhuman sense of the word, since he experiences sensations and perceptions. But in the sense of the word applicable to man—in the sense of a consciousness which is aware of reality and able to deal with it, a consciousness able to direct the actions and provide for the survival of a human being—an unfocused mind is *not* conscious. (*The Virtue of Selfishness*, 22)

31. In "Philosophy and Sense of Life," Rand discusses the process by which a man's "subconscious mechanism sums up his psychological activities, integrating his conclusions, reactions or evasions into an emotional sum that establishes a habitual pattern and becomes his automatic response to the world around him" (Rand, *The Romantic Manifesto: A Philosophy of Literature*, revised edition [New York: Signet, 1975], 26).

32. For further discussion of Prometheus' "curse," in relation to Rand's view of volition and moral character, see Onkar Ghate, "Breaking the Metaphysical Chains of Dictatorship," 244.

33. In *Atlas Shrugged*, Rand defines happiness, for example, as "that state of consciousness which proceeds from the achievement of one's values" (928).

34. "Saint" is a moral/aesthetic concept; it denotes a person conceived of as embodying a moral ideal. Rand discusses the need for concretizations of moral codes in "The Psycho-Epistemology of Art" (in *The Romantic Manifesto*). Jason Rheins has called my attention to a related discussion in "Art and Moral Treason" that sheds light on the role of the Saint of the pyre in *Anthem*. There Rand discusses Romantic art as the means by which a child learns

> the precondition and the incentive for the later understanding of [abstract] principles: the emotional experience of admiration for man's highest potential, the experience of looking up to a hero—a view of life motivated and dominated by values, a life in which man's choices are practicable, effective and crucially important—that is, a moral sense of life. (*Romantic Manifesto*, 146–47)

The Saint of the pyre plays a similar inspirational role for Prometheus at a key point in the story. In his second journal entry, Prometheus catches himself wondering about the lost words from the Umentionable Times and begs for the Council's forgiveness: "May the Council have mercy on us! . . . We shall not ask this question and we shall not think it. We shall not call death upon our head." It is in this context that he recounts the story of the Saint of the pyre, after which he writes: "What—even if we have to burn for it like the Saint of the pyre—what is the Unspeakable Word?" (51). It is the image of the Saint, Prometheus' early concretization of an individualistic morality, that inspires him to take this significant step towards conceptualizing that ideal and realizing it in his own life.

35. Leonard Peikoff, *Objectivism Through Induction*, Lecture 4 (audio tapes, Second Renaissance Books, 1998).

36. That hunger indicates that a physical need is significant. It represents a step towards grasping objectivity. According to Objectivism, though a man's values are chosen, they have a factual basis in his survival requirements. The underscoring of hunger shows that Prometheus recognizes that there is a factual component to values.

37. The only other time Prometheus describes himself as proud is in discussing the way he accepts his Life Mandate (26). He uses the term also to describe the Saint of

the pyre (51) and to describe Gaea's voice when she tells him that she followed him into the Forest (82). Later he associates it with the concept "I" (100).

38. All quotes in the following section are from lectures 3 and 4 of this series, except where otherwise indicated.

39. Rand, *Virtue of Selfishness*, 16

40. On this point see Onkar Ghate, "Breaking the Metaphysical Chains of Dictatorship," 228–29, 233–34.

41. Peikoff calls the sorts of values with which the thinker would begin "common sense values." They are things that the thinker can recognize as values and give some reason for, though he cannot yet philosophically validate them. Examples would include: food, shelter, clothing, friendship, strength, money, a job, knowledge, art. Because common sense values lack a full validation, it is possible that some of them will not be genuine values. But, if so, the thinker will find that they clash with the others and would ultimately be led to reject them.

42. Rand, *Virtue of Selfishness*, 27.

43. Rand, *Virtue of Selfishness*, 32.

44. Aristotle endorsed a moral standard much like the one Peikoff discusses. For further discussion of this sort of standard, including its relation to Rand's thought at different points in her development, see my "Aristotle as Ethicist" (audio tapes/CDs, The Ayn Rand Bookstore, 2003).

45. In the lectures Peikoff also stresses that when inducing a philosophical principle it is important to consider the principle in light of human history. As we have seen, Prometheus does in his final entry.

46. Gregory Salmieri and Allan Gotthelf, "Ayn Rand," *Dictionary of Modern American Philosophers* (London: Thoemmes, 2005).

47. I would like to thank the Ayn Rand Institute for hosting a colloquium at which I received valuable comments from Robert Mayhew, Shoshana Milgram, and especially Onkar Ghate. I would also like to thank Allan Gotthelf for helpful discussion of individualism and the concept "I," and Jason Rheins and Karen Shoebotham for comments on earlier drafts of this essay. Thanks are also due Jeff Britting at the Ayn Rand Archives, who went out of his way to provide me with archival material under time pressure.

# 13

# Freedom of Disassociation in *Anthem*

*Amy Peikoff*

Americans cherish the freedom of association as one of the basic freedoms guaranteed by the First Amendment. So do the citizens of other (relatively) free countries, as it is protected under analogous provisions in their law. Not surprisingly, this freedom is denied to the citizens of the dystopian society in *Anthem*. Citizens are prohibited from selecting their lovers (41), their friends (30), even their colleagues (24). To prefer any of one's "brothers," for the purpose of engaging in a joint endeavor, is to commit the "Transgression of Preference."

What may surprise readers of *Anthem* is the extent to which the citizens are denied the corollary freedom of *dis*association: the freedom to be alone when one chooses.

On the first page we learn that being alone is the "root of all evil." Equality 7-2521's act of keeping a journal, we are told in the opening paragraph, is a "sin"—a "base and evil" act. This is not because of the journal's subversive content, but simply because the writing is for no eyes but his own. To prefer to associate with certain of one's brothers is a transgression, but "there is no transgression blacker than to do or think alone" (17).

The founders of the society in *Anthem* understood that "to do or think alone," one must sometimes *be* alone. And they tried to ensure that no one ever would be. At birth, a baby is taken from its mother to live in the Home of the Infants, where all children live together until the age of five. The infants are always together, even when they sleep. "The sleeping halls were white and clean and bare of all things save one hundred beds" (20). They have similar sleeping arrangements in the Home of the Students, where they go to spend the next ten years of their lives. All students have the same schedule, arising and retiring at the command of a bell from a bell tower. All are taught identical lessons during the day, and at night they must recite in unison with their teachers: "We are nothing. Mankind is all. By the grace of our brothers we are allowed our lives. We exist through, by and for our brothers who are the State. Amen" (21).

At the age of fifteen, students are given their Life Mandates, and sent to different Homes according to their assigned Trades (26–27). None of these Homes, however, offers them opportunities to be alone; their life is again completely structured. In the Home of the Street Sweepers, to which Equality is assigned, there is again a bell that signifies when it is time for all to arise from their beds; and again they sleep in hundred-bed sleeping halls. All meals are eaten in common with one's fellow Street Sweepers. One performs his work in the company of others, too. Equality has two others in his assigned "brigade" (29). Evenings are consumed, first, by "Social Meetings," in which all citizens gather to hear speeches given by the Councils of the different Homes and visiting Leaders, and to sing Hymns. These meetings are followed by three hours of "Social Recreation." Often the entertainment consists of plays in which each role is performed by a chorus chanting in unison—even the actors may not act alone while on stage (27–28).

This is how citizens live, day after day, until they are forty. They then go to the Home of the Useless, where they will spend the rest of their days (usually not more than five years) free of toil, but nevertheless in a way that presumably allows for no opportunity to be alone (28). And if someone manages to find a spare minute and decides to go for a walk outside, he is reminded that citizens may not "walk through the City when they have no mission to walk there" (35). In other words, one must always be in the company of others, performing activities dictated by others, unless he is asleep—or supposed to be asleep. Equality describes this last as "the secret hour, when we awoke in the night and there were no brothers around us, but only their shapes in the beds and their snores" (23).

In sum, society is structured such that no one is allowed to be physically alone at any time, from the moment he is born until the day he dies.

Man is a being of both mind and body; thus the physical and the mental cannot be completely separated. Those steps taken by the Councils to prevent physical isolation are also effective in preventing mental isolation. Nonetheless, the Councils take additional steps to ensure (as far as possible) that no one ever thinks of himself as alone—i.e., as an individual. They first act to prevent a citizen from perceiving his own body as a separate entity, distinct from the bodies of his brothers. They do this by making all the Homes of the different Trades mirror free, which means that no one ever perceives his most distinguishing feature: his face (61-62). It is true that the Councils cannot prevent one from seeing his own limbs and the shadows cast by his body. But these are less distinctive, and in any event are seen only alongside those of one's brothers. In the third paragraph Equality writes, "it is strange to see only two legs stretched on the ground, and on the wall before us the shadow of our one head" (17).

Even if one may not perceive himself as a separate entity, he might still manage to *conceive* of himself as such, using his capacity for abstract thought. But the Councils have taken further steps to prevent this. The Hymns that are sung at the Social Meetings have themes such as "Brotherhood," "Equality," and "the Collective Spirit." The plays performed during Social Recreation are about "toil [with and for one's brothers] and how good it is" (28). Men are taught from an early age that they "have no cause to exist save in toiling for other men" (74). Further, they are taught that "the World Council is the body of all truth," and they are shown the following words, which are cut in marble above the doors of the Council's Palace:

We are one in all and all in one.
There are no men but only the great WE,
One, indivisible and forever. (19)

Further, the Councils prohibit the use of words which signify the concept of one's own person: "I," "me," "mine." Citizens are taught only "we," "us," and "our," and thus are encouraged to conceive of themselves as blending into the "great WE" with their brother men. "I" is the "Unspeakable Word"—those who manage somehow to discover this word and then speak it are put to death. This is the society's only capital offense (49).

But the Councils realize that, notwithstanding the highly controlled environment they created, some independent-minded citizens will occasionally "do or think alone" (17). They therefore deploy additional rules to sweep away any remnants of independent thought and action.

Some rules command citizens not to think about specific things. For example, as they approach the age of fifteen, the age at which their Life Mandate is assigned, the students are told, "Dare not choose in your minds the work you would like to do when you leave the Home of the Students." The Council of Vocations makes this decision for them (22). There is a "law which says that men may not think of women, save at the Time of Mating"—a time which comes only once a year (41). Because it is impossible for one with an active mind to avoid thinking about an explicitly stated topic—e.g., "Don't think about a pink elephant!"—such rules do no more than encourage citizens to steer their focus away from such thoughts when they arise, and make them feel guilty when they are unable—or unwilling—to do this.[1]

Other rules are aimed at independent thought as such. One is, of course, the explicit declaration that doing or thinking alone is the blackest transgression one can commit (17). Three other rules, however, target independent thought in general, but do so only indirectly. Two of these prohibit one from performing activities that are conducive to, or expressive of, thought: writing and drawing. One may not do either of these unless he has been so instructed by the Council of Vocations (17, 30). And, in any event, one may never write or draw something that will not be seen by others (17). Thus, these activities may never be engaged in as an adjunct to independent thought.

The third rule of this kind states that all citizens must agree on everything. Because it is impossible for volitional beings to agree on everything, in practice the rule means that no one may *state* a thought that differs from the thoughts of others. Consequently, if there are spare moments between their orchestrated activities, the citizens remain silent. They dare say nothing that has not been said or written by others, because they have no way of knowing whether others will agree (47). And even if something has been said or written by others, why should someone repeat it? After all, everyone is taught the same lessons and attends the same meetings. Finally, if one is unable to express independent thoughts, what is the point of thinking them? If Equality had not found the tunnel from the Unmentionable Times, which allowed him hours each night to express his thoughts in writing, he probably would not have remained mentally active for long.

The Councils, it seems, believe that still more must be done to achieve their goal. Apparently they realize that even in a highly regulated society that discouraged any independent thought, a citizen might stumble upon an opportunity to act alone—and would be tempted to do so. This is what happens to Equality and International when, during their work as street sweepers, they accidentally find an iron grate covering an entrance to a tunnel. Equality tells International that he is going down into the hole. International warns that such an action is forbidden even though, as Equality points out, the Councils do not know of the hole's existence: "Since the Council does not know of this hole, there can be no law permitting to enter. *And everything which is not permitted by law is forbidden*" (31, emphasis added).

This law, if strictly enforced, would ensure that no one can ever do anything alone, for it would eliminate the freedom of disassociation. One who obeyed this law could never perform an action that had not first been thought of—indeed, approved of—by someone else. A government that promulgates such a law represents "the ultimate inversion."[2] "Under a proper social system," by contrast,

> a private individual is legally free to take any action he pleases (so long as he does not violate the rights of others), while a government official is bound by law in his every official act. A private individual may do anything except that which is legally *forbidden;* a government official may do nothing except that which is legally *permitted*.[3]

Equality does not obey this law. With his descent into the hole, he commits his first overt action in rebellion against his society and against the ethics it embodies.

The rest of the citizens—with a few exceptions[4]—do precisely what the Councils intend: they relinquish their ability to engage in independent thought and action. What is the result? Equality observes:

> The heads of our brothers are bowed. The eyes of our brothers are dull, and never do they look one another in the eyes. The shoulders of our brothers are hunched, and their muscles are drawn, as if their bodies were shrinking and wished to shrink out of sight. And a word steals into our mind, as we look upon our brothers and that word is fear. (46)[5]

Equality says that he, too, feels the oppressive, pervasive fear "without name, without shape"—but only when he is among his brothers. His evening hours alone in the tunnel, away from the "odor of men," give him strength to endure the rest of the day. They provide him with so much joy that he fears the appearance of his "body is betraying [him]" (46). By contrast, the few of his brothers who have not yet surrendered their souls, but who have no reprieve from their plight, are beginning to show signs of breaking. One "cries without reason, in the midst of day or night." Another shows no signs of fear during the day; but at night he screams, "Help us! Help us! Help us!" (47).[6] It is not surprising that by the time men are sent to the Home of the Useless, "They do not speak often, for they are weary" (28).

Even Equality, the best among men in *Anthem*, is undercut by the Councils' teachings and institutions. After two years of independent study, after reinventing the electric light in defiance of the wishes of his fellow men, his first conscious thought is of what his invention could do for his brothers. He plans to present it to the World Council of Scholars, and believes they will reassign him to the Home of the Scholars (61). He is not deterred, even when his brothers torture and imprison him in the Palace of Corrective Detention. After escaping, he writes of his plans for the following day:

> We shall put before [the World Council of Scholars] the greatest gift ever offered to men. We shall tell them the truth. We shall hand to them, as our confession, these pages we have written. We shall join our hands to theirs, and we shall work together, with the power of the sky, for the glory of mankind. Our blessing upon you, our brothers! Tomorrow, you will take us back into your fold and we shall be an outcast no longer. Tomorrow we shall be one of you again. Tomorrow.(67)[7]

It takes two years of thinking, working, and writing alone in the tunnel before Equality converts the pride he takes in his work to feelings of pride in— and concern for the safety of—his physical body (61). And even then it is not until the World Council of Scholars threaten to destroy *his invention* that Equality decides to flee them (75). Up until that point he agrees to "Let the will of the [World] Council be done upon our body," even if it includes his being lashed "till there is nothing left under the lashes." His only concern is that the light be accepted by the Council and used by his brother men (72).

Rand also dramatizes other more specific consequences of the Councils' measures. First, having supplanted the personal singular pronouns, "I," "me," and "mine," with the plural, "we," "us," and "our," the Councils make it impossible to express personal emotions of friendship and love. As we saw above, friendship and love between individuals are considered Transgressions of Preference and are explicitly prohibited. But by regulating the words citizens may use, the Councils further succeed in regulating the emotions they may feel—or at least the emotions they can understand. Liberty comes closest to re-forming the forbidden concept of one's own person when she attempts to express her love for Equality. "We are one . . . alone . . . and only . . . and we love you are who are one . . . alone . . . and only" (87).

Some may find it difficult to believe that even the most all-encompassing totalitarian regime could eradicate such a basic concept as that of one's own person. Note, however, that it is more difficult to form a concept on one's own than it is to learn the concept from others. For example, imagine a child who is never taught the concept "ball" and therefore must form it on his own. Even in the case of a simple concept like "ball," forming the concept on one's own will result in a delay in grasping the concept, as compared to being taught the concept by others. So, by failing to teach young children the word "I," and by habituating them to use "we" instead, one might delay the forming of the concept of one's own person long enough to make the concept seem unnecessary. And in fact the concept *would* be unnecessary for a person who abides by all of the Council's rules and lives a life without a career, friendship, or love.

Because Rand's goal in *Anthem* is to exalt man's ego—man's spiritual essence (v)—much of her focus is on dramatizing the way in which a collectivist totalitarian regime destroys the ego. But another striking feature of *Anthem* is its portrayal of the technologically backward and intellectually stagnant society that is a product of that regime. For example, it takes twenty scholars to invent the candle, and then fifty years to get everyone to agree that it would be better than the existing technology: torches (68). We learn that the candle is the most recent technological advance and that it was "found only [!] a hundred years ago" (24). In addition, it is a "miracle" if a citizen lives to be forty-five (28). This short life span is owing in part to the fact that the society lacks electricity, and is therefore heavily dependent on human physical labor. But it is also due to the primitive state of medical care. Equality writes that in school he "learned how to bleed men to cure them of all ailments" (23).

This snail's-pace growth in human knowledge and technology is caused by the fact that no citizen is left free to "do or think alone." Life in the Home of the Students is aimed not at igniting a student's cognitive engine but at stalling it. The Home is a crowded environment in which no student can find a quiet place to contemplate what he is learning, even if he could find a spare moment to do so. Equality notes that in his tunnel, by contrast, "there is no sound of men to disturb us" (36). In addition, the teachers institute various policies aimed at discouraging true learning and understanding in favor of blind acceptance.

In a rational society, an intellectually active student treats the lectures he hears at school not as the end of an intellectual journey but as the beginning. He constantly asks questions, sometimes to himself but often out loud: "Is this true?" "How does this relate to that?" "What is the cause?" A good teacher encourages this sort of questioning while nudging the student in the direction of proper cognitive development. By contrast, in *Anthem*, the teachers recognize this sort of persistent questioning as a sign of independent thought, and they forbid it (23). A student prohibited from questioning in this way is unable to complete the mental integrations he is trying to perform, his only option being to absorb passively whatever the teacher presents, however incomplete and puzzling it may seem to him.

Equality is not only forbidden to ask questions about the lessons, he is also punished for being "born with a head that is too quick" (21). He says that he often understands what the teachers are teaching, even before they speak, and is unable to conceal this despite sincere efforts to do so. The consequence is that he is lashed for knowing his lessons too well (22). A teacher who is displeased at a student's mastery of his lessons seems like a contradiction in terms. Nonetheless, given the premises they accept, Equality's teachers could not possibly be pleased with him. Like his persistent questioning, Equality's ability to foreshadow the contents of his lessons means that he is thinking alone, committing one of the society's gravest transgressions. Even if his foreshadowing is not a departure from a lesson's *content*, it is a departure from the train of thought the teacher is conducting. Or, to extend the metaphor: it means that Equality has booked himself on an express train without permission to do so.

In forbidding his asking of questions and in lashing him for understanding his lessons too quickly, Equality's teachers are trying to keep him from thinking alone. And, because the only way one can truly think is to think alone—"There is no such thing as a collective brain" (v)—they are discouraging him from thinking at all. It is not surprising, then, that Equality learns more in two years of self-directed, part-time study—when he can follow his questions wherever they lead—than he does during his ten years of full-time study at the Home of the Students (36).

Equality later learns that even in the Home of the Scholars—the place nominally dedicated to thought and learning—the society's collectivist premises discourage independent thought and action. He presents his invention to the leading members of the World Council of Scholars and finds that they adhere to these premises in evaluating new ideas: "What is not thought by all men cannot be true," said one. "What is not done collectively cannot be good," said another. Because Equality worked on the box alone, and because his brothers do not agree with him that the box is evidence of "a new power" (electricity), the Council deems the box "useless" (73). They eventually decide that its very existence is a threat to their plans and their way of life, and conclude, "It must be destroyed!" (74).

Only those assigned to the Home of the Scholars are permitted to make advances in science and technology. And, if Equality's Life Mandate is indicative, those assigned to be Scholars are not the most intelligent, motivated, or curious students. Still, if these people, once assigned to the Home, were left free to think and invent, greater progress would be possible. But even the Scholars are not left free to think and direct their own research. As Scholar Solidarity 8-1164 tells Equality: "Many men in the Homes of the Scholars have had strange new ideas in the past . . . but when the majority of their brother Scholars voted against them, they abandoned their ideas, as all men must" (73).

Rand dramatizes the crippling nature of this policy—and, by implication, the value of the freedom it destroys—by showing Equality reinventing the electric light after only two years of independent study. True, Equality may be smarter than those assigned to the Home of the Scholars. However, he must conduct his research in the evenings, after long hours of monotonous physical labor. He has the constant pressure of knowing he is breaking the law and might be discovered. And the only materials he has to work with are those he is able to find in the tunnel or the city cesspool, or steal from the Home of the Scholars (35–36). Thus the real advantage he has over the Scholars is the freedom to direct his own thoughts and actions—the freedom "to do or think alone" (17).

Equality marvels at the fact that he is the only person "doing a work which has no purpose save that we wish to do it" (36). The ability to get away from his brothers and choose the work he wants to do, even for only a few hours per day, has given him "the first peace we have known in twenty years" (37). Later, after he escapes to the Uncharted Forest, it is the Sun that wakes him, not the bell rung by his brothers. He laughs aloud at the realization that he need not leap up immediately, as is customary in the Home of the Street Sweepers. Rather, "we could lie thus as long as we wished" (78). When for the first time he kills and cooks his own food, rather than eating whatever is served in the communal dining hall, he experiences a "strange new pride in eating" (79). Equality has been taught that what he is experiencing is "the corruption of solitude." But if that is true, he wonders, "what can men wish for save corruption?" (85).

Thus Rand dramatizes the value of disassociation from one's fellow man, by showing us, first, what is missing when this freedom is taken away, and then, what is regained when it is rediscovered.

Many people associate socialism with some nebulous sort of "free thinking," and believe socialism is compatible with First Amendment freedoms.[8] Consequently, when they read *Anthem,* they are likely to agree with the Macmillan reviewer who declined to publish the book on the grounds that Rand "does not understand socialism" (ix). But anyone who examines the facts about socialist regimes—fascist and communist, past and present—and who, like Rand, grasps their essence, will see that she knows what she is talking about.

Based on her and her family's experiences in Soviet Russia,[9] Rand, in *We the Living,* illustrates the ways in which the Soviet regime exerted control over its citizens' private lives.[10] However, this sort of totalitarian control is not some extinct relic of the Soviet Union. Similar control exists today in North Korea.

> Once a week every North Korean attends an obligatory indoctrination meeting and a criticism and self-criticism meeting. The latter is known in North Korea as a "balance sheet of life." Everyone must accuse himself of at least one political fault and must reproach his neighbor for at least two faults.[11]

Thus North Koreans must always be watching their own actions, as well as those of their neighbors, keeping in mind what might be said at the weekly meeting. The self-criticism requirement seems like it would be particularly effective at conveying a sense that one is never alone. Even though one need offer only one self-criticism per week, he must select that criticism from among all the possible criticisms that could be made about him. And in doing this, he will be judging himself—including all of his actions and thoughts—against the government's standard. Repeatedly applying the government's standards of evaluation to oneself, week after week, will cause one eventually to adopt those standards as one's own.

Historian Pierre Rigoulot writes that North Korea subjects its citizens to a "permanent ideological barrage . . . on a scale unknown elsewhere," and counts this among the "crimes of Communism."[12] Its bureaucratic apparatus, designed to control every aspect of its citizens' lives, is also among the most pervasive and effective.

> From the top to the bottom of the social ladder, the state and the Party, with their large organizations and police forces, control the citizens of the country in the name of "the Party's ten principles in the drive toward unity."[13]

If one chooses to join one of the government-instituted "cadres," he will "receive a number of privileges and material benefits." But, like the special ration cards and jobs reserved for party members in *We the Living,* the cadres' privileges and benefits come at the cost of living under "extremely tight control."

> They are forced to live in a special area, all their telephone conversations are closely monitored, and any audio or video cassettes in their possession are

regularly examined. Because of the systematic jamming of foreign broadcasts, all radios and televisions in North Korea can pick up only state channels. To make any journey, special permission is required from the relevant local authority and the necessary work unit.[14]

The ultimate goal of these measures is stated by a North Korean radio commentator who, in 1996, said, "The whole of society should be welded together into one solid political force, which breathes, moves, and thinks as one, under the leadership of a single man."[15] Nazi Germany under Hitler was similarly suffocating. Writes Leonard Peikoff, in *The Ominous Parallels:*

> In the totalitarian regimes, as the Germans found out after only a few months of Hitler's rule, every detail of life is prescribed, or proscribed. There is no longer any distinction between private matters and public matters. "There are to be no more private Germans," said Friedrich Sieburg, a Nazi writer; "each is to attain significance only by his service to the state, and to find complete self-fulfillment in this service." "The only person who is still a private individual in Germany," boasted Robert Ley, a member of the Nazi hierarchy, after several years of Nazi rule, "is somebody who is asleep."[16]

Hitler and the Nazis created the usual array of government agencies designed to control every aspect of society, culturally and economically.[17] And, as in *Anthem*, the government sponsored "lecture courses, art shows, vacation trips, and the like," in order to ensure that the German workers would not have too much leisure time to themselves.[18] In fact, government-sponsored activities began for Germans at the age of six, when they joined the Hitler youth. Had Hitler remained in power, he might have succeeded in turning the whole of Germany into a society like the one portrayed in *Anthem*, for the Hitler youth "declared that they would never speak of 'I' but only of 'we.'"[19]

Unfortunately, the suppression of individual thought and action exists to some degree in all of today's governments. Even the government of the United States—the country that began by declaring a man's inalienable right to pursue his own happiness—has slowly evolved into an institution that infringes on this right in countless ways. One can easily list, from memory, the acronyms of several government agencies, and thereby bring to mind the extent of their control over Americans' lives. There's the FDA (food and drugs), the NEA (arts), the NIH (health), the FCC (communication), and the FTC (trade). There's the EPA (environment) and OSHA (occupational safety), the DOE (education), the IRS (income), the SEC (investment) and the BATF (tobacco and firearms), just to name a few. The Mercatus Center at George Mason University reports that the 2003 edition of the Federal Register, which contains all the regulations imposed by federal agencies, is over 75,000 pages long and includes 3,643 new regulations.[20] If one engages in a regulated activity, and does not follow the regulation governing it, he is subject to fines or even jail time. Adding thousands of new regulations per year means that, with respect to an increasing number of activities, Americans do not have the freedom to do or think alone. Ayn Rand, writing in the 1960s, warns:

> we are fast approaching the stage of the ultimate inversion: the stage where government is *free* to do anything it pleases, while the citizens may act only by *permission;* which is the stage of the darkest periods of human history, the stage of rule by brute force.[21]

The freedom of disassociation is a significant freedom that is facing extinction. Even so, one might wonder why Rand's novella focuses on this freedom rather than on its more conventionally valued corollary, the freedom of association?

As we saw above, the government in *Anthem* has achieved what Rand has called the "ultimate inversion"—a society in which the government may do anything it pleases, while citizens can do nothing without permission from the government. The society had to be set up this way in order to eradicate what the Councils declared to be the blackest transgression, the root of all evil, "to do or think alone." Rand holds that a proper society is one conforming to the opposite principle, because she believes *doing and thinking alone are the root of all good.*

> It is my eyes which see, and the sight of my eyes grants beauty to the earth. It is my ears which hear, and the hearing of my ears gives its song to the world. It is my mind which thinks, and the judgment of my mind is the only searchlight that can find the truth. It is my will which chooses, and the choice of my will is the only edict I must respect. (94)

Rand holds that human good (happiness) can be achieved only through the exercise of reason; and a man can exercise his reason only if he is left free to think and then act on his own judgment. Reason is an attribute of the individual, and its function is to identify the facts of reality. A man can learn from others, but only if he does the work necessary to grasp the truth of what he is taught. If he is constantly in the company of other men, and bombarded by propaganda, and deprived of any opportunity to think quietly to himself, much of the content of his mind will be baseless, backed by nothing more than another person's arbitrary assertion. And he will have little opportunity to use his reason to question what he is told, to decide for himself what he believes is true and what actions he should take. Further, if he may act only by permission, he will not be free to act on his best judgment when others disapprove.

Rand believes that association with others—others of one's own choosing—can be a great value. However, this is true only under certain conditions. Accordingly, in a proper society, as part of the fundamental right to liberty, a man can decide when it is appropriate to be and act apart from his fellow men, and when to seek their company. In essence, as Rand illustrates in *Anthem,* even when there is value to be found in others' company, those others are only of secondary importance to him.[22]

Equality recognizes that some of the people in his city are a value to him—Liberty, International, and a few others. But he does not initially plan to return from the Uncharted Forest, even to be with Liberty, whom he dearly loves. She follows him, and finds him at an appropriate time—after he has realized that he is not "damned," that life in the Uncharted Forest is safe, enjoyable, and full of wonder (78–80).[23] However, note that even after finding his new home in the forest and discovering the word "I," he has no immediate plans to return to the city and find his friends. He says he will not return for these people until he has "read all the books and learned my new way, when my home will be ready and my earth tilled" (100).

Equality refers to these others as his "chosen friends," his "fellow-builders" who will help him "write the first chapter in the new history of man" (101).[24] So it is clear they could be of significant value. But even they are of secondary importance compared to that of his own study and learning. If Equality had lived in a proper society, and had received a better upbringing and education, he would not need to postpone his return to the city. But he realizes how much life in the collectivist society has impeded him and his thinking, and that this harm must be undone before he can create a proper society. He has been taught all his life that he is nothing compared to "the great WE," and that "There is no joy for men, save the joy shared with all their brothers"; and yet he learned that "the only things which taught [him] joy . . . belong to [him] alone, they come from [him] alone, they bear no relation to [his] brothers" (86). When he finally realizes the magnitude of the evil done to him through these teachings, he recognizes fully that he and his personally chosen values come first:

> I shall choose my friends among men, but neither slaves nor masters. And I shall choose only such as please me, and them I shall love and respect, but neither command nor obey. And we shall join our hands when we wish, or walk alone when we so desire. For in the temple of his spirit, each man is alone. Let each man keep his temple untouched and undefiled. Then let him join hands with others if he wishes, but only beyond his holy threshold. (96)[25]

## NOTES

1. Cf. Ayn Rand, *Atlas Shrugged* (New York: Random House, 1957; Signet thirty-fifth anniversary paperback edition, 1992), 406. Dr. Ferris explains why a government with totalitarian aspirations would enact laws one cannot possibly obey: "there's no way to rule innocent men."

2. Ayn Rand, "The Nature of Government," in her *Capitalism: The Unknown Ideal* (New York: New American Library, 1966; Signet expanded paperback edition, 1967), 336.

3. Rand, "Nature of Government," 331–32.

4. In addition to Liberty 5-3000, Equality mentions a few others who show signs of independent thought: "my friend who has no name save International 4-8818, and all those like him, Fraternity 2-5503, who cries without reason, and Solidarity 9-6347, who calls for help in the night, and a few others" (101).

5. Ayn Rand's vivid description here is based on personal observation. In her notes for *We the Living,* she describes those living under Communism in similar terms: "The perpetual fear . . . and hopelessness. A general degradation—men turning smaller than they usually appear." David Harriman, ed., *Journals of Ayn Rand* (New York: Dutton, 1997), 57.

6. In *We the Living,* Rand also dramatizes the way in which collectivism kills man's spirit. See Tara Smith, "Forbidding Life to Those Still Living," in *Essays on Ayn Rand's* We the Living, ed. Robert Mayhew (Lanham, MD: Lexington Books, 2004), 317-34.

7. The extent to which the citizens' spirits are broken is further illustrated by the ease with which Equality escapes from the Palace of Corrective Detention. "The locks are old on the doors and there are no guards about. There is no reason to have guards, for men have never defied the Councils so far as to escape from whatever place they were ordered to be" (67).

8. Even Pierre Rigoulot, author of a chapter on North Korea for *The Black Book of Communism,* is among them. Rigoulot finds it strange that "In a state claiming to base itself on socialism, the population is . . . carefully monitored and controlled." Pierre Rigoulot, "Crimes, Terror, and Secrecy in North Korea," in Stéphane Courtois et al., *The Black Book of Communism: Crimes, Terror, Repression,* trans. Jonathan Murphy and Mark Kraemer (Cambridge, Mass.: Harvard University Press, 1999), 559. In the same chapter he quotes a radio announcer saying "the whole of society should be welded together into one solid political force," describes the weekly meetings that all must attend, and then later complains that the government's policies are aimed at "deliberate total isolation" (558–59).

9. Ayn Rand told her literary agent in 1934, "The conditions I have depicted are true. I have lived them. No one has ever come out of Soviet Russia to tell it to the world. That was my job." Michael S. Berliner, ed., *Letters of Ayn Rand* (New York: Dutton, 1995), 18. The letters Rand received from her family, who remained in the Soviet Union after she had come to live in the United States, provide ample evidence that she was telling the truth. See Dina Schein Garmong, "*We the Living* and the Rosenbaum Family Letters," Mayhew, *Essays on Ayn Rand's* We the Living, 67–86.

10. Kira, the novel's heroine, must attend countless party meetings and events and perform actions that contradict her personal beliefs so she can keep her job and her ration cards. Rand, *We the Living,* 200, 205. She and her lover, Leo, are assigned apartment-mates by the government; they have no choice in the matter. Another character, Andrei, makes reference to his "personal affairs" in a conversation with a G.P.U. official. The official interrupts him, asking, "Your *what kind* of affairs, Comrade Taganov?" Rand, *We the Living,* Sixtieth anniversary paperback edition, 344 (emphasis in original). Andrei is an earnest communist who tries to be loyal to the party while retaining his capacity for independent thought. Another party member, Comrade Sonia, sees signs of this, and asks him, "Why do you think you are entitled to your own thoughts?" Rand, *We the Living,* 311.

11. Rigoulot, "Crimes, Terror, and Secrecy in North Korea," 558.

12. Rigoulot, "Crimes, Terror, and Secrecy in North Korea," 559.

13. Rigoulot, "Crimes, Terror, and Secrecy in North Korea," 558.

14. Rigoulot, "Crimes, Terror, and Secrecy in North Korea," 558–59.

15. Rigoulot, "Crimes, Terror, and Secrecy in North Korea," 558.

16. Leonard Peikoff, *The Ominous Parallels: The End of Freedom in America* (New York: New York, Stein and Day, 1982; Meridian paperback edition, 1993), 17.

17. Peikoff, *The Ominous Parallels*, 230.

18. Peikoff, *The Ominous Parallels*, 231.

19. Peikoff, *The Ominous Parallels*, 230, quoting Eugene Davidson, *The Trial of the Germans* (New York: Macmillan, 1966), 288.

Another thing that *Anthem* portrays accurately is the link between collectivism and economic and technological stagnation. One sees this most clearly in long-standing, economically isolated Communist regimes, such as the former Soviet Empire and Cuba. Looking at the economies of these countries, one will see that Communism is not, as Lenin promised, the ticket to prosperity and technological development. One scholar writes that "Soviet Russia's autocratic government, the driving force in developmental surges, tended in the longer run to retard innovation." Alan M. Ball, *Imagining America: Influences and Images in Twentieth-Century Russia* (Lanham, MD: Rowman & Littlefield, 2003), 267. Even China, whose economy benefits from relatively free trade with Western nations, cannot, in its present state, become "the next technology superpower." Editors of *The Economist* recently observed: "Its successes so far are restricted to a handful of firms, most are either protected or exceptional, rising through cracks in China's planned economy." They noted that a scholar searched for examples of hi-tech successes in China and reluctantly admitted he was able to find only a few. "The Allure of Low Technology," *The Economist*, vol. 369, December 20, 2003, 99.

20. The Mercatus Center, "2003 In Review," at http://www.mercatus.org/regulatory studies/ subcategory.php/177.html.

21. Rand, "The Nature of Government," 336.

22. See Ayn Rand, "Man's Rights," in her *Capitalism*, 320–28, and Rand, "The Nature of Government."

23. Perhaps soon after this point he could decide to seek her out, even though he thinks it is too soon for him to seek out his friends. After all, Liberty, as his lover, is a unique value to him. Or perhaps her leaving the City to find him shows that she is more independent, and therefore more valuable to him at this point in his development than are his friends who did not leave.

24. Equality chooses to bring a select few to him, rather than return to the city and try to incite a revolution, or otherwise attempt to build a society including all the citizens. This is because he recognizes that others are a value to him only if they are capable of adding to his knowledge or of producing and trading the products of their labor. See, e.g., Rand, "The Nature of Government," 329. And Equality believes that the life-sustaining achievements from the Unmentionable Times "are open to me, but closed forever to [most of] my brothers, for their minds are shackled to the weakest and dullest ones among them" (99–100).

25. Thanks to Robert Mayhew for many helpful comments on an earlier draft of this chapter.

# 14

## *Anthem* and Collectivist Regression into Primitivism

*Andrew Bernstein*

In *Anthem,* Ayn Rand depicts a global collectivism of the future utterly bereft of material advance. The people of that society have lost all of the progress in science, technology, and industry wrought by the thinkers of the past.

Equality 7-2521, a Thomas Edison of the future, covertly re-invents the electric light in a society that honors the "twenty illustrious men who had invented the candle" (68). It is a world in which "it took fifty years to secure the approval of all the Councils for the Candle, and to re-fit the Plans so as to make candles instead of torches" (74). At forty years of age men are worn out from toil and relegated to the Home of the Useless. "When a miracle happens and some live to be forty-five, they are the Ancient Ones" (28). In the century since the invention of the candle, no further progress has occurred; "the Council of Scholars knows all things" (23).

Where are the great technological developments of the nineteenth and twentieth centuries? Why have men lost the steamship, the automobile, the airplane? What has happened to electricity, telecommunication, nuclear power, space travel? Where are the advances in agricultural and medical science that so dramatically increased human life expectancy? In the universe of *Anthem,* it is not merely that progress has collapsed; human society has regressed into a second Dark Age, worse than the first. Why?

The conflict and the theme of the story center on the struggle between Equality 7-2521 and the collectivist dictatorship that suppresses him. From childhood, he "loved the Science of Things" (23), desiring, above all, to be a researcher, a discoverer of knowledge, an inventor. He believes fervently that "there are mysteries in the sky and under the water and in the plants which grow" (23)—mysteries whose secrets he yearns to uncover. So consumed with curiosity was he that in his early years he inundated his teachers with questions—questions that they could not answer—but which caused them to identify Equality 7-2521 as a boy with a joyously eager, active, independent mind.

The teachers did not approve. They did not admire the boy "with a head which is too quick" (21) for his brothers, and they frowned when they looked at him, expressing disdain for his superiority. "And we were lashed more often than all the other children" (22). When all men are mandated to be equal—equal absolutely, equal in talent and initiative, not merely in rights—then superiority is a sin.

It is also a threat. The Councils reigning over this collectivist world make clear, in theory and practice, that all attempts at freethinking and noncompliance are intolerable and will be ruthlessly suppressed. The Council of Vocations recognizes the unmistakable genius of the irrepressible boy and—because of such recognition, not despite it—condemns him to mindless manual toil for the rest of his working life. Because of strict laws prohibiting independent thought and action, the authorities imprison him for sneaking away to perform secret scientific experiments. When he brings to the World Council of Scholars the triumphant result of those experiments—a rudimentary form of electric light—the Scholars, supposedly society's wisest, most far-seeing members, are horrified. Because he has dared to think and act alone, they proclaim him worthy of death. If not for his escape into the Uncharted Forest, the Councils would have followed through on this threat and eliminated the only true genius of their society.

To rational individuals this policy of suppressing, even liquidating, the most advanced thinkers is inexplicable. But Ayn Rand makes clear the motives of the rulers. "What is not thought by all men cannot be true" (73), states one member of the Council of Scholars. "What is not done collectively cannot be good" (73), proclaims another. The brutal authoritarianism of this society follows logically from the fundamental nature of collectivism: the moral pre-eminence of society and the ensuing obligation of the individual to subordinate himself to its needs and dictates. Under such premises, a man has no right to his own life and, consequently, no right to his own mind. There can be neither need nor right to think when one's life and mind belong to the herd. The herd's leaders, not an individual, decide all aspects of his life. A recalcitrant loner who insists on challenging the supremacy of the tribe will not receive from it a benevolent response.

By far the most dangerous of such loners is the thinker, the intellectual, the man (or woman) of the mind. A rational thinker like Equality 7-2521 is concerned with facts, not society's beliefs or judgments; he looks at nature, not public opinion polls. If his research establishes that electricity can be harnessed to safely light men's cities, then he stands by this truth regardless of whether social institutions oppose him. Such a thinker, in colloquial terms, has "a mind of his own"; he adheres to his own judgment; he is not a follower or a conformist. But this is exactly the kind of individual who most threatens a dictator. A thinker, especially a genius capable of re-inventing the electric light, has the ability and the independence necessary to question the moral rectitude of a tyrant's regime.

Great minds—whether artists, scientists, inventors, etc.—generally do not limit their thinking to art, science, or technology. They think and often speak out regarding issues of personal morality and governmental policy. They are the men pre-eminently capable of identifying a dictatorship's iniquities; they have the cognitive capacity and the courageous independence to articulate their insights and potentially to rile the population against the regime. Thomas Paine and the other free-thinkers of the American Enlightenment who promulgated the revolution against the British monarchy form one illustrious historical example. (Not coincidentally, Ayn Rand's protagonist performs experiments in electricity quite similar to those performed by one of the greatest freethinkers and revolutionaries of that era: Benjamin Franklin.) The men of the mind constitute the gravest threat to a dictator's power.

And the men of brute force know it. History is filled with real-life instances that parallel the suppression of Equality 7-2521 by the Councils for the "crime" of thinking and thereby challenging the regime's arbitrary commandments. Leonid Brezhnev, for example, sentenced Nobel Prize–winning physicist Andrei Sakharov to internal exile in Siberia for protesting the 1979 Soviet invasion of Afghanistan. In the antebellum South, blacks were legally forbidden to seek an education; even free blacks were not allowed to attend school at their own expense. The Nazis burned books, as did the Khmer Rouge in Cambodia in the late 1970s. In Communist China, Mao Tse Tung was a vicious anti-intellectual: among other atrocities, he turned loose the juvenile thugs of the Red Guards to torment China's professors, teachers, writers, artists, etc., during the "Cultural Revolution" of the late 1960s. At minimum, thousands of Chinese intellectuals were murdered. Tyrants around the world incarcerate, torture, execute political prisoners, i.e., men whose only legal transgression is to question the regime's policies. Kill the head, these brutes realize, and the body follows. When man's mind is suppressed, his body will passively submit.[1]

Ayn Rand is exactly right: Equality 7-2521, the one great independent thinker of this society, is for that reason the Council's especial target. He, more than any of his peers, represents a threat to the regime's power. But when the thinkers are ruthlessly suppressed, what results for a nation's science and technology, its economy and its ability to progress? Certainly nothing positive.

Years after telling the story of Equality 7-2521, Ayn Rand wrote *Atlas Shrugged*, in which she dramatized the fate of a society abandoned by its leading thinkers. That novel—set not in the distant future, like *Anthem*, but in a possible foreseeable collectivist future—shows Western society moving inexorably toward the kind of collectivist dictatorship that, in a more fully realized form, utterly represses Equality 7-2521. With society's leading scientists, inventors, and entrepreneurs restricted, curtailed, and expropriated, the country's living standards plunge steadily toward the abyss. The hero of *Atlas Shrugged* liberates the thinkers by taking them out on strike against their oppressors, leading to the final collapse of the statist regime and to the revitalization of individualism and liberty—and of progress and prosperity. The society depicted in *Atlas Shrugged,* moving steadily into collectivism, is saved from the primitivist regression depicted in *Anthem* only by the hero's resuscitation of the principles of individual rights and political-economic freedom.

In *Anthem*, Ayn Rand's focus is on the obliteration of individuality and independent thinking by collectivism (and on the devastating results that ensue); in *Atlas Shrugged*, it is on the indispensable role that rational thinking performs in promoting human advance. Ayn Rand's overarching, interconnected theses in these novels—that the mind is the source of progress, that the mind requires freedom, and that the mind's suppression embodied in dictatorship leads inevitably to regression and collapse—is fully borne out by history and current events.

For example, America of the late-nineteenth century, after the abolition of slavery by the Thirteenth Amendment, was the freest country in history. Consequently, governmental suppression of the creative mind was at its historic low. Of many positive results, one was a torrent of advance in applied science, technology, and industrialization. Edison invented the phonograph, the electric lighting system, the motion picture projector; Bell, the telephone; the Wright brothers, the airplane. Henry Ford revolutionized transportation, George Eastman did the same in photography, and such American designers as William Lebaron Jenney and Louis Sullivan, by creating the first skyscrapers, wrought the same result in architecture. Such leading industrialists of the period as Andrew Carnegie, John D. Rockefeller, James J. Hill, and Edward H. Harriman vastly increased American production of steel, oil, and transcontinental rail service. These minds, and hundreds like them, given the freedom to think and to act on their thoughts, were the prime movers of America's ascension to world leader in material progress and prosperity. Even Charles Beard, generally no supporter of capitalism, observed of this era: "Nearly every year between the close of the civil conflict and the end of the century witnessed some signal achievement in the realm of applied science."[2]

Note also that, as a negative corollary to the connection between freedom and progress, the Dark Age depicted by Ayn Rand in *Anthem* has a historical antecedent in the era following the fall of Rome. The barbarian tribes that wrought the final demise of Rome and, with it, Classical civilization, were men of brute force, not of intellectual achievement. This did not change with their conversion to Christianity. The religion of the Dark and Middle Ages was, in its own fashion, equally antagonistic to intellectual advance. The

Catholic Church held what amounted to a theocratic dictatorship during the feudal era. It prescribed doctrine and proscribed freethinking. It burned heretics at the stake. Thousands were killed, for example, in suppressing the Arian heresy; and the repression of Manicheism was scarcely less brutal. As late as the seventeenth and eighteenth centuries, the *ancien regime,* of which Catholicism was an integral component, burned Bruno, threatened Galileo, intimidated D'Alembert, imprisoned Voltaire and Diderot.

The mind, the source of cultural advance, was subordinated to orthodoxy. Reason, forced to be the handmaiden of faith, was prudently silent. The great minds, born in any era, in this one were presumably on strike. For keeping one's mouth closed may be a preferred option to having it closed permanently. The practical result was, on Rand's premises, predictable. According to economist Angus Maddison, Europe showed zero growth in per capita income for the thousand years between 500 and 1500—and average per capita income stood at around $215 in 1500. The inability in a full millennium to rise out of the ashes of Rome's destruction would not be surprising to Ayn Rand. The mind's all-important role in man's life can be identified by the results of its suppression as well as by those of its liberation.[3]

The rebirth of reason initiated during the Renaissance reached its logical climax in the eighteenth century Enlightenment and the nineteenth century Industrial Revolution, described in part above. Great Britain, Europe's freest nation—the land of Locke, Newton, and the Glorious Revolution of 1688—liberated and celebrated the mind of commoners, the overwhelming preponderance of the population, to a degree far greater than any other country outside of North America. The result was that such "common" men as James Watt, Edward Jenner, George Stephenson, et al., proved quite uncommon as the creators of the steam engine, a vaccine for smallpox, and improved designs of locomotives and railroads. The Scientific, Technological, and Industrial Revolutions brought profound advances in medicine, agriculture, and manufacturing, leading to vastly increased real wages, per capita incomes, life expectancies, and populations.[4]

At the deepest level, the struggle of Equality 7-2521 against the collectivist dictatorship of the future exemplifies the eternal conflict between the freethinking human mind and the oppressors who, seeking unlimited power, attempt to silence their primordial foe. But Ayn Rand has added a unique twist on this theme. For she depicts a world that has regressed from a scientifically, technologically, and industrially advanced society to one of abysmal backwardness. The men of the Classical world had reached glorious achievements in the Humanities, to be sure, but their science and technology were crude by modern standards. The material collapse into the Dark Ages was consequently not that precipitous. But Ayn Rand, writing in the 1930s, and adamantly standing by her conclusions until her death in 1982, writes of a collapse from electricity, airplanes, telephones, modern medicine, etc., into a Dark Age at least as dark as its historical antecedent. This is a re-gression of enormous, historically unprecedented proportions. What factor, according to the author, makes such a relapse inevitable? Equality 7-2521 could ask himself the same question, and answer it, only after his discovery of the concept "I":

> But then he [man] gave up all he had won, and fell lower than his savage be-ginning.
> What brought it to pass? What disaster took their reason away from men? What whip lashed them to their knees in shame and submission? The worship of the word "We." (102)

So, the answer is: collectivism. Collectivism is even more repressive than reli-gion. National Socialism, Fascism and Communism—collectivism's twentieth century variants—constitute the most virulent form of thought control and, consequently, lead to the most oppressive form of statism in human history.

Religion, though irrational, possesses one last shred of respect for man's mind utterly lacking in collectivism. Religionists believe in a man's individ-ual immortal soul. Though such belief is a myth, in reality man does possess a consciousness not reducible to material processes—and the "spiritual," im-material component of human nature constitutes the individuating element in man. Further, this should be glorified, as religion sometimes seems to re-alize. Consequently, despite its insistence on the supremacy of faith over rea-son, religionists are led to a last grudging respect for man's consciousness or mind. For example, under Christianity men of genius undoubtedly risked their lives to express conclusions contradicting those of their faith; neverthe-less, they sometimes survived, occasionally even triumphed. Heroes such as Albertus Magnus, Thomas Aquinas, and Thomas More, though generally op-posed and in some cases even executed, were lauded for their independent reasoning by religious men and on religious premises. Because of religion's commitment to man's spirit, even under Islam a quasi–Golden Age of culture was able to occur during the European Middle Ages.

But no Golden Age did or could occur under Nazism or Communism. The age was not golden, but red with human blood. The collectivists do not glo-rify the individuating element in man. Rather, they anathematize and sedu-lously seek to exterminate it. Men are merely interchangeable, nameless ci-phers, like so many ants in a colony, and none have value in themselves. Individuality is utterly evil and must be suppressed. In *Anthem,* Ayn Rand shows a full collectivism accurately extended to its logical conclusion. Men not only possess no rights and exist to serve the state, but are also permitted no privacy: they sleep together in a barracks, eat together in a great hall, are permitted no personal friendships or relationships and forbidden any activi-ties undertaken on their own initiative. The final, crushing blow is the collectivization of the language: the extirpation from men's vocabulary of first person references and all concepts denoting individuality.

Under such premises and policies, no independent mind could gain the slightest degree of social acceptance. An individual could only be lashed, have his tongue ripped out, tortured, or executed. This, of course, is the fate of the Saint of the pyre—and to be burned at the stake would have been that of Equality 7-2521 had he not escaped. Such oppression of independent minds is the reason for that society's inevitable collapse into primitivism.

And this is the reason that the villains of *Anthem*—indeed of every novel in Ayn Rand's corpus—are collectivists. They represent the gravest enemy of the independent mind that Ayn Rand so properly glorifies.

## NOTES

1. Stephane Courtois, et al., *The Black Book of Communism: Crimes, Terror, Repression* (Cambridge: Harvard University Press, 1999), 19, 168, 513–38, 591, 803. Paul Johnson, *Modern Times: The World From the Twenties to the Nineties* (New York: HarperCollins, 1991), 655.

2. Charles and Mary Beard, *The Rise of American Civilization,* vol. 2 (New York: Macmillan, 1930), 411–12.

3. Angus Maddison, *Phases of Capitalist Development* (New York: Oxford University Press, 1982), 4–7.

4. J. H. Clapham, *An Economic History of Modern Britain,* vol. 1, *The Early Railway Age* (Cambridge: Cambridge University Press, 1926), 548–61. Peter Lindert and Jeffrey Williamson, "English Workers' Living Standards During the Industrial Revolution: A New Look," *The Economic History Review,* 2nd Series, 36 (Feb. 1983), 1–2, 4–7, 23–24. Jeffrey Williamson, *Did British Capitalism Create Inequality* (Boston: Allen and Unwin, 1985), 7–33. Clark Nardinelli, *Child Labor and the Industrial Revolution* (Bloomington, Indiana: Indiana University Press, 1990), 108–10, 144, 149, 156.

# Epilogue

## *Anthem*: An Appreciation

*Harry Binswanger*

[On April 11, 1998, The Ayn Rand Institute held an event in New York City to celebrate the sixtieth anniversary of the publication of *Anthem*. For the occasion, Harry Binswanger prepared informal remarks, which are reproduced here with only light editing, to preserve its character as an oral presentation. —Editor]

*It is a sin to write this.*

This has to be one of the most intriguing, attention-grabbing first lines ever written. It presents a paradox: the hero is writing that writing is wrong. And how can it be a sin to write down one's thoughts? Unless those thoughts are themselves sinful. And if some thoughts are sinful, then isn't man's mind in a straitjacket? Doesn't that make thought itself sinful?

*It is a sin to write this.* Seven short and simple words whisk us into the hero's conflict with the world—and within himself: his conflict with a world that holds thought to be sinful, his internal conflict deriving from his acceptance of, yet rebellion against, that world's standards.

When he finally solves his conflict, learns what sin and greatness really are, he is ready to carve into stone the word "ego." So, *Anthem* begins and ends with an act of writing. And the path of the book is the hero's tortured and ecstatic passage from "It is a sin to write this" to "The sacred word: EGO."

Once I had the rare pleasure of using *Anthem* in teaching a course on philosophy at Hunter College. One theme of the course was individualism vs. collectivism, so *Anthem* was an inescapable choice for an assigned reading. Sometimes we learn from our students, and in this course I was startled by a comparison one of my students asked about. He asked if *Anthem* was conceived as an answer to Plato, specifically to his "Myth of the Cave" in *The*

*Republic.* I never asked Miss Rand if she had intended it that way—I suspect not—but it makes a marvelous comparison. In Plato's myth, a group of people live chained underground, in a cave; they have always seen only shadows on the cave wall, which they mistake for true reality, of which they know nothing. One of them gets free, goes above ground and sees the real world and the sun that lights it. He returns underground, is rejected by the ignorant many, and is ultimately killed by them. In *Anthem*, the many are above ground, enchained by their collectivist ideas and values; the hero goes down into an abandoned tunnel to discover the truth, invents his own sun—an electric light—returns above ground to enlighten the others in his society, is declared evil and imprisoned; but he breaks free and goes on to found a new individualist society.

For Plato, the moral is that true knowledge comes from a passive revelation of a higher reality, and that the masses, who cannot comprehend it, will destroy the individual who does. For Ayn Rand, the moral is that true knowledge comes from an active, selfish investigation of this world, immersed in matter, and that the many who choose not to think are impotent before the individual who does. For Plato, the moral is the need to turn away from the material world; for Ayn Rand, the moral is the need to embrace and conquer the material world.

Let me turn now to style, perhaps *Anthem*'s most prominent virtue. The story is told in the first-person, through the hero's diary. A diary is addressed to oneself. It is written for objectification, not communication. The form presents both a difficulty and an opportunity. The difficulty is that it has to read as if it had been written in installments, almost contemporaneous with the events being related. The mood of the writing, therefore, has to change with the mood of the protagonist. Thus, the beginning of each chapter has to establish its—that is, the hero's—mood. For instance, Chapter V begins: "We made it. We created it. We brought it forth from the night of the ages." But Chapter VII begins: "It is dark here in the forest."

The opportunity the form of a diary offers is personal immediacy. Contrast the following two ways of writing expressing the same idea: "What—even if we have to burn for it like the Saint of the pyre—what is the Unspeakable Word?" (51). Now here's the same thought, expressed in the third-person: "Despite the risk of being burnt at the stake, like the Saint of the pyre, he wished he knew the Unspeakable Word." Through the diary form, we see the events through the hero's eyes, know only what he knows at that time, and have access to his innermost thoughts and feelings.

Further on style: ironically, *Anthem*'s "we" language, which dramatizes the basic evil the hero must overcome, has a positive value, literarily: it adds a certain timeless quality to the writing—similar to the "thou" and "thee" in biblical language; Ayn Rand wrote that the style was deliberately "archaic."[1] This enhances the timeless, non-journalistic, nature of the story.

*Anthem*, of all Ayn Rand's writings, is the most metaphysical in style. *Anthem* grabs you from its first sentence and sweeps you into Ayn Rand's spirit. By its rhythms and cadences it reaches, immediately, a metaphysical level, a level where the mundane and accidental have dropped away, leaving a solitary man facing existence. "It is dark here. The flame of the candle stands still in the air. Nothing moves in this tunnel save our hand on the paper. We are alone here under the earth. It is a fearful word, alone" (17). It is this metaphysical, almost surreal, setting that makes the hero's conflict translatable into one's own personal terms. The universal meaning is contained in the uniquely stripped-down particular, and that universal—man alone facing existence—resonates with any sensitive reader; it speaks to his deepest, inescapable, life-shaping concerns: how to confront existence, the meaning of life, man's relationship to man. *Anthem* speaks to these concerns whether the reader has reached their explicit formulation or holds them only implicitly as what Ayn Rand called "metaphysical value-judgments."

But the amazing thing about *Anthem* is its unalloyed benevolence. Not benevolence as mere cheeriness or gaiety, but as a fundamental conviction that life does have meaning, that the shackles can be thrown off—as the hero easily escapes from his prison cell by simply pushing on the rusty locks that have no power to hold him. It is the benevolence of recognizing that great things can be accomplished, and that, ultimately, nothing can hold one back but one's own errors—errors that cannot stand the light of the will to understand, maintained over the years of one's life. One feels that the hero of *Anthem* wins because he has to win, that the world of collectivism has no power to stop him once he realizes his own power. This is the precursor of the point in *Atlas Shrugged* when John Galt says to the world:

> I saw that there comes a point, in the defeat of any man of virtue, when his own consent is needed for evil to win—and that no manner of injury done to him by others can succeed if he chooses to withhold his consent. I saw that I could put an end to your outrages by pronouncing a single word in my mind. I pronounced it. The word was "No."[2]

In 1938, Ayn Rand wrote to her British publisher to ask for the right to review the design of the book, a right that is not ordinarily granted to authors.

> I would not ask for this [right] if this story were not more precious to me than anything I have ever considered writing. It is so very personally mine, it is, in a way, my manifesto, my profession of faith, the essence of my entire philosophy.[3]

What, then, is the philosophic message of *Anthem*? It is that man's ego is sacred. One's ego, one's life and self-awareness, is something wonderful, something to hold as infinitely precious, something to kneel before, the source of all the value in existence.

In this regard, I will close with my own favorite two brief passages from *Anthem*:

> For in the temple of his spirit, each man is alone. Let each man keep his temple untouched and undefiled. (96)
>
> I wished to know the *meaning* of things. *I* am the meaning. I wished to find a warrant for being. I need no warrant for being, and no word of sanction upon my being. *I* am the warrant and the sanction. (94)

Thank you, Ayn Rand.

## NOTES

1. See Leonard Peikoff, introduction to fiftieth anniversary American edition of Ayn Rand, *Anthem* (New York: Signet, 1995), x.

2. Ayn Rand, *Atlas Shrugged* (New York: Random House, 1957; Signet thirty-fifth anniversary paperback edition, 1992), 960.

3. Unpublished material (Ayn Rand Archives).

# Appendix

## Teaching *Anthem*: A Guide for High School and University Teachers

*Lindsay Joseph*

A perennial favorite in high school and college classes, *Anthem* is read by thousands of students each year. Young readers enjoy *Anthem*'s mysterious setting and exciting story line; they are drawn in particular to its courageous and inspiring hero.

Like other literary heroes, Equality 7-2521[1] possesses strength and valor. What sets him apart, however, is his ruthlessly independent mind. Whether he is choosing a friend, conducting a scientific experiment, or forming a new moral code to guide his life, Equality looks to reality; he refuses to blindly obey the dictates of his society. In this hero, readers find a man who stands proudly alone on the strength of the knowledge that he is right.

This heroic portrayal is especially valuable to *young* readers, who are forming their adult character and basic worldview. They are developing answers to such fundamental questions as: What kind of person do I want to be? Can I direct my life? Should I live for myself or for others? and, more broadly, In what kind of society do I want to live? Written as a prose poem, *Anthem* has few characters, a straightforward progression of events, and an austere style. Despite its apparent simplicity, however, this novella does convey answers to such broad philosophical questions.

This essay is intended as a guide for teachers as they help their students understand *Anthem* with greater depth and clarity. The teaching process begins by familiarizing students with the novella's content—what happened, who did it, and where. To aid in this comprehension and analysis, the chapter questions in the first section of this essay focus on the most important aspects of *Anthem*'s story line, characters, and setting. They require students to progress from mere factual recall to deeper interpretation—from identifying *what* to understanding *why*.

The next stage in the teaching process should be one of integration, because a story's concretes, even if clearly understood, are too numerous to retain as discrete units. Discussing the more abstract questions in the second part of this essay will help students to unite these concretes into a holistic grasp of character, storyline, and, finally, theme. In terms of characterization, this entails tying together a character's speeches, thoughts, descriptions, and actions to identify his central purpose. For instance, once students identify what motivates the governing Councils, their actions—from relegating Equality to the job of Street Sweeper to rejecting his invention—are more fully comprehended and easily recalled. In this second part, I also suggest methods of teaching the philosophical ideas contained in *Anthem*, and offer questions focusing on literary style.

Once students have achieved an integrated understanding of *Anthem*, they should be encouraged to relate their newfound knowledge to the world around them. Their knowledge is not useful if it is compartmentalized. The third part of this guide is designed to help students apply *Anthem*'s meaning to other areas of study, the real world, and their own lives. This is accomplished by means of advanced research projects and essay questions in the areas of literature, history, and politics, as well as personal response questions.

The final stage of literary study prompts students to clarify their thinking by expressing their ideas in writing. Suggested topics for creative and expository writing are contained in the last part of this essay.

## COMPREHENSION AND ANALYSIS

What follows is a list of content questions for each chapter of *Anthem*. They can be used to facilitate classroom discussion or to monitor student comprehension during independent study. They may also prove useful for regular homework assignments and for quizzes and unit tests.

### Chapter I

1. a) How would you describe the society in which *Anthem* is set? Some areas to consider are political structure, technology, social relationships, quality of life, and education.

   b) Would you want to live in this society? Why or why not?

2. Equality states that it is very unusual for men to reach the age of 45. Offer several possible explanations as to why life expectancy is so short in this society.

3. Religious terms of condemnation (such as "transgression," "sin," "curse," "crime," "evil," and "damned") appear throughout *Anthem*. For each of these terms:

a) Find several examples in which it refers to an act or character in the novel.

b) Explain why this act or character is condemned.

c) Argue whether you think it *should* be condemned, and why.

4. Ayn Rand intended Equality to stand out from his "brothers." Explain how she accomplishes this by contrasting Equality's character traits and physical qualities with those of his fellow men.

5. Why does the Council of Vocations assign Equality the job of street sweeper? Is it due to error, incompetence, or a more sinister motivation? Explain.

6. When do the events of *Anthem* take place—in the past, the present, or the future? How do you know?

7. a) How would your teachers react if you had Equality's "curse"?

b) Why do Equality's teachers disapprove of his quick mind?

8. a) At this point in the story, does Equality accept the moral teachings of his society?

b) If so, why doesn't he feel shame or remorse when he knows that he is committing a crime? Support your answer with textual evidence.

9. Would you want to be friends with someone like Equality? Why or why not?

## Chapter II

1. a) Re-read the account of Liberty 5-3000 (38–39).[2] Which character traits are revealed in this brief description?

b) Why does Equality give her a new name: "The Golden One"?

2. Find several examples of the ways in which this society tries to obliterate individuality by quashing personal choices, desires, and values.

3. Contrast Equality with the rest of the men living in this society.

4. Of the whole range of feelings possible to man (joy, excitement, anger, guilt, etc.), why is fear the prevalent emotion in this society?

5. Explain the following: the Great Truth, the Unmentionable Times, the Uncharted Forest, the Evil Ones, the Great Rebirth.

6. a) What word is Equality struggling to recapture?

b) Why is mentioning this word the only crime punishable by death? How does this word contradict the ideals of this society? What could its rediscovery possibly lead to?

## Chapter III

1. a) What does Equality discover in this chapter?

b) How important is this discovery? Describe four or five ways in which it would make life more productive and enjoyable.

2. Outline several of the Council of Scholars' beliefs and Equality's refutation of those beliefs.

## Chapter IV

1. Discuss the appropriateness of the new name given to Equality by Liberty: "The Unconquered."

## Chapter V

1. Equality understands that his invention will greatly benefit mankind; however, this was not his main motivation in conducting his experiments, and it is not the primary source of the great joy he experiences. Discuss.
2. Why is Equality so interested in seeing his own image at this point in the story? What emotion is he feeling?

## Chapter VI

1. What do the old locks and lack of guards in the Palace of Corrective Detention imply?

## Chapter VII

1. List four reasons given by the Council for rejecting Equality's invention. Are these the Council's real reasons for rejecting the gift? If not, what are?
2. What does Equality mean when he says, "We are old now, yet we were young this morning" (68)?

## Chapter VIII

1. What is Equality experiencing for the first time in this chapter, and what does he feel as a result?
2. Explain why Equality laughs when he remembers that he is "the Damned."
3. What does the Uncharted Forest symbolize?

## Chapter IX

1. Liberty contrasts Equality to his fellow men (82-83). Paraphrase this passage.

2. Equality questions the morality of his former society. Contrast what he was previously taught about solitude, good, evil, and joy to what he now believes.

## Chapter X

1. Describe the house and its contents in your own words, and explain why Liberty and Equality find it so strange.

## Chapter XI

1. What great discovery does Equality make in this chapter?
2. Explain the following quotes in your own words, and discuss how they might be applied to your life:
   a) "Whatever road I take, the guiding star is within me."
   b) "For the word 'We' must never be spoken, save by one's choice and as a second thought."
3. What does Equality now realize is the proper goal and purpose of his life?
4. In what ways is "I" like a god?
5. Re-read the incident with the Saint of the pyre (50). Does Equality now understand why the Saint felt joy and pride rather than pain and disgrace? Explain.

## Chapter XII

1. Why do the main characters take the names Prometheus and Gaea? Why weren't they allowed to choose their names in their old society?
2. What does Equality (Prometheus) plan to do in the future?
3. Equality (Prometheus) reaches the important realization that "To be free, a man must be free of his brothers" (101). Cite several examples from *Anthem* that illustrate what Ayn Rand means by this.

## INTEGRATION

Too often, students are taught how to analyze a work of literature, but not how to synthesize its elements into a conceptual whole. The following questions prompt the students to integrate *Anthem*'s discrete descriptions, actions, and dialogue in order to grasp its abstract meaning.

1. What does Equality finally understand about his society when the Council threatens to destroy his invention?

2. For each of the main characters, write a short description that captures his or her central character trait(s) and key motivation in the story.

3. *Anthem* is a heroic and inspiring story about the triumph of the individual's independent spirit. Even though, in the end, Equality is greatly outnumbered and the society he escapes is wallowing in primitive stagnation; it is a story of liberation and hope—not of despair. Discuss.

4. Aside from very rare exceptions (Equality, the Saint of the pyre) there is no opposition to the leaders in this society. Why is this? What ideas must these men have accepted to live a life of obedience, drudgery, and fear?

5. To fully control a man, one must not only enslave his body, but also destroy his mind. Discuss how the leaders in *Anthem* seek to accomplish this tyrannical practice.

6. Equality is a vivid illustration of man's free will—of how his choices determine his future. It is not an innate superiority that enables Equality to escape from his society. He is able to break free because he chooses to question when others choose to accept, he chooses to think when others choose to evade, he chooses to defy when others choose to obey. Discuss with reference to specific examples from the story. (Note to the teacher: This question addresses an aspect of the novel that students sometimes misinterpret. Young readers may mistakenly conclude that Equality succeeds because he was born with superior intelligence, strength, or ability.)

7. Ayn Rand identified *Anthem*'s theme as "the word *I*."[3] Explain the ways in which the characters and story line in *Anthem* illustrate this theme.

### Additional Questions on Literary Style

1. Figurative language is employed effectively, if sparingly, in this novella. Often, a well-chosen simile captures the essence of a character or the significance of an event. Discuss the meaning and significance of the following similes in *Anthem*.

   a) "We blew out the candle. Darkness swallowed us. There was nothing left around us, nothing save night and a thin thread of flame in it, as a crack in the wall of a prison" (59-60).

   b) "But International 4-8818 are different. They are a tall, strong youth and their eyes are like fireflies." (29).

   c) "[Liberty's] body was straight and thin as a blade of iron. . . . Their hair was golden as the sun; their hair flew in the wind, shining and wild, as if it defied men to restrain it. They threw seeds from their hand as if they deigned to fling a scornful gift, and the earth was as a beggar under their feet" (38-39).

d) "The shoulders of our Brothers are hunched, and their muscles are drawn, as if their bodies were shrinking and wished to shrink out of sight" (46).

2. Discuss the symbolic importance of the Uncharted Forest, Equality's manuscript, and the light bulb.

3. Comment on the irony of the characters' names.

4. Ayn Rand wrote *Anthem* in diary form, using first person major point-of-view. Discuss the merits of this form and point of view for this particular work. Consider: How is the diary form crucial to character development in *Anthem*? How does it help to reveal the setting and establish the nature of this society? How does it contribute to the mystery surrounding the Forbidden Word? How would using first person minor or third person omniscient point of view weaken the novella?

5. *Anthem* is replete with moral concepts typically reserved for religious reference: from "holy," "god," "revere," and "worship," to "sin," "transgression," "evil," and "damned." Even the title, *Anthem*, can be defined as "A religious choral song usually based on words from the Bible."[4] However, Ayn Rand's referents for these terms are diametrically opposed to those of religion. She worships not a supernatural deity, but the best in man. She glorifies not pain and self-sacrifice, but happiness and egoism. Discuss how the use of religious terminology in *Anthem* helps to convey Ayn Rand's radical moral code of rational egoism—the antithesis of religion's morality of self-sacrifice.[5]

### Teaching Philosophical Concepts

In order for students to comprehend *Anthem* fully, they need to be taught the precise meaning of the following concepts: altruism, egoism, collectivism, individualism, conformity, obedience, and independence.

Using the Socratic method, teachers can begin by posing straightforward questions about *Anthem*. For example, what does the society portrayed in *Anthem* consider to be good or virtuous? Garner several students' examples from the text, and then explain that they illustrate the moral code of altruism. Supply a precise definition for students to learn. Ask for further examples of altruism from modern society (i.e., former president Clinton's Volunteerism campaign). Next, discuss the opposite code of egoism. Repeat for each concept. Alternatively, the teacher can begin by supplying terms and definitions to the class. He can then ask students to find illustrations of each term from the novel and from real life. Students can consider personal experiences, current laws, newspaper articles, etc.[6]

## APPLICATIONS

In the following assignments, students are asked to apply their understanding of *Anthem* to literature, politics, history, and issues in our society. Students are encouraged to consider the ideas in *Anthem* while examining the world around them; in turn, research from these areas of study can help students develop a fuller understanding of Ayn Rand's ideas.

### Literature

1. Conduct a study of literary heroes. Consider, first, what is a literary hero? In addition to referring to the central character, this term "includes a moral evaluation and implies courage, honor, great strength or achievement, or some other noble quality . . . the hero is the doer of great deeds."[7] Compare and contrast Equality to a few of your favorite literary heroes. Discuss the qualities they share and make a case for which one, in your opinion, is the most heroic. Consider the quality of his soul, the severity of his opposition, and the significance of his battle. Characters to consider: Atticus Finch in *To Kill a Mockingbird*; Cyrano de Bergerac in *Cyrano de Bergerac*; Joan of Arc in Bernard Shaw's *Saint Joan*; Sir Thomas More in *A Man for All Seasons*; Henry Drummond in *Inherit the Wind*; Howard Roark in *The Fountainhead*; Jean Valjean in *Les Miserables*.

2. Compare and contrast *Anthem* to other anti-utopian novels, such as George Orwell's *1984*, Aldous Huxley's *Brave New World*, Yevgeny Zamyatin's *We*, or Ray Bradbury's *Farenheit 451*.

3. Contrast the hero in a Romantic work such as *Anthem* to the anti-hero in a Naturalistic work, such as Arthur Miller's *Death of a Salesman*.

4. Look up the Greek myths on Gaea and Prometheus, and explain why Ayn Rand chose these names for her characters in *Anthem*.

5. Contrast the story of Adam and Eve's expulsion from the Garden of Eden to the story of Equality and Liberty (Prometheus and Gaea) in *Anthem*. Include in your analysis the "sins" for which each was condemned.

6. In a letter discussing *Anthem,* Ayn Rand wrote that it "has the same relation to *The Fountainhead* as the preliminary sketches which artists draw for their future big canvases. I wrote [*Anthem*] while working on *The Fountainhead*—it has the same theme, spirit, and intention, although in quite a different form."[8] After reading both works, write a comparative essay with this latter statement as its thesis.

7. Liberty chooses "The Unconquered" as a fitting name for Equality. Similarly, William Henley's most famous poem is entitled "Invictus" (1875),

which is Latin for "Unconquered." Write a short essay on the similarities between the main characters in each of these works.

### Politics

1. In *Anthem*, Equality observes that "At forty, [men] are worn out . . . [and] are sent to the Home of the Useless, where the Old Ones live. . . . The Old Ones know that they are soon to die. When a miracle happens and some live to be forty-five, they are the Ancient Ones, and children stare at them when passing by . . ." (28). According to the World Health Organization's ranking of 191 countries (www.who.int), there is a huge discrepancy in the average life expectancy of various nations: it ranges from a high of 75 years in Japan to a low of 28.6 years in Sierra Leone. Why does life expectancy vary so greatly around the world? What are the main factors that determine life expectancy in a given country? Select several countries with high, medium, and low average life expectancies, and briefly research their political systems. Consider the following questions:
   a) Do citizens have the right to life, liberty, the pursuit of personal happiness, and ownership of private property? Do they enjoy freedom of speech, of the press, of assembly, of mobility, and of religion?
   b) How are their leaders chosen?
   c) To what extent does the government control and regulate the economy?
   d) Is the rule of law respected?
   Write a paper on your findings concerning the causal impact that a country's political system has on the life expectancy of its citizens.
2. In *Anthem*, Prometheus discovers the meaning of the word "freedom." He states that "To be free, a man must be free of his brothers. That is freedom. This and nothing else" (101). In fact, Ayn Rand defined freedom, in a political context, as "the absence of physical coercion."[9] This definition of freedom, however, stands in direct contrast to the one held by many modern thinkers, writers, and politicians—a common view of freedom, and one that Ayn Rand rejects: "Freedom must [entail] . . . an increased power on the part of the individual to share in the goods which a society has produced and an enlarged ability to contribute to the common good."[10] Write an essay contrasting these two definitions of freedom, and consider the form of government each would necessitate.
3. Is *Anthem* a realistic portrayal of life in a totalitarian society? Compare the fictionalized society in *Anthem* to a real dictatorship, past or present. Some options are Nazi Germany, Soviet Russia, Castro's Cuba, present day Iran, etc.

## History

While recounting man's struggle for freedom throughout history, Equality laments:

> At first, man was enslaved by the gods . . . then he was enslaved by the kings . . . he was enslaved by his birth, by his kin, by his race. But he broke their chains. He declared to all his brothers that a man has rights which [no men] can take away from him. . . . And he stood on the threshold of freedom. . . . But then he gave up all that he had won, and fell lower than his savage beginning. (101–102)

Ask the student to find a specific example from history for each of these five stages in mankind's political history, including an example from the twentieth century for the final stage. What, according to this novella, must man understand to enable him to pass through the threshold of freedom that, in the past, he so nearly reached?

## Our Society

1. How does our society treat independent thinkers, daring innovators, and successful entrepreneurs (like Equality)? Are they applauded or criticized? Write an essay on this topic, offering specific case studies to support your argument.
2. Our society appears to be in the midst of a crisis of personal responsibility. Everything from poverty to criminal behavior to obesity is blamed on causes beyond one's control. We hear the cry "It's not my fault! It's my family (or class or race or even fast food chains) that control my actions!" Such individuals claim that outside factors determine their destiny. Judging from *Anthem*, how do you think Ayn Rand would reply? Do you agree? Why or why not?

## Personal Response

The following is a suggested pre-reading assignment for students:

> The transition from adolescence to adulthood involves developing a personal identity—a sense of self. Write a paragraph that describes you, and explains what makes you uniquely you. Consider your future goals and dreams; what you value in a friend; favorite pets; preferred sports and hobbies; best-loved music, literature, movies, etc. And most significantly, consider your views about the nature of the world, your place in it, and how you should live.

Discuss with the students how and why they chose these values. This assignment can help the students to better understand the connection between the mind (thoughts, choices, etc.) and the self.

Then discuss with students the following questions after they have read *Anthem*:

> Review your pre-reading activity. Which of your ideas and personal values, goals, and loves would be allowed in the society portrayed in *Anthem*? Would any of them be forbidden? Why? What do you think of this?

This exercise can help students better understand the completely selfless society in *Anthem*. Students can see how living in this society would affect them directly. They will more fully understand Ayn Rand's conviction that the obliteration of the mind is the destruction of the self.

## WRITING ACTIVITIES

An inspiring piece of literature can present a wonderful opportunity to hone students' writing skills. Further, writing about a literary work can serve to further clarify students' thinking on a given topic. With this in mind, I offer the following suggestions for writing assignments on *Anthem*.

1. *Anthem* illustrates the importance of thinking and judging independently and of acting according to rational principles—even when "our brothers" oppose us. In light of the fact that smoking, drugs, shoplifting, and gang violence often involve peer pressure, write a letter to a magazine explaining *Anthem*'s benefits for young readers.
2. You are applying for a job to direct the movie version of *Anthem*. Write a letter to the producer in which you try to convince him to hire you. Your letter must indicate:
   a) Which actors you would cast as Prometheus and Gaea, and why. Explain how their acting skills and physical characteristics would enable them to portray these characters.
   b) A detailed description of the setting (geographical location or set design).
   c) An explanation of the theme of this novel, and its relevance and value to modern viewers.
   d) Other topics—musical suggestions for certain scenes, costumes, a description of the opening shot, etc.
3. Write a letter to Ayn Rand about *Anthem*. State your reaction to it (what you found particularly surprising, exciting, moving, etc.), and ask about those aspects of the novel that puzzled you. If applicable, comment on how Equality's struggle relates to your own life.
4. Write the "missing scene" from Chapter I, in which the Council of Vocations is deciding Equality's future profession. Are any of the Council members sympathetic to Equality? If so, would he dare to voice his

opinion? Ensure that you reveal the Council's true motives in assigning Equality the job of street sweeper.

5. Write a factual newspaper article about Prometheus' escape from jail, his surprise appearance at the World Council of Scholars, and his flight into the Uncharted Forest. Then, write an opinionated editorial about the same events, written by one of his "brothers."

6. Re-write the first meeting between Equality and Liberty from her perspective.

7. Re-write the scene about the Saint of the pyre from the Saint's perspective. What did he want to communicate to Equality?

8. Write a new ending for *Anthem* in which Prometheus is captured while attempting to rescue his friends. Include a court scene of Equality's trial before the Council for his "sins." How will Equality use his new understanding of morality to defend himself and his actions? (As a possible extension, act out this scene in class, and invite another class to judge.)

9. At the end of the story, Equality confidently declares that he is not afraid of his brothers. He knows that his new home is impassable to them, "For they have nothing to fight me with, save the brute forces of their numbers. I have my mind" (100). Write a short story in which the main character's intelligence, resourcefulness, and ingenuity (i.e., his mind) triumphs over his opponents' brute force or sheer numbers.

## CONCLUSION

As with Ayn Rand's other works of fiction, *Anthem* can be enjoyed and understood on several different levels. On the surface, it recounts a young scientist's heroic struggle to rediscover what has been lost to man: scientific knowledge, love, freedom, the very concept "I." Dig deeper and it is a commentary on collectivist societies; it depicts the poverty, stagnation, and despair that necessarily accompany the subjugation of the individual to the collective. On a more fundamental level, this work is an anthem to the very nature of man. It glorifies the independent mind as the self—as the source of one's ability to create, to value, to judge, to *be*—and thus as a thing to be worshipped. This guide should help teachers and their students to better understand *Anthem*, and thereby gain even deeper insight and inspiration from this important work.

## NOTES

1. For simplicity's sake, I shall henceforth refer to the hero of *Anthem* as "Equality."
2. For simplicity's sake, I shall henceforth refer to the heroine of *Anthem* as "Liberty."

3. Ayn Rand, *The Art of Fiction*, ed. Tore Boeckmann (New York: Plume, 2000), 36.

4. David B. Guralnik, ed., *Webster's New World Dictionary of the American Language* (New York: Meridian Books, Inc., 1961), 31.

5. See a fuller discussion of this topic in Leonard Peikoff's introduction to the fiftieth anniversary paperback edition of Ayn Rand, *Anthem* (New York: Signet, 1995), vi–vii.

6. For Ayn Rand's definition of these terms, see Harry Binswanger, ed., *The Ayn Rand Lexicon: Objectivism from A to Z* (New York: New American Library, 1986), and Allison T. Kunze and Jean Moroney, eds., *Glossary of Objectivist Definitions* (Gaylordsville, CT: Second Renaissance Books, 1999).

7. C. Carter Colwell, *A Student's Guide to Literature* (New York: Doubleday, 1968).

8. Michael S. Berliner, ed., *Letters Of Ayn Rand* (New York: Dutton, 1995), 314.

9. Ayn Rand, *Capitalism: the Unknown Ideal* (New York: New American Library, 1966; Signet expanded paperback edition, 1967), 46.

10. George Sabine, *A History of Political Theory* (New York: Henry Holt and Co., 1973), 658.

# Select Bibliography

*This bibliography is limited to books by Ayn Rand—and books about Ayn Rand and her philosophy, Objectivism—cited in this collection.*

Berliner, Michael S., ed. *Letters of Ayn Rand*. New York: Dutton, 1995; paperback edition, Plume, 1997.

Binswanger, Harry, ed. *The Ayn Rand Lexicon: Objectivism from A to Z*. New York: New American Library, 1986; paperback edition, Meridian, 1988.

Britting, Jeff. *Ayn Rand*. New York: Overlook Press. 2005.

Gotthelf, Allan. *On Ayn Rand*. Belmont, CA: Wadsworth, 2000.

Harriman, David, ed. *Journals of Ayn Rand*. New York: Dutton, 1997; paperback edition, Plume, 1999.

Kunze, Alison T., and Jean Moroney, eds. *Glossary of Objectivist Definitions*. Gaylordsville, CT: Second Renaissance Books, 1999.

Mayhew, Robert, ed. *Essays on Ayn Rand's* We the Living. Lanham, MD: Lexington Books, 2004.

Peikoff, Leonard, ed. *The Early Ayn Rand: A Selection from Her Unpublished Fiction*. New York: New American Library, 1984; paperback edition, Signet, 1986.

———. *Objectivism: The Philosophy of Ayn Rand*. New York: Dutton, 1991; paperback edition, New Meridian, 1993.

———. *Ominous Parallels: The End of Freedom in America*. New York: Stein and Day, 1982; Meridian paperback edition, 1993.

Rand, Ayn. *Anthem*. London: Cassell and Co., 1938.

———. *Anthem*. Los Angeles: Pamphleteers, Inc., 1946.

———. *Anthem*. Caldwell, ID: Caxton, 1953.

———. *Anthem*. Fiftieth anniversary paperback edition. Introduction by Leonard Peikoff. New York: Signet, 1995.

———. *The Art of Fiction: A Guide for Writers and Readers*. Edited by Tore Boeckmann. Introduction by Leonard Peikoff. New York: Plume, 2000.

325

———. *The Art of Nonfiction: A Guide for Writers and Readers.* Edited by Robert Mayhew. Introduction by Peter Schwartz. New York: Plume, 2001.

———. *Atlas Shrugged.* New York: Random House, 1957; Signet thirty-fifth anniversary paperback edition, 1992.

———. *Capitalism: The Unknown Ideal.* New York: New American Library, 1966; expanded paperback edition, Signet, 1967.

———. *For the New Intellectual.* New York: Random House, 1961; Signet paperback edition, 1961.

———. *The Fountainhead.* New York: Bobbs-Merrill, 1943; Signet fiftieth anniversary paperback edition, 1993.

———. *Introduction to Objectivist Epistemology.* Expanded Second Edition. Edited by Harry Binswanger and Leonard Peikoff. New York: Meridian, 1990.

———. *Philosophy: Who Needs It.* New York: Bobbs-Merrill, 1982; Signet paperback edition, 1984.

———. *Return of the Primitive: The Anti-Industrial Revolution.* Edited by Peter Schwartz. New York: Meridian, 1999.

———. *The Romantic Manifesto: A Philosophy of Literature.* Revised edition. New York: Signet, 1975.

———. *Russian Writings on Hollywood.* Edited by Michael S. Berliner. Marina del Rey, CA: The Ayn Rand Institute Press, 1999.

———. *The Virtue of Selfishness: A New Concept of Egoism.* New York: New American Library, 1964.

———. *The Voice of Reason: Essays in Objectivist Thought.* Leonard Peikoff, ed. New York: New American Library, 1988; paperback edition, Meridian, 1989.

———. *We the Living.* New York: Macmillan, 1936.

———. *We the Living.* Sixtieth anniversary paperback edition. Introduction by Leonard Peikoff. New York: Signet, 1996.

Schwartz, Peter, ed. *The Ayn Rand Column.* New Milford, CT: Second Renaissance, 1998.

# Index

# Contributors

**Michael S. Berliner** holds a Ph.D. in Philosophy from Boston University. He was executive director of the Ayn Rand Institute for its first fifteen years and previously taught philosophy of education and philosophy at California State University, Northridge. He created the first two catalogs of the Ayn Rand Papers at the Ayn Rand Archives and is currently compiling a definitive inventory. He is editor of *Letters of Ayn Rand* and Ayn Rand's *Russian Writings on Hollywood*. He has lectured throughout the United States and in Europe, Australia, and Israel on Ayn Rand's life.

**Andrew Bernstein** holds a Ph.D. in Philosophy from the Graduate School of the City University of New York and teaches at Pace University and SUNY Purchase. He is author of the novel *Heart of a Pagan* and of *The Capitalist Manifesto: The Historic, Economic and Philosophic Case for Laissez-Faire*. He lectures widely on topics relating to both Ayn Rand's novels and her philosophy of Objectivism. His website is www.andrewbernstein.net.

**Harry Binswanger** holds a Ph.D. in Philosophy from Columbia University. He taught philosophy at the City University of New York, Hunter College, from 1972 to 1979. During the 1980s, he was editor of *The Objectivist Forum*, a bimonthly journal devoted to Ayn Rand's philosophy. Since 1994, he has been professor of philosophy at the Objectivist Academic Center of the Ayn Rand Institute. He is author of *The Biological Basis of Teleological Concepts* and editor of *The Ayn Rand Lexicon* and of the second edition of Ayn Rand's *Introduction to Objectivist Epistemology*. He is currently writing a book on the nature of consciousness.

**Tore Boeckmann** is a writer whose mystery short stories have been published and anthologized in several languages. He edited Ayn Rand's *The Art of Fiction: A Guide for Writers and Readers*, and has lectured on Ayn Rand's literary esthetics in America and Europe. He is translator of the Norwegian edition of *Anthem*.

**Jeff Britting** is Archivist of the Ayn Rand Archives, a collection of the Ayn Rand Institute. He is author of the short illustrated biography *Ayn Rand*. He developed and associate-produced the Academy Award nominated documentary *Ayn Rand: A Sense of Life* and the feature film *Take Two*, and he co-produced the first stage productions of Ayn Rand's play *Ideal* and her novella *Anthem*. As a composer, he has written incidental music for eleven stage productions and three films, and is currently writing an opera based on an original libretto set in the Middle Ages.

**Onkar Ghate** holds a Ph.D. in Philosophy from the University of Calgary. He is a Senior Fellow at the Ayn Rand Institute, where he specializes in Ayn Rand's philosophy of Objectivism and teaches philosophy in the Institute's Objectivist Academic Center. Recent publications include "Postmodernism's Kantian Roots" and (co-authored with Dr. Edwin Locke) "Objectivism: The Proper Alternative to Postmodernism" (both in *Postmodernism and Management: Pros, Cons and the Alternative*), and an entry on Ayn Rand in the *Encyclopedia of Science, Technology, and Ethics* (forthcoming).

**Lindsay Joseph** received her Honors Bachelor of Arts and Bachelor of Education from York University, and her Honors Specialist Certification in the Teaching of English from the University of Toronto. For the past eight years, she has worked as a teacher and administrator at private schools in Toronto, Canada, where she specialized in writing curriculum, leading teacher-training workshops, and creating classroom resources. She is currently Executive Director of LePort School's Upper Elementary and Junior High, located in Southern California (www.LePortSchools.com).

**John Lewis** holds a Ph.D. in Classics from Cambridge University. He is Assistant Professor of History at Ashland University, where he is holder of an Anthem Fellowship for the Study of Objectivism. He has published numerous articles on ancient Greek history, law, and political thought. He is presently completing a monograph on the early Greek poet Solon of Athens and a book on the uses of a homeland defense strategy from the Greeks to the modern day.

**Robert Mayhew** is Professor of Philosophy at Seton Hall University. He is author of *Aristotle's Criticism of Plato's Republic*, *The Female in Aristotle's*

*Biology*, and *Ayn Rand and* Song of Russia*: Communism and Anti-Communism in 1940s Hollywood*. He has translated a play of Aristophanes (*Assembly of Women*), and has edited three volumes of unpublished material of Ayn Rand: *Ayn Rand's Marginalia*, *The Art of Nonfiction*, and (forthcoming) *Ayn Rand Answers*.

**Shoshana Milgram** [Knapp] holds a Ph.D. in Comparative Literature from Stanford University, and is Associate Professor of English at Virginia Tech. She has published articles on a variety of nineteenth- and twentieth-century figures in French, Russian, and English/American literature, including Napoleon Bonaparte, Victor Hugo, George Sand, Anton Chekhov, Fyodor Dostoevsky, Leo Tolstoi, Victoria Cross, George Eliot, John Fowles, W. S. Gilbert, Henry James, Ursula K. LeGuin, Vladimir Nabokov, Herbert Spencer, W. T. Stead, E. L. Voynich—and Ayn Rand. She is also author of introductions to editions of *Toilers of the Sea* and *The Man Who Laughs*, by Victor Hugo, and *The Seafarers*, by Nevil Shute. Her current project is a study of Ayn Rand's life up to 1957.

**Amy Peikoff** is BB&T Visiting Assistant Professor of Philosophy at the University of North Carolina at Chapel Hill. She holds a J.D. from the University of California, Los Angeles, School of Law and a Ph.D. in Philosophy from the University of Southern California. She has written articles on law and philosophy for academic journals and leading newspapers. Her current research interests include discovering and justifying the proper terms of legal protection for intellectual property.

**Gregory Salmieri** is a graduate student in philosophy at the University of Pittsburgh. He specializes in epistemology and ancient philosophy, and his research interests are focused on Aristotle's epistemology and methodology and on theories of concepts.

**Richard E. Ralston** received a B.A. in History from the University of Maryland after serving seven years in the U.S. Army. He then completed an M.A. in International Relations at the University of Southern California. He has been Managing Director of the Ayn Rand Institute, and Circulation Director and Publishing Director of the *Christian Science Monitor*. He is editor of two books, *Communism: Its Rise and Fall in the 20th Century* and *Why Businessmen Need Philosophy*. He is presently the Executive Director of Americans for Free Choice in Medicine.

**Darryl Wright** is Associate Professor of Philosophy at Harvey Mudd College. He has written and lectured on topics in ethical theory and the history of ethics, early analytic philosophy, and the philosophy of Ayn Rand.